Why Didn't Evangelicals "See Him Coming"?

Why Didn't Evangelicals "See Him Coming"?

Donald J. Trump's Deception and Dismantling of American Democracy

PAUL A. POMERVILLE

RESOURCE *Publications* · Eugene, Oregon

WHY DIDN'T EVANGELICALS "SEE HIM COMING"?
Donald J. Trump's Deception and Dismantling of American Democracy

Resource Publications
An Imprint of Wipf and Stock Publishers
199 W. 8th Ave., Suite 3
Eugene, OR 97401

www.wipfandstock.com

PAPERBACK ISBN: 978-1-6667-7645-4
HARDCOVER ISBN: 978-1-6667-7646-1
EBOOK ISBN: 978-1-6667-7647-8

08/25/23

Contents

Introduction

THE PRESIDENCY OF DONALD J. Trump, forty-fifth president of the United States, was not like any other in American history. Americans experienced a failure of imagination with this president. People were not able to fathom a morally corrupt sociopath without a conscience, ignorant of how government works, emerging as president and attacking democratic institutions to dismantle democracy—even inciting a violent insurrection on the United States Capitol to stay in power. After a single term in office, Trump left democracy hanging by a thread. Americans were stressed, confused, and reeling in his wake. Comparisons are made between Donald Trump and former presidents, and it only adds insult to injury, assuming an equivalency with others *that does not exist;* the comparisons made are only to "normalize him."[1] The damage Donald Trump inflicted on America's democracy is what fascist tyrants do. Americans didn't "see him *coming*"; they were stunned at his unpresidential manic antics, mesmerized by his unflinching anti-American rhetoric laden with lies as his gaslighting ripped through society by means of the internet. Astonishingly, Americans didn't "see him *going*" either, refusing to accept the results of a democratic election because Donald Trump said it was stolen from him! What is *that* all about?

Donald Trump's presidential legacy was his pathological antidemocratic rule, but the depth of his deception was unprecedented. Donald Trump "gaslighted" America. Gaslighting is a strategy of deception where lies are repetitive and continuous as they are streamed over time to manipulate and slowly change another's perception of reality. Psychologists say it is a common technique of abusers, dictators, narcissists, and cult leaders. In the assessment of Trump's presidency *there is no other issue more important to understand than his gaslighting of America*; it reveals who he is, opening the book of his pathologies. More important, gaslighting gives insight into what happened to American society; its effects have endured beyond his presidency, leaving an ugly anti-American mark on a sick society that

1. Drezner, *Toddler in Chief,* 207.

1

mirrors his pathologies. As a cunning master of deceit, Trump's presidency was shrouded in a mysterious fog that enveloped Americans—"a fog of lies"—more deceptive than the fog of war that descended on America during the Vietnam War. Two years after Donald Trump left office, he is still unaccountable for crimes he committed against democracy, and the enormity of the adverse effects of his gaslighting the American public are slowly being realized, as the fog of his lies and deception lifts. Numerous state and federal criminal investigations, as well as special select congressional hearings, have brought the reality of President Donald Trump's crimes to light—a virtual one-man crime wave has been brought into the bright light of day.[2] However, what happened during Trump's anti-American rule cannot be understood merely by an analysis of the man and his presidency, as important as that is for a return to democratic rule. *Americans must look within themselves to assess the damage.*

Friedrich Nietzsche, a German philosopher and culture critic, who often challenged Christian morality and attacked the ideas of the Christian religion, nevertheless had this important observation about human nature: "Whoever fights monsters should see to it that in the process he does not become a monster. And if you gaze long enough into an abyss, the abyss will gaze back into you." Nietzsche's look within himself revealed "a tortured spectacle, a mind rich in conflicts; for him, humanity consisted of inner expressions of competing wills."[3] There are consequences when people unguardedly and continuously contemplate evil. His observation about human nature refers to a central issue of Christian theology, *the vulnerability of sinful human nature to corruption.* Nietzsche referred to the function of conscience in humans—the ability to tell the difference between good and evil, an inner awareness of self, the freedom of choice, and that conscience is vulnerable to outside influences.[4] With Donald Trump, Americans were faced with a choice and many, including Christians, chose to follow a malignant narcissist sociopath and were gaslighted, tainted and complicit with the darkness he brought to American society. A prolonged gaze into the abyss of Trump's presidency revealed the influence of the lower angels of human nature in its "fallen state." For those who committed to him and gazed intensely, it was an occasion for the "evil of the abyss to stare back." From a Christian perspective, it is depressing to examine the tortured spectacle of American society manipulated by Donald Trump's gaslighting. Even investigating the dark story of Trump's presidency is depressing; nevertheless it

2. Slisco, "'Guilty as Sin'"; Litman, "Another Case"; Chait, "Trump's Greatest Triumph."
3. Leiter, "Nietzsche's Moral and Political Philosophy."
4. Leiter, "Nietzsche's Moral and Political Philosophy."

must be assessed and his dark deception must be exposed and brought into the bright light of day.

Christians are not naïve about evil; it is not a mystery in their worldview. The Bible centers on the origin of evil, a corrupt human nature, and its effects in life as well as its remedy. Evangelical Christians who followed and supported Donald Trump were schooled in the biblical reality of evil; they had a clear understanding of the dynamics of sin and depravity. Those who committed themselves to Donald Trump, not those who merely followed the Republican party's ideology when it had one, but Trump's "true believers," need to examine their commitment to him and the tragedy of his presidency *according to the biblical standard*. Many Americans did "see him coming," both Democrats and Republicans, investigative journalists, and professionals from the academic disciplines that focus on human behavior as well as many in the Christian community; they recognized the evil that Donald Trump represented and escaped the dark corrupting influence of his gaslighting. However, for distinct reasons that I will explore in the following chapters, there are millions of Americans from all the above groups that were overwhelmed by Donald Trump's blatant flood of lies and evil, not realizing who he was and that he set out to deceive Americans and dismantle their democracy.

It is not only the application of political science, psychology, and communication science that contribute to an understanding as to why millions of Americans and evangelicals didn't "see him coming." Along with the insights of those academic disciplines, biblical theology[5] gives an in-depth understanding of Trump and his presidency, because it focuses on individual spirituality, sinful human nature, the necessity for introspection, and the identification of evil. The Bible addresses the function of conscience and gives insights into fallen human nature. The "mystery of the gospel" in the Bible's history of salvation brings light and dispels the darkness of the abyss. Its view of fallen human nature is part of our investigation of Donald Trump, his gaslighting, and American society's susceptibility to it. Corrupt human nature also speaks to the salvation that Jesus Christ provided, a message of hope, forgiveness, and the possibility of reconciliation to God. The gospel message of grace and truth is that divine forgiveness is always preceded by human repentance in providing the ultimate answer to the problem of sin.[6] As Christians look into the depressing dark story

---

5. "Biblical theology" is distinguished from "systematic theology" in that it is theology found in the Bible; the biblical theologian's horizon is the Scriptures; the systematic theologian's horizon is the topical categories of a rationalistic Western system of theology—which is also founded on the Scriptures.

6. John 1:9–14.

of deception that Donald Trump brought to the American presidency, the gospel provides hope, light, and truth: "God is light, in him there is no darkness at all."[7] The truth of the gospel is an ever present redeeming thread in this book, because it brings refreshing insight and perspective for assessing Trump and his evil influence on America. Along with a multidisciplinary approach, therefore, I show how biblical theology plays a critical role in shedding light on Donald Trump, his presidency, and his unique deception that captured the American people.

For America to recover from Donald Trump's presidency and for any sort of reconciliation to occur in hyper-polarized America, it would be irresponsible to forget the tragedy of his presidency and move on, acting as though nothing extraordinary happened. Professionals know that any major action taken where lives are at stake requires a debriefing or after-action report to elicit lessons learned so that mistakes made are identified and not repeated. Trump's presidency must not be forgotten but exposed for what it was—*the introduction of neofascism to America* in an effort to dismantle and overthrow democracy.[8] Therefore, Trump's anti-American criminal actions must be understood and an assessment made of the damage that he inflicted on democratic institutions and American society. Why Trump's assault on democracy was not recognized as fascism speaks to both the nature and effectiveness of his gaslighting, as well as the naïveté of Americans to this type of authoritarian rule.

AMERICANS DIDN'T SEE A FASCIST TYRANT COMING

From the initial stages of his presidential campaign, Donald Trump intended to establish himself as a fascist leader and that involved dismantling American democracy. During the entire time he was in the Oval Office his words, deeds, and admiration for dictators confirmed his intention to be the first anti-democracy president of the United States of America. Focus on Donald Trump alone offers an incomplete analysis of the tragedy of his presidency. In Ruth Ben-Ghiat's *Strongmen: Mussolini to the Present*, she quotes Piero Gobetti, a former partisan under Mussolini: "Every country gets the gangster it deserves."[9] Gobetti's maxim recalls another, "It takes more than a dictator to destroy a democracy." "The people" are complicit in introducing fascism and bringing harm to democracy. Of course, this maxim includes the Christian community. Ben-Ghiat's book focuses on twentieth-century

---

7. 1 John 1:5; Col 1:3–29; John 1:9–14.

8. DeVega, "Philosopher Jason Stanley"; Reid, "Political Analyst Tells."

9. Ben-Ghiat, *Strongmen*, 251.

authoritarian rulers, and she includes Donald Trump. She advises, "To oppose authoritarians effectively we must have a clear-eyed view of how they manage to get into power and stay there."[10] The trouble is that Americans are not familiar with authoritarian leaders like Europeans are, especially the fascist type. Almost two and a half centuries of democracy made Americans naïve, unsuspecting targets for Donald Trump.

Former Secretary of State Madeleine Albright agrees with Ruth Ben-Ghiat regarding the nature of fascism; she says it should be viewed less as a political ideology than *a means for seizing and holding power*.[11] Mussolini said the deception employed in grasping power is sometimes slow and not observed by the public; he advised, "It is wise in seeking power to do so as one 'plucks a chicken'—one feather at a time."[12] Albright notes, "Every step in the direction of fascism—every plucked feather—causes damage to individuals and a society, each makes the next step shorter . . . we must recognize that despots rarely reveal their intentions and that leaders who begin well frequently become more authoritarian the longer they hold power."[13] Donald Trump experienced power and employed deception—the fascist role and mentality—during his dog-eat-dog ruthless and vindictive years doing business in New York State. He cultivated deception, lies, and a false persona portraying himself as a successful businessman and deal maker. His personal attorney, business advisor, and fix-it man Michael Cohen said that Trump's business model was "doing anything—and I mean anything—to win, [this] has always been his business model and way of life."[14] The numerous frauds, deception, and lies that were the norm in his business practices were carried over to Trump's presidency and at its end—with "the chicken almost completely plucked"—he attempted to overthrow the results of a democratic election, inciting an open violent insurrection on the US Capitol to stay in power in true fascist tradition.

In her book *Fascism: A Warning*, Albright describes a fascist as "someone who identifies strongly with and claims to speak for a whole nation or group, is unconcerned with the rights of others, and is willing to use whatever means are necessary, including violence, to achieve his or her goals."[15] She makes it clear that her warning is about Donald J. Trump, "whose statements and actions are so at odds with democratic ideals":

10. Ben-Ghiat, *Strongmen*, 250.

11. Albright, *Fascism*, 9.

12. Albright *Fascism*, 118, 119–20, 126, 230.

13. Albright, *Fascism*, 120.

14. Cohen, *Disloyal*, 10.

15. Albright, *Fascism*,11.

> In the process, [of his campaign and in the White House] he systematically degraded political discourse in the United States, showed an astonishing disregard for facts, libeled his predecessors, threatened to "lock up" political rivals, referred to mainstream journalists as "the enemy of the American people," spread falsehoods about the integrity of the U.S. electoral process, touted mindlessly nationalistic economic and trade policies, vilified immigrants and the countries from which they come, and nurtured paranoid bigotry toward the followers of one of the world's foremost religions.[16]

Since Albright wrote before the final days of Donald Trump's presidency, an update of her list of antidemocratic rhetoric and actions would include his unprecedented attempt to overturn a democratic election and incite a violent insurrection on the US Capitol—just as any other twentieth-century fascist dictator would.

From the beginning of his presidential campaign, Donald Trump appeared as a corrupt tyrant with fascist moves. In bold arrogance, he used fascist Mussolini's slogan "Drain the Swamp" to indicate that he would clean up government corruption. Instead, he did the opposite, bringing unprecedented corruption and a crime wave to the Oval Office. His "drain the swamp" type of bold lie was a diversionary tactic often used to cover up his fascist acts. He used psychological projection—blaming *others* for what *he* was doing; it was a behavior trait of his pathological personality disorders that added a grandiose dimension to everything he did or said. Anyone who has paid any attention whatsoever to the news media and television/cable news during the four-year presidency of Donald Trump has observed a fascist anti-democracy president in action. His fascist rhetoric was in the media ad nauseam. It was a dog-whistle of blatant racism and bold appeal to white supremacists in multicultural America disguised as immigration reform; *his racist message appealed to Americans who felt displaced by America's cultural diversity, deprived, and wronged by the government.* Dog-whistle, in the figurative sense, means a message communicated through certain coded words and phrases commonly understood by a particular group of people (Trump's base), but not others. In Christian theology, it refers to the use of coded words and phrases that appeal to people who feel deprived or wronged by society, *words and subjects that directly appeal to the self-centered sinful side of human nature;* words like racism, prejudice, hatred, "fight for your country" violence, "them and us partisanship," encouraging

16. Albright, *Fascism*, 5.

hatred and rebellion.[17] Flooding the public with these coded words, Trump incited his political base and *brought forth human nature's worst behavior,*[18] raising fears in those who opposed him, even putting members of Congress in fear for their political careers and fear of physical harm from Trump's fanatical base. In this fascist way, Trump effectively quashed the dissent of members of Congress as well as secured their vote by intimidation.[19]

AMERICANS DIDN'T SEE HIM COMING DUE TO GASLIGHTING

It is likely that a person under the onslaught of Trump's lies and deception either becomes aware that no other US presidency has even come close to the disaster of Donald Trump in the Oval Office, or they have been gaslighted and "see nothing wrong," having become accustomed to a malignant normality.[20] *Fascists, sociopaths, and malignant narcissists gaslight.* Gaslighting is not just another word for lying; it is a powerful scheme of deception and streaming lies recognized by the discipline of psychology and psychoanalysts. It takes place over time, with the goal of replacing another person's reality with the gaslighter's reality. It refers to the radicalization of a person or persons by another; the radicalization of young Muslim terrorists to the point where they will blow themselves up with a bomb, killing innocent people, is a contemporary example of this deception. Gaslighting has a powerful, dramatic psychological effect on the human psyche, *especially on narcissists.*

Donald Trump's gaslighting of America was unprecedented—an epic "Great Deception." The intensity of gaslighting was on a level above propaganda; no historic example of propaganda comes close to its effect on society, not even the use of propaganda in the rise of Adolf Hitler. In the Trump presidency, the effect of gaslighting on Americans and truth itself was unprecedented. The medium of communication he used for repeatedly streaming his lies was the internet; his deception would immediately reach millions of Americans—anyone with a television, computer, or a smartphone. The technology of the internet offered numerous social media information platforms, channels for unverified information, both

17. See biblical list of terms about "the acts of the flesh" or "self" in Gal 5:19–21, Col 3:5–9, and 2 Tim 3:1–5.

18. Bidar, "Obama Blames Social Media."

19. Kelly, "Liz Cheney Says."

20. Lifton, "Our Witness to Malignant Normality," §488, §494.

misinformation and disinformation,[21] along with widespread conspiracy theories that weaponized lies, created confusion, and weakened society's capacity for truth, Russian style. The new multi-sourced social media platforms, like Twitter, allowed Donald Trump to converse with Americans, gaslighting them incessantly. The lies and deception became an enormous liability for Americans who increasingly found it difficult to determine what was true. Instinctively, fascist Trump took advantage of the confusion, weakness, and social conditions that he created by gaslighting Americans. Lying and deception were always a winning approach in his life; now, in the presidency, the streaming of lies in gaslighting was the means for creating an alternate American reality—Trump's own twisted view of America. It was all set up for him to step in with fascist rule in the chaos he created.

Donald Trump's bold attempt to become America's first anti-democracy president was not done in secret; he boldly and openly attacked democracy's norms and institutions as Republican reform, allegedly to establish a Republican-style government and "Make America Great Again." He implemented the deceptive practice of gaslighting to cover up his fascist motives and intention to gain personal absolute power and wealth in his presidency. With Trump, the phenomenon of gaslighting took on a collective sense as large numbers of Americans succumbed to his constant streaming of lies. As president of the United States, the fascist tyrant had the perfect influential platform for mass deception—the presidential bully pulpit; the term took on a literal sickening meaning. Trump slowly "plucked the chicken," dismantling democratic institutions while gaslighting the public; he did so openly, loudly, and with great fanfare as preposterous lies accompanied each plucked feather. He was in the face of Americans daily, dominating the news media and controlling its narrative with a flood of audacious lies and false claims that diverted public attention from his anti-democracy agenda. Little did America realize that Trump's lifelong multiple pathological personality disorders were motivating his lies and erratic behavior and facilitating his attempt to assume the role of an antidemocratic leader; "truth" was under massive assault in American society. Yale professor of history Timothy Snyder summed up Trump's assault on democracy when he said, "Post-truth is pre-fascism."[22]

Stunned at first, the American Congress, media, and public were mesmerized by Donald Trump's audacious lies; the innocuous phrase "this is not normal" was heard over and over. The flood of lies so overwhelmed the media that press checks to determine the veracity of his claims could

21. Dhaliwal, "Barak Obama Says"; Lee, "Humanity's Worst Impulses."
22. Snyder, *On Tyranny*, 71.

not keep up with wave after wave of Trump's lies. Unfortunately, the propaganda damage of a lie was done merely in the telling, even though it was refuted afterwards—as Trump fully understood. In the *Washington Post's* Fact Check Project in 2021, Glenn Kessler stated that nearly half of Trump's 30,573 misleading claims and lies came in the last year of office. The spread of lies throughout his presidency was six lies a day in his first year, sixteen a day in his second year, twenty-two a day in his third year, and thirty-nine a day in his fourth year. The deluge of lies was the historic backdrop for the January 6 insurrection at the US Capitol. On his last day in office, Trump told five hundred lies in his Ellipse Mall speech just before the insurrection on the Capitol.[23] America was not prepared for a sociopath president who was a pathological liar—the great deception he launched.

Trump's seeming ubiquitous appearance in the media, repeating his lies over and over, in time made them appear to be true or at least worth considering (the gaslighting shift of reality phenomenon). Sociopaths lie. In the light of biblical theology, it is not farfetched to link Trump's intense lie phenomenon to his corrupt human nature and a supernatural edge of evil. Christians may recall the vitriolic encounter between Jesus and the Pharisees, the "gaslighters" in New Testament, when they questioned his deity and repeatedly lied about his identity. Jesus did not hesitate to attribute their lies to their father—the father of all lies—Satan.[24] *Why Donald Trump's extraordinary lie phenomenon was not a red flag to Christians staggers the imagination.* It makes a person nostalgic for times past in America society when honesty was the best policy. Today, truth no longer matters in political discourse; lies, deception, and conspiracy theories have taken over the political stage. Anne Applebaum, in *Twilight of Democracy*, states, "The emotional appeal of a conspiracy theory is in its simplicity. It explains away complex phenomena, accounts for chance and accidents, offers the believer the satisfying sense of having special, privileged access to the truth."[25] With his gaslighting, Trump brought massive, long-lasting confusion to American society. Even when the lying president is no longer in office, his lies continue to dominate and garner belief in a gaslighted Republican party, with his political base, and with millions of Americans. The effectiveness of Trump's gaslighting is demonstrated by the large number of Republican congressional members and his base continuing to propagate a proven, obviously false delusional Big Lie—that Joe Biden stole the 2020 election

23. Kessler, "Trump's False or Misleading Claims."

24. John 8:34, 44; see the development of this subject in chapter 7, "Hellenist Christians Expose Historical Gaslighting and Racism."

25. Applebaum, *Twilight of Democracy*, 45.

from him—almost two years after the election![26] Trump's gaslighting has damaged America's capacity for truth; it is in serious decline everywhere.

FASCISM AMERICAN STYLE

Historically, what a president says from the bully pulpit Americans tend to believe. After all, honesty has been a prominent keystone of American character—children are taught that lying is wrong. I do not claim that presidents never lie, but from my first awareness of an American president—thirteen presidents back to Franklin Delano Roosevelt—I have never associated repeated lying with any president, except Richard Nixon. The question is, Do presidents of the United States of America repeatedly and compulsively lie to the point of indicating a personal pathology? With Donald Trump the question does not have to do with the ethics of a lie—that question does not even exist in the mental process of a sociopath because he does not have a functioning conscience. The historical answer is no. Presidential historian Michael Beschloss states, "I have never seen a president in American history who has lied so continuously and so outrageously as Donald Trump, period."[27] The American public, the US Congress, and the Christian community were not prepared for Donald Trump, a president with marked immoral character and pathological personality disorders—*that were not borderline, but full-blown*—enabling him to continuously and boldly lie without any signs of shame or remorse. Of course, this greatly enhanced his gaslighting. No one expected a president that would lie and deceive with such alacrity. Did the Republican party do even a modicum of vetting with Donald Trump? Another obvious question is, Why would intelligent men and women of conscience, as well Christians schooled in biblical morality, not see him coming?

Donald Trump's admiration of Vladimir Putin, Russia's dictator—as well as other dictators—was clearly on display in his presidential campaign, throughout his presidency, and afterward. His adulation of Putin not only flagged his admiration for dictators but also his disdain for democracy and his intention to become a fascist president—with Russian help. Trump was the first president to "weaponize disinformation" Russian style. He began to show his colors when he fired James Comey, the FBI director, publicly admitting that it was to stop his Russia investigation. He also nullified the

---

26. Velshi, "Comity in Congress"; Niedzwiadek, "McCarthy after Ousting Cheney"; Collinson, "GOP's Devotion to Trump"; Choi, "One-Third of GOP"; Christopher, "Trump Effect"; Parsley, "Donald Trump Demands."

27. Timm, "Trump Vs. the Truth."

nation's intelligence services and their reports about Russia; he showed his distaste for intelligence briefings by ignoring and challenging agency assessments and the competence of professional career intelligence officers and then replacing them with his political sycophants that had no intelligence background.[28] On a world stage at Helsinki, on July 16, 2018, Trump appeared with Vladimir Putin and said to an international audience that he did not believe his American intelligence agencies when they said Russia interfered with the 2016 elections, because Putin firmly denied doing so!

To fully pave the way for his unlawful fascist style of wielding presidential power, Trump attacked democratic institutions. He took control of the Justice Department by appointing William Barr to the post of attorney general. Barr proved to be a corrupt, unscrupulous Trump sycophant, affording the president a strategic weapon for dismantling democracy—the Department of Justice. In an unprecedented violation of his office, Barr functioned as Donald Trump's personal lawyer, not as the chief law enforcement officer of the nation. Most notable was Barr's hijacking and quashing the crucial Robert Mueller *Russia Investigation Report* by not passing it on to Congress in a timely manner, but publishing his own ingenuous opinion in a four-page letter to Congress that denied the results of Mueller's two-year investigation and his three-hundred-page report as special counsel. Because of Barr's theory of presidential absolute immunity, he quashed Mueller's report.[29] Trump's corruption of the Department of Justice via Bill Barr allowed him to engage in a crime wave in office under the questionable legal theory of absolute presidential immunity; under its guise, Trump was free to attack democratic institutions—one at a time, just like "plucking a chicken"—as he dismantled America's democracy.

Donald Trump lied brazenly and continuously, denying that he had contact with Russians, gaslighting the American people on the subject, and calling the Russia investigation a hoax. *However, there was collusion with Russia in the 2016 election campaign.*[30] At the time, the truth concerning what Donald Trump was doing was hidden in the fog of his gaslighting. The major correction and refutation of Trump's lies and deceit was Special Counsel Robert Mueller's report on the Russia investigation, but Bill Barr effectively quashed it, keeping the proof of Trump's Russia contacts from the American public. Just before the presidential campaign, while Trump's lawyer Michael Cohen was running a major real estate deal for him in Moscow,

28. Vaillancourt, "Homeland Security Secretary Altered Report."

29. Wallace, "Judge Details"; Maddow, "Federal Judge Calls out Barr"; Tillman, "Mueller Memo Advising Barr."

30. Melber, "Trump Collusion Exposed in 2021"; Sheth, "U.S. Officially Designates"; Mazzetti, "G.O.P.-Led Senate Panel"; Mueller, *Mueller Report*, 44, 46–47, 138–39.

Trump blatantly and repeatedly lied to the American people saying, "There's no Russian collusion, I have no dealings with Russia . . . There's no Russia."[31] The proof that the 2016 campaign's collusion with Russia was not fully revealed to the American people until April 2021—five years later—is testament to the effectiveness of the mass radicalization phenomenon of Trump's gaslighting.

In the 2020 election, Donald Trump claimed election fraud, using psychological "projection" (a pathological trait of sociopaths *and children*) saying the election was stolen from him—a proven false claim—while the truth was that this was precisely what he did by unlawfully obtaining Russian help to steal the election from Hillary Clinton in 2016. The effectiveness of Trump's gaslighting is demonstrated in his maintaining the Big Lie that the election was stolen from him, while courts at state and federal level have determined the opposite conclusively, in over sixty baseless lawsuits filed by Trump's lawyers claiming election fraud; in each filing, the election was found to be fair and democratic. Rudy Giuliani and Sidney Powell filed some of the frivolous lawsuits and had their law licenses suspended, were fined, and sued. A judge recommended that Giuliani be disbarred for his lying and filing frivolous lawsuits.[32] Two years after the election, the Republican party and millions of Americans still embrace the Trump election motto "Stop the Steal" and still believe that Trump won the election! It should not escape notice that after Trump's obfuscating administration, the fog of deception is beginning to lift with a substantial amount of evidence released supporting that the 2016 election was stolen from Hillary Clinton. The irony of what has transpired and the lasting effects of Trump's gaslighting during his time in office should not be forgotten but remembered as lessons learned about a morally deficient, psychologically unfit, and deeply flawed human being's influence on American society.

Trump refusing to acknowledge proof of his election defeat years after a fair and lawful election is not an expression of the American value of never giving up; it is a manifestation of his pathological malignant narcissistic personality disorder. He perpetuated the Big Lie that the election was stolen from him; his pathology produced an unwillingness to accept defeat and he successfully transferred his pathology, causing members of Congress and millions of Americans *to follow a psychopathic delusion*.[33] Trump's pathological personality disorders enabled him to gaslight Americans and

31. Cohen, *Disloyal*, 160.

32. Benen, "Court Suspends Giuliani's Law License"; Durkee, "Ethics Complaint against Rudy Giuliani"; Larson, "Sidney Powell, Lin Wood."

33. Tansey, "Why Crazy Like a Fox," §2351, §2376–94.

Congress successfully with the Big Lie, and it ultimately led to a violent insurrection of the US Capitol. His followers stormed the Capitol building and assaulted police defending it, resulting in injuries to police, loss of life, property damage, and lasting trauma for the police involved as well as members of Congress.[34] Trump's ultimate purpose with the Big Lie was to incite an insurrection that would block Congress from certifying Joe Biden's win of the 2020 election. His wave of election crimes was part and parcel of his fascist attempt to stay in power. Trump's pathological bold use of the Big Lie, especially how he streamed his lies—gaslighting—was the main feature of his presidency; deception was the way he maintained his power, his political base, *and it is a major clue to the paradox of his Christian following*. It was fascism American style. His malignant narcissism enabled him to spin an unprecedented Great Deception; it partially explains why Americans did not see him coming, but it also reveals a complicit American society—those who elected and supported him—including evangelical Christians.

THE PARADOX OF DONALD TRUMP'S CHRISTIAN FOLLOWERS

Despite President Donald Trump's lawlessness, immorality, deception, and flood of lies, he has a Christian following. This book examines the paradox of many in America's Christian community following Donald Trump, a man of marked immoral and evil character, yet supporting his presidency as he slowly and openly dismantled democracy. Focus on the president's morality sometimes elicits the following response: "I don't care whether he is moral or not just so he performs his duties as president." This is an intellectually dishonest response for any intelligent person of conscience. Who would say morality is not important when engaging a babysitter? A business partner or financial advisor? A physical fitness coach for your wife? A date for your sixteen-year-old daughter? Furthermore, a *Christian* showing no concern for a president's moral character is a stark contradiction of the teaching of Jesus and biblical values—the foundation for Christian belief and life—which makes the issue of morality imperative.

The whole focus of biblical revelation and the Christian worldview is on the issue of morality, the fallen sinful nature of humans before a Holy God and their need for salvation from the power of sin and evil. Therefore, would not the issue of the moral character of the person that would occupy the most powerful office in the nation be an important Christian consideration? The framers of the Constitution thought so. It was not just

34. Hall et al., "At Least 1,003 People Have Been Charged."

their experience of evil under the British monarchy that led them to employ checks and balances in the US Constitution; at the time of its writing,
they were influenced by what the Christian faith revealed about the issue
of human morality, if not personally, then through their Christian wives,
family, and friends—and certainly through the influence of the Christian
community.[35] While I give a major emphasis to the behavioral sciences in
investigating the character of Donald Trump and his presidency, I suggest that Christian theology and biblical revelation (the Bible) provide an
in-depth understanding of the corruption of Donald Trump, his lawless
presidency, and the paradox of his Christian following. Often the findings
of the secular sciences, especially psychology, confirm the Christian viewpoint on human corruption and vice versa for determining what sort of
man occupied the Oval Office. The claim that Christian theology and the
Scriptures are a fundamental context for understanding Donald Trump and
his presidency should not surprise Christians, especially those who claim
to be "evangelicals," given the fact that the New Testament and teachings
of Jesus Christ focus on morality—the fallen condition of humanity and its
need for salvation. A Christian moral perspective is especially revealing for
understanding a contemporary fascist's self-focus; the pathological personality trait of no empathy is common with fascist leaders. This character trait
is the antithesis of a Christian's "focus on others" that is demonstrated fully
in the life of Jesus and anyone following in his steps. The analysis of the man
Donald Trump and his presidency, from both the perspective of psychology
and biblical theology in the following pages, provides an affirmative answer
as to whether the morality question is a valid consideration for selecting an
American president.

A sizable portion of the evangelical community ignored New Testament morality lessons of Jesus' teaching that would have assisted them in
seeing Donald Trump coming. *Christians face consequences for repeatedly
not responding to what they know to be true.* A failure to heed those morality lessons, in time, sets them up to be spiritually vulnerable for Trump's
gaslighting. Keeping focused on Jesus and incorporating his teachings is not
merely a pious notion; *it is a central biblical principle* in the teachings of
Jesus and the apostles in the New Testament (NT), as well as in the prophets
of the Old Testament (OT) Scriptures—the necessity for a faith response to
the word of God.[36] Jesus warned his disciples about this, because failure to

---

35. Lepore, *These Truths*, 43–45, 49–54, 59, 67–68, 72–75, 86, 92, 106–35; Meacham,
American Gospel, 3–12, 67–76, 146–78.

36. See representative Bible sources—Jesus' teachings, most focused on the "hypocrisy" of the Pharisees: John 8:12–45; 12:35–40; Matt 5:13–16; 13:1–23; Luke 6:46–49;
the apostles' teachings: 2 Tim 4:3–4; Titus 1:10–13; Heb 2:1–4; 3:12–19; Jas 1:21–27;

respond to what is known to be true marks the beginning of an erosion of Christian understanding and vulnerability to falsehood; in other words, a vulnerability to gaslighting.[37] Those in the Christian community that followed "in Donald Trump's steps" and ignored his moral character face several important questions: In committing to Christian nationalism, did they remain in vital contact with Jesus Christ and the gospel story of divine love in the NT and not become part of political hyper-partisanship—even hating others? Did they ignore a God-given capacity for empathy enhanced by salvation and disobey the command to love one another?[38] Did they remain faithful and obedient to God's Word, eternal truth—what it revealed about the nature of evil and the evil one?[39] Did they allow the supernatural endowment of the Holy Spirit—the Spirit of truth—to do his work in assessing the man Donald Trump?[40] Or did they experience a subtle shift of reality from following in Jesus' steps to following the extreme partisan politics of a sociopath? The warning to "keep believing" (i.e., keep responding to truth in life) is constant throughout the NT, because there was, and is today, a constant spiritual battle with the truth and falsehood in society. Ignoring the testimony of Jesus should not be taken lightly; many Christian martyrs surrendered their lives for it.[41]

JUST WHO ARE "EVANGELICALS"?

A complication arises in identifying American evangelical Christians today. The reporting and focus of the American media have rendered the term "evangelical" meaningless. It has focused on evangelical leaders that do not represent the leadership of the many Christian evangelical denominations and churches—the core of evangelical Christianity in America. In search of the sensational, the media has focused on pastors of megachurches and television-evangelists when reporting on evangelicals. Even more misleading is their focus on self-appointed prophets and their pseudo-apocalyptic type of Christianity—the far-right fringe of those calling themselves evangelicals that support Donald Trump.[42] Not helping in the identification of

the Old Testament prophets: Jer 7:28; 6:19; 7:23–26; 8:7–9; 9:13; 11:7; 13:8–11. See my book, *American Evangelical-Pentecostal Elephant in the Room.*

37. John 12:35–40.
38. John 15:1–17.
39. John 17:15–17.
40. John 14:15–17; 16:7–13; 1 Cor 12:7–11.
41. Rev 19:10.
42. Lemon, "Christian 'Prophet' Johnny Enlow"; Lemon, "Christian Pastor Claims

evangelicals is a very vocal and militant pseudo-Christian nationalism that is racist and does not represent mainline American Christian groups, let alone evangelicals. Reverend Nathaniel Manderson, from the American Baptist tradition, states about Christian nationalists:

> Currently and historically, they are nothing more than a political action committee. They have nothing to do with the foundations of the Christian faith. Their political agenda is based on hate, rejection, condemnation, and self-righteousness. The biblical Pharisees, who were the enemies of Jesus, used their political connections to have him killed. In our own time, these new Pharisees use their enormous political influence to reject foreigners, deny health insurance to millions, judge the poor as lazy, refuse any and all regulation of deadly firearms and stand in opposition to equality of opportunity. In short, they stand side by side with the oppressors on virtually every issue.[43]

All the reported minority groups in the media, even if taken together, hardly represent approximately one hundred million evangelicals in America! Such a diminutive media focus distorts the meaning of evangelical and renders a disservice to the core of American evangelicalism.

However, a myopic media focus does call attention to the silence of many mainstream evangelical and Pentecostal-charismatic churches that *did* see him coming yet tried to stay out of the political conflict, eliminating a Christian witness in a society in great need of one. Their silence raises questions about how Christians should be involved in politics and what the guidelines should be. Many evangelical and Pentecostal churches consider it sufficient to confine their preaching of the gospel to their Christian audience in the pew and any "outsiders" who happen to be present, engaging in foreign missions, and formulating internal doctrinal statements about American political issues. *This* is *not the same as an active Christian witness in American society*, calling out an immoral, dangerous, and corrupt president and his administration as well as calling out false Christian nationalism that ignores assaults on democracy and morality. Confining the church's witness to the Christian community falls short of Jesus' description of it as "the salt of the earth" and "the light of the world" (Matt 5:13–14). With the extreme danger that Donald Trump posed for American democracy, silence is complicity. The question remains, Does Christ's church have a prophetic responsibility to warn society of a danger like Donald Trump or not?

Biden"; Lemon, "Pastor Jonny Enlow Says"; Lemon, "Evangelical 'Prophet' Claims."

43. Manderson, "So Who Are 'Evangelicals'?."

Curiously, an example of such speaking out is found in the mental health profession; they rejected the "Goldwater gag rule" governing their profession at the emergence of Donald Trump, because they noted his danger to society. The Goldwater rule kept mental health professionals from commenting on public figures and from warning society about the danger of someone like Donald Trump. Despite the gag rule, psychiatrists spoke of the necessity to bear witness to the danger of a "malignant narcissist sociopath" president. They disregarded the gag order for the public good, speaking out and giving warnings about the pathological personality disorders of President Donald Trump that made him a danger to the public. They reached back historically to the basis that the American Psychiatric Association's guideline provided, which urged psychiatrists "to serve society by advising and consulting with the executive, legislative, and judiciary branches of the government." They also appealed to the Declaration of Geneva, established by the World Medical Association twenty-five years earlier, which mandated physicians speak up if there are humanitarian reasons to do so—this Declaration was created in response to the experience of Nazism.[44] The mental health profession's example of warning society of danger is discussed further at the end of chapter two. The profession's return to historical roots is an instructive parallel for the church; evangelicals should follow their example in reaching back in their evangelical roots for an appropriate response in the church's witness against evil in society today; such reaching back leads to Jesus' actions confronting the corruption of his generation.

To clarify the definition of evangelicals and avoid the media's contemporary minimalist view, I reach back a couple of generations in American history for a definition of evangelical. In 1980, I prepared a dissertation for a PhD in intercultural studies at Fuller Seminary's School of World Mission, "Pentecostalism and Missions: Distortion or Correction? The Pentecostal Contribution to Contemporary Mission Theology." An immediate task was to define evangelical to show Pentecostal Christians were part of the evangelical movement and then give their contribution to contemporary Christian missions. The definition of evangelical concerns *principles found in the central Christian tradition throughout history, originating in the evangel/good news of the New Testament.* Protestant Christians first appealed to the threefold Reformation principles of:

1. The authority of the Scriptures

---

44. A main source for the psychological assessment of Donald Trump is editor Bandy Lee's *Dangerous Case of Donald Trump*. Lee was a leader of the group of mental health professionals that rejected the misused and outdated "Goldwater rule."

2. Salvation by faith

3. The universal priesthood of believers.

The Reformation formula focused on the issues of that period of the church.

If we were to skip from the period of the Protestant Reformation forward to the time when I was preparing my dissertation, the term evangelical referred to seven principles that were agreed upon by the evangelical movement:

1. The authority of the word of God

2. Orthodoxy (correct belief)

3. Personal salvation by grace (through faith)

4. Dedication and commitment

5. Evangelism and missions

6. Ecumenism (*koinonia*, Christian fellowship)

7. Social concern (especially for the poor)[45]

An evangelical was a Christian that identified with this configuration of belief and practice. The seven principles span the history of the church from the Day of Pentecost in the first-century church to the present. Theoretically, no group was to be in focus with the seven principles; rather the focus was on New Testament principles of belief and practice. However, the evangelical movement in the 1980s hesitated in recognizing the Pentecostal movement that emerged at the turn of the twentieth century as well as the charismatic movement among mainline Protestant denominations and the Roman Catholic charismatic movement that emerged in the mid-1960s.

An inclusive notion of evangelicalism was confirmed at the turn of the twenty-first century with the worldwide Pentecostal-charismatic movement; it was not confined to any particular Christian body and membership numbers of the movement *in the countries of the Southern Hemisphere far exceeded* the population of evangelicals in the United States.[46] These four Christian movements emphasized the work of the Holy Spirit in the lives of Christians,[47] patterning it after first-century Christians in the New Testament. The global reality today is there are people from all the above designations of Christianity (mainline Christian denominations, evangelicals,

45. Willingham, "Truth behind the 'He Gets Us' Ads." See also the 1974 Lausanne Covenant, a unifying document of evangelical churches; the Lausanne Covenant gives a theological explanation for the "seven evangelical principles."

46. Pomerville, *Third Force*, 4–16.

47. Protestant theology categories: sanctification and pneumatology.

Pentecostals, charismatic-oriented Christians in both mainline Protestant churches and the Roman Catholic charismatic movement) that would ascribe to the "seven evangelical principles." The reason is that charismatic Christianity brought a unity of spiritual experience that penetrated a considerable number of Christians worldwide, bringing a dynamic new *eighth evangelical principle* from the New Testament into focus, in addition to the previous somewhat rationalistic seven principles. The eighth principle focused on the dynamic nature of the Christian faith made possible through the ministry of the Holy Spirit in the lives of Christians, and it was in accord with the Reformers' dynamic view of the word of God, which held the word of God was never separated from the Spirit.[48] Charismatic Christianity revealed the somewhat rationalistic and static nature of the seven principles influenced by the post-Reformation Western European Enlightenment on the Christian faith; *the eighth principle added a dynamic Holy Spirit dimension to each of the seven evangelical principles.* Therefore, the mention of a movement of Pentecostal-charismatic evangelical Christians—*850 million worldwide*[49]—puts the pinprick minimalist focus of the American media in perspective. The designation *evangelical* above shows that the Christian case for morality in evaluating a president of the United States of America is not an esoteric obscure minority viewpoint!

In the chapters that follow, I present reasons why some evangelical Christians didn't see Donald Trump coming and why millions of other Americans were also gaslighted and didn't see him coming either. Fascist Trump's successful gaslighting meant that historic American democratic reality was replaced with another reality—a twisted Trump authoritarian anti-American reality. Yale history professor Timothy Snyder said that many reasonable people make a mistake of assuming "that rulers who came to power through institutions cannot change or destroy those very institutions—even when that is exactly what they have announced that they will do."[50] Americans did not know what to make of Trump's bizarre intentions and actions, as he slowly dismantled democracy. Now they must become familiar with new words: "fascism," "narcissism," "pathological personality disorders," "presidential immunity," and "tyrant;" they must also recognize that old political terms like "freedom," "truth," "American," "history," "equality," "legal," and "racism" have been fed new meanings and are misused.

Donald Trump was not a student of the history of fascism nor was he led by ideology, but there were enablers in his cabinet that were familiar

48. Pomerville, *Third Force*, 112, 134–35, 191–95, 257–58.
49. Pomerville, *Third Force*, 7–9, 58–69.
50. Snyder, *On Tyranny*, 24.

with fascism and wanted to replace America's democratic republic with an authoritarian government. They informed him about historic fascism, its mottoes, and strategies, guiding him down the path of authoritarian rule—all with the support of the Republican party, which at first was silent, though later many in Congress joined him in his fascist crimes. Unfortunately, Trump's corrupt human nature, or if you want to say pathological personality disorders, were the perfect fit for fascist rule and a disastrous fate for American democracy. Although the founders of the Constitution anticipated the possibility of antidemocratic unscrupulous persons impacting democracy from within and included safeguards, even Congress was caught off guard by Trump launching a fascist attack on American democracy and its Constitution. Nobody was ready for, or even suspected, a *malignant narcissist sociopath had occupied the White House.*

PART I

Unprecedented

A Malignant Narcissist Sociopath—
in the White House

Chapter 1

The "Making" of a Tyrant

Tyrants are dictators gone bad.

ELIZABETH MIKA, CLINICAL PSYCHOLOGIST[1]

Being president doesn't change who you are,
it reveals who you are.

FIRST LADY MICHELLE OBAMA[2]

"WHO IS DONALD J. Trump?" This question involves understanding his multiple pathological personality disorders and how they impacted his unprecedented aberrant presidency. Yale historian Timothy Snyder said that Trump's performance in the Oval Office caused political scientists and historians to resurrect the ancient word "tyrant" as they searched for a word to describe him: "The Founding Fathers sought to avoid the *evil* that they, like the ancient philosophers called *tyranny.*"[3] Evil is a biblical word used freely by Christians and theologians. While the empirical sciences use the term, its origins are attributed to other than supernatural sources, but there is a striking similarity in theology and psychology as both describe the manifestation of evil and its impact on humanity. Psychology provides an important context in this book for an investigation of the bizarre mentality and manic actions of Donald Trump.

1. Mika, "Who Goes Trump?," §5187.
2. Paz, "Full Transcript of Michelle Obama's."
3. Snyder, *On Tyranny*, 10.

Prior to occupying the Oval Office, a popular view of Donald Trump's identity was his media persona in New York City. However, that persona was a creation of Donald Trump himself, a self-propagated "brand" accepted by the media. They saw him as (1) a man of great gifts, a smart and successful businessman—a deal maker—and savvy master manipulator of markets. According to clinical psychoanalysts, mental health experts, and professors of psychology they saw him as (2) a man afflicted with several personality disorders—sociopathy, malignant narcissism, and others, conducting himself not according to ideology, ethics, or policy but instinctively and uninhibitedly driven by those personality disorders.[4] This second view is similar to what Christian theology suggests; it uses different terminology and points to a different source and depth of human disfunction. In theological terms he is (3) a man acting in accord with a corrupt, even depraved, human nature revealing an inordinate focus on *self—what he wants*—an absence of empathy (no concern for others, what they want) with behaviors "of the flesh" due to a non-functioning ("seared") conscience.[5] Donald Trump's presidency did not sustain the media persona; rather, it quickly revealed his true identity. I turn to the description of Donald Trump as a tyrant because it introduces us to the second option about his identity, his pathological personality disorders that are found in tyrants, both ancient and modern. Clinical psychologist Elizabeth Mika notes, "All tyrants share several essential features: they are predominantly men with a specific character defect, narcissistic psychopathy (a.k.a. malignant narcissism)."[6]

A SOCIOPATH TYRANT EMERGES

When I first saw the title of Mary L. Trump's book, *Too Much and Never Enough*, I thought Mary was referring to Donald's wealth and primary life motivation—money. However, reading further, I understood that in the language of psychology her "too much and never enough" referred to the abusive development of Donald Trump in childhood, in an extremely dysfunctional family[7] with a sociopath father and a missing mother. When hearing the results of the 2016 election, Mary Trump responded, "It felt as though 62,979,636 voters had chosen to turn this country into a macro

---

4. Mika, "Who Goes Trump?," §5209.

5. See Gal 5:13–26 for the list of behaviors that flow from "the flesh." In contexts like this, the Greek word for flesh refers to the sinful state of human beings often presented as a power in opposition to the Spirit.

6. Mika, "Who Goes Trump?," §5196.

7. Trump, *Too Much and Never Enough*, 26.

version of my malignantly dysfunctional family"[8] The "too much" in Mary
Trump's book title referred to Donald's exposure to a sociopath father, who
humiliated family members, showed only self-interest, and to whom love
meant nothing; his pathological disability made him focus only on their
obedience to what he wanted. Mary says her uncle absorbed his father's
sociopathic traits as well as developed powerful and primitive defenses,
along with increasing hostility to others and seeming indifference to his
mother's and father's neglect. In addition, he developed a grievance attitude
along with bullying, disrespectful, and aggressive behaviors that hardened
into personality traits. Donald's attitudes and behaviors got the attention
of his sociopath father, but instead of showing his displeasure at them, he
reinforced, validated, and encouraged the behaviors—the very things that
made Donald unlovable and were the product of his father's abuse.[9] The
"not enough" in the book title referred to a lack of connection with parents
that cared about him, a missing mother due to illness for at least a year at
a crucial developmental stage when Donald was only influenced by his sociopath father who was not concerned with children. Therefore, emotional
needs of feeling safe, being loved, and valued were missing. Mary Trump
stated that he experienced parental deprivations in childhood that would
scar him for life.[10] According to the subtitle of Mary's book, occupying the
Oval Office made Donald "the World's Most Dangerous Man." Mary, Donald's *psychoanalyst* niece, was not engaging in hyperbole.

Mary Trump's book is important for determining who Donald Trump
is, not only because she has invaluable intimate experience as a family member but also because she has a PhD in clinical psychology from the Derner
Institute of Advanced Psychological Studies, is an experienced psychoanalyst,
and taught graduate psychology courses in trauma, psychopathology, and
developmental psychology in her career. The views Mary Trump expressed
about Donald are not gossipy speculations of a family member, but the viewpoint of a professional psychoanalyst schooled in developmental psychology.
Psychiatrist Dr. Bandy X. Lee, editor of *The Dangerous Case of Donald Trump*,
said that although Mary Trump was disinherited from her family because of
Donald Trump's evil machinations to obtain the family fortune, her presenta-
tion of Donald in her book was "professional and balanced."[11] Mary Trump
states, like most other clinical psychoanalysts that try to get complete picture
of Donald Trump and his psychopathologies and dysfunctional behavior, a

8. Trump, *Too Much and Never Enough*, 15.
9. Trump, *Too Much and Never Enough*, 25–27.
10. Trump, *Too Much and Never Enough*, 24, 26.
11. Lee, "Dr. Bandy X. Lee in Conversation."

thorough family history is needed. She gives that history along with a professional's insights and she starts with her sociopath grandfather.[12]

Fred Trump, Donald's father, was a high-functioning sociopath and
was able to pursue a successful real estate career that turned into a fortune at
the end of World War II, which Donald Trump finally inherited. Mary lists
the symptoms of sociopathy, the behaviors to which Donald was constantly
exposed, as a "lack of empathy, facility for lying, indifference to right and
wrong (non-functioning conscience), abusive behavior, and lack of interest
in the rights of others."[13] She states that children with a sociopath parent
guarantees a severe disruption for how they understand themselves; they
are unable to regulate their emotions and how they engage with others. The
severe impact of a sociopath father's behavior, especially if he is the only one
present, retards a child's development; this is evident in Mary's discussion
of the importance of "mirroring" in the development of a child's mind and
emotions. She states, "An attuned parent reflects, processes, and then gives
back to the baby the baby's own feelings."[14] Without mirroring, children
are denied important information about how their minds work and about
how to relate to others. Mirroring leads to higher levels of emotional intelligence and it is the "root of empathy."[15] Donald Trump did not experience
such "mirroring" from his sociopath father. He was confronted with toxic
antisocial sociopathic behaviors that his father "mirrored" and assimilated
them, making him a sociopath.

Mary Trump cites the opinions of armchair psychologists and journalists who referred to Donald Trump's mental state as malignant narcissism
or having a narcissistic personality disorder; she said that she had no problem with their diagnosis, because it meets all nine criteria outlined in the
Diagnostic and Statistic Manual of Mental Disorders (DSM 5). She admits
that what the armchair psychologists say is accurate, but they do not go far
enough in describing Donald Trump's personality disorders. Understand-
ably, for the layman who looks up the definitions of malignant narcissism
and narcissistic personality disorder, and see definitions that fit Trump perfectly, all the images and behavior that they observed on the news dozens
of times daily—for years—rang true. However, Mary Trump the clinical
psychologist suggests deeper pathological reasons. She says Donald's behaviors also meet the criteria for "anti-social personality disorder," which
comes under the diagnosis of "sociopathy," referring to the chronic level of

12. Trump, *Too Much and Never Enough*, 10–11.

13. Trump, *Too Much and Never Enough*, 24.

14. Trump, *Too Much and Never Enough*, 23.

15. Trump, *Too Much and Never Enough*, 23.

sociopathic behaviors of criminality, arrogance, and disregard for others. She is suggesting "comorbidity" or a combination of personality disorders for Donald Trump; in layman's language, she is describing the great depth and extent to which he will go to get his own way. Mary Trump is correct in saying labels only go so far, especially for the nonprofessional; they do not replace experience of earning an academic degree in the profession and practicing as a psychoanalyst, grasping the implications of pathological personality disorders in human relationships.

Another of Mary Trump's crucial psychoanalytic observations is that Donald may have had a long undiagnosed learning disability that for decades has shown his inability to process information.[16] She speaks of Donald's arrested development in early childhood not only involving emotional growth but cognitive growth also; the latter is repeatedly mentioned by members of Trump's cabinet interacting with him. They complain that he does not read anything and briefings must be heavily laden with charts, pictures, and simplified one-page summaries no matter how complex or important the issue, and after all these efforts he is still distracted and loses interest. Mary states, "Donald, who understands nothing about history, Constitutional principles, geopolitics, diplomacy (or anything else really) and was never pressed to demonstrate such knowledge, has evaluated all of this country's alliances, and all of our social programs solely through the prism of money, just as his father taught him to do."[17]

Donald Trump's obvious basic knowledge deficiency was the inspiration for Daniel Drezner's book entitled *The Toddler in Chief.* He suggests, "Trump's psychological makeup approximates that of a toddler."[18] He states that it is not only Trump's political opponents who frequently liken him to an immature child, but his closest political allies and subordinates draw the same comparison.[19] Drezner's book addresses the arrested cognitive and emotional development of Donald Trump as a child. Mary Trump notes that it is extraordinary after all the attention that Donald has received in the last fifty years *that he has been subjected to very little public scrutiny;* she states the reason is that he has always been "institutionalized"; his limitations were shielded from scrutiny due to his inherited wealth and never having to succeed on his own. However, she states that the pressures of the presidency mounted over three years in the Oval Office, "until the disparity between Donald's level of confidence required for running a country and

---

16. Trump, *Too Much and Never Enough,* 12–13.
17. Trump, *Too Much and Never Enough,* 15.
18. Drezner, *Toddler in Chief,* 3.
19. Drezner, *Toddler in Chief,* 8.

his incompetence has widened, revealing his delusions more starkly than ever before."[20] Echoing Michelle Obama, Mary Trump is saying that the presidency did not change Trump at all, it just revealed who he truly was—*a malignant narcissistic sociopath tyrant.*

PSYCHOLOGY'S DIAGNOSIS: PERSONALITY DISORDERS

Captain G. M. Gilbert, the army psychologist at the Nuremberg war trials (1945–49) said, "In my work with the defendants I was searching for the nature of evil and now I have come close to defining it—a lack of empathy. It is the one characteristic that connects all the Nazi defendants, a genuine incapacity to feel with their fellow men." Gilbert, who was Jewish, was assigned to watch over the defendants at the trials (war criminals of the Holocaust); he said, "Evil, I think, is the absence of empathy."[21] In his interaction with the war criminals charged with atrocities, Gilbert confirmed that the nature of evil was showing no empathy, *no concern for others.* His insight was consistent with the Judeo-Christian Scriptures and Christian theology. Empathy is an "others focus" the opposite of a "focus on self." Having no empathy is a violation of Christianity's royal commandment to love God with all the mind, heart, and soul—(the self)—and to love your *neighbor* as *yourself.* Having no empathy is the chief characteristic of Donald Trump's personality disorders; it provides a "consistent explanation" for his self-centered behavior displayed prominently throughout his presidency. Captain Gilbert did not speak of personality disorders as he attempted to find the underlying cause of the Holocaust perpetrators' horrendous behavior toward fellow human beings, but those who committed war crimes revealed a depth of cruelty and disregard for human life that caused him to turn to religious vocabulary—the nature of evil. As a psychologist, he was aware of his profession's terms to describe their acts of cruelty: It was the absence of empathy, showing no concern for others. He appeared to integrate both religious and psychological viewpoints in describing the perpetrators of the Holocaust by saying, "Evil is the absence of empathy."

Donald Trump: Pathological Personality Disorders

In searching for a way to describe the actions and mentality of Donald Trump, we are not forced into an either/or choice: psychology's "personality

20. Trump, *Too Much and Never Enough*, 13.
21. O'Neill, "Evil, I Think."

disorders" or the Bible's "depraved human nature." Captain Gilbert's example above suggests the possibility that both views are fruitful for understanding the behavior and mentality of Donald Trump. Both psychology and biblical revelation are interested in human conscience. According to Christian theology, it functions as the God-given ability to differentiate between good and evil, despite "corrupt human nature." Conscience is malleable; it can be taught and can be influenced by sin, even extinguished, but it is responsive to the divine influences of salvation. Psychology is especially interested in the development of conscience in childhood; its views on the arrested development of conscience explain pathological character traits in adult life; therefore, they clarify the adult behavior and mentality of Donald Trump.

Howard Covitz, psychoanalyst and professor of psychology, notes that Sigmund Freud was interested in the puzzling development of conscience. He thought a child begins life "with a sense that all are present to serve him"— with an intense *self-focus*. Eventually, he said that a child recognizes that "others" exist. At first, they do not realize their parents and "others" as complex beings with their own thoughts and relationships. "Freud discovered that the child's life changes dramatically when he realizes that others are subjects, just as he is, subjects in their own right."[22] He saw this as the healthy development of conscience in children, or "Guiding I." Those children who fail to accept others as subjects become adults with *personality disorders*.[23] Covitz cites typical characteristics seen in personality-disordered people; they:

1. Are incapable of understanding and responding in an empathic way to how others feel; people are like "pieces on a chess board" moved in order to win one's own way.

2. Have black and white thinking, splitting the world into friend or foe, those who support him and all those who are against him.

3. Have no need to evaluate how their actions may impact others and have little skepticism about the correctness of their behavior.

4. Have not developed respect for others' thinking, relationships, or efforts; does not value the accomplishments of others. There is no appreciation, therefore, for organizations, government structures, conventional practices, and laws. "They may appear civilized but are not socialized."

5. Since they are like points 1–4, they show no ability "to see more than one not-unreasonable view, a monomania of sorts."

22. Covitz, "Health, Risk, and Duty," §3738.
23. Covitz, "Health, Risk, and Duty," §3744.

6. Since they are like points 1–5, they display a limited capacity to distinguish the real from the wished for or imagined and, because of this, demonstrate a ready willingness to distort the truth.[24]

Anyone who has observed Donald Trump on cable news knows that the above characteristics of personality-disordered persons describe his behavior and rhetoric and are a description of his mental state; the characteristics listed above are also the subject of numerous books written about Donald Trump in his presidency. It is helpful to note that all the pathological characteristics described above have one issue in common: an inordinate interest in "getting one's own way."

At this point, it is helpful to see definitions for what Mary Trump and other mental health experts, as well as journalists, have described as Donald Trump's mental state and erratic behavior: *sociopathy/psychopathy* and *malignant narcissism*. In the discussion above, Mary Trump mentioned that Donald's behavior and mentality certainly fit the term "sociopath," but then suggested comorbidity, or several pathological disorders, including *antisocial personality disorder*. The three often mentioned diagnoses are:

> Sociopathy: A sociopath is a term used to describe someone who has antisocial personality disorder (ASPD). People with ASPD cannot understand others' feelings. They will often break rules or make impulsive decisions without feeling guilty for the harm they cause. "Psychopathy" is sometimes considered synonymous with "sociopathy"; it is traditionally a personality disorder characterized by persistent anti-social behavior, impaired empathy and remorse, and bold disinhibited and egotistical traits.
>
> Antisocial Personality Disorder (ASPD): is characterized by a long-term pattern of disregard for, or violation of, the rights of others. A weak or nonexistent conscience is often apparent, as well as a history of legal problems or impulsive and aggressive behavior.
>
> Malignant Narcissism: is a *psychological syndrome* comprising an extreme mix of narcissism, antisocial behavior, aggression, and sadism. Grandiose, and always ready to raise hostility levels, the malignant narcissist undermines families and organizations in which they are involved and dehumanizes the people with whom they associate.[25]

---

24. Covitz, "Health, Risk, and Duty," §3744–56.
25. Wikipedia, "Talk:Sociopath."

Sociopathy is the newer term used for psychopathy.[26] The definitions and characteristics of sociopathy, psychopathy, and antisocial personality disorder overlap with one another and at times are contradictory, depending on the system of personality disorders one follows; however, they all track with Covitz's characteristics of personality disorder above. The significance of "malignant narcissism," which encompasses the above three mentioned personality disorders, is that it is *a common factor in the mental makeup of tyrannical leaders.* The terms *dictator* and *tyrant* are used interchangeably, but not all dictators are tyrants; a tyrant is a dictator gone bad.[27]

In the discussion of malignant narcissism, the emphasis should be on "malignant" or the pathological dimension of narcissism, because all people to some degree are narcissistic; having a sense of self-worth or importance as a human being is healthy. Narcissism, therefore, should be considered on a scale or spectrum (zero to ten for instance) that allows for normal narcissism to move on a scale to moderate narcissism and then proceed to pathological or malignant narcissism.[28] *If American society is narcissistic, moving beyond the normal and moderate, then a president with malignant narcissism disorder would find a connection for influencing a narcissistic society;* the society, in turn, would receive what he has to say.[29] The malignant narcissistic leader and narcissistic society equation makes the narcissistic president's gaslighting effective and seductive; he just tells people what they want to hear. Logic dictates that all presidents have been narcissistic to a moderate degree; if not, they would hardly run for president! However, psychoanalysts speak of *malignant* narcissism (eight to ten on the spectrum), describing it as a "severe mental sickness." Erich Fromm, who coined the term in 1964, described it as "the quintessence of evil," characterizing it as the most severe pathology and the root of the most vicious destructiveness in humanity.[30] Malignant narcissism describes how far a person will go in disregarding "others" to "get their own way." Fromm developed his theory of malignant narcissism diagnosing Adolf Hitler; he was a Holocaust survivor.

Lance Dodes, a retired Harvard Medical School professor, said concerning Donald Trump:

> The best diagnosis for Trump is that he is a malignant narcissist. It contains the narcissistic part, which is no big deal alone—lots of people are narcissistic—but the malignant part is the

26. Free Dictionary, "Psychopathy."
27. Mika, "Who Goes Trump?," §5196, §5191.
28. Malkin, "Pathological Narcissism and Politics," §1442–99.
29. Mika, "Who Goes Trump?," §5272, §5346.
30. Wikipedia, "Malignant Narcissism."

sociopathic dimension. These terms suggest that Trump is a very primitive man. He is also a man who has a fundamental deep psychological defect. It is expressed in his inability to empathize with others and his lack of genuine loyalty to anyone. You will notice that Trump wants everybody to be loyal to him, but he is loyal to nobody.[31]

Dodes uses the term "primitive" for Trump in the sense that he has a psychological defect that is basic to the development of human beings—no empathy toward other fellow human beings; "primitive" refers to arrested development early in childhood in recognizing "the other." He says, "The failure of normal empathy is central to sociopathy, which is marked by an absence of guilt, intentional manipulation, and controlling or even sadistically harming 'others' for personal power or gratification. People with sociopathic traits have a flaw in the basic nature of human beings."[32]

"Crazy Like a Fox" or "Crazy Like Crazy"?

Dr. Dodes's discussion of the failure of normal empathy raises a central question about the mentality and behavior of Donald Trump: Is he crazy like a fox—just being clever—or are his actions showing something more serious? Dodes asks, "Could his words and actions be expressions of a significant mental derangement?" His answer is an emphatic, "Yes."[33] He goes on to say that sociopathy always means a lack of empathy, but there is the sense in which sociopaths have a sort of "empathy of the predator," giving him a perceptive acumen, making him a genius at manipulation—at getting his own way—leaning toward "crazy like a fox." He is not saying that Donald Trump is a genius operating at a high level of cognitive functioning and intelligence. Dodes uses "crazy like crazy" to indicate that Trump has a "significant mental derangement."[34] He appears to be searching for a low-level term in the function of humanity, one that expresses a dysfunctional human state, a primitivity or "animal-like primal cunning"; the animal kingdom is the context of his discussion of empathy. Psychoanalysts, especially those who have experienced extreme manifestations of evil like the Holocaust (Erich Fromm and US Army psychologist Captain Gilbert), appear to struggle with describing such a fundamental dysfunctional humanity in psychological terms and use the term "evil."

31. Neuharth, "What Exactly Is 'Malignant Narcissism'?"

32. Dodes, "Sociopathy," §1940.

33. Dodes, "Sociopathy," §1934.

34. Dodes, "Sociopathy," §2015–21.

Mary Trump's view of Donald's arrested cognitive development in childhood does not see Donald as a genius with high-level human intelligence, cognitive skills, and knowledge either. She sees the opposite—an arrested cognitive and moral development, lacking in basic understanding about the world and "how things work," due to his personality disorders. Her discussion of Donald goes in the opposite direction—"crazy like *crazy*"—but with the understanding that his personality disorders give him an edge in human interaction—an evil cunning that shows no concern for others (no empathy): lying with a straight face, a malignant narcissistic self-focus that is unhesitating in deception and lying, threatening revenge, creating fear, and showing no remorse. Dodes also leans in that direction with the mention of a "dysfunctional state" and a "primitivity" or an "animal-like primal cunning" that approaches Christian theology's view of depraved human nature that is susceptible to supernatural evil, resulting in behavior at a lower level of humanity. In biblical terms, the "acts of the flesh" refers to an extreme self-focus and lack of concern for "others." Instead of being separated from reality—crazy—Trump's pathologies add an "evil edge" to his reality (he is open to supernatural evil), but he is aware of what he is doing.

Christian theology generally agrees with Dodes's diagnosis, his descriptions of sociopathy and malignant narcissism, and psychology's view of arrested development in early childhood leading to what psychology describes as pathological personality disorders. The Christian view is that there is a flaw in the basic nature of human beings, a basic disorder in humanity also, but refers to it as "corrupted, depraved human nature" in spiritual beings created in the image of God.[35] The image of God was "marred" by disobedience to God (sin), leaving humanity open to the power and influence of supernatural evil. The Christian worldview speaks directly to the depth of depravity in humans that psychoanalysts sometimes struggle to describe and assign the term evil. The concurrence of the two viewpoints is centering on the lack of empathy—a deficient "others-focus" in human relationships. The lack of empathy is also prominent in the fundamental human problem of relating to God—an inordinate "self-focus." As helpful as Dodes's psychological terms are for describing the "aberrant and excessive destructive behavior" of Donald Trump, at times they fall short in describing the depth of evil behavior. Christian theology provides a necessary discussion and focus on the dysfunctional mentality and behaviors of the human condition but in the context of human nature's need for God's transforming power in experiencing salvation.

35. 1 Cor 2:6–16; Gen 1:26–27.

CHRISTIAN THEOLOGY'S DIAGNOSIS: FALLEN HUMAN NATURE

The empirical science of psychology provides helpful viewpoints of hu-man behavior that describe Donald Trump's aberrant behavior. Christian theology supplements those viewpoints with an explanation of the nature, depth, and origins of evil. Biblical theologians speak of a "salvation history" in the Bible, showing an epic conflict between good and evil, dating back to the creation that centers on human sin and the damage done to humanity. The Bible is a book that deals with humanity's need for salvation before a Holy God. First, it speaks of humans inheriting Adam's sin, because he was progenitor of the human race;[36] second, it reveals that all humans have in fact committed sin.[37] In the biblical context, evil is a serious central matter for humanity in an ultimate sense both for this life and for eternity. Third, the "good news" that Jesus proclaimed in the New Testament is that all who have faith in him receive God's salvation—eternal life.[38] The epic "heavenly conflict" is between God and Satan; "the Tempter" is a created heavenly be-ing, a "fallen angel," and a provocateur that brings a supernatural dimension of evil and power to bear on human beings created in the image of God; his purpose is to destroy God's creation, working through fallen human nature.[39] Jesus taught his apostles a prayer that focused on the problem of evil and the evil one, the Lord's Prayer.[40] The power described in the prayer is Jesus' gospel of the kingdom of God, referring to Christ's triumph over evil. Jesus demonstrated the power of his heavenly kingdom by (1) casting out demons in his ministry, (2) his redemptive death on the cross and resur-rection, and (3) giving the gift of the indwelling Holy Spirit that provides Christians with an inner life power to overcome sin and the influence of evil in this life, as they continue to exercise their faith in Jesus.[41]

Empathy and the "Others-Orientation" of Christianity

According to Mary Trump and other mental health experts, Donald Trump is afflicted with several pathological personality disorders; he is a malignant

36. Rom 5:12–14.
37. Rom 1:18–31.
38. Rom 1:16–17; 5:1–8; John 17:2–3.
39. Gen 3:1–15; Job 1:6–12; John 8:44; Rom 5:12–17.
40. Matt 6:9–13; the Lord's Prayer is in the larger context of Jesus' Sermon on the Mount.
41. Rom 5–8; John 20:31.

narcissist sociopath; these conditions indicate a basic flaw in human beings that results in their inability to empathize with others. Christian theology's diagnosis of fallen human nature indicates the same inability in spiritual terms. This is expressed in the royal commandment mentioned by both Moses and Jesus in the Bible.[42] It was not possible to "love others" as God intended when a sinful human nature propelled a person in the opposite direction—a focus on self.[43] In his Sermon on the Mount, Jesus quoted the royal commandment from the Old Testament Scriptures about "loving others as oneself" to a generation of Jews that had lost contact with the meaning and purpose of the law of Moses. The royal commandment spoke of a complete reverence and love for God from the heart and loving "others" as oneself; Jesus citing this royal commandment to the religious leaders of Israel revealed how far that generation was from God in their Jewish exclusiveness and "hatred" of gentiles (non-Jews). The condition of the human heart that the royal commandment anticipated—loving others as oneself—was made a living reality by Jesus' gospel of the kingdom of God,[44] *because it provided for a spiritual inner transformation called "new birth."* Jesus explained the impact of salvation in humanity as being "born again," due to the Holy Spirit's inner transformation of "the old corrupted humanity," and a *continuing* work of the Holy Spirit in a new humanity where the self is being transformed into the likeness of Jesus.[45]

Therefore, a heavenly transformation (by God's power) of the inner life dominated by a sinful nature and its unrestrained focus on "self" was, and is, critical. Spiritual new birth speaks of an inner transformation that is received through repentance of sin and faith in the gospel. The gospel's power in this regard is extremely relevant and full of insight for the central problem of racism in America today—a hatred of others, their races, and cultures—involving the belief that one's own race and culture is superior and has the right to rule another's (a perverted "others" orientation).[46] Enabling a person to love others as oneself concerns a process in life in which the

---

42. Deut 6:5; Lev 19:18; Matt 22:37–40.

43. Romans 6:6 and 7:5 reference the "realm of the *flesh*" or the sinful state of humans, the old self (7:25), going in the wrong direction; Rom 8:3–8 references the mind and flesh or the old self needing salvation. Galatians 5:13–15 says "don't indulge the flesh," in the old self, but *"love your neighbor as yourself;"* 5:19–21 refers to "acts of the self" or evidential behavior of the old self-centered sinful nature in verses 22–25; the fruit of the Spirit is evidential behavior of the new self (6:15) *controlled by the Spirit in loving others* (my emphases).

44. John 3:3–8.

45. Rom 6–8; Eph 2–3; 1 Cor 2.

46. Pomerville, *Cross-Cultural American*, 172, 178, 181–90.

Holy Spirit transforms Christians into the image of Christ; it is incremental in a Christian's life of continuing faith.[47] The necessity for the inner life to be transformed by God was the focus of Jesus' Sermon on the Mount; he showed the law of Moses, an outward legal code, could never enable people to "love others as oneself."[48] It required the transformation of inner life by a faith response to Jesus and his gospel of the kingdom of heaven.

For the Christian, biblical theology is not just another theory describing the functioning of the mind, conscience, and human nature; it is viewed as an explanation of ultimate truth and ultimate evil, God's revelation about sinful humanity needing salvation.[49] It focuses on empathy as psychology does, considering it a key element in basic human nature, but the Bible elevates empathy to what seems impossible heights, humanly speaking. It commands love for others, even showing love toward enemies. God-like love in the human heart liberates the corrupted self-focus of fallen human nature; then, that love is "let out" as they focus on others in a life of faith. The response of the human self to others as love speaks of a divine quality of human behavior. Divine love is present in the lives of redeemed humanity as a gift of grace. Loving does not depend on or require the worthiness of the object loved, but the presence of divine love itself is the motivation for reaching out to others—it is an "other-focus" from God. The Bible speaks of the new redeemed self-infused with God's love, due to the indwelling Spirit of God in the human heart.[50]

The person with faith in Jesus' gospel of the kingdom of heaven receives the fundamental benefits of his death on the cross: (1) the forgiveness of sins, and (2) the gift of God's Holy Spirit. This twofold expression of God's love in salvation fulfilled his ultimate intention to live and rule in the hearts of people through the gift of God's Spirit. This "great salvation" was the occasion for God's love to be poured out into the hearts (minds) of those having faith in Jesus by way of the Holy Spirit's indwelling presence, making it possible to "love your neighbor as yourself."[51] The Holy Spirit not only transforms sinful human nature, freeing it from the power of sin, but he also creates a "new man or woman" with a heart (mind) free to live a holy life in confronting the power of evil.[52] The twofold benefit of salvation for living among other human beings was made possible by God's love for

47. Matt 5–7; see John 3:3, 5–8; Rom 1:17.
48. Rom 7:9–25; 8:1–11.
49. Rom 1:19, 21, 24–25, 28–31.
50. Rom 5:5, 8; Col 3:10.
51. Gal 5: 13–14; 22–26.
52. Col 3:1–17; 1 Thess 4:1–10.

sinful humanity and his sending Jesus Christ into the world; it was the oc
casion for Jesus to express his love "for others" by the sacrifice of himself.
Given the example of God's salvation through Jesus Christ, the enablement
for an "others-orientation" in "loving others" is from God and it is the sine
qua non of the Christian life.

MALIGNANT NARCISSIST TRUMP: AN OTHERS-ORIENTATION?

Donald Trump, to say the least, does not exhibit any indication of the
spiritual transformation or behaviors indicated by Christian salvation. His
personality disorders preclude the mental and emotional response required
for receiving salvation—humbling oneself in repentance, showing sorrow
for sin, turning away from it, and submitting to God; instead, his mentality
and behavior show no awareness of God and no empathy—no others-orientation whatsoever. Furthermore, he shows no evidence of a functioning
conscience; instead, Donald Trump's words and behavior are evidence that
*he is driven by a "fallen human nature" without empathy and the mitigating
function of conscience.*[53] In biblical terminology he lives in "the realm of
the flesh," revealing an advanced stage of the effects of the power of sin—
a seared conscience and depraved mind and character. His actions clearly
follow the self-orientation of the old corrupt human nature described in
Scripture; hardly anyone would describe him with behavior like "the fruit of
the Spirit" reflecting an others orientation, or describe him as "loving others
like himself."

In his Sermon on the Mount (Matt 5:1—7:27), Jesus contrasts those
who are transformed by the power of the kingdom of heaven in salvation
with the Jewish people of his generation and other generations after the exile who corrupted the law of Moses. Starting with "the Beatitudes" (5:3–12),
Jesus said, "Blessed" (having divine spiritual favor) are "the poor in spirit,"
"they that mourn," "the meek," "those who hunger and thirst for righteousness," "the merciful," "the pure in heart," "the peacemakers," and "those persecuted because of righteousness." Note: The character of Donald Trump
is the opposite of these characteristics of the children of the kingdom; he
does not share a single one of them. As Jesus continues with the Sermon,
he describes the words and behaviors of the children of the kingdom of
heaven, contrasting them with the words and behaviors of those without
faith in him, *those operating under the law who were controlled by a fallen
sinful human nature:* (1) anger, (2) adultery, (3) hardness of heart, (4) oath

53. See also Col 3:5–9.

taking to ensure one's truthfulness, (5) revenge, (6) no love, (7) greed, (8) obsession with money and ignoring God, (9) judging others and lies in the name of religion (false prophets), and (10) disobedience to and failing to put the word of God into practice (Matt 5:21—7:27). Again, these words and behaviors precisely describe Donald Trump. The words and character of the children of the kingdom in the Sermon on the Mount (given below) are clearly not a description of the words and behavior of Donald Trump:

1. "Reconciling" with one who personally offends versus anger, insults, and character assassination

2. "Not even looking a woman lustfully" (personal morality) versus actual adulteries (for Trump, adulteries that were public knowledge, but also his admissions on a "hot mike" about how he sexually abused women)

3. Monogamy and morality versus the Jewish custom of a certificate of divorce, frequently divorcing for any reason due to male hardness of heart (immorality)

4. Simply telling the truth always versus "not breaking an oath" (giving a rationale why one is truthful)

5. Settling lawsuits generously without protracted trials, going the second mile with an adversary, giving to those who want to borrow versus an eye for an eye revengeful response to insults and manipulation of justice through unending lawsuits

6. Loving enemies and praying for those who persecute you, showing that you are the child of God because God does the same versus the Jewish saying "love your neighbor and *hate* your enemies"

7. Empathic generosity—not calculating—and genuine spirituality versus greed, obsession with wealth, and the worship of money, showing a false persona of charitable giving that hides pseudo-religiosity

8. Priority in seeking God's kingdom, contentment with the necessities of life with faith in God versus ignoring God, obsessing with earthly personal wealth and worrying about it, and worshiping money

9. Not judging others but "in everything, doing to others what you would have them do to you" and discerning evil versus hypocritical judging of others projecting one's personal evil onto others, deceived by false prophets, and pseudo-spirituality (Trump holding up a Bible in front of a riot-ravaged church)

10. Behavior that obviously indicates "good fruit"—behavior from true spirituality of the heart, showing obedience to God's word, putting it into practice versus behavior of the flesh, ignoring God's salvation and standard of morality (Matt 5:17—7:21)

The above character and behaviors are so removed from Donald Trump's pathological personality, evil speech, and behavior that anyone suggesting that they describe him is delusional; none of it was demonstrated in accord with the reality displayed by his public persona over five years.

The Old Testament Scriptures also present Christians with numerous descriptions of evil and wickedness that coincide with the traits of psychology's pathological personality disorders; some quotes from Proverbs are virtual portraits of Donald Trump:

- "Wisdom will save you from the ways of wicked men, whose words are perverse, who have left the straight paths to walk in dark ways, who delight in doing wrong and rejoice in the perverseness of evil [sadism], who are devious in their ways" (Prov 2:12–16).

- "A troublemaker and a villain who goes about with a corrupt mouth, who winks maliciously with his eye, signals with his feet and motions with his fingers [Donald Trump's mafia boss-like evasive speech and body language communication], who plots evil with deceit in his heart—he always stirs up conflict . . . There are six things the Lord hates, seven that are detestable to him: haughty eyes, a lying tongue, hands that shed innocent blood, a heart that devises wicked schemes, feet that are quick to rush into evil, a false witness who pours out lies and a person who stirs up conflict in the community" (Prov 6:12–14, 16–19).

- "The wise in heart accept commands, but a chattering fool comes to ruin; the mouth of the righteous is a fountain of life, but the mouth of the wicked conceals violence; whoever ignores correction leads others astray; whoever conceals hatred with lying lips and spreads slander is a fool; a fool finds pleasure in wicked schemes" (Prov 10: 8, 11, 17–18, 23; a "fool" in Proverbs is a person who is gullible, without moral direction—an undeveloped or seared conscience and inclined to evil: Prov. 1:4, 7).

- "Whoever loves discipline loves knowledge, but whoever hates correction is stupid; the advice of the wicked is deceitful; a person is praised according to their prudence, and one with a warped mind is despised; the righteous care for the needs of their animals, but the kindest acts of the wicked are cruel; those who chase fantasies [conspiracy theories] have no sense; the way of fools seems right to them but the wise listen to advice; fools show their annoyance at once, but the prudent overlook an insult; the words of the reckless pierce like swords; the Lord detests lying lips, but he delights in people who are trustworthy; a fool's heart blurts out folly" (Prov 12:1, 5, 15–16, 18, 22–23).

Since the Bible so fully describes evil and wickedness and its descriptions so easily apply to the actions and words of Donald Trump, why didn't evangelical Christians "see him coming?" The answer to this question goes deeper than his immorality, lying, hatred, absence of love, and despicable behavior. The Christian community had a heads up from the Scriptures, especially in the teachings of Jesus that are foundational for Christian belief and living, not to mention Christ's indwelling Spirit of truth.[54] The paradox of evangelicals following Donald Trump at the very least indicates a lack of a faith response to the Scriptures, not listening to what God's Spirit says, where self-deception is the result. Many evangelicals failed to apply the truth of the gospel—as revealed in the teachings of Jesus[55]—in their politics and in following Donald Trump. They appear to have suspended Christian belief and Scripture in their political lives and replaced indispensable biblical standards with what they wanted to hear from a malignant narcissistic sociopath.

Part of the answer to the question why evangelicals did not see him coming is that Donald Trump is fundamentally a "deceiver." Both psychology's personality disorders and biblical theology emphasize this character trait in assessing Donald Trump. The first suggestion as to Trump's identity was his media persona: a smart and successful businessman, a master "dealmaker," a millionaire playboy; however, *this was the deceptive propaganda and image Trump created and peddled about himself that was swallowed by millions.* Michael Cohen, Trump's personal attorney, characterized his boss as the typical "con man." A news media hungry for the sensational was conned and complicit in propagating a false image of Donald Trump to the public. Cohen states, "His alleged business acumen was the only basis for considering him for the presidency and it was false."[56] Donald Trump was not "a smart and successful businessman"—*he was by spirit and pathology a con artist and thief;* the history of Trump's false persona and failures prior to his presidency is the topic of the next chapter.

---

54. 1 Cor 12:10.

55. Some representative Bible sources: Jesus' teachings in John 8:12–45; 12:35–40; Matt 5:13–16; 13:1–23; the apostles' teachings in 2 Tim 4:3–4; Titus 1:10–13; Heb 2:1–4; 3:12–19; Jas 1:21–27; the Old Testament prophets in Jer 7:28; 6:19; 7:23–26; 8:7–9; 9:13; 11:7; 13:8–11.

56. Cohen, *Disloyal*, 12.

Chapter 2

The "Making" of a Con Man

Every country gets the gangster it deserves.

RUTH BEN-GHIAT, *STRONGMEN*[1]

I knew him better than even his family did, because I bore witness to the real man, in strip clubs, shady business meetings, and in unguarded moments when he revealed who he truly was: a cheat, a liar, a bully, a racist, and a con man.

MICHAEL COHEN, TRUMP'S PERSONAL ATTORNEY[2]

DONALD TRUMP: BUSINESSMAN OR CON MAN?

BEFORE HIS PRESIDENCY, DONALD Trump "conned" his family, his banks, those with whom he did business, the public, the IRS, the Justice Department, his personal lawyer, and the media. He cheated everybody. His identity as a con man was hidden by deception in his business dealings, by his attorney's cover up of his sexual exploits, with the help of the media, and elite New York society's appetite for salacious stories about the "clown from Queens" and his sexual prowess.[3] His media persona as a successful businessman was the product of his own making, as he lied about business successes, taking credit for his father's business acumen, and covering up

1. Ben-Ghiat, *Strongmen*, 250.
2. Cohen, *Disloyal*, 12.
3. Trump, *Too Much and Never Enough*, 138.

his failures. With those who called him on his "cheating" he was ruthless, using threats, doubling down with vicious acts of revenge, and tying up his adversaries in court with frivolous lawsuits to avoid an accounting for his lawless behavior. Any notion of success was due to his inherited wealth and his father's name and business acumen. While supported by his father in his business dealings, he was fine. When he was on his own, it was a different matter altogether; his incompetence brought failure and courted disaster; he only escaped by fraudulent schemes—"running his cons."

The chapter shows Donald Trump is a con man. His pathological personality disorder traits are apparent in his business activities. One could say that Donald's personality disorders *gave him a devious and cruel business edge*, revealing the core of his con man persona. Trump is a functional malignant narcissistic sociopath. His personality disorders give him a grandiose view of himself, revealing what is behind his compulsive criminality; he shows no empathy for anyone, striking out at anyone or anything that gets in the way of his getting what he wants. Trump's actions can also be described as depraved human nature at work. The psalmist says human nature is capable of unlimited manifestations of evil: "From their callous hearts [the wicked] come iniquity; their evil imaginations have no limits" (Ps 73:7–10). Captain Gilbert, army psychologist at the Nuremberg war trials, noted that even behind the actions of the perpetrators of the Holocaust, psychological terms were inadequate in capturing the depth of cruelty of their actions; he had to revert to religious vocabulary to explain the lack of empathy that he saw in them. At times, we need to do the same in assessing Donald Trump as a con man; he has no empathy or concern whatsoever for his mark or victim; the no empathy factor in his self-centered scheming, his pathological self-focus, is the polar opposite of the divine "other-focus" so prominent in biblical theology. On the other hand, con man Donald Trump is defined by no empathy, a "what's in it for me?" attitude, caring nothing for those caught in his con.

Dr. Dodes stated that a person with "three or more" of the characteristics listed below has pathological personality disorders; however, Donald Trump in his business career reveals "the whole list." They are not qualifications for a successful businessman! Both Mary Trump and Michael Cohen show they are the basis for his business failures.

1. Failure to conform to social norms with respect to lawful behaviors

2. Deceitfulness, as indicated by repeated lying or conning others for personal profit or pleasure (sadism)

3. Impulsivity or failure to plan ahead

4. Irritability and aggressiveness, as indicated by repeated physical fights or assaults

5. Reckless disregard for safety of others

6. Consistent irresponsibility, as indicated by repeated failure to sustain consistent work behavior or honor financial obligations (bankruptcies, failure to pay wages and debts)

7. Lack of remorse, as indicated by being indifferent to or rationalizing having hurt, mistreated, or stolen from another

8. Evidence of conduct disorder (impulsive aggressive, callous, or deceitful behavior that is persistent and difficult to deter with threats or punishment)

Dodes stated that other systems of diagnosis use different words: sadistic, unempathetic, cruel, devaluing, immoral, primitive, callous, predatory, bullying, dehumanizing;[4] all of these describe Donald Trump in his business dealings. I will note the presence of the above list of traits in Trump's major business dealings, using parentheses and italics, but not in every occurrence to avoid repetition.

PSYCHOANALYST MARY TRUMP: "CLOSE-UP" OF A CON MAN

What characterizes Donald Trump's business dealings is not success but abysmal failure. My primary sources for Trump's business dealings prior to his presidency are Mary Trump, Donald's niece, and Michael Cohen, his personal attorney; both had an insider's view of Trump in his business dealings—Mary for decades and Cohen for a little more than a decade. Mary Trump, Donald's psychoanalyst niece, not only had insights into Donald's behavior in the family, but he also hired her to write a book on his business dealings, giving her access to people and documentation of his business transactions. After his *Art of the Deal* book, Donald hired Mary to write *The Art of the Comeback* for him. When she started researching for the book, Donald was about to experience his *fourth bankruptcy*.[5] True to character, he did not tell Mary that he already had a contract with Random House to publish the book, and its editor did not know that Donald had hired Mary. After weeks on the project, she had not been paid and she mentioned it to Donald; he pretended to not know what she was talking about; she told him

4. Dodes, "Sociopathy," §1970–81.
5. Trump, *Too Much and Never Enough*, 146.

she at least needed money to purchase equipment for the writing project. While he was receiving $450,000 a month on a budget the bank put him on after a previous bankruptcy, he hardly paid her anything.[6] Donald gave her no helpful input for the book; he did not want to open up about his business dealings or that he was cheap. Random House discovered Mary was writing for Donald and they wanted a more experienced writer; finally, Donald had the book publisher fire Mary.[7] (*Deceitfulness; consistent irresponsibility; cruelty; no conscience; lack of remorse; unempathetic; failure to conform to social norms.*)

In Donald Trump's business association with his father in the 1970s, Fred knew that Donald was not suited for the "unglamorous, tightly budgeted, and highly regimented routine of running rental properties."[8] Mary said that Fred used Donald's arrogance and shamelessness to break into the Manhattan market; he let Donald play the business crowd up front and Fred got things done behind the scenes. Any success was due to Fred's business acumen, wealth, and name; he did not overlook Donald's incompetence as a businessman, but Fred knew he had enough talent for both. Fred put millions of dollars into projects with Donald "out front," because he knew that he could use the "skills" that Donald was able to employ: "self-promotion, shameless liar, marketer, and builder of brands," something that Fred was not able to do.[9] When Donald Trump married Ivana in 1976, Roy Cohn, Fred's lawyer, had Ivana sign a prenuptial agreement because Donald's only source of income was his father.[10] (*Consistent irresponsibility; repeated failure to sustain consistent work behavior; deceitfulness, as indicated by repeated lying or by conning others for personal profit or pleasure; sadism.*)

The Con Man's Business Disasters

Doing business with Donald changed drastically in the 1980s when he became fixated with casinos in Atlantic City and his brutal ineptitude was revealed. Fred advised Donald against it and told him that he did not want to be involved; the Atlantic City business ventures were completely outside of Fred's purview. In 1985, Donald Trump purchased a three hundred million dollar casino *sight unseen*; a year after, he bought Harrah's, which Donald renamed "Trump Plaza." This was the first chance Donald had to

6. Trump, *Too Much and Never Enough*, 147.
7. Trump, *Too Much and Never Enough*, 151.
8. Trump, *Too Much and Never Enough*, 102.
9. Trump, *Too Much and Never Enough*, 103.
10. Trump, *Too Much and Never Enough*, 107.

succeed without his father. According to Mary Trump, "The two casinos were competing with one another and eventually would be cannibalizing one another's profits." She said Donald "didn't understand and refused to learn that owning and running casinos was vastly different from owning and running rental properties in Brooklyn."[11] Donald's third casino, the Taj Mahal, opened in Atlantic City and declared bankruptcy just a year later. While the Taj was open, it kept the other two casinos from making any money. The Plaza and Castle lost a combined fifty-eight million dollars the year the Taj opened. The three properties carried ninety-four million dollars in annual debt; the Taj alone needed more than *one million dollars a day* to break even.[12] Fred was forced to become involved, as he attempted to bail Donald out of trouble.[13] (*Evidence of conduct disorder, impulsive aggressive; callous or deceitful behavior that is persistent and difficult to deter with threats or punishment; impulsivity or failure to plan ahead; consistent irresponsibility, as indicated by repeated failure to sustain consistent work behavior or honor financial obligations; bankruptcies; failure to pay wages and debts.*)

Mary reports that in 1979 Fred Trump and his companies loaned money to Donald to bail him out of pressing casino debt. Donald borrowed $1.5 million in January, $65,000 in February, $122,000 in March, $150,000 in April, $192,000 in May, $266,000 in June, $2.4 million in July, and $40,000 in August, according to records filed with the New Jersey casino regulations.[14] Donald's business ventures carried billions of dollars of debt; by 1990 his personal obligation was $975 million; previously, he bought Mar-a-Lago for $8 million (1988), a yacht for $29 million, and in 1989 bought Eastern Airlines Shuttle for $365 million. Mary Trump, who had more than a pedestrian knowledge of these business activities, said, "The sheer volume of the purchases, the price tags of the transactions kept everybody, including the banks, from paying attention to his fast-accumulating debt and questionable business acumen."[15] (*Impulsivity or failure to plan ahead; lack of remorse, as indicated by being indifferent to or rationalizing having hurt, mistreated, or stolen from another; consistent irresponsibility, as indicated by repeated failure to sustain consistent work behavior or honor financial obligations; bankruptcies; failure to pay wages and debts. His grandiosity and readiness to raise hostility levels show the traits of a malignant narcissist and should be added to the above casino ventures and loans from banks.*)

11. Trump, *Too Much and Never Enough*, 134–35.

12. Trump, *Too Much and Never Enough*, 136.

13. Trump, *Too Much and Never Enough*, 103, 133.

14. Trump, *Too Much and Never Enough*, 107.

15. Trump, *Too Much and Never Enough*, 134.

Finally, the bank had to deal with an out-of-control Donald Trump to protect their loan investments. Mary stated that in May 1990, they fronted Trump money to cover his business operations, putting him on a *$450,000 a month allowance*—almost five point five million dollars a year "for having miserably failed."[16] The allowance was for personal expenses, his apartment in Trump Tower, his private jet, and the mortgage on Mar-a-Lago. Donald had to meet with the bank weekly to hold his spending in check and to monitor if he was selling off his luxury assets; Mary states that he was on a short leash for the first time in his life. Legally, he had to pay back his bank loans, and he chafed under the restrictions and violated them by continuing to spend money that he did not have, purchasing a $250,000 engagement ring for his fiancée and giving Ivana ten million dollars as part of a divorce settlement. The bank warned Donald but took no action against him, confirming to Trump that he could do whatever he wanted. Concerning Donald's casino ventures, Mary Trump said, "In Atlantic City, he had become unmoored from his need for his father's approval or permission. He no longer needed to talk himself up; his exaggerated assessment of himself was simultaneously fueled and validated by banks that were throwing hundreds of millions of dollars at him and a media that lavished him with attention and unwarranted praise."[17] Saying that Donald Trump was a con man is a gross understatement; it does not begin to describe the extraordinary extent to which used his father's name and money to present himself and his phony "brand."

Donald Trump was disdainful about Trump Management run by his father, calling it a "two-bit operation," but it was more than solvent. Fred paid himself $109 million from 1988 to 1993 and had tens of millions in the bank. The Trump Organization that Donald ran was in serious trouble, and he was still on the luxurious bank allowance; finally, banks refused to loan him money.[18] Mary said that Donald was not only ill-suited to run the day-to-day business of rental properties but was ill-suited for running any business at all, "even one that played to his strengths of self-promotion and self-aggrandizement and taste for glitz."[19] Far from showing any appreciation for his father who attempted to bail Donald out of trouble, Donald decided to run a con on his father and siblings, to get control of his father's fortune and get out from under the control of the bank. (*Consistent irresponsibility, as indicated by repeated failure to sustain consistent work behavior or*

16. Trump, *Too Much and Never Enough*, 137.
17. Trump, *Too Much and Never Enough*, 137.
18. Trump, *Too Much and Never Enough*, 140.
19. Trump, *Too Much and Never Enough*, 142.

honor financial obligations; lack of remorse, as indicated by being indifferent to or rationalizing having hurt, mistreated, or stolen from another; evidence of conduct disorder: impulsive aggressive, callous, or deceitful behavior that is persistent and difficult to deter with threats or punishment.)

A Heartless Sociopath Turns on His Family

Fred began to show signs of dementia and was sidelined from the business; Donald took advantage of this by colluding with Fred's lawyer Irwin Durben and his accountant Jack Milnik to draft a codicil to Fred's will that would put Donald in complete control of his estate, his empire, and all its holdings after he died. Donald would have control of even the smallest expenditure of money, and his siblings would be powerless to do anything about it. The lawyer and accountant brought the codicil to Fred to sign on a day when he was lucid; they told him that it was his original intention, but the shrewd businessman emerged long enough that Fred was incensed and refused to sign it.[20]

Fred's wife called her eldest child, Maryanne, to warn her; she was a former prosecutor with a knowledge of trusts and estates; she referred Donald's con to her lawyer husband, and he had a colleague uncover Donald's tax fraud scheme. Eventually, Fred's will and testament was rewritten, and Maryanne, Donald, and Robert (Trump's living children) were named executors. Whatever Donald would receive from the will, an equal amount would be given to Maryanne and Robert. Fred Jr., Mary's father, was deemed a "rebellious and disappointing eldest son," because he wanted to become an airline pilot and did so successfully, rejecting his father's desire that he would lead the Trump empire. His father pressured him constantly and humiliated him for wanting to become a "bus driver"; Fred Jr. responded by becoming an alcoholic and losing his job with the airlines, passing away at the early age of forty-two.[21] Therefore, no consideration was given to his remaining children, Mary and Fritz, in the inheritance from Fred Sr.[22] As the dementia worsened, Donald treated his father with contempt as though the condition was his fault. Fred died on June 25, 1999. Robert became the "point man" for the surviving children in seeing their inheritance was divided between the surviving children; Donald did not care if the children of Fred Jr. got anything; he did not want to be bothered.

20. Trump, *Too Much and Never Enough*, 143.
21. Trump, *Too Much and Never Enough*, 51–52, 57–67, 74, 94, 116, 122.
22. Trump, *Too Much and Never Enough*, 144.

Although Mary and her brother Fritz were children of Fred's eldest but deceased son, both Fred Jr. and his children were disinherited. Instead of receiving 20 percent of their father's share of Fred's estate, dividing it evenly among the siblings, they were only made part of a separate bequest made for the grandchildren, an amount that was less than a tenth of 1 percent of what their aunts and uncles inherited.[23] However, Mary and Fritz had the power to hold up the disbursement of funds for probate; they had to sign off on it. They would not sign unless they received their father's share of the inheritance. At the death of Fred, they also discovered the monthly checks they were receiving from the core of Fred's business, Midland Associates' Land Leases, were *priceless*.[24] Then things turned ugly: "Uncle Rob" told them if they did not sign off on the will, they would bankrupt the Midland Associates and Mary and Fritz would spend the rest of their lives paying taxes on money they did not have. Also, Maryanne had the medical insurance for Fritz's child canceled, and his monthly medical costs were expensive.[25] When Mary's grandmother died on August 7, 2000, her will was the same as her husband Fred's, with the exception that Mary and Fritz had been removed from the bequests! Mary said, "My father and his entire line had now been effectively erased."[26] Mary was forced to sue for any inheritance; Donald's "codicil con" on his family not only failed to get him out of financial trouble, but the cruelty he showed to his elder brother's children made him enemies that would stall access to his father's inheritance for a decade. (*All of Dodes's traits indicating pathological personality disorders as well as Donald's malignant narcissism, in his business dealings with family, his cruelty, lack of conscience, lack of empathy, and remorse become increasingly worse.*)

Trump's "Big Con"—1995 to 2005

About two years after Trump's family "codicil con," Donald, Maryanne, and Robert suddenly realized they needed each other and conspired to avoid paying potentially hundreds of millions of dollars of estate taxes that would be due on Fred's empire; they had to work together to avoid the government taking it over.[27] Their solution (very probably Donald's, as he ran the same con from 2006 to 2021)[28] was to avoid paying taxes on Fred's hold-

23. Trump, *Too Much and Never Enough*, 157, 167–68.

24. Trump, *Too Much and Never Enough*, 169–71.

25. Trump, *Too Much and Never Enough*, 174.

26. Trump, *Too Much and Never Enough*, 177.

27. Trump, *Too Much and Never Enough*, 157, 185–91.

28. Crane-Newman and Sommerfeldt, "Trump Organization, Allen Weisselberg";

ings by forming a shell company called "All County Building & Supply Maintenance." The shadow company's main purpose was to siphon off money from Trump Management (Fred's empire) through large gifts disguised as "legitimate business transactions" to Donald's Trump Organization. All County bought items for Trump's buildings and a secretary would bill the items to Fred's buildings with a 20 to 50 percent markup. Trump and siblings would then pocket the difference. This way, they would receive "millions in gifts from their father, skirting fifty-five percent tax on gifts over a certain value that would have cut the total significantly."[29]

The con was so effective that when Fred died in 1999, Trump Management (Fred's empire) showed only $1.9 million in cash and no assets larger than $103 million and an IOU from Donald. They claimed the estate value was $51.8 million, but they sold it for *$705.6 million* in 2004, and the banks financing the sale for a single buyer (Schon) valued the properties *at $1 billion.* Mary Trump said, "In one fell swoop my uncle Donald 'the master deal maker' left $300 million on the table."[30] Mary explained that during Fred's life he had transferred hundreds of millions of dollars to his children. Donald had received the equivalent of $430 million, "much of it through questionable means: loans that he never repaid, investments in properties that had never matured, essentially gifts that had never been taxed."[31] These funds did not include $170 million, Donald's share of the sale of Fred's empire. The above information was a huge deviation from Donald Trump's consistent claim/lie that he was "a self-made man," only receiving a small loan from his father of one million dollars to start his business career![32] (*Almost all of Dr. Dodes's pathological personality traits would apply here on Trump's big con, with emphasis on failure to conform to social norms with respect to lawful behaviors, outright criminal acts.*)

Trump's Current "Big Con"—2006 to 2021

In *Too Much and Never Enough,* Mary Trump referred to a landmark *New York Times* investigation and subsequent article in October 2018.[33] It exposed and alleged fraud, illegal activities the Trump business engaged in over decades. *New York Times* journalists had researched the article for over

Shamsian, "Trump's Apparent Confirmation."

29. Pramuk, "Trump Committed 'Outright Fraud.'"
30. Trump, *Too Much and Never Enough,* 191–92.
31. Trump, *Too Much and Never Enough,* 190.
32. Trump, *Too Much and Never Enough,* 197.
33. "Donald Trump Self-Made Sham," Editorial.

a year, analyzing one hundred thousand pages of documents focused on Donald Trump's business dealings and his 1995 tax returns; it was the longest, most detailed article ever published by the news organization—fourteen thousand words.[34] *Where did the New York Times get this trove of "hard documentation evidence" about Donald Trump's business dealings for their landmark article:* "Donald Trump and the Self-Made Sham?" The landmark article indicated that its journalists dug out the information; none of the follow-up articles at the time stated otherwise. An article, "How Times Journalists Uncovered the Original Source of the President's Wealth"[35] did not mention anyone other than their journalists: Suzanne Craig, David Barstow, and Russ Buettner. Was this the whole story on the source of the article, or was there a "deep throat"?

In June 2017, a woman knocked on Mary Trump's door; she said, "Hi my name is Suzanne Craig, I'm a reporter for the *New York Times*."[36] At first, Mary did not want to talk to any reporters and refused comment, but she accepted Craig's business card. Later, Mary decided to call Craig, because she saw the damage her uncle was doing to American democracy through his policies as president; she saw how Donald was attacking democratic norms, endangering alliances, and oppressing vulnerable people. She told Craig that she wanted to help but did not know if she still had access to documents relating to her lawsuit that was settled years before. Arriving at her attorney's office, she found thirty banker's boxes that lined two walls and filled a bookshelf about her lawsuit. After an hour and half of reviewing the documentation, she said to her attorney, "Remind me, why did we settle the lawsuit?" He responded that her grandfather's estate was only worth thirty million dollars and expenses were adding up at the time; *however,* Mary was holding documents that revealed the estate had been worth close to *one billion dollars* when Fred died, she just did not know it yet. Mary Trump decided to take Donald Trump down.[37]

In 2017, Mary Trump's identity as the source of the *New York Times's* article was kept secret. She said, "I hadn't fully grasped how much of a risk I was taking. If anybody in my family found out what I was doing, there would be repercussions—I knew how vindictive they were—but there was no way to gauge how serious the consequences might be. Anything would pale in comparison to what they'd already done [to her]."[38] Perhaps the first

34. Delkic, "How Times Journalists Uncovered."
35. Delkic, "How Times Journalists Uncovered."
36. Trump, *Too Much and Never Enough,* 185.
37. Trump, *Too Much and Never Enough,* 186–88.
38. Trump, *Too Much and Never Enough,* 188.

mention of Mary being the source of documentation in the tax fraud of 1995 to 2005 was Mary's book *Too Much and Never enough*. The other was an article from *The Daily Beast* on July 7, 2020: "Revealed: The Family Member Who Turned on Donald Trump." This "successful con," in terms of Donald and siblings not being charged and prosecuted (the statute of limitations had expired in the 1990s), was not discovered until October 2, 2018, with the *New York Times*'s landmark article. However, like most criminals, Donald Trump stuck with the same modus operandi that was working for him. The above information about Donald Trump's "big con" (1995 to 2005) should sound familiar to those who have been monitoring the Manhattan District Attorney Alvin Bragg's criminal case against the Trump organization and its chief financial officer, Allen Weisselberg, and New York Attorney General Letitia James's civil investigation of Donald Trump and his children for tax fraud currently in the news.[39]

The historical precedent for Donald Trump's current big con, regarding fifteen years of fraud and tax evasion (2006 to 2021), was the same type of con that he ran in the years 1995 to 2005. The cases are similar and appear to be from the same Trump playbook. Neal Katyal, former Acting Solicitor General, stated that, with the new indictment against the Trump Organization that reaches back fifteen years with fifteen felony charges, he labels the company as a "criminal organization." He explained that the charges of fraud and tax evasion usually involve a sentence of five years; this is what having "two sets of financial books" means according to the law.[40] The old 1995 to 2005 case indicates a pattern with the Trump organization's business dealings that is important for establishing intent in the new indictment by New York prosecutors. In *The Daily Beast* interview with Mary Trump in July 2021, she stated that "the kind of charges in the new indictment against Donald is like the strategy he worked on me to avoid paying taxes."[41] It is possible, maybe even probable, that Mary Trump and her trove of documented hard evidence made her the "deep throat" in Donald's latest New York big cons.

39. The New York AG James's civil investigation of Trump's taxes started in July 2021; it was still ongoing in October 2022, with AG James suing (indicting) Donald Trump and his children; at the time of writing about this incident in July 2021, I used the title, "Trump's Current Big Con 2006 to 2021." Trump's current big con is ongoing now (2006 to 2022). See my chapter 9.

40. Melber, "Trump's Business Was Just Labeled"; Jackson, "Ex-Trump Organization CFO."

41. Daily Beast Staff, "Ivanka Just Might Flip."

THE CON MAN AND HIS CONSIGLIERE

Michael Cohen's account of Donald Trump's business dealings prior to his presidency presents an image of Donald as a con man and the Trump Organization as a criminal enterprise. Cohen and Trump's admiration of the mafia crime families of New York gives an important identity context to Donald and his business dealings.[42] Cohen was drawn to Trump because he saw him as a "Mafia Don," even down to Donald's imitation of Don Corleone's gruff voice and mannerisms.[43] Trump's desire to make casinos a central part of his brand invoked the image of Las Vegas casino-type mob personalities, adding to his crime boss persona.

In his teens, Cohen worked for a club and gym called El Caribe, a mob hangout where he would watch and emulate the "wise guys" from the Gambino and Lucchese families. Cohen described the gangsters:

> They always had a specific kind of energy around them, a charisma that I found compelling. They were constantly joking around and playing tricks and pulling pranks on each other, which I liked, and which came to be how we acted at the Trump Organization—like gangsters, but in suits and ties. At the same time, the men in the El Caribe [sic] demanded and commanded respect. They were gangsters, and the sense of fear that people felt around them—that I felt around them—was very powerful.[44]

When his father saw Michael acting and dressing like a gangster, he told him to "cut it out."[45] While Michael did not continue emulating gangsters in outward ways, nevertheless the mafia image of illicit power was the context for Cohen's portrayal of Trump and his organization—and his own behavior as consigliere—throughout his book.

The Unthinkable: A "Mob Don" without a Moral Code

An actual difference between the mafia crime families and Donald Trump's organization is that a mafia "don" is governed by cultural rules, codes, and traditions of "the family," especially unswerving loyalty to the family. On the other hand, in the Trump organization Donald is loyal to nobody but himself, cheating everybody. The mafia context and Trump's deviation from the

42. Cohen, *Disloyal*, 64.

43. Cohen, *Disloyal*, 35, 73; *"Don"* is a term referring to a respected and feared leader; Don Corleone was the leader of the mafia crime families in the movie *The Godfather*.

44. Cohen, *Disloyal*, 52–53.

45. Cohen, *Disloyal*, 59.

loyalty code speaks to Michael Cohen's book title, *Disloyal*; Cohen was not disloyal to Trump, but Donald cheated him, the one who was loyal in protecting Trump for over ten years. Despite the obvious violence and criminality of a regular mafia organization, at least it is controlled by culture, family, and loyalty codes. It is more "righteous" (the secular sense of the term) than Donald Trump's organization, which deployed its own kind of violence and criminality by an uncontrollable sociopath and the limitless power of evil in fallen human nature. Cohen states that Trump loved trafficking in violence and threatening violence; during his election campaign in a Las Vegas rally in 2006, he urged the crowd to beat up a protester, saying, "I'd punch him in the face."[46] The tough guy talk is a lie. Donald Trump is a coward and bully.[47]

Michael Cohen said his role with Trump was a fix-it consigliere. Trump had other lawyers to deal with matters when he was in the right; Cohen states he was Trump's personal lawyer when he "was in the wrong," like the mafia lawyer covering up the mob boss's crimes and violence, dishonesty, unethical dealings, and sexual immorality from the view of the public, his family, and his wife.[48] He says, "No tactic or ruse was too low, including preying on the weak or vulnerable—in fact, that became Trump's business model perhaps because he'd gone broke so many times himself only to be bailed out by his Daddy that he knew just how defenseless the insolvent really are."[49] Obviously, Cohen does not reveal any of Trump's criminal activities that would incriminate himself; however, he gives examples of Trump's business deals that reveal cruelty, bullying, deception, stiffing those to whom he owed money, and taking his victims to court to cover up his frauds and unethical deals.[50] Trump Tower, one of Trump's most prominent brand landmarks, was also the site where felons, gangsters, and an infamous Haitian dictator resided. Resident mobsters, both American mafia and Russian gangsters, ran criminal operations out of the hotel from 1984 to 2014. Anatoly Golubchik, Vadim Trincherov, and Michael Sall ran a betting and money laundering syndicate out of the hotel. The Lucchese mafia family associate, Robert Hopkins, was convicted for operating New York's biggest gambling ring out of a condo in the tower. In 2014, Helley Nahman owned the whole fifty-first floor and was imprisoned for running a one hundred million dollar poker and sports gambling ring; he was pardoned by Donald

46. Cohen, *Disloyal*, 85; "Pride is their necklace; they clothe themselves with violence" (Ps 73:6).
47. Trump, *Too Much and Never Enough*, 49.
48. Cohen, *Disloyal*, 40.
49. Cohen, *Disloyal*, 64.
50. Cohen, *Disloyal*, 24–28, 30–34, 38–49.

Trump in his last days in office.[51] Since Michael Cohen does not delve into Trump the con man's criminal activity, it is necessary to point out that Trump's cons were essentially criminal in nature, involving various financial crimes; a con often was a "theft." Donald Trump is fundamentally a thief.[52]

What Cohen found especially vile in his consigliere duties was the "catch and kill" cover-up operations for Trump's predatory sexual behavior and sexual assaults. The catch and kill was essentially "to find, stop, and spin or twist any story or rumor that could harm the interests or reputation of the rich and powerful, like blackmail, threats and intimidation"; it was to sow doubt, confusion, and even fear.[53] Cohen discovered that Rhona Graf, Trump's assistant, had a file cabinet that was full of files on Donald's catch and kill cases.[54] Prior to Cohen's time with Trump, David Pecker of the *National Enquirer* performed the "catch and kills" for him. Cohen describes Pecker as a man having a "virtually complete lack of morality, basic decency or shame, compounded by a brazen willingness to cover up rapes and assaults and despicable acts of all varieties, provided he was benefitting a powerful man and that he would receive a favor in return"—he was a Trump "mirror associate." However, Cohen said that Pecker was like him (Cohen) a fixer, but he used the tabloids.[55]

Michael Cohen was a successful lawyer with his own small firm, a multimillionaire who did not need a job with Donald Trump. Trump's power drew Cohen in; he wanted to become part of it. In his first meeting with Trump, Cohen stated ominously, "Within the first few seconds of our meeting Donald had lied to me, directly, demonstrably and without doubt." The lie concerned Cohen having such a great deal on the apartment he bought in Trump Towers. It was not true; Cohen said that it was a silly, harmless, childish lie.[56] Nevertheless, in seeking to be associated with Donald Trump's power, this was not the last time Cohen would overlook Trump's lying, lawlessness, and vile behavior. He was drawn "into Trump's centrifugal force, precisely the way a con man draws a mark into his world."[57] However, what is also true of the con man is the saying "it is not possible to con an honest man." Cohen's iron-willed lust for power at any cost inevitably and relentlessly pulled him like a magnet into Donald's world of lawlessness, cruelty,

51. LoveProperty Staff, "Shocking Secrets."
52. See chapter 10.
53. Cohen, *Disloyal*, 69.
54. Cohen, *Disloyal*, 73.
55. Cohen, *Disloyal*, 70.
56. Cohen, *Disloyal*, 19, 23.
57. Cohen, *Disloyal*, 49.

and shame. Because of his pathologies, Donald never showed remorse. Cohen mentions his regret repeatedly in his book, concluding that he was not really a lawyer but a "surrogate and attack dog with a law license."[58] His experience as a successful attorney drawn into the lawless, cruel, and shameful world of Donald Trump is an example of how Americans who are somewhere beyond normal on the scale of narcissism respond to the malignant narcissist con man Donald Trump and become his mark.

Trump Conning His Consigliere

Michael Cohen did not give any indication that he recognized Trump's pathological personality disorders and deception in a technical sense, but he described their results over and over in plain language—especially how they affected him. Without any mention of "gaslighting" as a technique of sociopaths and fascist-type leaders, he asks himself why he was caught up in Trump's ridiculous lie that Barack Obama was not born in the United States. Trump's "birtherism" con is a classic case of Trump gaslighting the American people.[59] Cohen explains his surprising behavior:

> The truth was that I didn't just passively not protest Trump's transparently false accusations against Obama; I actively, rabidly, incessantly, insistently repeated the lies and innuendo, knowing in my heart that it was wrong—but unable to stop myself. I know that's not much of an explanation. I know it sounds like a cop out, and hardly the most likable trait a man might offer in his defense. But that is what it feels like to lose control of your mind—you actually give up your common sense, sense of decency, sensitivity, even your grip on reality. It was like having a mental illness: the reality was hard for outsiders to grasp, in all of its dimensions. The fact that I'd departed from reality, in my desire to please the Boss, meant that I really and truly had actually taken leave of my senses.[60]

Whether conscious of Trump's gaslighting or not, Cohen gave an accurate description of those affected by it, a devious mode of deception that Donald Trump learned from his sociopath father.

Elizabeth Mika, a clinical psychologist, describes the players in the deceptive method as "a three-legged beast:" (1) the tyrant, (2) his followers, and

58. Cohen, *Disloyal*, 83.

59. Cohen, *Disloyal*, 100–103; see chapter 5 in this book for Trump's gaslighting on this specific topic of "birtherism" with Barack Obama.

60. Cohen, *Disloyal*, 103.

(3) society at large. Society is the third leg because "seldom do tyrants arise in a vacuum."[61] According to Mika, the third leg provides the ripe ground for collusion in what social scientists call the toxic triangle; all are bound together by narcissism; "it animates the beast while, paradoxically and not eating it alive, bringing its downfall in due time."[62] Mika says the three-legged beast remains invisible and "somehow" seems to evade comprehension; she refers to all three legs or participants in the triangle being unaware, because "narcissism is blind to itself."[63] The deceptive process starts with the narcissistic tyrant gaslighting, and his unseen, subtle deception over time changes the other person's view of reality. Mika does not mention gaslighting specifically, but speaks of a malignant narcissist's deception in general terms as "manipulation," "lying," "making delusional promises which one does not intend to carry out," and "scapegoating": *She refers to a process of deception.*

Mika speaks of the narcissist having "no empathy but striving to gain control over others." Regarding people's susceptibility to gaslighting, she states, "Our human propensity to submit to inhumane rules established by pathological authority cannot be overestimated."[64] I add the idea of gaslighting here, as the basic mode of deception for understanding the modus operandi of tyrant and con man Donald Trump. Mika tells us that, in the toxic triangle, Donald Trump and Michael Cohen are not the only ones drawn together through a "binding narcissism," but a narcissistic society—competitive, hyper-partisan, racist, and unequal with people bearing grievances—*is also complicit and drawn into the toxic triangle;* then through a democratic election, "America gets the gangster it deserves." Therefore, Mika's three-legged beast analogy provides a fundamental insight into our main question, "Why didn't evangelical Christians see Donald Trump coming?"[65]

DONALD TRUMP: UNFIT BUSINESSMAN, UNFIT PRESIDENT

While I have only briefly described the failings, toxic business deals, and devious character of Donald Trump, sufficient evidence has been presented to show that he was not a successful businessman; rather, the two personal

61. Mika, "Who Goes Trump?," §5175–78.

62. Mika, "Who Goes Trump?," §5175–78; Mika's comment here is prophetic, as Trump's personality disorders "did him in"; see chapter 10.

63. Mika, "Who Goes Trump?," §5328.

64. Mika, "Who Goes Trump?," §5422.

65. The toxic triangle theme is developed further in the chapters focusing on "gaslighting."

witnesses closest to him for decades in his business dealings (Mary Trump and Michael Cohen) portray him as a con man. Another primary source for Trump's state of mental health, especially his fitness for president, is discussed throughout the book *The Dangerous Case of Donald Trump: 27 Psychiatrists and Mental Health Experts Assess a President.* This volume provides a basic scientific analysis of Donald Trump's pathological personality disorders from a number of mental health experts, crucial information for understanding Donald Trump, his presidency, and his followers. The book leads us to important issues about Donald Trump's presidency: (1) the psychiatric and mental health profession *recognized the danger Donald Trump posed for American society and made an ethical decision to speak out with a warning,* and (2) they advocated psychological vetting of presidential candidates to determine their mental fitness for office. Donald Trump was not only unfit as a businessman and dangerous to others but the same held for his candidacy for president—he was unfit and dangerous for the most powerful office in the nation.

The psychiatric and mental health profession is regulated by a Goldwater rule that states diagnoses of celebrities and political figures should not be given when they are not under psychiatrists' care. In 2016, twenty-seven prominent psychiatric professionals objected to the rule imposed on their profession, saying that it contradicted the profession's basic ethic—"to do no harm"; post-Donald Trump's presidency their number was in the hundreds.[66] The silence of the profession regarding the danger of Donald Trump would have done just that—"caused harm" by not warning society of the danger he posed with his pathological personality disorders.[67] The issue of Donald Trump bringing his dangerous pathologies to the office of the president—the most powerful person in the nation—was the driving force behind their duty to warn, and they became a "witnessing profession," combining their scholarship with activism.[68] Diagnosing is one thing, and the duty to warn of a public danger is another; for mental health professionals, it was just a matter of "seeing what you see and saying what you know."[69] Dr. Bandy X. Lee, editor of *The Dangerous Case of Donald Trump,* stated further, "Possibly the oddest experience of my career as a psychiatrist has been to find that the only people not allowed to speak about an issue are those who know the most about it."[70]

66. Davis, "Interview with Dr. Bandy X. Lee."
67. Lee, "Our Duty to Warn," §722, §728.
68. Lifton, "Our Witness to Malignant Normality," §539.
69. Lee, "Our Duty to Warn," §835.
70. Lee, "Our Duty to Warn," §722.

The objection to diagnosing the president's pathological disorders while he was not under any psychiatrist's care was not logical or valid. Trump's personality disorders proved that he would never allow personal examination. Moreover, due to the type of personality disorders Donald Trump demonstrated, characteristics of narcissistic psychopathy are known and observable in childhood and occur in a narrow and inflexible character structure. The profession had already proven that written accounts—case files—of patients had been accepted in the profession as sufficient to render diagnosis without having the patient present for diagnosis.[71] Trump's ubiquitous presence was observed publicly and documented over five years, providing more than sufficient evidence of his pathological personality disorders; in fact, it provided more evidence than if a psychiatrist had diagnosed Trump personally. After five years of Donald Trump in your face daily in the media multiple times, you did not need to be a psychiatrist to know he was mentally deranged. The duty of the profession to warn society and protect it from danger was clear. Even police officers, without professional psychiatric knowledge, routinely remove persons from the public legally when they show aberrant and dangerous behavior and bring them to psychiatric facilities for examination.

After the psychiatric profession observed Donald Trump's aberrant behavior in the presidency, another danger became evident that caused them to speak out—his brazen violation of democratic institutions, harmful policies toward the vulnerable in society, acts threatening the viability, even the existence of democracy. He committed crimes in the presidential office for which he was not held accountable, and there was the danger of all this becoming *normalized*. Lecturer in psychiatry and psycho-historian Robert Jay Lifton states:

> Because he is president and operates within the broad contours and interactions of the presidency, there is the tendency to view what he does is simply part of our democratic process—that is, as politically and even ethically normal. In this way, a dangerous president becomes normalized, and malignant normality comes to dominate our governing (or, one could say, our anti-governing) dynamic.[72]

The danger that Lifton described is *exactly what happened in Donald Trump's presidency*; now post-Trump, it is the arduous task of new president Joe Biden to overcome a malignant normality that has been normalized.

71. Glass, "Should Psychiatrists Refrain?," §2935, §2948–54, §2960, §2983, §3070, §3152; Gilligan, "Issue Is Dangerousness," §3198, §3209, §3227–64.

72. Lifton, "Our Witness to Malignant Normality," §512.

In considering the psychiatric and mental health profession's noble attempt to warn society of the dangerous nature of Donald Trump as a "witnessing profession," it recalls a view of biblical theology that it is the church's responsibility to warn society and actively witness about the danger of Donald Trump. Is not the church in its fundamental nature and purpose a *witnessing* body of Christians? Is it not a *prophetic* institution in the sense of being sent into the world to call out evil in society, while proclaiming the truth of the gospel with Jesus' promise that the "hates of hell" would not prevail over it?[73] Or is it just another institution in narcissistic American society? The core of evangelical Christianity in America, not the pseudo-apocalyptic fringe or Christian nationalism mentioned previously, was as silent about the evils of Donald Trump and his presidency as the Republican Senate. I return to this question, but I mention it here because of the irony—the psychiatric profession doing what the church should have done.

The second question the psychiatric and mental health profession calls our attention to is not just the danger that Donald Trump posed for society but his fitness or qualification for the office of the presidency. Prudence Gourguechon described the basis for the removal of a president in the Twenty-Fifth Amendment to the Constitution and asks what it means specifically when it says the president "shall have the ability to discharge the powers and duties of the office." She asks, "What is the standard the Vice President and Cabinet use to remove an unfit president?" This also calls to question why there is not a clear standard for vetting presidential candidates. She says we must have a rational, thorough, and coherent definition of the mental capacities required to carry out the duties of the presidency.[74] Even at the low level of police officers, as officials in local government, candidates take civil service examinations on physical, cognitive, and psychological fitness along with a background investigation to determine fitness for their job—*but not presidential candidates?*

Gourguechon points to the US *Army Field Manual* 6–22 *Leadership Development* as having the kind of testing that a candidate for president or removal could be required to take. The leadership test focuses on "ego function" (psychoanalysis) and "execution functions" (developmental psychology) that measure higher level mental capacities that enable one to perform

73. Acts 1:8; John 15:26–27; 16:7–10; Matt 5:13–16 ("salt of the earth" and "light of the world"); Matt 16:16–19 (Peter's confession that *Jesus is the Christ*, being the rock on which the church is built); Jesus warned society also in his ministry (Matt 4:17; 23:1–39) as well as his apostles when they were with him (Matt 4:19; Luke 10:1–16, 20–24).

74. Gourguechon, "Is the Commander in Chief Fit?," §7556, §7568.

as responsible adults; the tests are apolitical, unassailable standards.[75] The US Army test focuses on five crucial qualities of responsible leadership:

1. Trust: Leaders shape the ethical climate of their organization while developing trust and relationships that enable proper leadership.

2. Discipline and self-control: A leader demonstrates control over his behavior and aligns his behavior with core Army values: "Loyalty, duty, respect, selfless service, honor, integrity, and personal courage."

3. Judgment and critical thinking: These are complex, high-level mental functions that include the abilities to discriminate, assess, plan, decide, anticipate, prioritize, and compare. A leader with the capacity for critical thinking "seeks to obtain the most thorough and accurate understanding possible," the manual says, and he anticipates "first, second and third consequences of multiple courses of action."

4. Self-awareness: Self-awareness requires the capacity to reflect and an interest in doing so. "Self-aware leaders know themselves, including their traits, feelings, and behaviors," the manual says. "They employ self-understanding and recognize their effect on others."

5. Empathy: Perhaps surprisingly, the field manual repeatedly stresses the importance of empathy as an essential attribute for Army leadership. A good leader "demonstrates an understanding of another person's point of view" and "identifies with others' feelings and emotions."

Gourguechon said she originally wanted to include "truthfulness and capacity for reality testing" in the Army model; then it occurred to her "that the absence of attention to the requirement for honesty in the Army manual might well be because the capacity to be truthful and know the difference between fantasy and reality is a bedrock given, and therefore it would not occur to the framers of the Army's leadership guide to mention it. Of course, under the conditions of combat, not facing the truth of impending death but resorting to fantasy would be disastrous for oneself and others. Regarding a presidential candidate, however, truthfulness does not seem like such a given, but it is, as the presidency of Donald Trump demonstrated in damage done to democracy, damage to others in his administration that were maligned and fired, and eight hundred thousand American deaths in the COVID-19 pandemic. Gourguechon says Trump "fails in all five areas, with numerous examples of his behavior to support that determination."[76] The definition of "sociopath" rules out the possibility of the above listed qualities

75. Gourguechon, "Is the Commander in Chief Fit?," §7575.
76. Gourguechon, "Is the Commander in Chief Fit?," §7715.

of leadership. Many evangelicals and Americans did not see the New York playboy, womanizer, and con man coming. Actor George Clooney knew Trump at that time and said he remembers Trump was just a "knucklehead always chasing girls."[77] Propped up by inherited wealth that he squandered on casinos, visualizing himself as member of "the rat pack" of Las Vegas, and emulating a mafioso, Donald Trump was inept at everything but the cons he ran. He appeared like a pathetic cruel joke as president of the United States.

77. Associated Press, "George Clooney Says."

Chapter 3

The "Un-Making" of American Democracy

Make America Great Again! Drain the Swamp! America First!

DONALD TRUMP SLOGANS FROM WHITE SUPREMACISTS, BENITO MUSSO-
LINI, AND WWII ISOLATIONISTS[1]

*The Strongman's rogue nature also draws people to him. He proclaims
law-and-order, yet enables lawlessness. This paradox becomes official policy as government evolves into a criminal enterprise, Hitler's
Germany being one example and Putin's Russia another.*

RUTH BEN-GHIAT IN *STRONGMEN*[2]

THE COMPARISON OF DONALD Trump with other presidents is a fool's er-
rand. The previous two chapters showed him to be a fascist tyrant and a con
man who was unfit for the presidency, an immoral white-collar criminal
with incapacitating mental disorders that were the signature characteristics of *tyrants*.[3] When comparing past presidents, it is customary to look
at what they "made" of their presidency to determine their legacy. However, with Trump's presidency, what immediately captures your attention
is democracy's "un-making"—the damage done to American democracy

---

1. Albright, *Fascism*, 24; Snyder, *On Tyranny*, 52, 123; Levitsky and Ziblatt, *How
Democracies Die*, 39.

2. Ben-Ghiat, *Strongmen*, 251.

3. Dodes, "Sociopathy," §2053.

that he was sworn to protect. He attacked democratic institutions and, in the end, attempted to overthrow a *democratic election* that he lost, conspiring to overthrow the American government in a violent insurrection at the Capitol! Comparing Trump with other presidents is a foolish attempt to assign *normalcy* to his presidency.[4] To understand Donald Trump, one should make comparisons with other *fascist tyrants*, not presidents of the United States. History will record Donald Trump's legacy as the "un-making" or "dismantling" of American democracy.

In this chapter and the following, I focus on a narrative of events that define Trump's presidency: (1) the emergence of a fascist candidate, (2) fascist assaults on democratic institutions, and (3) commission of fascist-like "election crimes." I show the step-by-step process of a fascist, what Trump *did* in the "unmaking of America." I hope to correct an American fascist knowledge deficiency, showing how fascist Donald Trump set out to dismantle American democracy.

THE ROLE OF A FASCIST TYRANT: DISMANTLING DEMOCRACY

In her book *Fascism: A Warning*, Madeleine Albright said Benito Mussolini's campaign slogan was "Drain the Swamp"; it was a promise to make Italy clean and safe. Then he did the opposite, corrupting the justice system by suspending the jury system and due process, rigging the votes to gain control of parliament to make it fascist, kidnapping and murdering his political opponents, abolishing political parties, eliminating freedom of the press, and securing the right to name municipal officials himself. He took control of the national police, abused political power to further his control of government, and seduced the Vatican in gaining the right to approve all bishops; all of these attacks perpetrated against society and its democratic institutions were implemented with the goal of introducing a "fascist century" in Italy, making fascism the "doctrine of an age of fascism."[5] Ruth Ben-Ghiat reports the same about Mussolini's promises to "tame corruption in Italy": twenty years later fascism had become a symbol for many Italians of "racketeering, exploitation of the weak, injustice, immorality," an informer reported in 1942.[6] The fact that Mussolini actually did drain the swamps of the Pontine Marshes, establishing a new town, Aprilia, among others in 1938, and the fact that the location of the White

4. Christopher, "Watch: Mary Trump Goes Off."
5. Albright, *Fascism*, 24–25.
6. Ben-Ghiat, *Strongmen*, 225.

House *is* on previous "swamps of Pennsylvania Avenue" makes the "draining the swamp" slogan ironic.[7]

Fascist Comparisons

In 2016, Donald Trump also promised America he would "drain the swamp," erase corruption from government, and "make it honest";[8] then he did just the opposite, corrupting government institutions, officials, his followers (including evangelical Christians), the Republican party, and was impeached for putting the presidential office and its influence "up for sale." Nevertheless, he continued with his fascist attempts to gain and maintain power at all costs by disregarding and spreading disinformation about a deadly pandemic that resulted in the deaths of eight hundred thousand Americans. He incited racism and white supremacy by his racist rhetoric and actions, giving his political base "permission" to inflict unprecedented violence on American citizens of color.

After losing the election in 2020, he continued his assault on democracy by publicly denying the results of a democratic election and corrupting the Department of Justice by pressuring it to overturn the election; he also pressured local Republican officials to challenge election results in their states and continued to corrupt the democratic election process by causing frivolous lawsuits to be brought into scores of America courts, demeaning the rule of law. As a defeated president in his final days in office, he pardoned numerous political cronies that committed felonies on his behalf, prevented the peaceful transition of power to his successor, and finally launched a coup d'état to stop the confirmation of Joe Biden's election win. He incited his followers to storm the Capitol in a violent assault on police that resulted in injuries and even the loss of human lives; for this, Trump was impeached *again*, achieving the infamous distinction as the only American president to have "bookend" impeachments in his presidency—one at the beginning and one at the end. In comparing Donald Trump with one of modern history's most infamous fascists, Mussolini, he more than qualifies as a fascist tyrant.

Madeleine Albright's comparison of Donald Trump and Benito Mussolini (Il Duce) as fascists tyrants reaches beyond their attacks on democratic institutions to *amazing similarities in their character and actions*. Albright states the following about Il Duce's character: he had a "talent for theater" and had "little respect for the courage of his adversaries"; his threats, "grandiosity" in rhetoric and action resulted in people giving him whatever he

7. Widmer, "Draining the Swamp."
8. Parton, "Trump Administration Drained."

demanded; he relished the job of governing but "never worked as hard as his publicists said," yet he felt that he had to rule absolutely, having full trust in his own judgment—there was no satiating his hunger for power. His aggressive manner was extreme as he marched with his "blackshirts" armed with muskets yelling his fascist credo: "Believe! Obey! Fight!" telling the people to "live dangerously." He had an uncanny ability to fleece the public, persuading them to give him their gold wedding rings; he was sure he knew what the masses wanted—a show. He flaunted masculine virility and was "an epic-level philanderer." Prior to one of his speeches, he even took credit for the sun breaking through the clouds (in his inauguration speech); he used the symbolism of color and dress with both men and women in his rallies, often pointing to and mocking reporters and preliminary speakers, with his audience following up with cat calls and boos. He had a penchant for putting his name on products, and he flaunted his peculiarities and antisocial manners: He didn't think it was sanitary to shake hands, he didn't smoke, he didn't drink, and he was a poor listener who didn't like to hear other people talk. He was inept at governing, not understanding how society worked, and refused the counsel of good advisors, telling them his instinct was better than their judgment; he told a gathering of intellectuals, "Only one person in Italy is infallible" and then told a reporter, "Often, I would like to be wrong, but so far it has never happened."[9] To avoid confusion, I should note that the previous description was about *Mussolini*, not Donald Trump! Albright notes that Mussolini tried to govern well; he did drain the swamps and built new towns, improving Italy's infrastructure; he also gave attention to the elderly and disabled and funded prenatal health clinics and summer camps for children;[10] in this example, it is clear we are not talking about sociopath Donald Trump. The two leaders were not contemporaries or related by blood, but the amazing details of Mussolini's character and actions corresponding with Donald Trump can be attributed to the fact that both were fascist tyrants, but stopping at this would miss an important point.

How does one account for such amazing correspondence in the rule and character of the two men? It was not Donald Trump's historical scholarship that enabled him to mimic a dictator that he admired but had never read anything about. Steve Bannon or Stephen Miller, Trump's fascist advisors, may have mentioned some anecdotal fascist facts to Trump, but that would not account for the amazing similarities. Rather, the similarities of the two men are explained *by their common pathological personality disorder, malignant narcissism.* Dr. Lance Dodes said personality disorders were

9. Albright, *Fascism*, 23–28.
10. Albright, *Fascism*, 24.

a common factor in the mental makeup of tyrannical leaders. One could envision Il Duce as a gregarious person, laughing and enjoying life (at the expense of others), not sharing Trump's antisocial pathology or sociopathy. Brooding Donald Trump is obsessed with plotting evil and revenge, emulating the perpetual victim, and he doesn't laugh.[11] As a sociopath, Trump appears to be even further along the scale of narcissism into the "malignant range" than Mussolini or, we could say in theological terms, Donald Trump represents human depravity in a more advanced stage of extreme self-indulgence and evil than Il Duce. It *is* possible to explain the similarities between Benito Mussolini and Donald Trump by *a common corrupt human nature*, their following the dictates of "the flesh" and intensified by supernatural powers of darkness. With these comparisons, any hope about Donald Trump changing his fascist persona as a tyrant and con man and becoming "presidential" was naïve dreaming. Mussolini's malice and cruelty found expression in foreign wars against the peoples of North Africa, while Trump's cruelty and malevolence focused on the vulnerable, poor, sick, and disadvantaged persons of color *in his own country*. In Albright's comparison of Mussolini's behavior with Donald Trump, however, the names could be switched and her tongue in cheek description would still be accurate.

In a new documentary film *The Meaning of Hitler* by Michael Tucker and Petra Epporlein, the directors point out parallels between the Führer and Donald Trump; the documentary is based on the 1978 book with the same title by Sebastian Haffner. The directors (Epporlein is from East Germany) note parallels between fascism in 1930s Germany and the mirror image of what is happening in America with white supremacy today; they say the contemporary language used in America during the march in Charlottesville was borrowed from the Nazis in the 1930s.[12] The parallels the directors note involve both Hitler and the German nation at that time with Donald Trump and America today:

1. Personal likenesses: Hitler is "loveless, family-less, having no friends, he only has his cult followers"; with Hitler and the following parallels below, we see the pathological personality disorders the two fascists share.

2. Appeal to "victimization": Both Hitler and the German nation had a victim complex; the "politics of grievance" and "politics of personality"—"We are being victimized!"—a malignant narcissistic

11. Comey, *Higher Loyalty*, 241.
12. Carey, "'Trump Is No Hitler, But . . . .'"

leader was seducing a narcissistic nation, all very familiar and parallel with Trump and America today.

3. Give others permission to indulge in violence: Both fascists leaders incited violence in their rallies; Trump incited police: "Get tougher," and he also incited violence toward protesters at rallies: "Take him out and beat the crap out of him"; Hitler launched a violent "Beer Hall Putsch" that failed like Trump's failed coup on January 6, 2021, but in Hitler's case, he later conspired in setting the Reichstag fire (set to blame Communists) and followed up by killing over one thousand of his opposition, to become fascist dictator of the nation.

4. Replace the State with chaos: Hitler created chaos with the Reichstag fire and then stepped in to provide order—a fascist state; from the beginning, the Trump administration was chaotic; he fostered chaos, enjoyed it, and thrived in implementing devious strategies to destabilize, discredit, and do away with democracy—which he then would have opportunity to substitute his own fascist rule. Tucker and Epporlein state that Donald Trump has created chaos on a level never seen before.

5. Exploit technological advancement: Hitler exploited "the Hitler bottle," a microphone with a condenser that enabled him to reach not just five hundred people but hundreds of thousands at one time with clear, amplified speech that electrified his audiences. Trump had the internet and was able to exploit it in gaslighting society, taking full advantage of social media platforms with immediate control and unusual success.

6. Revise history: The directors state this is a central element of right wing extremist thinking. Hitler and Joseph Goebbels's propaganda machine was extremely successful in revising and covering up Hitler's illegitimate rise to power and his attempt to exterminate European Jews. During Donald Trump's administration, his gaslighting covered up his illegitimate rise to power with Russian assistance and a monumental number of presidential serial crimes, enabling him to remain in office. The efforts of Donald Trump and the Republican party to "revise the history" of the insurrection on the Capitol on January 6, 2021, is a cover-up attempt in recent history; it is also audacious, when you consider they started the revising only seven months after its occurrence, and all of America watched it happen on television and smartphones! It is important to understand that using the term "revision" of history with a provable event—such as the results of the 2020 election—just means Republicans decided to construct *a delusional lie about it*. The

Big Lie that the election was stolen from Donald Trump increased in influence for more than two years; this reveals something powerful was taking place.

It is understandable that a sociopath driven by pathological personality disorders would propagate a provable lie such as denying there was an insurrection and claiming a stolen election, but a majority of the Republican Senate was (and is) also complicit in the lies. What is *their* excuse? How does one explain the Republican party propagating an obvious election lie and the belief of millions of Americans in the lie? The effective use of propaganda in Trump's fascist rule has had an amazing and lasting effect on America. *The damage done to American democracy and lingering malignant normality in society will be difficult to reverse.* Even though Trump is no longer in office, pathological delusion drives him in "stop the steal" campaigns. Why does the Republican party follow the delusion about a stolen election? Aside from the fact that Donald Trump still maintains control of the Republican party to continue raising money, they have united under the delusional Big Lie that the election was stolen from Trump in a desperate effort to return him and themselves to power. The delusional unity has mutated and expanded into an attempt to revise Trump's fascist history of concerted attempts to restrict the vote, overthrow elections, and incite an insurrection to overturn an election.[13] The Republican party's contemporary efforts to restrict the vote and the attempt to revise the racist history of America, rejecting critical race theory, echoes the historic issue of restricting the "Black vote" and attempting to cover up *the wider racism of America's past that has never been resolved.*[14]

The previous comparisons of President Donald Trump with twentieth-century fascist dictators provide an accurate facsimile of Trump's behavior in his two presidential campaigns (2016 and 2020). Trump's pathological personality disorders determined the character of the campaigns, they bore the signature of a fascist tyrant. American political experience has not provided examples of fascist dictators that would forewarn Americans of the tyranny of a fascist president. Even after Trump's four-year presidency, narcissistic gaslighting shrouded their experience with him and millions of Americans accepted his presidency as a necessary "malignant political normalcy."

13. Cillizza, "Kaleigh McEnany Is Gaslighting."
14. Lepore, *These Truths*, 311–37.

THE SEED THAT KILLS DEMOCRACY

The Trump era brought a fascist candidate to the presidency, fascist tactics to the White House, fascist serial crimes committed against democratic institutions, and a violent fascist coup to the Capitol of the American Republic. It seems trivial, in comparison with these demonstrative violent events, to note that all of them were ushered in by "a loss of forbearance and civility" in political discourse. Harvard professors Levitsky and Ziblatt state, "Norms of toleration and restraint served as the soft guardrails of American democracy, to avoid a kind of partisan fight-to-the-death-type politics; they say that such extreme partisan polarization can kill democracies."[15] The authors add that democracies run better when mutual toleration, accepting one another as legitimate rivals, and forbearance prevail; in other words, when attempts to reach across the aisle and the exercise of restraint in behavior and rhetoric keep democracies alive. At the time of writing this chapter,[16] the most outstanding characteristic of political discourse on the floor of Congress is the *absence of restraint;* it ranges from name calling to physical intimidation[17] and even attempts to carry firearms to back up verbal intimidation.[18] Donald Trump did not start this trend of incivility, but *his pathologies gave it a definitive personal mark that was contagious, and its residual effect is with us even after he has left office.*

The Loss of Civility and Forbearance

Hyper-partisanship had already been growing in political discourse for decades in America, but by the time Barack Obama became president many Republicans began to question the legitimacy of Democrats and abandoned forbearance for "winning by any means necessary."[19] Did the emergence of the first African American president precipitate this failure of forbearance, especially in the Republican South? When Donald Trump emerged as a presidential candidate, both Republicans and Democrats abandoned forbearance, especially Republicans, as the "politics is war" idea of Newt Gingrich[20] found full release; political campaigns were reduced to winning

---

15. Levitsky and Ziblatt, *How Democracies Die,* 10–11.

16. August 2021.

17. Jankowicz, "Marjorie Taylor Greene Chased."

18. McAuliff and Greene, "'I Am Someone's Daughter'"; Epps, "No, You Can't Carry a Gun"; Kaplan, "Nancy Pelosi."

19. Levitsky and Ziblatt, *How Democracies Die,* 11.

20. Coppins, "Man Who Broke Politics."

by any means necessary. The "gloves came off" in election campaigns when racist candidate Donald Trump came on the political scene; the absence of restraint in his case was due to his sociopathic personality disorders that made him impervious to forbearance and civility—they were not in the inventory of his pathological corrupt personality, but racist rhetoric and actions were. At first, the general lack of forbearance in politics provided an excuse for Trump's brash, overly aggressive, callus behavior and open racism, as he attacked and maligned his opponents. However, candidate Trump's behavior and rhetoric became worse with the pressure of public exposure. In the wake of his personality disorders, he trampled convention, ignored the rules of debate, cut off debate moderators frustrating their attempts to restore order, and appeared to delight in the shock and confusion. With threatening rhetoric and the actions of a bully, Donald Trump paced the debate stage, intimidating with his physical bulk, and hovered over the first female presidential candidate, Hillary Clinton, a sixty-eight-year-old grandmother. Former President Barack Obama said that Hillary was perhaps the best qualified presidential candidate ever, with her long and varied government service. She stood her ground against the bully and political novice with a curious fixed smile.

Eventually, forbearance and civility in politics came to an abrupt halt under the onslaught of Donald Trump's pathological personality disorders. It was not just Trump's incivility with others in the debates and campaign that was dangerous, but his corrupt words and behavior functioned as a "dog whistle," inciting other politicians to engage their "lower nature," adopting a "win at any cost" politics until incivility took over political discourse and was increasingly evident in American society, especially with Trump's political base. Trump's pathologies found full ugly expression in his presidential campaign against Hillary Clinton. At the presidential debate with Joe Biden, incumbent Donald Trump was the epitome of a madman. He did not come as nominee to debate with another nominee; he maintained and abused presidential prerogatives (as he always did), ignored the rules of the debate, and verbally attacked debate monitors while maligning and talking over his opponent with half-sentence disjointed ravings. America saw firsthand what the behavior of a malignant narcissistic sociopath raging in the White House was like during Donald Trump's frightening four-year presidency.

Professors Levitsky and Ziblatt provide warning signs to help identify authoritarian rulers before they become president and have the power to damage democracy. They say Americans should begin to worry when a politician: (1) rejects, in words or action, the democratic rules of the game, (2) denies the legitimacy of opponents, (3) tolerates or encourages violence, or (4) indicates a willingness to curtail the civil liberties of opponents, including the media.[21] While the authors say that a politician showing even *one* of these key indicators of an authoritarian should be cause for concern, Donald Trump showed them all in spades, both in his presidential campaigns and in his presidency. He set out to gain and retain the power of the presidency illegally, in the effort to amass personal wealth just like any other fascist tyrant.[22] The unprecedented corruption, lawlessness, propaganda, and attempt to gain and retain power at any cost is the "thumbprint of fascism" in Donald Trump's presidency; latent prints are everywhere; he corrupted everything he touched. Citizens of Eastern European countries need no explanation of the political forensics of fascism, nor would citizens of countries in Latin America, Asia, and Africa; they are familiar with the fascist thumbprint, having experienced its cruelties throughout their sociopolitical existence. *This was not the case with Americans.* Now with the aftermath of Donald Trump's fascist rule, historically naïve Americans may become aware of the latent print of fascism under Donald Trump and repudiate him based on forensic evidence, *or they may not.* Three indisputable facts exist about the Trump phenomenon: (1) American voters elected a fascist president, (2) the Republican party did not stop his attempt to dismantle democracy, and (3) those who publicly resisted his fascist moves were relatively few. Was there anything that could stop the tyrant?

PATRIOTS: THORNS IN THE SIDE OF FASCISTS

In Timothy Snyder's little handbook *On Tyranny: Twenty Lessons from the Twentieth Century*, he gives an answer for stopping a tyrant by describing the mindset and actions of responsible citizens in a democracy. I focus on only three out of his twenty short lessons that describe people who become "a thorn in the side of fascists," and they often mark the beginning of the end for fascists. Snyder encourages people to (1) stand out, (2) be a patriot, and (3) be as courageous as you can. They should stand out: "Someone has to. It is easy to follow along. It can feel strange to do or say something different. But without that unease, there is no freedom. Remember Rosa Parks. The moment you set an example, the spell of the status quo is broken, and others will follow." "Standing out" means not being silent in the face of tyranny and following your conscience in resisting it. From our point in history, the actions of Rosa Parks seem ordinary, but at that time and place "she

21. Levitsky and Ziblatt, *How Democracies Die*, 26.
22. Alexander and Behar, "Truth behind Trump Tower Moscow"; Salant, "You're Still Paying for Trump's Visits."

stood out!"[23] Be a patriot: "Set a good example of what America means for the generations to come. They will need it." Snyder says patriots focus on serving their country and wanting America to live up to its ideals.[24] Be as courageous as you can: Snyder says, "If none of us is prepared to die for freedom, then all of us will die under tyranny."[25]

"Standing Out" as a Courageous Patriot

The mindset and actions of the Republican Senate were the antithesis of Snyder's advice during Trump's presidency; as a whole, its members did not "stand out"; there were few patriots, and most were cowards. They were silent and would not stand according to conscience against his tyranny (a public declaration from Senator Mitt Romney from Utah was an exception, as well as a few others); rather, they *enabled* Trump in his tyranny. Donald Trump claimed to be the quintessential patriot, cleaning up a corrupt government to "Make America Great Again" (MAGA), but he brought unprecedented corruption to the White House and proved to be a saboteur as he dismantled American Democracy. The slogan that was embroidered on red MAGA baseball hats was a ubiquitous bold lie, a "psychological projection"—he was destroying America! Snyder refutes Trump's fake patriotism—he says it is not patriotic (1) to dodge the draft and to mock war heroes and their families; (2) to compare searching for sexual partners in New York with military service in Vietnam; (3) to avoid paying taxes when working families do; (4) to admire foreign dictators and cultivate relationships with them; (5) to call upon Russia to intervene in an American presidential election; (6) to cite Russian propaganda at rallies and share an advisor with Russian oligarchs. Snyder states, "The point is not that Russia and America must be enemies. The point is that patriotism involves *serving your own country*."[26]

Donald Trump is also the antithesis of "be as courageous as you can"; his fake tough guy bully persona was, as Benjamin Disraeli said, "Courage is fire, bullying is smoke." Trump's bullying and tough-guy image was "smoke" covering for his insecurity and cowardice; it covered his cowardly acts like firing people who disagreed with him without facing them (unlike Trump's reality show "The Apprentice"), having others do it for him or doing it by tweet under the most cruel circumstances. Trump hid behind presidential privilege and manipulated the justice system, claiming immunity for his

23. Snyder, *On Tyranny*, 51.
24. Snyder, *On Tyranny*, 113–14.
25. Snyder, *On Tyranny*, 115.
26. Snyder, *On Tyranny*, 112–13.

criminal acts and filing frivolous lawsuits backed up by inherited wealth; he did so to avoid facing up to wrongful actions and crimes committed both in and out office. His self-imposed "institutionalization" (hiding behind employees, officials, and lawyers) throughout his business life and in the White House protected him from public scrutiny. His pathological antisocial behavior and rejection of reality revealed his fear of others discovering his inadequacies and the possibility of losing control; it all adds up to fundamental cowardice. Only sycophants and those Trump gaslighted would describe him as a stand-up guy.

FBI Director James Comey—Trump's Thorn

Of the relatively few people in government service who "stood out" as "patriots" and were "courageous as they could be" in confronting Donald Trump, the person who embodied these qualities was the director of the FBI, James Comey. Of course, there were others who both publicly and privately showed Snyder's three personal attributes, but James Comey was one of the first who "stood out" in his resistance to Trump's fascist moves in personal interaction. Comey stood up to Trump's mafia-boss-like threats and intimidation partly because he had prosecuted *real mafia bosses*. His personal resistance to Trump's attempt to corrupt him and the organization of the FBI is fundamentally patriotic and courageous in his one-on-one contacts with Trump. He was certainly "a thorn in his side" early in Trump's steamrolling fascist presidency; it inevitably led to Comey's firing under extremely cruel circumstances. Yet Comey provided an example for others to follow, not just in the FBI but also for career diplomats serving in Trump's administration who at his first impeachment "stood out" as patriots and were courageous. In a sense, Comey's example was the beginning of the end for Trump's fascist rule. Patriots like Robert Mueller, Adam Schiff, Eric Swalwell, Alexander Vindman, Marie Yovanovich, Mitt Romney, Liz Cheney, Adam Kinsinger, and others would "stand out," risking and losing careers in the effort.

James Comey played a leading role in defending the rule of law and the institution of the FBI, even before Donald Trump's fascist attacks on him. Under the Bush administration in 2003, Comey was appointed deputy attorney general under Attorney General (AG) John Ashcroft. He became embroiled in the controversial issue concerning the legality of torturing terrorists in the custody of American intelligence agencies. In Operation Stellar Wind, he opposed President Bush and his administration, defending Ashcroft's view that it contradicted America's rule of law. When Ashcroft became ill, Comey took his place as acting attorney general, and the Bush administration put intense pressure on him to make torture legal. He resisted the pressure for a while, but finally resigned on principle—because torture was prohibited by the rule of law.[27] When Comey was appointed director of the FBI, replacing Robert Mueller in 2013, he emphasized "good leadership" and held "honesty" and commitment to the rule of law in the highest regard. He had prosecuted mafia bosses and it was inevitable that he would see through Donald Trump's fascist moves—mafia-boss-like tactics—and clash with him.[28]

A fascist that intends to gain power by any means quickly comes up against the rule of law in American democracy; since the rule of law is a major roadblock in any illegal attempt to gain power, a fascist must weaken, discredit, and eventually replace the rule of law. Donald Trump attempted to do this personally with James Comey and failed. Comey was director of the FBI in a precarious period for the rule of law. Early on, before Donald Trump arrived on the political scene, the Russian government began its illegal activities to influence America's presidential elections. Comey also had responsibility for supervising the Hillary Clinton email investigation that started in July 2015.[29] These career challenging events were the catalyst for James Comey to "stand out," "be a patriot," and "be as courageous as he could." Although he was not directly involved in the investigation as to whether Clinton illegally used her private email system, allegedly exposing classified government documents, he was in charge.[30]

At the beginning of the investigation, it was unlikely that the Department of Justice would prosecute Clinton; the FBI had to consider what her state of mind was—what she was thinking—with the emails; did she know what she was doing or was she just "sloppy," with no criminal intent? Comey had planned to announce on July 5, 2016, that the FBI had thoroughly investigated Hillary Clinton for a year regarding her use of her email system, and the FBI believed there was no prosecutable case. It was finally decided that no criminal intent was involved but that she was unsophisticated about internet technology and security.[31] On October 27, only twelve days before the election, additional emails were found on Anthony Weiner's computer; his wife was Huma Abedin, assistant to Hillary Clinton, and hundreds of thousands of emails from Hillary's personal domain were on a laptop; the

27. Comey, *Higher Loyalty*, 85–97.
28. Comey, *Higher Loyalty*, 130–32.
29. Comey, *Higher Loyalty*, 160.
30. Comey, *Higher Loyalty*, 167; Strzok, *Compromised*, §62–67.
31. Comey, *Higher Loyalty*, 164, 182–85; Strzok, *Compromised*, §62–67.

FBI could not ignore this.[32] Comey "stood out" in announcing the investigation was completed and then had to announce it reopened when these further emails were discovered close to the 2016 presidential election. The political implications of reopening the Clinton investigation so close to the election were negative for her election bid; furthermore, the optics of reopening the investigation would look like the FBI was politically involved.

Comey was faced with a dilemma. He faced two bad choices: (1) telling Congress about reopening the Clinton investigation—"speak" (a really bad choice), or (2) "conceal" (a catastrophic choice). The FBI's leadership discussed the two choices internally, and also with the Justice Department, but in the end they all left the decision to Comey. He made his decision based on defending the reputation of the FBI and the Justice Department, institutions representing the rule of law. If he did not speak and Hillary Clinton won the election and then it became known she was being investigated by the FBI, the Justice Department would lose the public trust. Therefore, he chose to tell Congress about the reopening of the investigation (he "stood out," was "a patriot," and was "as courageous as he could be").[33] While great clamor followed the optics that Comey allegedly was "helping Trump get elected," it is ironic there was not similar outrage over Russia actually helping Trump get elected, according to hard evidence from Special Counsel Mueller's investigation. This demonstrates the effectiveness of Trump's gaslighting in getting the public to believe a lie.

Trump's Struggle to Remove the Thorn

Leading up to Donald Trump firing James Comey, there were *nine* occasions when he tried to get Comey alone or called him on the phone, without witnesses, pressuring him to be "loyal" (to Trump). It was mob-boss-like intimidation, but Trump did not do this in a forthright way, instead using nonconfrontational, cowardly tactics to subtly corrupt Comey because he feared him. James Comey knew exactly with whom he was dealing—having faced mafia bosses before and tactics of criminals that he prosecuted—but Donald Trump did not know with whom he was dealing; his personality disorders blinded him. Comey had a "higher loyalty" in his commitment to truth, exposing lies, and with his stress on good leadership; this is who he *was*, based on his experience as a prosecutor in respecting the rule of law and from the influence of Christian values. When Trump attempted to compromise and corrupt him, Comey knew what Trump was doing in each

32. Comey, *Higher Loyalty*, 192.
33. Comey, *Higher Loyalty*, 194–98.

of nine occasions; he was able to think ahead and determine how he would resist his corrupting influence and somehow document it. Whether it was phone calls or when Trump deceptively connived a solitary meeting with no other witnesses, immediately afterwards Comey made notes about what was said and reported what transpired to the FBI leadership and the Justice Department.

On January 6, 2017, at Trump Tower the heads of the NSA, NIB, FBI, and CIA gave an intelligence briefing to Trump and the White House staff. Comey was surprised that Trump and his staff were speaking openly of their plans to spin the intelligence they had just received. After the intelligence briefing, Comey was to brief Trump alone on the sensitive and salacious details of the Steele Dossier in a more private setting.[34] In this first meeting with Trump alone, Trump started his conversation by mentioning that he hoped Comey would stay on as director of the FBI. Comey thought this was strange, because it was common knowledge the director had a ten-year term, so the comment was out of place. Comey then continued with his task and told Trump about the media possessing the Steele Dossier that had salacious details about Trump's contact with prostitutes in Moscow. He explained his purpose was to inform Trump so that he would be aware that the document was "out there."[35] Comey assured Trump that there was no investigation into the incident. Trump repeatedly denied the Moscow reports as "fake news." He then denied even staying overnight in Moscow, calling the whole thing a "political witch hunt." The second contact with Trump was a phone call; Trump started the call with saying, "I hope you stay on as director." This was obviously an indirect threat about Comey keeping his job. Comey replied that he intended to stay on as FBI director. Trump's reason for the call was the Steele Dossier; he claimed it was leaked by the government, but Comey explained that it was not a US government document and they did not leak it.[36] Comey noted that in the three years he was director of the FBI with President Obama, he never had a phone call with him or private meetings. This lack of personal contact between the FBI director and the president was a "long-standing tradition." Sociopath Trump cared nothing for traditions.

The third contact, on January 22, 2017, was a reception at the White House for all law enforcement heads, to thank them for their service with the media present. Comey said he was wary about even being there, as the FBI and its director were not supposed to be on anyone's political team, and he supposed the optics with the cameras of the news media might suggest

34. Comey, *Higher Loyalty*, 220–21.

35. Comey, *Higher Loyalty*, 223.

36. Comey, *Higher Loyalty*, 226.

it. He was intent on safeguarding the integrity and independence of the agency, so he stood in the back of the room. Trump was scanning the crowd while he spoke and called the head of the Secret Service, who was standing next to Comey; the man went to the president and Trump hugged him. Trump continued to scan the room and finally called out Comey's name, asking him to come forward for the photo op. Comey thought it was a disaster and determined that he would not hug him. As Comey approached, he put out his hand to shake to avoid the hug; nevertheless Trump tried to pull him in for the hug, but Comey was stronger; as unobtrusively as possible, he used his strength to avoid the hug but he got something worse in exchange. Trump put his mouth close to his ear and whispered the same indirect threat: "I'm really looking forward to working with you." Unfortunately, it looked like a kiss. Then Trump motioned for Comey to stand next to him; Comey refused, returning to the back of the room, and slipped out of the reception.[37]

On January 27, 2017, twenty-one days into Comey's relationship with Trump, he invited him to dinner at the White House (solitary contact number four). Before the dinner, Comey spoke with Jim Clapper at an FBI event, telling him about the invitation to dinner. Clapper said he was probably invited along with others, as he heard of others being invited to dinner. Upon arrival at the White House, Comey saw that he was the only guest. Comey said that he noted a menu listing the items for dinner, but "didn't know that his job security was on the menu." After discussing the calligraphy of the menu, Trump abruptly asked, "So what do you want to do?" Comey thought it was a strange question. Then before Comey could speak, Trump began a long monologue on the directorship of the FBI, mentioning that he could "make a change in the Director of the FBI," and if he (Comey) wanted to walk away, he could. Trump asked him, "What do you think about it?" Comey told him that he knew that he could change the FBI director any time he wished, but he wanted to stay on and finish his term in a job that he enjoyed and that he thought he was doing well in, and that the president could always depend on him to tell him the truth. Trump responded, "I need loyalty. I expect loyalty."[38] At that point, Comey was silent and there was a "stare down" contest; Trump ended the standoff by changing the subject.

Trump continued their conversation as though nothing had transpired, although it was not a conversation. Comey described it: "It was very hard to get a word in. For the rest of the meal, pausing only now and then to eat, he spoke in torrents, gushing words about the size of his inauguration

37. Comey, *Higher Loyalty*, 231–32.
38. Comey, *Higher Loyalty*, 236–37.

crowd, etc."[39] Comey said his speaking style was a tactic: "His method of speaking was like an oral jigsaw puzzle contest with a shot clock. He would, in rapid-fire sequence, pick up a piece, put it down, pick up an unrelated piece, put it down, return to the original piece, on and on. But it was always him picking up the pieces and putting them down. The barrage of words seemed designed to prevent a genuine two-way dialogue from ever happening. Then there was the baffling, unnecessary lies."[40] Trump ended his manic monologue by asking Comey how he ever became director of the FBI, and after Comey's answer Trump told him again, "I need loyalty." Comey paused and answered: "You will always get honesty from me." Trump paused, "That's what I want, honest loyalty," he said. Comey said that he would always get "honest loyalty" from him, and it appeared to satisfy Trump as some sort of "deal" in which we were both winners.[41] Comey went home and wrote a memo on the meeting for the FBI.

On February 8, 2017, Comey was invited to the White House to see Reince Priebus, chief of staff, because Priebus had no experience in working for the government and wanted to understand about the relationship between the director of the FBI and the president, he said. After Comey's explanation, Priebus asked if Comey wanted to see the president and Comey said no. Priebus told Comey to sit, and he would go down the hall and see if the president was there. His meeting with Priebus was a setup to get Comey in front of the president again—contact five. When Comey arrived, Trump started into one of his manic monologues again, centering on an interview that he had on Fox News with Bill O'Reilly. O'Reilly asked Trump if he respected Vladimir Putin; he answered that yes, he did respect him and then said, "I respect a lot of people." O'Reilly said, "But he's a killer." Trump said, "There are a lot of killers. We've got a lot of killers [in America]. What do you think? Our country's so innocent?"[42] As Trump's monologue continued, he never stopped talking—thereby leaving the impression that his hearers agreed with his preposterous opinions due to their silence. About this devious tactic, Comey states, "His assertions about what 'everyone thinks' and what is 'obviously true' wash over you unchallenged, as they did at our dinner, because he never stops talking. As a result, Trump pulls all those present into a silent circle of assent."[43] Comey knew what Trump was doing, so he jumped into his monologue, saying, "But we are not killers." Comey said

39. Comey, *Higher Loyalty*, 238.
40. Comey, *Higher Loyalty*, 239–40.
41. Comey, *Higher Loyalty*, 243.
42. Comey, *Higher Loyalty*, 248.
43. Comey, *Higher Loyalty*, 249–50.

Trump's whole demeanor and facial expression changed: hardening, eyes narrowing, jaw tightening, then it was gone like Comey had said nothing. The meeting was over.[44] Trump's sociopathy assisted him in his bully tactics, but he remained a coward.

A week later, on February 14, 2017, Comey was back in the Oval Office for a counterterrorism briefing with the president, Mike Pence, the CIA director, the director of the NHS counterterrorism, and Comey's new boss, AG Jeff Sessions. After the meeting, Trump dismissed all but Comey for solitary contact number six; he said, "I want to talk about Mike Flynn." Flynn had resigned the previous day, and Comey sent FBI agents to question him about Russia sanctions and Flynn lied to the agents. Sessions, Kushner, and Priebus were at the door sticking their heads in, trying to be present in the conversation, but Trump waved them off; there was a large group outside the door waiting to talk to the president. Alone with Comey, Trump said in his indirect mob boss threatening way, "I hope you can see your way clear to letting this go, he [Flynn] is a good guy. I hope you can let this go."[45] It was a clear case of Trump criminally obstructing justice. Comey did not agree to let Flynn go. After the meeting, Comey prepared a memo to the FBI about what the president asked and discussed it with the FBI leadership: McCabe, Jim Rybicki, and the FBI general counsel Jim Baker; Comey asked Rybicki to arrange for him to meet with Attorney General Jeff Sessions to report the incident. Comey told Sessions that, as his boss, it was his duty to see that he (Comey) did not have any further solitary meetings with the president. Sessions did not respond, only shook his head and looked down at the table. Afterwards, Comey had his chief of staff contact Session's chief of staff, making the same request. Nevertheless, Comey struggled with the situation for the next three months.

A Cowardly Dismissal

In the next three months, Trump made three calls to Comey: March 1, 2017, a call "just to know how Comey was doing," obviously an intimidation call; March 30, 2017, when Trump said the Russia investigation was "a cloud impairing his ability to lead the nation," claiming there was "no Russia," "no hookers in Russia," and no "golden showers" thing; he asked what Comey could do to lift the cloud. He also mentioned that he did not know why there was an FBI investigation between Russia and the Trump campaign, stressing that Comey needed to get the information out that he

44. Comey, *Higher Loyalty*, 249–50.
45. Comey, *Higher Loyalty*, 255.

was not under investigation. Comey reported the call to Assistant Attorney General Dana Boente (Sessions had reclused himself from the Russia investigation). The third call, April 11, 2017, Trump asked Comey what he had done about the Russia investigation and "getting out" information that Trump was not under investigation. Comey noted that he appeared to be irritated. He told Trump in truly clear terms that the proper way to voice his concerns was through the "traditional channel" and to contact the leadership of the Department of Justice with his concerns. Comey reported the call to the acting attorney general.[46] I give the details of encounters here to show how relentless, devious, and cruel the malignant narcissist-sociopath Donald Trump was in attempting to compromise the leader of a critical law enforcement institution, committing the crime of obstruction of justice and then attempting to eliminate an important obstacle in his lawless pursuit of total power. It was just the beginning of Trump's crimes in the presidential office, but Trump discovered that if he wanted to eliminate an important obstacle, a thorn in his side in his illegal pursuit of power, that he could not corrupt James Comey but would have to fire him. Trump would not only unjustly fire James Comey, but he would humiliate him with as much cruelty he could devise.

On May 9, 2017, when Comey was in Los Angeles at a diversity agent recruiting effort, he was addressing the agents from the FBI office when he saw on the television monitors in the back of the room that he had been fired. He told the audience that he would have to get to the bottom of the news report and finished his speech. Comey's assistant in Washington, DC, received a letter about his termination from an official from the White House, then emailed the dismissal letter to him. Comey boarded the helicopter for the return trip to Washington, and it was covered by the media. Trump was watching television and saw the images of Comey returning on the FBI helicopter and called Andrew McCabe, angry that Comey was still using FBI property to fly back, and asked him to launch an investigation into it. McCabe said that would not be necessary as *he* authorized it for Comey's safety. Trump blew up and insulted McCabe's wife, who had lost an election in Virginia, asking him how it felt to be losers; he also commanded that Comey not be allowed on FBI property, but that his personal effects be boxed up and sent to him. There is no doubt that being fired from the FBI was a crushing blow for Comey; he later said that Trump "eats your soul in small bites."[47]

46. Comey, *Higher Loyalty*, 257–61.

47. Albert, "Comey: 'Trump Eats Your Soul.'"

However, the thorn in Trump's side left a fatal wound. The firing of James Comey was not the end of Donald Trump's confrontation with the rule of law, but the beginning of an intense scrutiny of his crimes in office. Comey's example of resisting Trump would break the spell of his apparent invincibility and ruthlessness. The memo Comey wrote to the Justice Department when Trump asked him to back off the Flynn investigation and let him off—Comey kept a copy at home and it was evidence that Trump committed a felony. Comey could not trust the Department of Justice leadership to follow through with a criminal investigation, so, thanks to Trump, he now was a private citizen and could pass the memo on to a friend, a former prosecutor, with instructions to give it to a news reporter. Then, the flap over the news coverage of Trump's apparent interference with Flynn's investigation contributed and led to *the appointment of Robert Mueller on the Russia investigation.* In addition, on June 8, 2017, Comey testified publicly before the Senate Select Committee on Intelligence that wanted to hear about his interactions with President Trump! Comey gave the committee a written statement that included the nine private contacts he had with Donald Trump where he attempted to corrupt and gain personal influence over the FBI in covering up his crimes.[48]

Jim Comey's firing and its aftermath was "the beginning of the end" for Donald Trump, because at the time of this writing[49] there are renewed calls for the new attorney general, Merrick Garland, to indict Trump for the crimes enumerated in the Mueller investigation and his crimes of obstruction of justice during all his investigations, including two impeachments and their trials. The second impeachment, concerning Trump's role in the insurrection of the Capitol on January 6, 2021, led to a bipartisan Congressional Special Panel investigating the "January 6 insurrection" and a Department of Justice investigation of both participants and planners of the insurrection. We have not yet seen Donald Trump's final attempt to dismantle American democracy, as Trump's crimes continue while he is out of office. In the next chapter, I focus on the unparalleled absolute presidential immunity that Trump claims in all his crimes that led to his criminal unaccountability, first in the Mueller investigation of Russia's influence on the 2016 election and then in all his other crimes against democracy.

48. Comey, *Higher Loyalty,* 270–71.
49. August 2021.

Chapter 4

"Plucking the Bald Eagle"

Justice delayed is justice denied.

A LEGAL MAXIM

When the sentence for a crime is not quickly carried out,
people's hearts are filled with schemes to do wrong.

THE BIBLE, ECCL 8:11

BENITO MUSSOLINI'S METAPHOR FOR engaging in fascist rule, "plucking a chicken," becomes repulsive when applied to American democracy: "plucking the bald eagle." The eagle represents America's strength and freedom protected by law, and such an ignominious end to America's sacred symbol conveys an unthinkable image—American democracy suffering violence, indignity, and mutilation. When voters elected Donald Trump as president, the unthinkable image became an American reality. Plucking the bald eagle is an apt metaphor for the contempt that fascist tyrant Trump showed for the American way of life, attacking its rule of law and democratic institutions and attempting to overthrow a democratic election together with the indignity of a violent insurrection on America's Capitol. Although Trump's fascist anti-American acts were uncovered by Special Counsel Robert Mueller's investigation on Russia election interference, resulting in an unprecedented two impeachments by Congress, between those impeachments was a veritable *one-man crime wave for which Donald Trump was not held accountable.*[1]

1. Slisco, "'Guilty as Sin.'"

The ex-white-collar career criminal of New York became the serial criminal of Washington, DC, committing a host of felonies against democracy. Chapter 2, "The 'Making' of a Con Man," focused on Donald Trump's corrupt business dealings and financial crimes in New York. When he became president, the office of the presidency did not change who he was; it revealed who he was. Trump did not stop committing financial crimes;[2] he ignored the soft guardrail of democracy of providing his tax returns; had he submitted them, it would have immediately revealed his financial crimes. However, President Donald Trump's financial crimes paled in comparison to his *crimes against democracy*. As a fascist president, his crimes shifted to assaults on democratic institutions, plucking the bald eagle one feather at a time.

IS A PRESIDENT ABOVE THE LAW?

Some people may object to the notion that President Donald Trump committed "crimes," because he was not convicted of a crime while in office. In the case of Donald Trump, this logic is like "straining at a gnat and swallowing a camel."[3] President Trump was not convicted of a crime, but that did not mean that he didn't commit crimes. He was caught red-handed committing numerous crimes that were documented in the investigations of Special Counsel Robert Mueller, the US Congress in two impeachment hearings, and by a select committee looking into the insurrection of January 6, 2021. The fact that President Trump was never called to account for these crimes and placed under oath to answer for them is an unprecedented miscarriage of justice, occurring repeatedly in his presidency. He was shielded from the due process of law and consequences for his lawbreaking *by the office of the presidency and a novel theory of "absolute presidential immunity."* This was *not* the intention of the framers of the United States Constitution for a president. The House Permanent Select Committee on Intelligence's report in its investigation of Donald Trump and Ukraine crimes (first impeachment) begins with a quote from the first president of the United States on the role of the Constitution. In his farewell address, President George Washington warned of a moment when "cunning, ambitious, and unprincipled men will be enabled to subvert the power of the people and to usurp for themselves the reins of government, destroying afterwards the very engines which have

2. Fahrenthold, "Ballrooms, Candles and Luxury Cottages"; Wang, "Trump-Appointed Ambassador"; Mangan, "Tax Firm Mazars Fires Trump."
3. Matt 23:4.

lifted them to unjust dominion."[4] His words were an indictment of the forty-fifth president of the United States, Donald Trump. Seven years after the adoption of the US Constitution, there was still a keen awareness regarding the office of the presidency being occupied by a man that George Washington described; the founders of the Constitution were also aware of kings that abused their power; the last thing they would want in such a document is the notion of absolute presidential immunity!

A Presidential Immunity Shield: Permission to Commit Crimes?

A multilayered immunity shield for criminal activity was provided for the man described in the previous three chapters—Donald Trump—an amoral, malignant narcissistic sociopath, a career criminal without a conscience who was clearly unqualified for public office by any measure. An immunity shield for such a man was a recipe for plucking the eagle, making Trump virtually above the law in America's revered democracy. In his presidential above-the-law status, the man was free to commit a series of fascist crimes focused on democratic targets that a fascist dictator must "pluck," weaken, discredit, and replace. Trump overtly and covertly began attacking American democracy's constitutional norms, traditions, and institutions. He engaged in criminal activity in doing so, until it caught the attention of the FBI and led to the Mueller investigation on the influence of Russia in the 2016 presidential election, as well as two congressional impeachment investigations that were both election-related. The seven conditions that made up an unprecedented immunity shield for the crimes of the president were:

1. a novel legal theory of presidential immunity,

2. a compromised Department of Justice with corrupt Attorney General Bill Barr,

3. compromised and discredited intelligence services,[5]

4. a corrupt Republican-controlled Senate,

5. a manipulation of the justice system by Trump "weaponizing" lawsuits, delaying criminal charges for years,

6. coerced government officials under presidential threat of being fired and under the threat of physical harm from Trump's fanatical base, and

---

4. House Intelligence Committee, *Impeachment Report*, 7.
5. Stephanopoulos, "Trump Decimated the Intelligence Community."

7 a president with pathological personality disorders that enabled him to lie profusely and deceive without signs of guilt or remorse.

Under this umbrella of presidential immunity, fascist Donald Trump was able to commit crimes with impunity as he dismantled American democracy.

The nature of Trump's crimes in a lawless presidency pointed to his goal of fascist rule. To perpetuate presidential power and stay in office, he assaulted the guardian and legal path to power in a democracy—the core institution of democratic elections. His "election crimes" were (1) his presidential campaign colluding with Russia, giving him an edge in the electoral college vote in key states (2016 election); (2) committing obstruction of justice repeatedly in both of Congress's election-related impeachment hearings, as well as in the Mueller investigation into Russian interference in the elections; (3) ignoring lawful subpoenas and refusing to allow government witnesses to appear at congressional impeachment hearings; (4) tampering with the witnesses in those hearings; (5) in the first impeachment, attempting to purchase foreign influence to tarnish his opponent Joe Biden in the 2020 elections;[6] (6) attempting to corrupt the democratic election process itself by asking the Department of Justice (DOJ) attorney general after the election to pressure local election officials in key states to change their vote-count to overturn a democratic election that he lost to Joe Biden in 2020;[7] and finally, in true fascist form, (7) in a desperate attempt to stay in power, he attempted to retain power by planning and inciting a violent insurrection of the US Capitol to stop Congress's confirmation of Joe Biden's win of the election on January 6, 2021. Anyone else committing crimes like those cited would be charged with serious felonies, if not treason; however, President Trump was above the law and unaccountable for them all. Claiming that Trump was a one-man crime wave is not hyperbole; the above cited crimes are just the tip of the iceberg.

Absolute Presidential Immunity: An Unconstitutional Notion

The emergence of absolute presidential immunity is a historic novelty; its dangers were recalled in the presidency of Richard Nixon. However, under the circumstances of a president like Donald Trump—an amoral, malignant narcissistic sociopath, a career criminal without a conscience—the notion of absolute presidential immunity was not only unconstitutional but

6. Mueller, *Mueller Report*, 2:200–202.

7. Maddow, "Federal Judge Calls out Barr"; Wallace, "Judge Details What Daniel Goldman Calls."

a license for him to commit crimes in the presidency. Rules and laws had always been of little concern to him; *sociopaths always feel that they can do whatever they want.* For Trump, presidential immunity meant that he was free to pursue his lawless quest for fascist rule; his serial crimes against democracy would be excused and he would be unaccountable. Presidential attorneys, a corrupt attorney general, and a complicit party-majority in the Senate were only part of Donald Trump's multilayered, unprecedented immunity shield. On the advice of his White House attorneys and corrupt Attorney General William Barr,[8] Trump claimed presidential immunity for all his words and actions while in office; in effect, he claimed to be above the law. One of Trump's attorneys, William Consovoy, said that Trump could shoot someone on Fifth Avenue and not be indicted; he has immunity until he leaves office.[9] They were attorneys. They knew the importance of legal precedent for such an outrageous view in case law; the claim was a sham.

Insufficient Case Law

Case law is law established by decisions of courts, especially appellate courts in published opinions; it is law based on judicial decisions rather than legislative action; it is law based on previous judicial decisions and precedent rather than statutes.[10] In determining whether a previous case is relevant and can be used, "a binding precedent or authority" must be found; this means finding a principle or rule established in a previous legal precedent that is either binding on or persuasive to a court, when deciding subsequent cases with similar issues of fact.[11] "Similar issues of fact" in case law are that (1) the case in question is essentially the same as the case of application; (2) the resolution of the case in question is similar to the case of application; (3) the significant facts of the precedent case are also relevant to the case of application; and (4) no additional facts appear in the case of application that might be treated as significant.[12] This sharpening function for determining what "similar issues of fact" are in case law clearly shows that previous adjudications of presidential immunity do not meet "binding precedent" requirements for Donald Trump's claim of immunity. *There are no previous cases of a rogue president committing multiple felonies!* Trump's case deals with an entirely different set of facts—intentional and repeated

8. Savage and Stern, "Judge Calls Barr's Handling"; Stern, "Federal Judge Says."

9. Pierson, "Trump Could Shoot Someone."

10. Free Dictionary, "Case Law."

11. Wikipedia, "Precedent."

12. Free Dictionary, "Case Law."

abuses of presidential power and crimes. Furthermore, the Trump case "adds additional facts" (multiple felonies) that make previous adjudications on presidential immunity very "dissimilar." Nevertheless, Trump's lawyers claimed it anyway and got away with it.

Case law that covers the frequency and depth of criminal behavior that rogue president Donald Trump represented does not exist. Presidential immunity has only been tested/adjudicated in the courts under normal presidential circumstances, such as a president threatened with lawsuits or political criminal charges that may interfere with and impede his carrying out the duties of office. The case of a president needing immunity in normal circumstances is not what characterizes Donald Trump's presidency! Rather, in constitutional terms, his presidency is characterized by continuous abuse of presidential power and lawlessness in office, a flood-tide of high crimes and misdemeanors. Obvious evidence for this abnormal presidency is two congressional impeachments bracketing one presidential term, one at the beginning and one at the end. A rogue president that intentionally engaged in committing multiple felonies against democracy has not yet been adjudicated in federal courts or the Supreme Court in a way that fits the present instance. Case law with presidential immunity like Trump's presidency *does not exist, because a serial-criminal president like him has never existed in American history.* Previous adjudications of presidential immunity lack a binding legal precedent for his case; they have only tested the concept of presidential immunity under normal presidential circumstances that are *not* similar to the Trump presidency—a virtual crime wave in office.[13] Later, the issue of absolute immunity appeared in federal court and the Supreme Court in 2019 and 2021 when Donald Trump claimed presidential immunity to avoid surrendering his federal tax returns; at that time, judges expressed indignation, calling the notion of absolute immunity "repugnant," and it was rejected.[14]

Nevertheless, in the gaslighting-induced fog of Trump's lawless presidency, the notion of absolute immunity allowed him to bluff his way through investigations by refusing cooperation with the investigations, intentionally obstructing them (a felony), and firing those who led the investigations (FBI Director James Comey and his successor, Acting Director Andrew McCabe) or attempting to fire, as in the case of Special Counsel Robert Mueller.[15] At the time, Mueller even referred to the absolute immunity shield and the

13. Buchanan, "Tracking 30 Investigations"; see also chapter 9.

14. Stempel, "Judge's Order Releasing Trump's Tax Returns"; Dwyer, "Supreme Court Rejects Immunity."

15. Mueller, *Mueller Report,* 2:198.

difficulties it would present, if he was filling the usual prosecutorial role and making prosecutorial judgments in building a case for prosecution—which he was not—because of the given presidential immunity assumption of the Justice Department that a sitting president could not be indicted. Mueller's task as special counsel was to gather evidence of crimes in the Russia investigation so Congress would indict the president in a presidential impeachment.[16] The abnormal role for a prosecutor, not indicting a person after building a criminal case against him, is a key point for understanding the Mueller investigation and his report. However, that Justice Department policy was later discovered to be merely a "departmental internal personnel directive"!

Acting on his alleged above-the-law status, Donald Trump proceeded to commit crimes against democracy until he accrued for himself an unprecedented, infamous, historical achievement of being the only president that the US Congress impeached (in effect indicted) twice for "high crimes and misdemeanors." In those bookended, essentially criminal, indictments, the Senate trials were not traditional trials with witnesses testifying,[17] because President Trump tampered with the witnesses and refused to let them testify; it was a sham trial where a complicit Republican Senate majority gave a not guilty vote on a purely partisan basis, ignoring the overwhelming evidence presented and refusing to convict Trump. A conviction would have resulted in removing him from office (in the first impeachment trial; in the second impeachment he was already out of office). Trump refused to appear in person to declare his innocence in both congressional trials, neither of them had the appearance or function of a trial, and Trump did not submit to interviews in the investigations; he was never under oath, he only flat out claimed absolute immunity. When he was pronounced not guilty in the first impeachment, Trump's take was that he could commit crimes in office with impunity.

JUSTICE DELAYED IS JUSTICE DENIED

In all the above-listed crimes of Donald Trump, he did not face justice due to the unconstitutional notion of absolute presidential immunity, a signature issue of Attorney General Bill Barr. Prior to his confirmation as attorney general, Barr sent a nineteen-page document to Congress outlining his belief in presidential immunity.[18] In the middle of the Mueller investigation,

16. Mueller, *Mueller Report*, 2:195, 2:344.

17. Swalwell, *Endgame*, 336–37, 339, 344–45, 351, 353.

18. Schiff, *Midnight in Washington*, 167.

Barr sent a letter to the acting AG, Rod Rosenstein, claiming the Mueller investigation was illegitimate based on his specious "unitary theory of the Executive," giving sweeping powers to the president.[19] Under that immunity notion from Barr, implemented by Trump's attorneys, Trump refused to give testimony in the investigations into his criminal activities; it allowed him to continue to obstruct all of the investigations against him with impunity. Barr politicized the Justice Department, firing US state attorneys general handling cases filed against Trump and replacing them with Trump sycophants.[20]

Most crucial in Barr's protection of the president was *quashing the Mueller Investigation Report, which contained evidence of ten counts of criminal obstruction of justice* for Trump's interference in the Russia investigation and incidents of obstruction of justice in the first impeachment investigation.[21] For Trump, quashing the report amounted to a "get out of jail free" card. After Trump vacated the White house, and after a two-year court battle, presidential attorney McGahn finally agreed to testify in the House Judiciary Committee with damning testimony under closed doors in May 2021, but it was two years too late for the impeachment trial in the Senate and the Russia investigation. This Trump delay tactic and a corrupt attorney general demonstrated two of the layers of Trump's unprecedented presidential immunity shield, rendering him above the law."[22] Barr quashing the Mueller report was a despicable act of betrayal and abuse of his office. Eric Swalwell said a letter had been received by the Justice Department, signed by one thousand former federal prosecutors, senior officials of the Justice Department, serving prosecutors, and US attorneys, some Republican and some Democrat, stating that there was more than enough evidence to indict Trump for obstruction of justice.[23]

Throughout his life, Donald Trump avoided justice by weaponizing lawsuits, filing baseless and endless lawsuits and frivolous motions, backed up by a bevy of lawyers and his inherited wealth. Then with the power and protections of the office of the presidency, he continued to avoid civil and criminal legal scrutiny by the same means, never appearing in a court under oath (a problem for a pathological liar). In the impeachment investigations, prosecutors knew of Trump's delay tactics and knew that he would

19. Swalwell, *Endgame*, 9.

20. Leonnig and Rucker, *I Alone Can Fix It*, 192–96.

21. Mueller, *Mueller Report*, 2:210–320, 2:344.

22. Polantz, "Ex-WH Counsel McGahn"; Diaz, "2 Years Later"; Lowell, "Trump Plans to Sue."

23. Swalwell, *Endgame*, 12.

draw out their investigations for years, as the above example of his attorney McGahn demonstrated. In Mueller's Russia investigation, McGahn would have testified about Trump's crime of obstruction of justice; he had already told Trump that he would tell the truth if called as a witness, threatening to resign. The threat of filing lawsuits to delay changed the whole demeanor of the impeachment investigations as well as their outcomes, because such delays would be impossible for impeachment prosecutors to justify politically, in a high-profile case, and the public would not tolerate it. Delays always worked for Trump.

The above seven factors that made up the unprecedented shield of immunity for Trump's crimes led to a more intolerable situation; in effect, they gave the fascist president permission to continue committing crimes and dismantle democracy, slowly plucking the eagle with impunity. The rule of law under Trump amounted to an unprecedented assault on Lady Justice; blindfolded and grasping the scales of justice, she is symbolic of impartiality and letting evidence stand on its own and speak for itself, but Trump never got indicted, let alone faced a trial where evidence against him would speak for itself.[24] Justice degenerated to the point where the fundamental premise of justice—a fair trial—was denied; an unwillingness to see evidence and hear testimony of witnesses in a fair trial was denied by the Republican-led Senate in two impeachment hearings. With Donald Trump, the maxim "justice delayed was justice denied" was like a drumbeat throughout his presidency. Trump's actions in delaying and perverting justice are historic; his strategies are known, yet the crimes that he committed in the presidency and afterwards are still not addressed, and he has still not been held accountable. Justice never catches up with Donald Trump. *It appears that he has found the Achilles heel of the American justice system.*

Trump's immunity shield protected him from the consequences of committing crimes that led to a trial; it was a continuing flagrant affront to the American judicial system, as well as evidence that a lawless fascist occupied the Oval Office. There should be no doubt that from the beginning, Donald Trump was set on dismantling democracy just like any other fascist. Ed Kilgore's article "Trump's Long Campaign to Steal the Presidency: A Timeline" states there is a false impression currently being disseminated that the insurrection of the Capitol was "improvised on January 6, 2021," when in fact Trump's efforts dated to shortly after the 2016 election.[25] Kilgore is correct in speaking of a timeline of Trump's "stealing election" events; it reached back to when he was elected to office with Russian interference in

24. Wikipedia, "Lady Justice."
25. Kilgore, "Trump's Long Campaign."

the election, giving him an advantage in the electoral vote. The House Select Committee's investigation into the Capitol insurrection of January 6, 2021, is a bookend Trump steal-the-election event, matching the earlier bookend steal-the-election event in July 2015—the start of Trump's fascist presidential campaign. The timeline between these bookend crimes is littered with Donald Trump's illegal attempts to gain and maintain presidential power—his "election crimes." Trump's Russia contacts even preceded the election campaign, when his personal attorney, Michael Cohen, met with Russians in November of 2015 and Trump was a "person of interest" in FBI investigations involving Russia.[26]

RUSSIAN INTERFERENCE WAS NO HOAX

In Donald Trump's election campaign and presidency, Russians are everywhere: government officials and diplomats, emissaries, Kremlin FSB agents (federal security service), lawyers, oligarchs, businesspeople, investors, realtors, and thugs; they associate freely with Donald Trump and family members, his presidential campaign, US government officials, and with his friends and associates. What explains this sudden "Russia presence" in American political circles? Were it not for historical fact, one might think that Russia was an ally of the United States instead of a cold war enemy since World War II. The presence of the world's preeminent authoritarian government, led by one of the world's most ruthless, richest dictator-tyrants, Vladimir Putin, and the president of the United States in amiable dialogue was not merely an oddity but was evidence of Donald Trump's total disdain for democracy and his personal desire to be a world-class rich fascist leader just like Putin.[27] The day when Russian influence was thought to be far off, a continent geographically far away, was now forgotten history; in 2016, the Russians were in our own backyard, even appearing in the White House in private conversations with the victorious fascist candidate Donald Trump! When representative Eric Swalwell asked his colleagues if any of them had contacts with Russians, the answer was zero. But in these times, he said, "In the Trump forest if you shake a tree a Russian falls out of it."[28]

While enjoying the relaxed security of the White House and its president, the Russians were still covertly attacking and undermining American democracy just as they always have; they had not changed, America's ideology had not changed; Donald Trump had arrived in the White House!

26. Strzok, *Compromised*, §51.
27. Alexander and Behar, "Truth behind Trump Tower Moscow."
28. Swalwell, *Endgame*, 99.

The FBI and America's intelligence agencies were reporting Russia's interference in American elections as early as March 2013.[29] In 2015, Russians hacked into computers of US government officials, federal and state, stealing documents from Democratic national election campaign servers, Hillary Clinton's computer, as well as American election records. In his book *Compromised: Counterintelligence and the Threat of Donald J. Trump*, FBI counterintelligence supervisor Peter Strzok said, "In late December 2016 the director of national intelligence published a report confirming the same intelligence that we [the FBI] had been receiving throughout the presidential campaign—Vladimir Putin and the Russian government were interfering with our electoral system to undermine faith in the election, hurt Hillary Clinton's prospects, and help Trump get elected."[30]

FBI Investigations: Russian Interference in US Elections

The American public knew all about the Clinton email investigation; it dominated the news, but the public knew nothing of the Russian election interference investigation involving Donald Trump; only a few in the FBI knew about it.[31] Donald Trump took advantage of the resulting imbalanced press coverage of information on the two investigations, exploiting the lack of information on the ongoing investigation involving himself and Russia. Traditionally, this was FBI policy about ongoing investigations—they did not announce them. Using psychological projection and manipulation of the media, Trump shifted the public's attention from *his Russia* involvement to Hillary's email investigation, blowing it out of proportion and flat out lying about it. The Clinton misstep with emails was miniscule compared to the crimes Trump committed in handling classified information while president, as he tore documents up in front of witnesses, put them in burn bags, flushed documents down the toilet, and then, when leaving the White House, stole dozens of boxes containing classified documents and hid them at Mar-a-Lago.[32] The Clinton email investigation was the beginning of Trump's explosive and very effective media campaign vilifying her by gaslighting and using projection to mischaracterize her—*she* was a criminal

29. "Hillary Clinton Email Investigation," Ballotpedia.

30. Strzok, *Compromised*, §51.

31. Strzok, *Compromised*, §62–67.

32. O'Donnell, "Goldman on Trump Keeping"; Graham, "Incredible Vanishing Trump Presidency"; Shafer, "Opinion: How Trump Flushed"; Litman, "Another Case Where Trump's Flagrant Misconduct"; Concepcion, "Report: Presidential Diarist Says Trump."

and should be "locked up"—when *he* was historically the most notorious criminal ever to occupy the White House.

After an exhaustive investigation in July 2016, the FBI found no crime or criminal intent on the part of Hillary Clinton and therefore no charges were filed against her.[33] Even when other emails were found after the FBI closed their initial investigation on Clinton and the case was reopened, investigators found no wrongdoing in the new documents, and she was not charged in the follow-up investigation either.[34] For Trump, the truth about Clinton misusing her computer was not the point; the point was repeating a bold-faced lie publicly (that she was a criminal) in his gaslighting game, to turn the public against her. *It worked.* The fact that the Trump campaign was cup to its neck in Russians" was unknown to the public at the time, as was the FBI's investigation of Russian interference in America's elections; the FBI's interest in Trump had been ongoing for years. Due to Donald Trump's history of dependence on Russian money since the 1980s,[35] together with his current public false statements of "no Russia involvement whatsoever" that combination of contradictory facts meant that FBI Counterintelligence was duty-bound, for the first time in the history of the American presidency, *to consider whether a president may have been compromised and was acting as an agent of a foreign adversary*—Trump was a "subject of interest" for the FBI.[36] In counterintelligence investigations, the point is not to gather evidence of guilt for prosecution of an individual but to determine if a person is being "compromised" by a foreign power and is therefore vulnerable to blackmail and may be forced to commit acts against the interests of the United States.[37] The counterintelligence investigation of Donald Trump, as usual with the FBI, was done without public knowledge, especially since it was so close to an election. The question was "whether a compromised candidate for the United States presidency was part of this new Russia interference in American elections."[38] It is a monumental irony that Donald Trump's presidency began and ended with counterintelligence investigations of the Espionage Act; at the beginning, the notion of him being compromised by Russians may have appeared far-fetched, but at the end of his presidency

33. Strzok, *Compromised*, §51.

34. "Hillary Clinton Email Investigation," Ballotpedia.

35. Strzok, *Compromised*, §84–90.

36. Strzok, *Compromised*, §95.

37. Strzok, *Compromised*, §84–90; this was the same point in Trump not submitting his tax returns during his entire presidency.

38. Alexander and Behar, "Truth behind Trump Tower Moscow."

his disloyalty to democracy was not only plausible but clear; the FBI was investigating him for a crime that would bring the lawless president down.

Russian Collusion in the 2016 Presidential Election

Donald Trump was certainly vulnerable to compromise. His financial dependence on Russian money, as Eric Trump freely admitted,[39] his business dealings with Russia, and curious relationship and praise for Russia and Putin pointed in that direction. Trump's claim that he had no dealings with the Russians had joke status with the FBI, due to the trove of information they had about Trump and his organization's dealings with Russia prior to, and including contacts in, the presidential campaign.[40] In the same time period as the Clinton email investigation (2015), and later in 2016, the FBI had plenty of evidence that Trump's campaign was meeting with Russians in order to sway the election in his favor:

1. Michael Cohen, Trump's personal lawyer, emailed Dmitry Peskov, Russian government press secretary, about a real estate project in Russia known as "Trump Tower Moscow"; then-candidate Trump signed a letter of intent in November 2015 and pursued the project through June 2016.[41] Cohen met with Russian officials and businessmen numerous times.

2. George Papadopoulos, Trump's campaign foreign policy advisor, in May 2016 met with Joseph Mifsud who told him that the Russian government had "dirt" on Hillary Clinton in the form of thousands of emails. Papadopoulos had a Facebook account for communicating with Russians, and he contacted Ivan Timofeev, a high-level Russian officer.[42]

3. Jared Kushner, Paul Manafort, and Donald Trump Jr. met with Russian lawyer Natalya Veselnitskaya and Rinat Akhmetshin,[43] former Soviet counterintelligence officers,[44] on June 9, 2016, at Trump Tower; Veselnitskaya claimed to have documents that would incriminate Hillary Clinton as "part of Russia and its government's support of Donald Trump"; on June 14, 2016, the Democratic National Committee (DNC)

39. Firozi, "Eric Trump in 2014."
40. Bump, "Again: There's No Evidence."
41. Mueller, *Mueller Report*, 1:45.
42. Strzok, *Compromised*, §1944, §2094.
43. See chapter 10 on the Trump stolen classified documents investigation.
44. Suskind, *List*, 204.

said the Russian government hackers had infiltrated the DNC and obtained opposition research for Trump as well as other documents; on July 22, 2016, WikiLeaks posted thousands of documents with information about the Clinton campaign. In July 2016, WikiLeaks first released emails stolen from the DNC by the intelligence directorate of the general staff of the Russian army (GRU).[45]

4. Carter Page, Trump campaign foreign policy advisor, in 2013 was contacted by Russian agents that the FBI had identified (and subsequently charged) in New York. In July 2016, he traveled to Moscow to give speeches and presentations, including the commencement address to the New Economics School.[46]

5. Mike Flynn, national security advisor and US army lieutenant general, had conversations with Russian GRU leadership and then covered them up. He swore to judges that he lied to FBI agent Strzok and other FBI agents. In 2015, he attended a dinner in Moscow celebrating Russian Television's tenth anniversary; he sat with Putin.[47]

6. Paul Manafort, Trump campaign chairman, was a long-term business associate with Konstantin Kilimnik, a Russian FSB agent (the old KGB). Manafort passed internal polling data to Kilimnik regarding key electoral college states in the 2016 election. Manafort also had links with oligarch Oleg Deripaska and pro-Russian Ukrainians.[48]

7. Rick Gates, Trump campaign aide, with Paul Manafort passed the polling data to Russian FSB agent Konstantin Kilimnik in 2016.

8. Robert Mueller indicted *twelve Russian agents* for interfering in the 2016 elections.[49]

9. In 2016, Jeff Sessions, Trump's first attorney general, met several times with Russian ambassador Kislyak; Erik Prince, associate of Steve Bannon, contacted Kirill Dmitriev.

Most of the above Trump associates and campaign officials were indicted and convicted in a court of law, some for obstruction of justice and others for conspiracy against the United States in violations of the Foreign Agents Registration Act (FARA). *Mueller indicted thirty-four people (twelve Russians)*

45. Mueller, *Mueller Report*, 1:46.
46. Strzok, *Compromised*, §2281–97.
47. Strzok, *Compromised*, §2309–14.
48. Mueller, *Mueller Report*, 1:46; Strzok, *Compromised*, §2309; Sneed, "Unsealed Manafort Docs."
49. Strzok, *Compromised*, §5346.

and three Russian companies for over one hundred crimes.[50] Nevertheless, at the time of the election campaign in 2016, the lies of Donald Trump and Rudy Giuliani[51] and members of Trump's presidential campaign who were essentially Russian collaborators carried the day. The sixty-eight-year-old grandmother Hillary Clinton was branded a criminal—and worse—in the minds of millions of Americans. The probable Russian-compromised candidate Donald Trump was elected president of the United States by an electoral college majority while losing the popular vote. This contradictory picture of two opposite realities cries out for an explanation. It is typical of the gaslighted Trump presidency. The ironic injustice is overpowering. Our Electoral College is an antiquated and undemocratic part of the electoral process; Russian agents took advantage of it to help Donald Trump get elected. Trump would exploit it even further in attempting to invalidate the 2020 election that he lost.[52]

Not until 2021, when the fog of Trump's gaslighting lifted, did the truth emerge that Donald Trump's election campaign *did in fact collude/ conspire with Russians* to gain an advantage over presidential candidate Hillary Clinton in the 2016 elections. Two reports: the *Mueller Investigation Report* (a two-year-long investigation by a special counsel) and the Senate Intelligence Committee's *Final Report* (a bipartisan, three-year-long investigation resulting in one thousand pages) give extensive evidence of the Russians colluding with the Trump 2016 election campaign and Donald Trump's obstruction in the investigations. However, at the time, Trump saw to it that both reports were quashed. In the same manner, the reports were discredited by Donald Trump's sycophants Attorney General Barr and Republican Senator Rubio; with their political viewpoints, both men gave conclusions that ignored the overwhelming evidentiary conclusions.[53] In a state or federal court of law where the evidentiary rule of law is maintained by strict legal procedures, such blatant ignoring of evidence would never have been allowed. The deceptive, politically induced fog that overwhelmed the truth at the time, now years later is beginning to burn off. As a clear-eyed assessment of the documented evidence is freshly examined, apart from the Trump gaslighting campaign that was at its height when the reports were released and quashed, the truth emerged. Paradoxically, after Trump left office, he was not charged with the ten felony counts of obstruction of justice

---

50. Cummings et al., "Mueller's Investigation Is Done."

51. Skolnik, "'Throw a Fake.'"

52. See chapter 10 regarding Trump's interference with state "electors."

53. Gazis, "Senate Intelligence Committee"; Shuham, "Intelligence Committee's 1,000 Page Russia Report"; Von Rennenkampff, "Republicans Incriminate Trump."

that Mueller had gathered evidence for in his indictment, although his associates were indicted and convicted in the same investigation.

While Donald Trump was demonizing Hillary Clinton in 2016, his campaign manager, Paul Manafort, and Rick Gates were contacting a Russian FSB agent, Konstantin Kilimnik, passing on critical campaign strategy and election polls on key battleground states to assist Trump in an electoral college win. This information was then used by hackers of the GRU in a sustained program of disinformation before the 2016 elections. Special Counsel Robert Mueller indicted the three men: Manafort was convicted for lying about his contacts with Kilimnik during the Mueller investigation along with other federal charges (but paroled by Donald Trump just prior to leaving office), Rick Gates pled guilty and cooperated with the Mueller investigation, and Kremlin FSB agent Kilimnik is still at large.[54]

UNDERSTANDING THE MUELLER INVESTIGATION AND REPORT

On May 17, 2017, Robert Mueller was appointed by Rod Rosenstein to continue the ongoing FBI investigation formerly led by Director James B. Comey.[55] As special counsel, Mueller was commissioned to find "any links and/or coordination between the Russian government and individuals associated with the presidential campaign of Donald Trump" and "any matters that arose or may arise directly from the investigation."[56] In Mueller's report, he explained that the terminology "links" and "coordination" intended by the Special Counsel Order were not legal terms, nor was "collusion," which was so often used in the news media, but he said the appropriate legal term was "conspiracy," which was synonymous with "collusion."[57] The investigation uncovered "numerous links" to Russia's interference,[58] numerous cases obstructing justice by many in the Trump presidential campaign, including the president himself, as well as other conspiracy-related federal crimes. Mueller reported that "the Russian government interfered in the 2016 presidential election in sweeping and systematic fashion" and that their campaign to interfere favored presidential candidate Donald J. Trump and

54. Melber, "Trump Collusion Exposed"; Sheth, "U.S. Officially Designates"; Mazzetti, "G.O.P.-Led Senate Panel"; Mueller, *Mueller Report*, 1:44, 1:46–47, 1:138–39.

55. Schiff, *Midnight in Washington*, 132.

56. Mueller, *Mueller Report*, 1:20.

57. Mueller, *Mueller Report*, 1:20.

58. Mueller, *Mueller Report*, 1:42, 1:167.

disparaged candidate Hillary Clinton.[59] Mueller made it clear that his report did not exonerate Donald Trump on the crime of obstruction of justice.[60]

The central stipulation Mueller cited for not charging Donald Trump was his pre-investigation decision not to take a traditional prosecutorial judgment outcome role, because the Justice Department's office of legal counsel (OLC) issued "an opinion," finding that the "indictment or criminal prosecution of a sitting President would impermissibly undermine the capacity of the executive branch, to perform its constitutionally assigned functions."[61] Previously, I stated that this OLC "immunity opinion" did not fit rogue President Donald Trump's case; in his case, it did not undermine his "constitutionally assigned presidential functions"—it undermined his criminal activities! Case law did not exist with a "binding legal precedent" and "similar issues of fact" that would support the OLC opinion.

Nevertheless, when Mueller started his investigation as special counsel, he was duty-bound to follow the guidelines of the OLC; further, he determined that it would be unfair to indict the president when he would not have opportunity to defend himself in a criminal trial.[62] The role Mueller took, therefore, was investigating and gathering information related to "links and coordination" of the Trump campaign with Russia, showing their interference in the presidential election. His role in relation to Trump's misconduct would be like that of a prosecutor gathering evidence of a crime for a grand jury. As special counsel in the Russia investigation, he would only gather evidence of Trump's crimes, and the evidence was supposed to be presented to Congress in a report.[63] Upon receiving the Mueller report, Congress would then determine articles of impeachment and order an impeachment hearing. Mueller was to indict and prosecute others that may have committed crimes prior to and during his investigation. Because Mueller did not indict Donald Trump with a crime does not mean he did not commit crimes; it meant that the indictment and trying of crimes by the president was not his mission as special counsel. The Mueller report, therefore, did not exonerate Trump; to indict or exonerate was not Mueller's or the report's purpose. Of course, after a two-year Mueller investigation, Congress was waiting for the report on Russian interference in the US elections, but Trump's attorney general, Bill Barr, had other nefarious plans for the report.

59. Mueller, *Mueller Report*, 1:41–42.
60. Mueller, *Mueller Report*, 2:203, 2:210–320, 2:344.
61. Mueller, *Mueller Report*, 1:194.
62. Mueller, *Mueller Report*, 1:195.
63. Peck and McLean, "Mueller Report Rules."

Mueller summarizes his "nontraditional prosecutorial judgment role" in gathering evidence of any links or coordination between the Trump campaign and Russia under nontraditional legal constraints, stating that "difficult issues would need to be resolved" by Congress later—issues like absolute presidential immunity and Trump's alleged above-the-law status. At the end of the summary, Mueller said regarding Trump, *"If we had confidence after a thorough investigation of the facts that the President clearly did not commit obstruction of justice, we would so state . . .* while this report does not conclude that the President committed a crime, it also does not exonerate him."[64] For the layperson, Mueller's explanation may appear as cryptic "lawyer-speak," if one does not consider its context—that he was not investigating to charge Trump with a crime; that was Congress's task. However, in contradiction to the special counsel's findings, Trump new appointee Attorney General William Barr took it upon himself to exonerate Trump!

William Barr's Deception—Quashing the Mueller Report

After being in office only thirty-seven days, William Barr performed a massive injustice that extended even beyond Trump's presidency influencing his unaccountability for crimes he committed in office and afterwards. On March 22, 2019, Special Counsel Robert Mueller submitted his report of over three hundred pages to new Attorney General William Barr, representing a two-year-long investigation of his team of FBI investigators, believing it would be forwarded to Congress. Two days after having received the report, Barr sent "a four-page summary" of Mueller's report to Congress in a letter! With astounding arrogance and dismissiveness, Barr gave his opinion in the summary, making two points that contradicted Mueller's findings: (1) that Mueller did not find evidence of conspiracy or coordination of the Trump campaign with the Russian government in its election interference and (2) that Mueller did not draw a conclusion as to whether President Trump committed obstruction of justice.[65] Both points were gross misrepresentations of the Mueller report findings. With extreme haste and superficial treatment of a three-hundred-page document from a two-year investigation, in two days Barr showed unusual professional disrespect for Robert Mueller, a man above reproach with sterling prosecutorial credentials and career with the law enforcement community, contradicting him in the attempt to exonerate Trump with his bold lie about Mueller's report; then, Barr immediately

64. Mueller, *Mueller Report*, 2:344.
65. Mueller, *Mueller Report*, 1:21.

released "his summary" to the public![66] Further, in Barr's second point above, he totally disregards Mueller's clearly stated purpose that he would not take the traditional prosecutorial judgment role (indicting), which explains why Mueller did not draw a prosecutorial conclusion; it was due to a procedural pre-investigation decision (the OLC "opinion").

On August 19, 2022, the OLC "opinion memo" that Barr cites as a basis for not charging Trump with obstruction of justice was ordered released to the public. A Washington, DC, circuit chief judge found it to be "a public relations message" of the Justice Department about how to announce the possibility for charging a president; it was not a Justice Department opinion! Barr had the memo sealed as "privileged" and then published his own opinion contradicting Mueller's two-year investigation results that revealed evidence for charging Trump with ten counts of obstruction of justice. It was a historic shameless subterfuge by a corrupt Bill Barr.[67] It was not that Mueller found no evidence of the president committing obstruction of justice; the contrary was true—Mueller documented massive evidence showing Trump committed obstruction of justice in a series of election-related crimes, finding evidence for ten counts of obstruction of justice.[68]

Barr clearly dissembled with his summary of the Mueller report. Adam Schiff said that "it was a deliberate and monstrous deception." It attempted to conceal content regarding the president's culpability in committing obstruction of justice.[69] With Barr's first point, whether there was a conspiracy, Mueller documented massive contacts between Russians and the Trump campaign, and Barr ignored all of this;[70] "his summary" was blatantly false and revealed dissembling.[71] Almost four years later, Barr continued to lie about quashing Mueller's report but was challenged and debunked.[72] Rachael Maddow cuts through all of Barr's lies and mischaracterizations about Mueller's investigation:

> The investigation into Donald Trump's Russia scandal, led by former Special Counsel Robert Mueller, led to a series of striking findings: The former president's political operation in 2016 sought Russian assistance, embraced Russian assistance,

66. Mueller, *Mueller Report*, 1:22–25.

67. Tillman, "Mueller Memo Advising Barr."

68. Mueller, *Mueller Report*, 2:203, 2:210–320, 2:344.

69. Schiff, *Midnight in Washington*, 173.

70. Mueller, *Mueller Report*, 1:42, 1:167.

71. Savage and Stern, "Judge Calls Barr's Handling"; Stern, "Federal Judge Says."

72. Melber, "'Trolls' and 'Liars.'"

capitalized on Russian assistance, lied about Russian assistance, and took steps to obstruct the investigation into Russian assistance.[73]

AG Barr was a central piece of Trump's immunity shield protecting him from the consequences of his criminal activities; his hijacking and discrediting the Mueller report that was supposed to be given to Congress was only the first occasion where he politicized the Justice Department. Barr's "nothing happened here" summary of the Mueller report, when Mueller charged thirty-four people, six former Trump aides, dozens of Russians, and three companies with over one hundred crimes[74] is ironic; *it is an introduction to the corruption of the Justice Department under William Barr.*

FIRST TRUMP IMPEACHMENT: THE "PERFECT PHONE CALL"?

Donald Trump said, "It was just a phone call . . . it was a perfect phone call." No, he was caught plucking the bald eagle. The phone call was an abuse of presidential power, a presidential "high crime" according to the Constitution of the United States. The phone call and Trump's efforts to stop Congress's investigation were criminal acts that led to his impeachment on December 18, 2019, as the House of Representatives found Trump guilty (in effect indicting him) of Article I, "abuse of power" and Article II, "obstruction of Congress." An irony to note is that this attempt by Donald Trump to corrupt an election was not an isolated event. This "perfect phone call" to Ukrainian President Zelenskyy to obtain foreign assistance in slandering Trump's political opponent Joe Biden took place on *July 25, 2019, the day after Mueller's report on Russia interference in 2016 was quashed by Bill Barr*! Trump had just dodged an investigation of his campaign's collusion with the Russians and his obstruction of justice through the devious efforts of William Barr, and the next day sociopath Trump repeats his folly. This reveals two things about the president's misconduct: It was not an isolated occurrence but the "tip of the iceberg"[75] of presidential crimes, abuse of power, and obstruction of justice that occurred repeatedly in his presidency, and Donald Trump has no respect for law or rules of any kind, due to his multiple pathological personality disorders that eliminate such concerns.

---

73. Benen, "Investigation into the Russia Investigation."

74. "Mueller Report," *BBC News*; see chapter 9 for a continuation of the analysis of the Durham investigation.

75. House Intelligence Committee, *Impeachment Report*, 10.

Any insight into the character of Trump and his presidential crime wave must consider his motivation; he is empowered by his pathological personality disorders; he does whatever he wants. In Trump's mind, both Bill Barr quashing the Mueller investigation and the first impeachment meant that he could do anything he wanted, including crimes against the United States. I revisit this discussion of Trump's unaccountability in chapter 9. Sociopath Trump learns nothing from his close call with the Mueller report; rather, he is emboldened in his lawless quest to dismantle democracy.

The Toddler in Chief

Rejecting advice, insisting on having one's own way, and not doing what someone else wants is an established pattern in the presidency of Donald Trump. Rejecting the advice of others is a pathological trait of malignant narcissistic sociopaths. Personality disorders begin in childhood when there is no adult corrective intervention to discourage foolish, self-centered behavior and the resulting tantrums of a child. Mentally and socially, Trump has never grown up. Mary Trump described Donald Trump's childhood where his sociopath father was the only parent influencing him; since he did not care about Donald's foolish, self-centered behavior, eventually personality disorders developed along with "arrested cognitive and moral development," and Donald became a sociopath like his father. In his book *The Toddler in Chief*, Daniel Drezner refers to this abnormal childhood development and claims that Donald Trump behaves more like a "toddler in chief" than the commander in chief. Drezner's source of evidence for this claim is more than a thousand instances reported by Trump's own supporters that have also made the comparison and characterized Trump as having "the maturity of a petulant child," rather than an adult in his seventies.

Drezner's claim is that Trump's "psychological makeup approximates that of a toddler."[76] Donald Trump told biographer Michael D'Antonio, "When I look at myself in the first grade and I look at myself now, I'm basically the same. The temperament is not that different."[77] Trump himself, as well as his family and associates, agree that his psychological makeup has remained unchanged from when he was a very small boy. When adult sociopath Trump is confronted with bad behavior, wrongdoing, or a crime, he consistently uses a childish but effective strategy with a gaslighted public—psychological projection: "*I* didn't do anything wrong; *you* did!" He deftly shifts attention from himself to his accuser, no matter how absurd

76. Drezner, *Toddler in Chief*, 1.
77. Drezner, *Toddler in Chief*, 7.

the contention or whatever the circumstances show. In addition, due to his antisocial tendencies, throughout Trump's adult life his lack of social development and personal limitations have had little public scrutiny, because of his wealth and "institutionalization"—he not only has been shielded from public scrutiny (lack of socialization), but he never needed to succeed on his own.[78] Many of the biographies of Trump make a similar point: Trump has experienced little emotional or psychological development since he was a toddler. Drezner said that Tim O'Brien, the author of *Trump Nation: The Art of Being the Donald*, warned *Politico* that after Trump's election "we now have somebody who's going to sit in the Oval Office who is lacking in a lot of adult restraints and [has] immature emotions."[79] Tim O'Brien's warning was diplomatic in his gross understatement.

Those who worked with Trump in Congress and the White House know all too well his toddler-like behavior; they lamented that the White House had become like a daycare center, although they would not say so in his presence. Drezner states, "The Mueller report confirms that when Trump aides have testified under penalty of perjury, they frequently characterize the President as possessing the emotional and intellectual maturity of a small boy."[80] Chuck Schumer described Trump as throwing a temper tantrum when he didn't get funding for "his wall" (at the US-Mexico border). Sally Yates said Trump was behaving "like a spoiled two-year-old holding his breath." Speaker of the House Nancy Pelosi said about Trump's stubborn resistance during the 2018 and 2019 government shutdowns, "I'm a mother of five, grandmother of nine. I know a temper tantrum when I see one." Later she commented on his "short attention span" and a "lack of knowledge of subjects at hand."[81] Frequently, Trump's lack of knowledge is mentioned by those who worked with him. Speaker of the House Paul Ryan said, "I'm telling you he didn't know anything about government. I wanted to scold him all the time." Governor Chris Christie said, "He acts on impulse. He doesn't grasp the inner workings of government."[82] These observations are not just anecdotal and limited to a few that worked with Trump, but they represent a pattern of childish behavior observed by reporters, his family, supporters, biographers, political allies, and those who wanted him to succeed as president. The "toddler" observations speak of Trump's unfitness for presidential office and confirm his pathological personality disorders;

78. Trump, *Too Much and Never Enough*, 13.
79. Drezner, *Toddler in Chief*, 8.
80. Drezner, *Toddler in Chief*, 14.
81. Drezner, *Toddler in Chief*, 3.
82. Drezner, *Toddler in Chief*, 13.

in short, they revealed who the man was. Trump's childish influence on his associates in the White House destroyed careers and introduced extreme cruelty in working relationships, until forbearance and civility no longer existed in the White House or in the Republican party.

Donald Trump's pathological personality disorders started early in childhood. He not only experienced arrested emotional and moral development (conscience), but he also experienced arrested cognitive development. Trump did not have the slightest idea what a "perfect phone call" was for a president talking with a Ukrainian leader. The call was just stupid. On October 3, 2019, in a public press interview, a reporter asked Trump what he hoped Volodymyr Zelenskyy would do after the July 25, 2019, phone call. Trump replied, "Well, I would think that, if they were honest about it, they'd start a major investigation into the Bidens. It's a very simple answer." (For a very simple "man-boy.") In the same press interview, Trump publicly invited China also to do an investigation into Joe Biden, showing no understanding of the crime he committed.[83] After Trump lost the election on December 27, 2020, he made another "perfect phone call" to his corrupt Department of Justice, requesting that the acting attorney general, Jeffrey Rosen, inform Georgia election officials to "just say the election was corrupt and leave the rest to me." Deputy Attorney General Richard Donoghue documented the phone call recording the crime.[84] Then on January 2, 2021, Trump made another "perfect phone call" to Secretary of State Brad Raffensperger in Georgia, saying, "All I want you to do is this. I just want you to find 11,780 votes, which is one more than we have. Because we won the State."[85] In the book of Proverbs, a record of Israel's wisdom, it addresses the above repeated lack of moral constraint: "The tongue of the wise adorns knowledge, but the mouth of the fool gushes folly," and "fools despise wisdom and instruction" (Prov 15:2; 1:7). The Hebrew word rendered "fool" in Proverbs denotes a person who is morally deficient.[86] Fools don't keep their ignorance to themselves; it "gushes" out of them, affecting those around them, and in Trump's case—a nation.

Trump knew the Russia investigation was a major problem, and he had numerous contacts with James Comey, director of the FBI, attempting to have him stop his investigation. He was advised by many in his cabinet to exercise caution in contacts with Russians and any statements about elections,

83. Drezner, *Toddler in Chief*, 13.

84. Lowell, "'Just Say the Election Was Corrupt.'"

85. Smith et al., "'Trump Begs Georgia Secretary"; Kanefield, "New Evidence of Trump Election Illegality."

86. See also NIV text note on Prov 1:7, "*fools* despise wisdom and instruction."

but he ignored their advice and fired the director of the FBI. After the Russia investigation, Trump watched Congress interview witnesses on television in the Ukraine impeachment investigation. Any adult of normal intelligence would have heeded the cautions of associates. However, the next day after the Mueller investigation was finished, he committed the same crime with Ukraine! Trump did not show even the slightest constraint in his behavior; he does whatever he wants. Malignant narcissists do not listen to advice; they feel they do not need advice because they think they already know better than anyone else what to do. They are trapped in their ignorance. Sadism is part of the personality disorder; Trump enjoys exasperating others as well as enjoying the chaos he creates. Psychologically, Trump is often like a petulant child, rejecting correction, undisciplined, and ruled by his ignorance—especially about the workings of government.

Americans did not realize who Donald Trump was and did not see him coming, even after his bizarre behavior and fascist rhetoric during his presidential campaign; nevertheless, *they voted him into office*. What is even more startling is that, after four years of facing full-blown fascism, Trump's childish antics, his stupidity, and his dismantling of American democracy, a year after he left office millions of Americans not only still supported him but venerated him as a populist "folk hero" even to the point where they believe his pathological delusions about a stolen election. What are we to think about this malignant normality and Americans being comfortable with fascist rule? In plain, everyday speech, Jack Holmes of *Esquire* responded to this apparent American gullibility and inexplicable hero worship of Donald Trump:

> You ever think about how they were going to bulldoze the American republic for *this guy*? A rich-kid fail-son who inherited all his daddy's cash and squandered it many times over before clawing himself back into putative solvency through a game-show hosting gig where he pretended to be a businessman, all the while treating people—especially women—like absolute dog [s***] everywhere he went for his entire life? It's almost like the aggressive mediocrity was part of the appeal, a statement of power, that a guy who knew nothing about anything and nodded along as someone called his own daughter a "piece of [a**]" on the radio could still become president if he said the right things about the right people. Of course, it was only possible through the absurd technicalities generated by our system of electing our presidents.[87]

87. Holmes, "They Were Going to Bulldoze."

Holmes's frustration recalls Ruth Ben-Ghiat's quote from *Strongmen,* "Every country gets the gangster it deserves."[88] The quote speaks of a shared moral culpability the American public has in connection with the rule of a "fascist strongman." It also calls for an explanation as to why serious intelligent Americans ignored obvious immorality, lying, deception, crimes, and the anti-American values of Donald Trump. In other words, why didn't Americans see him coming? In addition, now that he has left the presidency, why do Americans still hold such delusional "realities" about Trump and what he did in his presidency? The remaining chapters of this book provide a major insight, if not a definitive answer, to these questions. In an already toxic American society, a malignant narcissist sociopath president unleashed a perfect storm of mass deception that mental health professionals call "gaslighting." Underestimating this deceptive strategy makes it impossible to understand the man, his presidency, and America's culpability in the damage Donald Trump did to American democracy. Tens of millions of Americans have done so today and see him as just another ex-president.

88. Ben-Ghiat, *Strongmen,* 250.

PART II

America's Great Deception

Chapter 5

"Gaslighting"—Stealing America's Reality

Like a maniac shooting flaming arrows of death
is one who deceives their neighbor and says,
"I was only joking!"

PROV 26:18–19

THE TERM "GASLIGHTING" ORIGINATED from a 1944 movie, *Gaslight*, starring Charles Boyer and Ingrid Bergman with Joseph Cotton and Angela Lansbury. The plot involves a young woman who, in a whirlwind romance of two weeks, marries a man that insists she move to London where she has no friends and is isolated from the outside world. Her husband then begins to slowly manipulate her into believing she is going insane. He accuses her of kleptomania in situations that he sets up with his sleight of hand deception and causes her to doubt her sanity by *dimming and brightening the house's gas lights. She begins to think it is all in her own mind.* As with his sleight of hand tricks, the husband denies the gaslighting ruse. His motive is to acquire his wife's jewels by having her committed to a mental institution. The husband, who is a thief and a murderer, is also a master manipulator; he attempts to steal the reality of the young, innocent wife by imposing his own malicious reality. His attempt is foiled by the wife, involving a police inspector who uncovers the husband's deception.[1] Psychology coopted the term "gaslighting" to describe the actions of manipulative persons having

1. Wikipedia, "Gaslight (1944 film)."

pathological personality disorders that attempt to steal another's reality and impose their own.

GASLIGHTING IS MORE THAN PROPAGANDA

Gaslighting is more than just lying or propaganda; it is a process of deception, a way to stream lies to manipulate a person into questioning their reality and ultimately accept the gaslighter's reality. In the case of all who gaslight, it is helpful to recognize this strategy of deception as a process of "stealing the reality of another" with lies. In a certain sense, a lie is an attempt to steal another's reality, often contradicting what the other perceives to be true. Gaslighting, however, infers a more elaborate scheme of stealing another's reality; continuous lies are presented over time in a conflict of wills where the gaslighter slowly replaces another's reality with their own. The absence of empathy is a common factor in gaslighters; psychologists note that the absence of empathy assists the gaslighter, it is a basic defect of the human condition. Christian theology also links a lack of empathy with a fundamental defect in the human condition—a fallen sinful human nature—a spiritual state where a lack of empathy or an inordinate self-focus is the opposite of caring about others; it also explains gaslighting consequences when truth is disregarded or twisted, leading the liar further into moral darkness. The New Testament view of human beings as fallen spiritual beings takes a lot of the mystery out of what is going on in the minds of humans, especially in terms of understanding the self's responsibility toward truth.

It is important to remember that Donald Trump is a sociopath. He is devoid of empathy and conscience; there remains only a perverted will to control and destroy the reality of another. He has no feelings for others; he is totally focused on himself, his reality, and his goals. He engages in gaslighting naturally, or primitively, from a basic corrupt human condition; he experiences no inner conflict himself; he creates outer conflict with others to control them. Clinical psychologist Elizabeth Mika states:

> Not having the inhibitions and scruples imposed by empathy and conscience, he can easily lie, cheat, manipulate, destroy, and kill if he wants to—or, when powerful enough, order others to do it for him. The characteristics indicative of narcissistic psychopathy is observable already in childhood. Biographies of tyrants . . . note the early manifestations of vanity, sensation-seeking, and impulsivity often accompanied by poor self-control, aggression and callousness, manipulativeness, and a strong

competitive drive and desire to dominate coexistent with a lack of empathy and conscience.[2]

The last sentence of the quote above agrees with psychoanalyst Mary Trump's diagnosis of Donald Trump having arrested emotional development; the frequent observation is that as an adult he appears like a "toddler in chief." Having no empathy or conscience means the gaslighter's will is focused entirely on what the self dictates; the gaslighter's will is intact and excessively focused—this is helpful in establishing intent in the gaslighter's commission of a crime. The gaslighter knows what he is doing even though obsessively focused on achieving what he or she wants.

While Mika focuses on tyrants and their manipulation of the masses, more gaslighting occurs in personal relationships on a smaller scale in social settings: abusers in a family or marriage, cults, and political parties. In *Psychology Today*, psychologist Stephanie Sarkis gives warning signs of gaslighting in relationships with others:

1. "They tell blatant lies."

   Even if you know it is a lie, they tell you with a straight face; they are setting up a precedent. Once the huge lie is told, you're not sure if anything they say is true; "keeping you unsteady and off-kilter"—that is the goal.

2. "They deny they ever said something, even though you have proof."

   This makes you question your reality. Maybe they didn't say or do a thing. "The more they do this, the more *you* question *your reality* and start accepting theirs." (After all, the president said, "I've never met so and so, I don't know him or her," although photos of them together are public record.)

3. "They use what is near and dear to you as ammunition."

   They attack your core values (democracy, your spirituality, your children, your identity, your country, your rights, your health); "they attack the foundation of your being."

4. "They wear you down over time."

   Gaslighting is gradual, with multiple lies, degrading and then ramping up. "Even the brightest, most self-aware people can be sucked into gaslighting."

2. Mika, "Who Goes Trump?," §5208.

5. "Their actions do not match their words."

   Look at what they *do*. What they *say means nothing*; it's just *talk*; what they *do* is the issue.

6. "They throw in positive reinforcement to confuse you."

   The person cutting you down, "telling you that you don't have value," praises you for something you did; this creates uneasiness: "'Well, maybe they aren't so bad.' Yes, they *are*." Again, this is done to keep you off-kilter—and "to *question your reality*." What you were praised for probably served the gaslighter.

7. "They know confusion weakens people."

   "Gaslighters know that people like having a sense of stability and normalcy" (e.g., their culture). "Their goal is to uproot this and make you constantly question everything," and a human tendency is to look to the person who will help you feel more stable—the gaslighter.

8. "They project" (a favorite Trump pathological response).

   "*They* are a drug user or cheater, yet they are constantly accusing *you* of that. This is done so often that you start trying to defend yourself and are *distracted* from the *gaslighter's own behavior*."

9. "They try to align people against you."

   Gaslighters are *master manipulators, finding people that will stand by them no matter what*—"they use these people against you." "'This person knows that you're not right.'" "A gaslighter is a *constant liar*." He or she makes you feel like you don't know who to trust and turns you to the gaslighter—isolating you and giving the gaslighter more control.

10. "They tell you or others that you are crazy."

    This is the most effective tool of the gaslighter, "because it's dismissive. The gaslighter knows if they question your sanity, people will not believe you when you tell them the gaslighter is abusive or out of control. It's a master technique."

11. "They tell you everyone else is a liar" (all is "fake news"; only what Trump says is true).

    Fake news makes you question your reality (objective truth). "You've never known someone with the audacity to say this, so they must be telling the truth, right? No. It's a manipulation technique. It makes people *turn to the gaslighter for 'correct' information*"—a lie.[3]

3. Sarkis, "11 Red Flags of Gaslighting," my emphasis added.

The warning signs indicate the gaslighter is an extremely manipulative person in getting their own way, a primary goal of people with personality disorders. The content of each of the above warning signs is useful for recognizing the tyrant Donald Trump as a gaslighter motivated by sociopathy and malignant narcissism; his gaslighting had phenomenal impact on American society over a five-year period.

Trump's Gaslighting: An Unprecedented Impact

A toxic anti-American reality exists and persists in America. Why? Donald Trump has gaslighted America; a sociopath president has purposefully transferred his sick, delusional, anti-American reality to millions of Americans by mass radicalization (gaslighting); it is now their reality. The list of events below indicates the effectiveness of Trump's gaslighting. The proof is in our face every day in America. Scanning the cable news networks across the board on a single day in October 2021, the following images of *ex-president* Donald Trump appeared:

- On stage at an "overturn the election rally" in Georgia; Trump lying about a stolen election
- At the White House standing behind a podium with the presidential seal and bracketed by American flags
- In a foreign country appearing with world leaders
- Maligning Congress member Alexandria Ocasio-Cortez
- Standing with cabinet member Hope Hicks at the White House
- Standing with his red tie gleaming, giving a power fist
- Shaking hands with President Macron at the G7 in France
- In Texas, stooping down to greet Governor Greg Abbott in a wheelchair
- Standing with the White House in the background

The above nine media images almost a year after he left the presidency do not represent the reality of America in October 2021. They represent Donald Trump's reality of a stolen election. He is no longer president of the United States. He does not reside in the White House. President Joe Biden lives there, because he won the presidential election in November 2020 and Donald Trump lost. Not only is Trump not accepting the reality of a lost election, in October 2021 the news media used images from the previous year, a false reality corroborating Trump's fantasy. Trump chooses to think that he is still president and gaslights the public with his delusion, because his malignant narcissism causes him to reject the election loss.[4] What is the media's excuse?

Trump's malignant narcissism is part of his multiple personality disorders; they have developed to an extreme point where he stubbornly refuses to accept reality that is obvious to others. His narcissism is extreme—malignant—not like American society's narcissism of a lesser degree. Trump's day-to-day mindset on the loss of the election is delusional. A delusion is defined as a "rigidly held demonstrably false belief which is impervious to any contradictory facts."[5] A person may not be able to perceive the contradictory facts, or they just reject the contrary facts because they do not like them. Trump continues to obsess about the reality that he lost the election into October of 2021, a year after he lost. His personality disorders give him an abnormal inordinate stubbornness; it is not that he is delusional in the sense that he cannot see the reality of October 2021 that he lost the election; rather, his will is abnormally strong in creating another reality—that he won the election and he does not accept the reality that he lost. He still acts like he is president,[6] speaks like he is president, and continues to claim the election was stolen from him; it is a grand charade. Despite all the facts to the contrary, he continues gaslighting in his attempt to steal America's reality and replace it with his own pathological reality. Losing the election did not change who he was; it revealed who he was—a malignant narcissist who chooses not to face reality; he creates his own. Some of the October 2021 fake images listed above appear to be photoshopped or staged. Is this a result of the media's attempt to normalize Trump? Why else would photographs a year old be used with current news, especially during a Trump campaign where he pushes the election was stolen the previous year? Or is it due to Trump's gaslighting? The media incidents show the imprint of Trump's demented reality transferred to America.

The above list of nine "fake" images of reality in a single day of October 2021 indicate that malignant narcissist Trump's gaslighting was effective. It is easy to underestimate what "effective" means here. A year after he lost the presidential election, he has been expelled from social media sites, and a sick Trump false reality persists in the minds of millions of Americans. Five years of Trump gaslighting the American people with continuous lies, violent rhetoric, race-baiting, and his incredibly ignorant and non-empathetic response to a lethal pandemic have had a lasting effect. His vigorous manic

4. Howe, "'Crime of Century!'"

5. Gartner, "Donald Trump Is: A) Bad," §2184.

6. Acosta, "How Trump Is Pretending."

efforts to overthrow the results of a democratic election—including a vio lent insurrection—have taken a toll on society. American reality has been stolen. Trump's delusional reality remains.

A careful observer of the news media may also recognize radical changes *in American behavior* after Trump's gaslighting; the observer may wonder why such violent, unprecedented events like those listed below were still emerging in October of 2021:

- Increased incidents in passenger violence on airplanes[7]

- An unprecedented number of mass shootings, some in schools, involving children

- Unprecedented "police-citizen-contact" shootings

- Targeted violence against Asian Americans

- Unprecedented incivility and lack of moral control in society,[8] even on the floor of Congress

- Unusual aggressive violence by women[9]

- A historic refusal, sometimes violent, in accepting vaccines during a deadly pandemic, considering it an issue of "personal rights" rather than public health

- The spread of outlandish conspiracy theories with millions of Americans believing them

- A mistrust of science in a scientifically advanced nation

- During a deadly pandemic, Americans refusing simple prevention measures of wearing a mask and "social distancing," some even reacting with physical violence and homicide

- A new phenomenon of violence—driving cars/trucks into crowds of people

- After Donald Trump's bold, in-your-face presidency of lies, Americans at all levels publicly lying without remorse

By July 2022, this list of incidents from October 2021 had multiplied and deepened, becoming even more evident in American society, showing a segment of society unable to control inner impulses, lacking moral control, and acting out with excessive exhibitions of evil. *Scores of millions share Donald*

7. Obeidallah, "Why the Explosion?"
8. Luscombe, "Why Everyone Is So Rude."
9. Luscombe, "Why Everyone Is So Rude."

Trump's delusional reality, and the resulting bizarre behavior of Americans demonstrates it daily. In Trump's warped mind, he continues to think and act like he is still president of the United States, like he is running a shadow presidency.[10]

During the presidency of Donald Trump, a perfect storm of circumstances converged in American history, enabling him to gaslight society with unprecedented results. As mentioned in chapter 1, social scientists speak of a perfect storm environment in society as it becomes "a toxic triangle." The three elements that converged to create Bermuda triangle-like conditions are (1) a narcissistic sociopath anti-American president, (2) connecting with a narcissistic, discontented segment of American society, (3) where the narcissistic tyrant used an unprecedented communication tool—the internet's social media platforms (Twitter, Facebook, Instagram, YouTube, etc.)—to gaslight vulnerable, gullible Americans. We are talking about something more than a condenser in a microphone to project a speaker's voice to a larger audience—the fascist's means of disseminating propaganda in 1939 Germany. The modern convergence of the above three perfect storm factors provided a sociopath anti-American president *with a popular, immediate, repeatable, and continuous influence on Americans daily wherever they are, bombarding them with his unfiltered manic thoughts, lies, and conspiracy theories via their smartphones.*

Ironically, while the internet opened unheard of vistas of information and knowledge, it also led to the "dumbing down" of America and release of humanity's worse impulses.[11] Further, previously traditional news media operated under the discipline of a regimen of truth verification, requiring multiple sources of confirmation on issues reported to maintain factual integrity of what was published. Jonathan Haidt, a social psychologist at New York University, stated about social media platforms, "Twitter can overpower all the newspapers in the country."[12] He refers to the number of Americans with smartphones and the fact that a tweet does not follow a regimen of truth verification; rather information is unverified; an opinion may be sent by a fool or a maniac. The result of the new technology was that Donald Trump replaced American reality by "tweets"; millions of Americans received his twisted anti-American reality, replacing their own. The unique technology allowed the unleashing of an intense propaganda scheme of gaslighting by a sociopath, who weaponized the internet with a

10. Cillizza, "Yet More Evidence."
11. Lee, "Humanity's Worst Impulses."
12. Haidt, "Why the Past 10 Years."

flood of lies, conspiracy theories, and deception that penetrated deeply in the American psyche, resulting in a toxic society.

In order to grasp President Trump's gaslighting influence in perfect storm conditions, one must recognize the frequency of his public appearances and the volume of lies that he streamed to people. He was able to dominate cable news because he was the president, but he also took advantage of the internet's social media platforms to gaslight Americans via their smartphones. We had a "tweeting president" in the middle of the night and in the early morning hours. It is not hyperbole to say that the American people experienced President Trump as a *psycho-political tornado.*[13] To understand the tornado effect of his influence in perfect storm conditions, the first list above of nine post-presidential appearances on cable news in October 2021 must be multiplied by at least four (four times nine equals thirty-six Trump contacts with Americans per day—a conservative estimate). In a single day in 2020, he sent thirty-three tweets.[14] Those tweets would be sprinkled with his 30,573 lies in four years, twenty per day if averaged, and you would begin to see the fire hose of Trump's demented reality and lies gaslighting Americans. It all added up to a slow, continuous theft of American reality by high-tech stealth, leaving many with Trump's demented anti-American reality. The second list of events above, the violence, incivility, and behavior not reflecting American values is evidence of Donald Trump successfully transferring his anti-American reality to unsuspecting Americans. The damage that his gaslighting brought to America is inestimable; it has had a lasting effect, and it is not immediately clear how America's reality is to be restored.

This chapter focuses on Donald Trump's gaslighting, how he stole American reality from millions of Americans and replaced it with his delusional sociopathic reality. The modern gaslighting effect in America is not just Joseph Goebbels's propaganda and a jazzed up mike. The depth of Trump's gaslighting and its lasting effect on Americans was historically unprecedented; it is more attuned to what previously was known as "brainwashing" individuals. Gaslighting shows that a more dangerous deception was going on than in 1939 Germany, because it was implemented by a malignant narcissistic sociopath wielding an unprecedented communication tool daily on an entire society. Trump's gaslighting impacted an entire political party[15] and 45 percent of the nation's voters.[16] This Russia-like weaponiz-

---

13. Teng, "Trauma, Time, Truth, and Trump," §4031.
14. Cole, "Donald Trump Sent."
15. O'Donnell, "Rep Schiff: Trump Completely Remade."
16. Cooper, "'There Has Been a Coup.'"

ing of misinformation, disinformation, and bold lies took place in America under the unprecedented circumstances of a fascist tyrant in the presidency. Trump's success in gaslighting was a major part of why evangelicals didn't see him coming; they were among the unsuspecting, psychologically vulnerable Americans that accepted his delusional reality and lies about America. His gaslighting also is the reason why millions of Americans (after he has left office) are still not aware of the damage he did to American democracy. Today, a significant number of Americans remain gaslighted, having had the reality of American democracy stolen from them. They now cooperate with Trump in creating and spreading his fascist anti-American reality; even Republican members of Congress are complicit. Many Americans are not even aware their reality has been exchanged for Trump's and are living a malignant normality in a truly toxic society created by Donald Trump, not able to distinguish appearance from reality.[17]

TRUMP'S FIVE-STEP GASLIGHTING SCHEME

In her book *Gaslighting America*, Amanda Carpenter gives a more simplified model of gaslighting used in politics. She observed instances of gaslighting in her journalism career as a reporter for the *Washington Times* and as a political contributor for CNN. She also identified gaslighting in Washington, DC, when she was a speech writer for South Carolina Republican Senator Jim DeMint and communications director for Republican Senator Ted Cruz. Carpenter focuses on the gaslighting of Donald Trump as a manipulating politician; she has no illusions about who he was; she states, "Trump was dangerous. Nothing about him was conservative, civil, or reliable in my mind, he was crude and lied all the time, seemingly for fun."[18] She sees gaslighting as an elaborate scheme with the goal of gaining control over people.[19] Carpenter identifies five steps or phases in Donald Trump's gaslighting scheme that he used in political situations:

- "Stake a claim.
  Often what is claimed is a lie that is difficult to challenge or prove otherwise, like a conspiracy theory challenging an election; in politics that may be risky, but it gets the attention of people and is an attempt to create a new false reality that would chip away at replacing democratic American reality.

17. Karem, "Why Won't Donald Trump Go Away?"
18. Carpenter, *Gaslighting of America*, 49.
19. Carpenter, *Gaslighting America*, 15.

- Advance and deny.
  Advance the false claim by creating speculation on it while appearing noncommittal, even denying it; Trump's phrases for introducing this step are "maybe it's true, I don't know"; "other people say"; "a lot of people think"; "I've got a lot of questions."

- Create suspense.
  Keep the media focused on the claim "soon we will know . . ." or "very soon there's an audio tape coming out . . . ." Sometimes this step is drawn out over weeks, months, or even years.

- Discredit opponent.
  Attack the personal character and motives of an opponent.

- Win.
  Declare victory, *whatever* the outcome is or the circumstances are."[20]

Carpenter views gaslighting as a psychological term for what happens when a master manipulator like Trump lies so brazenly that people end up questioning reality as they know it. Over the course of the 2016 campaign, she said:

> I cannot tell you the number of times I heard reporters and political observers ask one another questions like 'Can you believe what Trump said?' or 'Is this really happening?' It was all so unreal. We simply couldn't believe what we were seeing and hearing with our own eyes and ears. Oftentimes, Trump says something for so long and so confidently—and with so much outside support [the Republican party]—that you can't help but wonder if he isn't right. That's gaslighting.[21]

Carpenter's gaslighting model is helpful in identifying phases of gaslighting that Trump used to discredit or destroy enemies or cover up his crimes; it was a major strategy for streaming lies and deception in his presidency.

In *Gaslighting America*, Carpenter illustrates the five steps of gaslighting that Trump employed with his conspiracy theory of "birtherism," regarding Barack Obama's place of birth. Step one: Stake a claim—President Obama was not an American citizen. Trump started step two: advance and deny with "*A lot of people* think he was born in Kenya." Trump denied that he believed it, but while a guest on *The View* television show on March 28, 2011, he said, "*but I've got a lot of questions.*" On Fox News on March 28,

---

20. Carpenter, *Gaslighting America*, 15.
21. Carpenter, *Gaslighting America*, 14.

2011, he said, "I'm starting to wonder myself if Obama was not born in the country." With step three: Create suspense, he kept the media focused on himself and his view of birtherism for six weeks, saying, "Soon we will know." On *Morning Joe*, April 16, 2011, Trump stated, "Very soon there's a tape of Obama's grandmother who saw him born in Kenya." This was an outright lie. Obama produced his birth certificate on April 27, 2011. There was no tape.[22]

However, in August 2012 Trump tweeted, "An extremely credible source has called my office and told me @BarackObama's birth certificate is a fraud"—another lie. In 2014, Trump was still pushing birtherism, tweeting: "All hackers . . . hack Obama's college records (destroyed) and check place of birth."[23] A university poll in 2016 found 77 percent of Trump supporters believed Obama was "definitely" or "probably" hiding information on his private life.[24] Steps four and five, discredit opponent and win, show the extreme cunning of Donald Trump by discrediting both of his major enemies at the time. On September 2016 (close to the election), Trump summoned the press corps to the Trump Hotel in Washington, DC, stating that "he would make a major statement about Obama's birth." He revealed step four, discredit opponent, by discrediting his *real opponent*—Hillary Clinton—and claimed victory (step five: win) by stating that Hillary Clinton and her campaign of 2008 started the "birtherism" controversy! Then Trump said, "I finished it!" He admitted Obama was born in the United States of America, but made Hillary Clinton responsible for birtherism—*his opponent in the 2016 election*! Then, of course, Donald Trump put on a full court press gaslighting effort to portray Hillary Clinton as a criminal in his 2016 election campaign. The word "diabolical" comes to mind.

Although Amanda Carpenter was aware of the gaslighting phenomenon, she sprinkles conspiracy theories throughout her book that were proven false.[25] As a loyal Republican, she was gaslighted herself during the Obama administration.[26] In 2016, when she was working with CNN, she personally experienced being a target of Donald Trump's gaslighting. The *National Enquirer* published an article that claimed Ted Cruz had five affairs with women that worked for him; the cover of the *Enquirer* showed a photograph of a group of women and Amanda Carpenter was in the group (step

22. Carpenter, *Gaslighting America*, 9–11.
23. Carpenter, *Gaslighting America*, 12.
24. Carpenter, *Gaslighting America*, 12.
25. Carpenter, *Gaslighting America*, 34.
26. Carpenter, *Gaslighting America*, 38.

one: Stake a claim).[27] She said there was no doubt in her mind that Donald Trump was responsible for including her as one of Cruz's affairs. Although the Cruz campaign said the article was "pure garbage," Trump continued his gaslighting. The *Washington Post's* Chris Cillizza described Trump's statement about the *National Enquirer's* article as "perfectly Trumpian." It *was* precisely that, because it involved projection and contained so many elements of Trump's trademark gaslighting steps; Trump said:

> I have no idea whether or not the cover story about Ted Cruz in this week's issue of the *National Enquirer* is true or not, but I had absolutely nothing to do with it, did not know about it, and have not, as yet, read it [step two: advance and deny]. I have nothing to do with the *National Enquirer* and unlike "Lyin'" Ted Cruz I do not surround myself with political hacks and henchman and then pretend total innocence [step four: discredit opponent]. Ted Cruz's problem with the *National Enquirer* is his and his alone, and while they were right about O.J. Simpson, John Edwards, and many others, I certainly hope they are not right about "Lyin'" Ted Cruz [step three: Create suspense]. I look forward to spending the week in Wisconsin, winning the Republican nomination [step five: win] and ultimately the Presidency in order to Make America Great Again.[28]

The statement was riddled with lies and the mindset described in the previous list of warning signs of gaslighting. Remember, the *National Enquirer* was frequently a tool of Donald Trump in his business career in New York; owner David Pecker and Trump concocted frequent similar "catch and kill" operations,[29] using the magazine to target and demean Trump's enemies.

The Fascist's Gaslighting Target: Democratic Elections

In American constitutional tradition, democratic elections represent "the will of the people" in their selection of a president to lead the nation. However, in fascist tradition, President Donald Trump gaslighted "the people" and targeted democratic elections. "The people" were the enemies of narcissistic sociopath Trump; "the will of the people" idea was the opposite of fascist concern; they represented a potential threat to whatever he wanted— total power. Because Trump has no empathy, no love for others, no loyalty to anyone, and no friends, "the people" were merely pieces on a chessboard;

27. Carpenter, *Gaslighting America*, 56–58.
28. Carpenter, *Gaslighting America*, 64–65.
29. See chapter 2, "'Making' of a Con Man."

they existed to be gaslighted and be conformed to his will, his desires, and his winning. With sociopaths, *people are disposable.* They have reckless disregard for people; they lie to people, deceive them, and dispose of them without remorse. The Bible aptly describes the deceptive sociopath's lack of concern for the welfare of people: "Like a maniac shooting flaming arrows of death is one who deceives their neighbor and says, I was only joking!"[30] The mindset of a sociopath is the opposite of showing empathy or caring anything about other people; a depraved state is indicated; at times, caring for people is replaced by *sadism*—enjoying the sufferings of others. The safety, desires, aspirations, and the reality of other people are of no concern to a narcissistic sociopath; their interest is only in bending the reality of others to the shape of their own reality—getting their way. Donald Trump lied to everyone, but he specifically singled out people to gaslight that became major obstacles to his gaining complete power. He attempted to gaslight and get rid of people that were a thorn in his side: James Comey, Hillary Clinton, Robert Mueller, Adam Schiff, and others. In short, democracy was the enemy of anti-American Donald Trump; his specific target in gaslighting was democratic elections, to impose his will over "the will of the people." The sociopath's fixation on self was the polar opposite of the democratic principle—"the will of the people." What malignant narcissistic Trump wanted was all that mattered—complete control—and nothing or no one would stand in the way of his autocratic aspirations and delusional reality.

Donald Trump's fascist goal was to slowly dismantle democracy and achieve total power. When he first set foot in the political arena, he set his sights on controlling American *elections.* In taking over democracy, a key target for fascists is elections, the institution that represents the legal road to power. A fascist dictator must weaken, discredit, and emasculate (1) the rule of law—a major roadblock to an illegal pursuit of power (the Department of Justice), (2) traditions of democratic institutions—the guardrails of constitutional government, and (3) the procedures of a democratic election, the vote and the Electoral College. Trump had to undermine the American public's confidence in all three. He had to fundamentally change the notion of a right to vote by suppressing and undermining it; in the end, an *anti-American* Republican party followed him in devising multiple ways to suppress the vote. He began his attack on democratic elections even before he was elected president, he continued the attack while he was president, and then, after he left office, he resumed his attack. In a flurry of attempts to overturn the results of a democratic election that he lost, he manipulated the courts by filing frivolous election lawsuits, personally intimidated state

30. Prov 26:18–19.

electoral officials, manipulated his crazed base to intimidate his opponents and voters, and finally incited a violent insurrection of the US Capitol to change the states' electoral votes.

Anti-American Donald Trump gaslighted many people in his presidential campaign and in his presidency; those who were thorns in his side had to be eliminated as he attempted to impose authoritarian rule. In all his tactical gaslighting incidents there was one overarching strategic gaslighting scheme—a big gaslighting effort—to discredit democratic elections. After he left office, this major gaslighting effort became known as the Big Lie— that the 2020 election was *stolen from him*. The intended message of the Big Lie was that democratic elections are corrupt and not to be trusted. At first, he did not openly campaign against democratic elections; he slowly stole the American reality that they were reliable; he gaslighted Americans until many accepted *his reality that they were not only unreliable but that an election was stolen from him*! When Trump fired up his fanatical base—those who had accepted his reality of a stolen election—they were motivated to do his threatening and violent dirty work.

Before the 2016 election, from the very beginning, Donald Trump was set on dismantling democracy—just like any other fascist would. Why would Trump in his presidential campaign before the 2016 election, when he knew that he had Russia working behind the scenes to help him win, say "the election is rigged?" He said, "If I lose, the election was rigged." Why would he say this? Was it anxiety about losing the election to Clinton? No. Trump is a sociopath; anxiety of this kind is not part of his mental inventory. Instead, sociopaths have supreme confidence, even a grandiose delusionary vision of who they are and what they can do. Trump saying the election was rigged was step one: stake a claim in his gaslighting scheme: "democratic elections are dishonest, rigged, and not to be trusted."

After the 2016 election, elected President Donald Trump began step two: advance and deny that elections were not to be trusted. This is the man who said the elections were rigged before he was elected. Now, as the new president, he put forth the denial that Russia interfered in the election to help him win; it was a hoax, "There is no Russia!" He claimed that he was duly elected; he said other elected presidents did not have their election challenged like him with investigations; why was he being persecuted? During the whole impeachment process, Trump created suspense, step three. For weeks, witnesses in the impeachment (number one) testified that Trump committed a crime; but Trump said it was a "perfect phone call," taking steps to cover up his criminal act. His refusal to participate in the impeachment caused people to wonder, Will he be impeached? Will he be removed from office? He clearly committed crimes but would the Republican-led Senate convict him? Would he be held accountable? Finally, Trump was impeached for his crimes, but he was not held accountable by a complicit majority Republican Senate that refused to convict him, regardless of overwhelming evidence. Although he was "censured by the House," most people wondered what that meant: It must not be too serious because he was still president! People wondered, Was Trump guilty or not?

Practically, Trump advanced the notion that elections were not to be trusted by committing crimes against them for which he was not held accountable: (1) He and his campaign colluded with Russia to win the electoral college votes in key states in 2016; then, (2) in 2019 he called the president of Ukraine on the phone, using the power of his office to collude/extort a foreign power to obtain "dirt" on his political opponent in an election, introducing step four: discredit opponent; (3) he obstructed justice by his war against the impeachment hearings; and (4) he suborned and threatened witnesses, preventing them from testifying. One "winning" public message for Trump was that democracy and the rule of law were weak—after all the crimes he was accused of he was still president. Impeachments did not stop him; Trump's gaslighting scheme in stealing the reality of free and fair elections in a democracy was not over; in a second impeachment, for inciting an insurrection on the Capitol and attempting to interrupt the confirmation of a democratic election, he was impeached again but was not convicted by the Republican Senate in lock-step with him. After being indicted twice by Congress, Trump declared victory (step five: win). Ironically, Trump said that he won and it was all a farce.

In focusing on Donald Trump's personal guilt and his gaslighting, we should not lose perspective by assigning guilt only to his criminal actions. There were *those who enabled his criminal acts*, both those close to him and in wider society. With the toxic triangle idea about society, the first leg was the malignant narcissist who gaslights; the second leg was the disgruntled narcissist part of society that responds by accepting, aiding, and abetting his antidemocratic reality; and the third leg was *a narcissistic society at large*. I have addressed the first and second legs of the toxic triangle, but I have not said much about society at large, the third leg: those who didn't see him coming and still revere an American democratic republic; this group is the focus of the next chapter.

Chapter 6

Gaslighting Disables Your Capacity for Truth

Woe to those who call evil good and good evil, who put darkness for light and light for darkness, who put bitter for sweet and sweet for bitter. Woe to those who are wise in their own eyes and clever in their own sight.

THE PROPHET ISAIAH[1]

Truth has perished; it has vanished from their lips.

THE PROPHET JEREMIAH[2]

SOMEHOW, MILLIONS OF AMERICANS follow a sociopath ex-president and have accepted his delusional, absurdist reality where up is down, black is white, darkness is light, lies are true, and a presidential election loss does not make an ex-president. When sociopath Trump lost the election, suddenly elections were no longer important nor was the right to vote in America valid. A year after Joe Biden won the 2020 election, most of the Republican political party had accepted Donald Trump's delusional, absurdist reality that the election was stolen. On the floor of Congress, a Republican congresswoman boldly wears a mask that says "Trump Won!" *Somehow*, the Big Lie that the election was stolen from Trump has become the Republican party's

1. Isa 5:20–21.
2. Ps 52:2–4; Jer 7:28.

platform for the 2022 and 2024 elections—not Republican beliefs, principles, or ideology.[3] *Somehow*, millions of Americans have accepted Trump's absurdist reality and are comfortable with the Big Lie and an antidemocratic reality.[4] They see the upside-down world through the eyes of a fascist narcissistic sociopath. Malignant narcissist Trump's gaslighting deception was and is still intentionally focused on disabling the inner capacity of truth in others. He maliciously attacks and manipulates American public reality, creating a crisis of truth with a flood of lies and false conspiracies, inserting his delusional anti-American reality into the American consciousness. As sure as American history recorded the economic Great Depression, it will also note Donald Trump's presidency as the political "Great Deception."

According to the view of psychology and Christian theology, Donald Trump's pathological gaslighting has rendered the capacity of truth dysfunctional in many Americans. Both disciplines explain how a person's capacity of truth can be susceptible to Trump's gaslighting and cause a malfunction of one's capacity for truth. Trump continues to perpetuate the Big Lie that the election was stolen from him; it is the theme of the ex-president's continuous "overturn-the-election rallies" and it has become the mantra of his public dialogue. Social media platforms have refused him access because he and his mantra represent a pathological delusion. Many Americans and evangelical Christians didn't see the malignant narcissist coming. They not only have failed to see him coming, but after he left—after experiencing four years of his gaslighting—they are still unable to see the effect his pathological disorders have had on society that are demonstrated every day. They no longer recognize topsy-turvy behavior; it has become a *malignant normal* for them.

The following headlines appeared in the news media in a one-month period (October 2021). Seven out of the eight incidents below happened on the same day:

- "Father Allegedly Shoots Son Because He Wouldn't Stop Playing Guitar"

- "A Man Reported Killing a [Muslim] Man in His Driveway, Authorities Say. He Was Arrested 11 Days Later."

- "Workers in These 3 States GA, IL, KY Are Quitting in Droves"

- "Donald Trump Jr. Sells Tees Mocking Alec Baldwin's 'Rust' Movie Set Tragedy"

3. Frum, "Revenge of the Donald."

4. Beals, "Poll: 50 Percent of Republicans"; Williams, "Juan Williams: Trump Is Killing."

- "Steve Bannon Suggests Merrick Garland, FBI Involved in 'Coup' Plot to Oust Trump"

- "Texas Man Sentenced to Life in Prison for Beating [Two-Year-Old] Toddler to Death after She Put Her Shoes on Wrong Feet, Days before Her Birthday"

- "Democrats Say GOP Lawmakers Implicated in Jan 6 Should Be Expelled"

- "Charlie Kirk [Tea Party Trump Activist] Gets Asked at TPUSA Event: 'How Many Elections Are They Going to Steal before We Kill These People?'"[5]

With the passage of time, media headlines reveal even more bizarre behavior of Americans until violence is unprecedented. Could Trump's perfect storm of gaslighting American society, plus his encouraging gratuitous uncontrolled violence and his unaccountability have caused the inexplicable exploding inner rage in day-to-day American life? Has he left a lasting violent mark on the American psyche? The answer of both psychology and biblical theology is yes. Examples in the news media of incivility, intolerance, and explosive violence in society multiply from week to week. Even new manifestations of uncontrolled violence and bizarre crimes emerge, such as "looting gangs," scores of looters (fifty to one hundred) in malls and department stores committing in daylight smash and grab robberies. There are incidents of unprecedented flagrant violence in sports events: in football games tacklers punching ball carriers after play ends when they lay on the turf, spectators physically attacking referees, fist fights among spectators as well as between opposing teams, and spectator demeanor toward players so insulting and cruel that they are ejected from a basketball game. This is not to mention America's mass shootings in public malls and in schools where children are the victims. An innocuous phrase repeated over and over during Trump's presidency was "this is not normal." It also can be applied in the aftermath of his presidency, because gaslighting did not stop, nor did the unprecedented violent behavior. It is as though a silent disaster of biblical proportions has occurred in America that makes biblical language seem appropriate: "they invent ways of doing evil and, having a depraved mind, they do what ought not to be done. They are filled with every kind of wickedness, evil, greed and

5. Doliner, "Father Allegedly Shoots Son"; Shammas, "Man Reported Killing"; Rosenberg et al., "Record Number of Workers"; Dutton, "Donald Trump Jr. Selling Shirts"; Lambe, "Steve Bannon Suggests"; Lambe, "Texas Man Sentenced"; Beitsch, "Democrats Say GOP Lawmakers"; Idliby, "Charlie Kirk Gets Asked."

depravity. They are full of envy, murder, strife, deceit, and malice. They are gossips, slanderers, God-haters, insolent, arrogant and boastful."[6]

Both biblical theology and the mental health profession suggest that this unprecedented violence and bizarre evil behavior in society today is the result of the influence of *a malignant narcissistic ex-president's effective gaslighting of Americans over a five-year period*. Having succumbed to it, Trump's followers and the wider society have become like him, acting out his manic reality. In decades of adult professional life in America, including seventeen years as a police officer and seven years training police agencies across the country, I have seen and experienced all kinds of human depravity and bizarre behavior, but I have never heard or experienced anything close to this violent portrait of America. *Somehow, the gaslighting of a narcissistic president found a narcissistic connection in society that brought out the worst of human nature in Americans.*

GASLIGHTING AND SELF-DECEPTION

For over half a decade, Trump bombarded Americans with his manic psychopathic delusions and deception, using the internet to reach and effectively gaslight susceptible Americans. When I speak of susceptibility to Trump's gaslighting, I refer to the toxic relationship of a narcissistic president and a narcissistic American public. Complicity shifts from the gaslighter to the gaslighted. It is a story of *self-deception*. An analysis of the effectiveness of Trump's gaslighting must probe beyond the gaslighter, Donald Trump, to those gaslighted—American society. Tyrants do not arise in a vacuum, just as tyranny does not spring on the world unannounced.[7] In the case of Donald Trump, the tyrant was elected by the American people. It is as Ruth Ben-Ghiat states in *Strongmen*, "Every country gets the gangster it deserves." These gaslighting insights suggests that *pathologies may be identified widely in American society that match those of "strongman" Donald Trump*. A simple gaslighting truth is that Americans chose to follow Trump because they liked what they saw and heard him say, no matter how absurd, immoral, and delusional it was. Millions of Americans saw him coming, were simpatico, and were seduced by his gaslighting. Psychology and its practitioners explain how gaslighting compromises a person's capacity for truth.

Psychologists say there is a common mindset in those gaslighted with the gaslighter that makes them susceptible. Thomas Singer, psychiatrist and Jungian psychoanalyst, says, "I hypothesize a direct link between Trump's

6. Rom 1:28–30.
7. Mika, "Who Goes Trump?," §5351.

personal narcissism and the collective psyche of those American citizens who embrace his perception of America and who feel that he understands and speaks to them." He adds, "There are ways in which Trump mirrors, even amplifies, *our* collective attention deficit disorder, *our* sociopathy, and *our* narcissism. Therefore, *this is less about diagnosing a public figure than about recognizing our own pathology*."[8] Singer extends susceptibility and culpability to the "American group self." He speaks of the "shadow of the American psyche" being released—its worst side—when people are influenced by Trump's gaslighting. The American group self's spirituality, or lack of it, represents "the lower angels of humanity" being incited and then unleashed in people. These are not the words of a theologian but a psychoanalyst! Singer says when this part of the collective American psyche is activated "the most primitive psychological forces come alive for the purpose of defending the group and its collective spirit or Self." He explains:

> Trump tapped into the negative feelings that many Americans have about all the things we are supposed to be compassionate about—ethnic, racial, gender, and religious differences. What a relief, so many must have thought, to hear a politician speak their unspoken resentments and express their rage. Trump tapped into the dirty little secret of their loathing of various minorities.[9]

Singer says what makes Trump's narcissism so dangerous "in its mix of shadow (his attacks on all sorts of groups of people) and Self elements (his self-aggrandizing, inflated sense of himself and those for whom he pretends to speak) is that it plays to the unholy marriage of Self and the aggressive, hateful, and violent elements in the collective psyche."[10] Another way of expressing Singer's statement is that Trump incites the worst in sinful human nature, probing the depths of evil, and that evil is unleashed by society. His concluding remark: "But one of the most disturbing thoughts about the Trump presidency is that he has taken up residence not just in the White House, but in the psyches of each and every one of us."[11] This is true of those who have been gaslighted by Donald Trump during his presidency; for some, he has taken up a permanent residence. Although he is no longer the resident of the White House, *his absurdist reality* of up is down, black is white, wrong is right, and lies are true *continues*. The capacity for truth in Americans has been compromised by Trump's gaslighting; *his* pathological

8. Singer, "Trump and the American Collective Psyche," §4933–39.

9. Singer, "Trump and the American Collective Psyche," §5046–51, §5063.

10. Singer, "Trump and the American Collective Psyche," §5047–79.

11. Singer, "Trump and the American Collective Psyche," §5114.

unreality has replaced American reality. The evil of Donald Trump does not leave America when he leaves the White House; it remains in American society, which he has effectively gaslighted.

HUMAN NATURE'S POSITIVE SIDE: A CAPACITY FOR TRUTH

I have shown similarities between psychology's description of Donald Trump's pathological personality disorders and biblical theology's other side of the coin view of corrupt human nature. Psychology describes its personality disorders, sociopathy, antisocial disorder, and malignant narcissism as "basic defects in humanity." Biblical theology and Christian theology (systematic theology) also reveal there is a basic defect in humanity—"sinful human nature." There is an image of God in human nature that has been marred by the presence and power of sin. Since the comparison of the two viewpoints have had to do with the basic defects in humanity so far, I have addressed only the negative side of human nature. When I speak of humanity's capacity for truth, I examine the positive side.

Human Equipment of "the Self"

Staying with the comparison of the two disciplines regarding the human self, Christian theology's view of the human self is fundamentally spiritual. Psychology speaks of the "human spirit," but Christian theology does so in a different sense, giving the human spirit a supernatural dimension: "But it is the spirit in a person, the breath of the Almighty that gives them understanding" (Job 32:8). Without giving the full Christian view of the positive side of human nature, which is greatly affected by God's salvation, for the purpose of comparison I assume[12] the science of psychology and Christian theology would agree to the following basic human equipment of "the Self": (1) a human spirit or spiritual being; (2) a rational mind along with emotional intelligence, feelings about human interaction; (3) a conscience providing moral capacity, what is good or bad; (4) will, freedom of choice (which determines whether the capacity for truth remains functioning or atrophies); and (5) a survival instinct in protecting one's life and

---

12. Psychology is not my chosen academic field of study. I recognize this and therefore "assume." Perhaps it is assuming too much to describe psychology's view of this positive side of self, but I do so to emphasize the point of "self-deception" in responding to Trump's gaslighting; the simplification is an operational description of the Self for both sciences.

avoiding danger ("fight or flight" reaction, which may be a combination of all the equipment functioning and focusing on danger). People may choose whether to use this equipment or capacity for truth in responding to the inner voice of truth and morality or choose to ignore it and respond to a lie because that is what they want to hear.

Both psychology and Christian theology agree that this basic equipment of the Self is open to outside influences; therefore, the freedom of choice is an all-important human attribute in maintaining one's capacity for truth. In childhood other factors are determinative, but in adulthood choice is prominent. Christian theology holds that if adults choose not to follow their inner capacity for truth, suppressing it and not using it, *its demise is set in motion*.[13] I describe here the dynamics of self-delusion: ignoring what is true or choosing to go against what one knows to be true. When people follow what they want to hear rather than hear what their inner voice of truth and reality is saying, *it is the beginning of the disablement of their capacity for truth*. This is especially true for Christians when specific outside influences are believed to be supernatural: immoral, bad demonic influence or good Holy Spirit influence. Everyone's capacity for truth did not fail under Trump's gaslighting; many Americans and Christians of every stripe engaged their capacity for truth and chose to resist his lies and deception— they saw the sociopath coming.

A MALIGNANT NARCISSIST GASLIGHTS A GULLIBLE NARCISSISTIC SOCIETY

Donald Trump's gaslighting left his pathological mark on the minds and behavior of Americans. A year after he lost the election, his popularity and influence are surprisingly strong. This loyalty to Trump is undisturbed despite evidence of his criminal activity in office, his being impeached twice, his trying to overturn a democratic election, and his inciting a violent insurrection on the Capitol of the United States! Many Americans have been deeply affected by Trump's malignant narcissistic political tornado; they reflect his reality and pathologies in their thinking and behavior. They have been gaslighted. As mentioned in chapter 2, clinical psychologist Elizabeth Mika observed there are "three wobbly legs" to what political scientists call "the toxic triangle" in society: (1) the malignant narcissist leader, (2) his close followers, and (3) society at large; they are all bound together *by narcissism*. She states the toxic triangle is a "narcissistic collusion." The malignant narcissist leader's rhetoric appeals to both his narcissistic close followers and

13. Rom 1:18, 24–32; John 12:35; 2 Thess 2:9–11.

narcissistic society at large, an unhappy society that feels they have been deprived and are victims. The main ingredient, narcissism, somehow remains
invisible to the participants and observers.[14] A gullible American public
does not recognize they have become desensitized to "normal" thought and
behavior; they have been gaslighted and have become accustomed to a malignant narcissistic abnormality.

The toxic triangle of narcissistic collusion addresses our ongoing question: Why didn't evangelicals see him coming? *The answer is that some did
see him coming and liked what they saw and heard.* Trump's malignant narcissistic message clicked with their narcissism, Christians included. With
the third leg of the toxic triangle, society at large, the narcissism is at the
lower levels of the narcissistic scale (perhaps four to five on the zero to ten
scale); it is not as empowered and pathological as Donald Trump's malignant narcissism, but over time narcissistic society moves toward him on the
scale, slowly becoming more like him. Mika explains the simplicity of a narcissistic public responding to the "charisma" of a malignant narcissist tyrant:

> [The charisma] is simply their ability to tell others what they
> want to hear, to make them go along with whatever scheme
> they've concocted for the moment. Their glibness is something
> that easily fools normal people, who do not understand the kind
> of pathology that results from a missing conscience.[15]

Trump's delusion that he didn't lose the election was a direct result of his
pathological narcissistic personality disorder; he would not accept the loss;
he chose to resist the reality of a lost election, and a narcissistic public would
not accept it either and chose to avoid the crash of their dreams. Therefore,
it was easy for Trump to recruit "stop the steal" followers, even though joining him would amount to their accepting his concocted pathological reality,
the Big Lie that the election was stolen. The toxic triangle suggests a simple
answer to why people in society act out like Trump: They willingly respond
to a malignant narcissist. Mika explains the identification of the close followers (second leg, Trump's base) with the narcissistic tyrant:

> Through the process of identification, the tyrant's followers
> absorb his omnipotence and glory and imagine themselves as
> powerful as he is, the winners in the game of life. This identifica-
> tion heals the followers' narcissistic wounds, but also tends to
> shut down their reason and conscience, allowing them to engage
> in immoral and criminal behaviors with a sense of impunity

14. Mika, "Who Goes Trump?," §5271.
15. Mika, "Who Goes Trump?," §5254.

engendered by this identification. Without the support of his narcissistic followers, who see in the tyrant a reflection and vindication of their long-nursed dreams of glory, the tyrant would remain a middling nobody.[16]

Mika speaks to the explosive gratuitous violence of Trump's base and wider society, illustrated by the news headlines shown at the beginning of this chapter. She explains how people are "set up" for the violence by having their capacity for truth (reason and conscience) shut down. The revenge, victimhood, and aggrievements that Trump frequently expresses are permission for his aggrieved, bloodthirsty base and members of wider society to engage in violence—like they did at the January 6 violent insurrection at the Capitol, or perhaps with the mass shooting phenomenon in schools, with children as victims. Of course, the sense of impunity the public feels is based on *Trump's actual continuing unaccountability for his crimes and violence*, making his perceived permission even more enticing for his followers, producing a reckless disregard for the rule of law in American society.

Post-Trump Stress Disorder (PTSD)

A year after he lost the election, Donald Trump's influence remains strong because *Americans have been deeply affected by his malignant narcissistic political tornado*. The stress of his absurdist reality—up is down, black is white, wrong is right—mirrors the stress and confusion that many have suffered previously under narcissistic attacks in their lives, triggering the memory of them and reopening old narcissistic wounds. This description of the stress from Trump's gaslighting is like the recurring traumatic memories and horrors that combat veterans experience, in that something triggers the memories of the traumatic stress, the psychological wound is reopened, and the veteran experiences the previous war trauma afresh. Psychologists call this Post-Traumatic Stress Disorder (PTSD). Betty Teng, a psychotherapist specializing in trauma cases, likens the trauma that Donald Trump unleashed on American society to their experiencing "Post-Trump Stress Disorder" (the meaning of PTSD I will use throughout this section). She does not attempt humor with the comparison but wants to show the psychological similarities between the two traumatic stress experiences.[17]

Trauma therapist Teng states that survivors of traumatic experiences, stressful relationships, and histories have the trauma-memory of them

16. Mika, "Who Goes Trump?," §5277, emphasis mine.
17. Teng, "Trauma, Time, Truth, and Trump," §4031.

triggered by "the incessant barrage of aggressive words and daily reports of the erratic conduct of a powerful, narcissistic and attention-seeking world leader."[18] She states that Trump's narcissistic compulsive personality keeps the American public "fixated on his toxic behavior and stuck in a state of chaotic, meaningless crisis" and "the speed of new troubling information in exploding in-boxes leaves a person exhausted, confused and overstimulates the brain, like trying to drink from an internet fire-hose."[19] She says, "By drinking from the Internet's fire-hose, we not only end up still thirsty, but we may get seriously hurt in the process." Teng says because we are not machines, this fire hose rapid information affects us: "This onslaught of information disallows us from taking the time to truly consider any of it and we open ourselves to believing dangerous and unchecked falsehoods."[20] Furthermore, combat veterans and public victims are left speechless when the treatment and cure for PTSD is *communication*; the combat veteran articulating their trauma is the cure; the healing is in the verbal reiteration of the trauma.

Mika states *pathological social conditions* that may have caused former narcissistic wounds are making millions of Americans vulnerable and susceptible to Trump's gaslighting:

> It takes years of cultivation of special conditions in a society for a tyranny to take over. Those conditions invariably include: a growing and unbearably oppressive economic and social inequality ignored by the elites who benefit from it, at least for a time; fear, moral confusion, and chaos that come from that deepening inequality; a breakdown of social norms; and growing disregard for the humanity of a large portion of the population and for higher values. In effect, we could see that the pre-tyrannical societies, whether nominally democratic or based on other forms of political organization, exhibit signs of a narcissistic pathology writ large.[21]

Previous traumatic personal experiences where narcissistic wounds occurred in relationships, family, divorce (750,000 each year in the US),[22]

18. Teng, "Trauma, Time, Truth, and Trump," §4006.

19. Teng, "Trauma, Time, Truth, and Trump," §4082, §4095.

20. Teng, "Trauma, Time, Truth, and Trump," §4082, §4095.

21. Mika, "Who Goes Trump?," §5351–57; Elizabeth Mika is Polish and received her degree in clinical psychology from Adam Mickiewica University in Poznan, Poland. She is well-versed in Europe's fascist leaders and governments and has a view of political science from an Eastern European perspective.

22. Vuleta, "35 Encouraging Stats."

childhood trauma, abuse, and rape may be reopened by "Trump induced trauma." People have experienced life conditions that produce societal grievances: the experience of disadvantaged underclass communities in the heart of America's major cities, historic systemic and generational racism, and a lost war (the American civil war) where active racism is still current and locally condoned long afterwards, especially in the American South, although the Vietnam war is a more contemporary source of trauma. Inequalities of any kind in society, as well as the impact of natural disasters, mean that millions of Americans were and are today vulnerable and susceptible to Trump's narcissistic attacks. *His appeal to social grievances and constant revenge-seeking triggers emotions and the memory of previous narcissistic abuse returns, reopening the old narcissistic wounds.* However, it is not just the uneducated, the poor, and the disadvantaged in society that are susceptible to narcissistic Trump-induced trauma, because susceptibility involves narcissism that cuts across socioeconomic strata, affecting all classes and cultural groups in America.[23]

The horrendous after-effects of Trump's gaslighting—his Great Deception—are still with us: incivility, intolerance, disregard for law, and an *unprecedented, inexplicable, explosive inner rage in Americans.* The after-effects are reported daily in the news media. It took a mentally sick president to reveal how sick American society was and is. All malignant narcissist Trump had to do was find people that wanted to hear what he had to say, people that wanted to hear his lies and absurdist reality. He did not need to go searching for them—a *narcissistic American society was waiting with open arms and minds to hear him.* Soon, some Americans found themselves involved in anti-American lawless violence in a Trump-stressed society that, before he arrived on the scene, they never would have even contemplated doing (e.g., the insurrection of the Capitol and the regrets of many participants). Trump's gaslighting was like a dog whistle that unleashed the dark side of sinful human nature of many Americans; the problem is that once the genie is let out of the bottle, it is difficult to put him back. The psychoanalyst's description of the narcissistic gaslighter's effective appeal to narcissistic society above coincides with the apostle Peter's description of "gaslighters"—false teachers in his day; he shows uncanny detail that coincides with psychology's description of the same deceivers and deceptive process (2 Pet 2:1–22). He speaks of the difficulty of putting the evil back in the bottle, as he discusses the appeal of "false teachers"—gaslighters that seduce the "unstable" and "their following the corrupt desires of the flesh" (sinful human behavior); the false teacher's effective appeal is the gaslighter sharing "a corrupt sinful human nature" with the gaslighted.

The above explanations of psychology and trauma psychoanalysts about the effects of malignant narcissistic sociopath Trump's gaslighting and the public's otherwise inexplicable bizarre behavior and violence *are spot on.* Since Trump is no longer in office, a new president and others are left to deal with the damage he did to American society and democracy. No one could repair the damage Trump did to America in one presidential term; it may take decades, even generations. Furthermore, Trump did not go away after leaving office; he is still gaslighting and he is in the face of Americans even more than before, continuing his efforts to replace democracy with authoritarian fascist rule—while criminally unaccountable, as though nothing has changed. He will not stop; it is who he is, a malignant narcissistic fascist who failed once, but his personality disorders enable him to persevere until he gets his way: absolute power in America's damaged democracy.

One of the tasks of the media in American society is to expose and condemn, but this has not always been the case in the post-Trump presidency. In an article written by Bill Press, "Breaking News: Media's Frame Is Helping Trump," the author points out that Joe Biden does not get credit in the media for anything, no matter how much he accomplishes. At a time when Trump's involvement in the January 6 insurrection is increasingly clear, revealing his one-man crime wave, and multiple civil and criminal indictments are going forward in the courts, the media focus on Trump is that of a pitiful, poor loser rather than a dangerous seditionist.[24] Why? Media interviews of Trump ignore his past disastrous leadership, his delusional mantra of a "stolen election," and corruption of the Republican party; he is asked for his opinion, even on foreign affairs, comparing him with former presidents—*normalizing him.*[25] Normalizing in the media suggests that Trump's gaslighting was more pervasive than those who saw him coming realize. Did Trump's gaslighting create a pool of narcissistic followers in every corner of American society—the media included? Therefore, those whose capacity for truth did not fail them: some in the media, some Christians,[26] some members of Congress, and some other Americans who did see him coming must continue to stand up and "stand out" as "living thorns," exposing and condemning Trump's absurdist antidemocratic reality and criminal actions. The danger of Donald Trump is not over *until he is exposed and convicted in court for his crimes.* Until then, his gaslighted image that he created

---

24. Press, "Breaking News: Media's Frame."
25. Ngan, "North Korea Slams Feeble Biden."
26. Eph 5:11–16.

for himself remains—a patriot trying to "Make America Great Again"—and at least 40 percent of Americans think that false image is true.

Those who claim the name "evangelical," especially, must remain true to their name and "stand out," following the example of Jesus himself, his apostles, and the early church as they confronted gaslighting in Israel's culture—a corrupt Judaism that was not anything like the ancient faith of Israel. It was an affront to morality, the message of the prophets, and the truth of the gospel. Jesus' followers left contemporary evangelicals a successful model for confronting gaslighting. First-century Jewish Christians confronted a gaslighted Jewish culture yet were faithful to the gospel message and overcame the false teaching of the day concerning a Messiah-king and an earthly Jewish kingdom. They suffered *Jewish persecution* for their testimony about Jesus—the suffering Messiah-king with a heavenly kingdom, who was savior of the world. Then as martyrs they gave the same "witness unto death" message about Jesus, as they were persecuted by the Roman government. The biblical gaslighting story that follows in chapter 7 illustrates the necessity for evangelicals to keep a Jesus focus and witness to his redemptive sacrifice on the cross (a suffering savior); a lack of Jesus-focus was not just a problem for first-century Christians but for every century that followed; it is an unsuspected contributing reason for the diminished spirituality of American evangelicals today.

Chapter 7

Hellenist Christians Expose
Historic Gaslighting and Racism

Be careful, be on your guard against the yeast of the Pharisees and Sadducees. . . Walk while you have the light, before darkness overtakes you. Believe in the light while you have the light, so that you may become children of light.

<small>JESUS OF NAZARETH[1]</small>

You will ever be hearing but never understanding; you will be ever seeing but never perceiving. For this people's heart has become calloused; they hardly hear with their ears, and they have closed their eyes. Otherwise, they might see with their eyes, hear with their ears, understand with their hearts and turn, and I would heal them.

<small>THE PROPHET ISAIAH[2]</small>

---

1. Jesus identified Pharisees and Sadducees as the first-century "gaslighters" (Matt 16:6, 12); then he stated how gaslighting affects what Christians do with the truth (John 12:35–36). The exodus and its metaphors "yeast" and "light" in the epigraph are what ties Jesus' words together in the two Gospel passages. The metaphors refer to an unbelieving generation of Jews that "died in the wilderness" after the exodus. Jesus applied that fateful journey of an unbelieving generation to the first-century unbelieving "adulterous generation" that rejected him, the suffering Messiah.

2. Isa 6:9–10.

A MAJOR BIBLICAL EXAMPLE of gaslighting took place in the first century that is documented throughout the New Testament. Evangelical culture and history have masked its importance, resulting in a Pollyanna view of the early church. Hellenist Luke, author of the Gospel of Luke-Acts of the Apostles document, tells of a Hellenist band of brothers that exposed the presence of a Jewish cultural tradition that functioned as racism in the nascent church, most of which were Jewish Christians. The tradition's roots were not in the ancient faith of Israel but in a corrupt religious tradition that had gaslighted Israel since their exile. It resulted in a cultural *Israel focus* and torah life over a *Jesus focus* and faith in his gospel, causing many Jewish Christians to turn back from following Jesus. Therefore, the New Testament repeatedly emphasizes "continuing to believe." A Jesus-focus is fundamental for spiritual life, whether at its beginning when confessing him as savior or when one continues to believe in him as Lord throughout life.[3] According to Jesus and the apostles' teaching, the consequences for *not continuing to believe are severe.*[4] This may not be so clear for some evangelical Christians because of their emphasis on belief at the point of conversion—a crisis experience. I do not address the issue of eternal salvation here,[5] but *the necessity of maintaining Jesus' presence in a life of faith.*[6]

A major movement of Jewish Christians gaslighting in the early church was led by former Pharisees that had become Christian. "The circumcision" brought a corrupt view of the ancient faith of Israel into the church, advocating Christians follow a corruption of torah-life after believing the gospel. Many Jewish Christians lost their Jesus focus and embraced a torah life again, even though the Spirit of all prophecy bore witness to Jesus.[7] John's Gospel, primarily a theological-oriented document, was written at the end of the first century to warn Christians of a renewal of this return to torah heresy that had been introduced by the circumcision group sixty years previously. Now its ugly head raised again. After the destruction of Jerusalem and the temple in AD 70, the temple order was transferred to the synagogue where doctors of the law, Pharisees, were in charge and they reignited their attack on Christianity. Former Pharisees in the church were emboldened to push their return to the torah heresy and attack the truth of

---

3. Rom 1:17.

4. Jesus' teachings: John 8:12–45; 12:35–40; Matt 5:13–16; 13:1–23; the apostles' teachings: 2 Tim 4:3–4; Titus 1:10–13; Heb 2:1–4; 3:12–19; Jas 1:21–27; the Old Testament prophets: Jer 7:28; 6:19; 7:23–26; 8:17–19; 9:13; 11:7; 13:8–11.

5. John 17:3, 11–12.

6. John 15:26—16:1, 12–15.

7. Rev 19:10.

the gospel once again at the end of the century.[8] Christians still worshiped in the synagogues as well as house churches in the diaspora, and the return to torah emphasis was a threat to those that John supervised; he had seen and experienced the heresy decades previously. The theme of John's Gospel, therefore, is *continuing to believe*—John focused his entire Gospel on the problem.[9]

The first time John experienced the return to torah movement, it turned into a major conflict between an Israel-centered corrupt Judaism and a Jesus-centered gospel. In times of persecution, it presented a great temptation for ethnic Jewish Christians in the church to escape it. The key issue for that predominantly early Jewish church was to maintain *Christian identity* apart from what seemed to be a natural cultural tendency—allowing torah-life to be the focus of their faith. However, the core problem was not the Torah, the writings of Moses; it was allowing an intrusive, corrupt, Israel-centered Judaism of the Pharisees—the yeast of the Pharisees—to become the center of their faith instead of their new faith in Jesus. The biblical examples of this corrupt Judaism gaslighting had a specific history, and it was not the ancient faith of Israel but postexilic Jewish history. It was (1) Israel's exile, decline, and attempt to reconstitute Israel "as in the days of Moses" leading to the first century; (2) Israel's first-century corrupt religion and culture of the Pharisees; (3) Jesus of Nazareth confronting this gaslighting of the Pharisees; and (4) after Jesus' ascension, the early Jewish church and apostles confronting gaslighting *in the church*. All the incidents of gaslighting in the church involved the attempt to replace the Jesus-centered gospel with a corrupt Israel-centered Judaism that was the centerpiece of unbelieving first-century Jewish culture. Former Pharisees, now Christian-Judaizers, promoted this false identity issue. Therefore, Jewish Christians struggled over whether their ethnic heritage as Jews—"Israel the nation" or "Jesus the savior of the world" was to be preeminent in their lives. This struggle between Israel's corrupt Judaism and Jesus' gospel *is the contextual plot of the entire New Testament*. After Jesus' ascension, the identity issue was crucial for the Christian faith: (1) for the integrity of the gospel message, (2) for spiritual life of Christians, and (3) for the ongoing witness of the church in the world.

Would not evangelicals experience a similar loss of Jesus focus if in their history they were gaslighted and faced the same identity crisis and spiritual consequences? Would they not have to make the same momentous decision today as the early church did to avoid spiritual decline? My purpose

---

8. Bruce, *Gospel of John*, 215.

9. John 21:31 and 1:1–18.

in providing biblical examples of gaslighting below is not just to show the danger an excessive Israel-focus was for Jesus, the disciples, and the predominantly Jewish church in the first century—*as helpful and enlightening as that is for the interpretation of the New Testament*—but to provide a warning. Would not nearly two centuries of an Israel-centered Dispensational theology influence evangelicals today? It is not only possible but probable that it would tend to crowd out the centrality of Jesus, not only in their view of salvation history but by bringing a dominant *Israel-focus* in their thinking that tended to *diminish their Jesus-focus, leaving some in a compromised spiritual state, vulnerable, and susceptible to the deceptive gaslighting of Donald Trump.* The following biblical examples of gaslighting in the Jewish historical context (Israel in exile and first-century Israel) provide specific illustrations of spiritual decline that describe some evangelical Christians that are on the wrong side of this identity issue of Jesus-focus and Israel-focus today. First, I examine the biblical example of gaslighting Israel in and after their exile, to illustrate the origins of a corrupt Israel-centered Judaism that influenced the first-century church. Second, I examine an Israel-centered Dispensational theology originating in the history of evangelicals that still captivates evangelicals today.

POST-EXILE GASLIGHTING IN ISRAEL

Just after Israel's exile in Babylon, when they returned to Jerusalem, the religious leaders, scribes, and doctors of the law attempted to recreate the ancient nation of Israel. This was a natural inclination, but at cross-purposes with God's intention to create a new Israel six hundred years later by sending the suffering servant of the Lord, Jesus the Messiah who would create a new people of God, born not according to Jewish ancestry or nationality, but born according to God's Spirit.[10] The circumstances of coming out of exile with a desire to reinstitute the nation of Israel were much different than the circumstances of the exodus of Hebrews from Egypt that led to the "ancient faith of Israel." What resulted with the returning Jewish exiles, on the other hand, was that the scribes and doctors of the law created the "religion of Judaism."[11] What they created was in great contrast to what God had formerly created in the ancient faith of Israel, in giving the pristine law of Moses in the exodus. Postexilic Judaism held that the hope for the Messiah was for a messiah-king that would establish an earthly Jewish kingdom, not a suffering messiah-redeemer for all nations with a heavenly spiritual

10. Isa 53; Gal 6:15–16; John 1:9–13; 3:5–8.
11. Rom 10:1–21, especially 10:1–3.

kingdom. They imposed their corrupt Judaism on the Israelites through gaslighting over six hundred years. Israel was gaslighted with a *corruption of the ancient faith*. The hope for the Messiah chronicled in the books of Moses was a suffering Messiah-redeemer for all nations with a heavenly spiritual kingdom.

Therefore, after the exile, the view of Moses's messianic hope was replaced with the notion of a messiah-king that would establish an earthly ethnic-Jewish kingdom like King David's kingdom. In their "PTSD" (traditional sense) after the exile, the scribes and doctors of the law created and proclaimed a message of the messiah that the people wanted to hear. John Bright states, "In and after the exile a succession of godly, yet very practical men took hold of Israel's faith and made it into the religion of Judaism."[12] According to Israeli scholar Yehezkiel Kaufmann, "The ancient fall of Jerusalem was the great watershed of the history of Israelite religion; at the fall of Jerusalem, the early life of the Israelites ended and the history of Judaism began."[13] The *pure stream of the law of Moses in the ancient faith of Israel* became polluted, and Israel's living faith turned into *the static religion of Judaism*.

The post-exile circumstances were nothing like God's creation of the people of God in and after the exodus. At that time, there was a faith in the presence of God (an ontological "there-ness" of God) whose miraculous power was demonstrated in their deliverance from Egypt. In view of the fall of Jerusalem, the Israelite exiles questioned the presence of God, causing the spirit of prophecy to die; their religious emphasis turned to the written word of Scripture alone (epistemology, what was said about God), without experiencing the dynamic word of the prophets and the reality of God's presence. There was a shift from the "there-ness" of God among them to where that living presence gave way to *the overpowering dynamic of culture and human religious activity*. Their creation of Judaism was a retreat from the ancient faith of Israel. The religious leadership focused on the human efforts of the scribes and doctors of the law (the gaslighters) to preserve the Scriptures and Jewish identity; they were the forerunners of first-century gaslighting Pharisees.

The postexilic strategy of the scribes and doctors of the law was to form a law community, and its purpose would be the "scrupulous observance of the law."[14] Their function was to give a prescriptive commentary of the written word of God. The exile in Babylon and servitude under Persian,

12. Bright, *Kingdom of God*, 170.

13. Kaufmann, *Religion of Israel*, 447–51.

14. Bright, *Kingdom of God*, 170.

Greek, and Roman rule profoundly influenced their interpretation of the Scriptures and the content of their corrupt oral tradition for six hundred years. In the process of a fundamental change in their culture in the exile, there was a subtle shift from a heartfelt faith in the activity of the living God among them (there-ness of God, a confrontation with the reality of his presence) to human efforts at law keeping and protecting themselves from the nations surrounding them. Feelings of protection from the nations evolved into a first-century hatred of gentiles. Israel was no longer a faith-community; *there was no expectation that God would do anything.*

The result of gaslighting a corrupt Judaism over the centuries was that Jews in the first century were unable to recognize the arrival of Jesus, the suffering Messiah-redeemer with a heavenly spiritual kingdom (as the Isaiah quote notes in the epigraph above—it is the most quoted prophetic text in the NT); that reality about the Messiah had been replaced with hopes of a messianic earthly king and kingdom. Then Jesus came announcing his kingdom as "the good news of *the kingdom of heaven*."[15] A gaslighted, corrupt Judaism had almost obliterated Israel's capacity for truth, because the Pharisees and Sadducees continued to implement the postexilic gaslighting scheme and message in the first century. It not only challenged Jesus' message of the "good news of the spiritual kingdom of heaven," it caused a major conflict in the predominantly ethnically Jewish Christian church. In other words, this corrupt Judaism versus gospel conflict became the plot of the entire New Testament.

JESUS CONFRONTED GASLIGHTING

Jesus told his Jewish disciples to be careful and be on their guard against the "yeast" or gaslighting influence of the Pharisees and Sadducees, because they were the purveyors of a false notion about a messiah-king and an earthly kingdom. The Pharisees continued their gaslighting by teaching the corrupt Israel-centered, postexilic Judaism; *the last thing first-century Jews wanted to hear was a message about a "suffering" messiah-savior and a "heavenly" spiritual kingdom—especially one that included gentiles.* Most were expecting an earthly king like David to replace Roman rule. The notion of a political messiah prevailed. Despite the centrality of sacrifices in the ancient faith of Israel, the spiritual meaning of blood sacrifice had declined, eroded over six hundred years of gaslighting, except for a very small remnant in Israel that received Jesus the Messiah at his arrival. The Messiah's forerunner, John the Baptist, faithfully proclaimed the irreplaceable issue of

15. Matt 4:17; see also chapters 5–7 in Matthew's Gospel.

sacrifice and a suffering Messiah-Savior when he announced Jesus as "the Lamb of God who takes away the sin of the world."[16] Jesus confronted and critiqued first-century Jewish religious rule, not the ancient faith of Israel. According to Moses, the gospel was the fulfillment of that ancient faith; Jesus confronted the governing corrupt religious rulers, the Pharisees, and Sadducees, and their gaslighting of a corrupt Judaism. Jesus openly and vehemently condemned them and their perversion of Israel's ancient faith. He was furious with their human traditions and religious leaders that had nullified the word of God through their oral traditions that had placed a great burden on the Jewish people.[17] Evangelicals that try to use Jesus to justify their silence in not confronting the evil in Donald Trump and his presidency *greatly misrepresent him.*

Centuries of postexilic gaslighting had replaced the reality of the ancient faith of Israel in the minds of first-century Jews; a suffering messiah-savior for all humanity with a spiritual kingdom was no longer expected. Jesus said they were an "unbelieving generation"[18] and he was astounded by the lack of faith in Israel under the religious rule of the Pharisees.[19] Due to prolonged gaslighting, many in Israel, especially the religious leaders, had "hardened hearts" and were impervious to the truth—they were like the path soil in Jesus' parable of the soils.[20] Their capacity for truth was not only dysfunctional, but their sinful human nature was open to the influence of the evil one.[21] From the beginning, the religious leaders tried to kill Jesus. The first-century generation of Jews were thoroughly gaslighted with a corrupt Judaism. Hardened hearts meant their capacity for truth was gone and the worst of corrupt human nature was ready to be unleashed on Jesus and his disciples.

Gaslighting Affected Jesus' Jewish Disciples

Jesus' warning to his *Jewish disciples* to "*be careful, be on your guard against the yeast of the Pharisees and Sadducees*" was not a pedestrian, off-the-cuff comment. The corrupt Judaism of the Pharisees was imbedded in the disciples' culture; it was *their mindset* throughout the time Jesus was physically

16. John the Baptist, his followers, and family as well as a limited number of others—a remnant of faithful Jews—believed in Jesus; see Luke 1–3.

17. Mark 7:1–13; Matt 11:28–30; Luke 11:46.

18. Mark 9:19.

19. Luke 7:9, 11:29–32; Mark 6:5–6; Matt 6:30–34.

20. Matt 13:1–23.

21. John 8:34–59.

with them. Their capacity for truth was seriously impaired for hearing and receiving his teaching. Peter illustrated all the disciples' dullness to Jesus' teaching.[22] As Jesus condemned the corrupt Judaism of the Jews, Peter frequently challenged him and attempted to correct him. On one occasion, nearing the end of Jesus' ministry, Peter had just made his confession that Jesus was the Messiah come from God. Jesus started to speak of his crucifixion, but Peter interrupted him saying that would "never happen"—the notion that Jesus had to die did not fit his gaslighted idea of the messiah-king. Jesus responded to Peter, "Get behind me, Satan."[23] The notion that the Son of God would be anything other than a crucified savior was satanically inspired. The obtuseness of the Jewish disciples when they were with Jesus is illustrated in all the Synoptic Gospels; they had been thoroughly gaslighted just as most of that generation of Jews had. There was little room for a suffering Messiah in their minds; it was crowded out by a messiah king and an earthly Jewish kingdom. Although the Jewish disciples' capacity for truth was almost gone, not comprehending much of what Jesus taught, he was successful in raising their faith to the level that they believed he "came from God."[24] Their capacity for truth would dramatically change on and after Pentecost. The impact of the Pharisees' gaslighting on Jesus' disciples while he was with them in his physical body is illustrated in the following paragraph.

The Synoptic Gospels show Jesus beginning his ministry proclaiming the good news *of the kingdom of God*. He went everywhere demonstrating the *spiritual power of his heavenly kingdom* by healing the sick, raising the dead, and casting out demonic spirits. When Jesus was still with the disciples, he sent them out to declare the same message—the immediacy and power of the heavenly kingdom of God, and they returned rejoicing at experiencing the kingdom's power in healing and overcoming the power of Satan.[25] The message of the cross, the Messiah's sacrifice for the sins of the world, was not part of their message when they were with Jesus. He began talking to them about his death and resurrection near the end of his ministry, but the disciples did not know what he was talking about.[26] The core of Jesus' teaching while he was with them was *the power of the heavenly kingdom of God*. The Sermon on the Mount was a comparison of Jesus' good news of the kingdom with the corrupt Judaism of the Pharisees; Jesus' parables of the

22. Matt 15:15–16.
23. Matt 16:21–23.
24. Matt 16:13–16; John 6:1–70.
25. Luke 10:17–20.
26. Luke 18:31–34.

kingdom were numerous. Hellenist Luke's Gospel-Acts was originally one document; the Gospel of Luke part centers on Jesus' *international* kingdom of God. In his Gospel, Luke includes an incident after Jesus' resurrection where Jesus scolded the disciples for not grasping what the Scriptures said about his suffering (Luke 24:25–32); then immediately following, turning to the Acts part of Luke's document, he records the resurrected Jesus spending forty days speaking to the disciples about the kingdom of God and telling them of the necessity to wait for *the Holy Spirit* to come upon them in power (the spiritual, heavenly kingdom) (Acts 1:3–5). However, even after Jesus' forty-day seminar on the spiritual kingdom of God, the disciples ask, "Lord, are you at this time going to restore the kingdom to *Israel?*"[27] Their hopes were still on a Jewish earthly kingdom! However, Jesus commanding them to wait for the coming of the Holy Spirit would change that notion and, in time, enable the disciples to proclaim the message of a crucified but resurrected, living, heavenly Messiah to gentiles; many early Jewish Christians were perplexed at this absurdity.

Jesus understood the reason for the disciples' little faith. John's Gospel provides five chapters that describe Jesus' preparation of the disciples for his death on the cross *and for the conflict that they would encounter in facing a corrupt Judaism in Jesus' absence.* Jesus' conflict with a corrupt Judaism was a prototype of what the disciples and the early Jewish church would experience in their conflict with unbelieving Jews and the religious leader's gaslighted message of a corrupt Judaism. Chapters 13–17 of John's Gospel contain unprecedented information in the New Testament, explaining the role of the Holy Spirit taking Jesus' place; the Spirit of Truth or *paraclete* (in Greek), which means "the one called alongside to help," is repeatedly used in the chapters. The Holy Spirit would come upon them on the Day of Pentecost and their capacity for truth would come alive in every respect, enabling them to witness against both the evils of the religious rule of the Pharisees and the secular rule of Rome.[28] The Spirit would remind them of what Jesus taught and assist them in correcting their gaslighted mindset about an earthly messiah-king and Jewish kingdom. However, the Holy Spirit's work was not automatic; *a response of faith was required* by the disciples to effect the incremental change in their cultural perspective; the function of choice was still part of the disciples' capacity for truth. With all the divine empowerment, they would still have to choose to "walk in the Spirit" rather than follow corrupt human nature, "the flesh," and any fears they may have had about abandoning their culture. The apostle Paul explains the spiritual

27. Acts 1:6.
28. John 15:26–27; 16:7–11.

dynamics involved in this process when Christians face such a choice in his Romans letter.[29]

Even with the Spirit's help and the restoration of the disciples' capacity for truth, resisting the pull of their culture was a struggle of faith. Again, the apostle Peter provided an example of the struggle for liberation from the influence of a corrupt Judaism, especially a hatred for gentiles.[30] A fundamental hatred of gentiles was embedded in first-century corrupt Jewish culture. With Christians, faith was necessary to overcome that hatred; they had to respond to the prompting of the Holy Spirit, engaging a renewed conscience and inner capacity of truth to overcome such feelings. This response of faith was necessary so that they would not respond to what they wanted to hear or what may have been an easier road for them in the light of an intense gospel-Judaism conflict in Jewish society. Many Christians chose the easy way out of the stress in this conflict, ceasing to believe and yielding to the gaslighting of the Judaizers[31] siding with them to avoid the stress. When Jesus gave his disciples the warning "walk while you have the light, before darkness overtakes you," he meant that they must *live according to the truth*—continue to believe—responding to the truth in whatever the circumstances they encountered in Jewish society. Failure to do so would mean the demise of their capacity for truth and the process of darkness—lies and deception—overtaking them.[32] This is the biblical message for evangelicals today.

A Gaslighting-Resistant Hellenist Band of Brothers

After the euphoria of the coming of the Holy Spirit upon the Jewish apostles and disciples at Pentecost, the Acts of the Apostles shows the international mission of the church necessarily shifting from Pharisee-controlled Jerusalem to the gentile city of Antioch in Syria. Jewish Christians (including the Twelve) were sluggish in responding to the Holy Spirit and Jesus' Great Commission to *leave Jerusalem*, bringing the gospel message to Judea, Samaria, and the world beyond (i.e., the despised gentile world). The gaslighting of a corrupt Judaism for six hundred years impacted the early Jewish church; it was their culture, and they held religious cultural values about the

29. Romans 7:5–25 is a detailed description of the Christian's supernaturally empowered Self's capacity of truth, as they choose to respond to the power of the Spirit rather than the desires of fallen sinful human nature.

30. Acts 9:32–11, 17; 15:6–11.

31. Gal 3:1–3; 4:9–18; 5:2–13; 6:12–16.

32. John 12:35–36.

centrality of Jerusalem, the Jewish nation, its temple, and hatred of the gentiles *that would not be easily set aside.* The corrupt Judaism of the Pharisees was racist at its core. At first, the extreme Israel-focus of a corrupt Judaism revealed itself very subtly in discrimination against Hellenist (gentile) widows in the church.[33]

Stephen and other Hellenist Christians were appointed to take care of the situation, because the Jewish apostles felt they should not be tasked with "waiting on tables";[34] instead, they would give themselves to prayer and ministry. Hellenist author Luke may have written the "waiting on tables" comment tongue in cheek. As it turned out, the Jewish apostles targeted the resistant gaslighted Jews of Jerusalem. However, Stephen and his Hellenist "band of brothers" had been successful in ministry to *gentiles* in Jerusalem's Hellenist synagogues—besides their waiting on tables! Stephen, "a man full of God's grace and power, performed great wonders and signs among the people"; he was unstoppable in proving the *crucified* Jesus was the Messiah to Hellenist Jews that were influenced by a corrupt Judaism. Disgruntled at losing arguments, some false witnesses reported Stephen to the Jewish Sanhedrin for "blasphemous words against Moses and God," for "never stopping his speaking against this holy place [the temple] and against the law," as they said.[35] A Hellenist Jew by the name of Saul of Tarsus may have even heard Stephen's preaching and argued with him.[36]

After Stephen's arrest, in his defense before the racist Jewish Sanhedrin, with subtle irony Hellenist Stephen attacked their corrupt gaslighted view of the law, Moses, and their notion of holy places (holy temple and a holy land); essentially, he ridiculed their entire theology of holy places and the "presence of God." He started his factual historical account of Israel by telling them that God told their beloved patriarch Abraham *to leave his country and people to go into a foreign land!* He said God would show him that he had no inheritance in it, and that the Israelites would be four hundred years in a country not their own, as mistreated slaves, before returning to worship in Canaan (Acts 7:3). Stephen pointed out that their revered ancestors Joseph, Jacob, and Moses *were in foreign lands as foreigners* (Egypt, Midian, the Sinai Desert)—*but God was with them.* Then he reminded them that because of a worldwide famine, the patriarchs all ended up in *Egypt and died there!* Jacob's bones were returned to Canaan, but he was buried

---

33. Acts 6:1–7.

34. Jesus' message of washing the disciples' feet had not yet sunk in (John 13:1–17).

35. Acts 6:11, 13–14.

36. Acts 6:9.

in the family tomb in (hated) Samaria—a tomb that Abraham *bought from a Hittite*.[37] In his extremely irritating picture of the patriarch's history in foreign lands, Stephen was fearless and relentless; he reminded them that *Moses was born in Egypt and educated in the wisdom of the Egyptians.* When Moses tried to liberate their ancestors from Egypt, his own people rejected him, and he fled to Midian where he settled as a foreigner with his *two uncircumcised Midianite sons*! After forty years, God appeared to Moses in a burning bush *in the desert near Mount Sinai* and said, "Take off your sandals, *for the place where you are standing is holy ground*" (Acts 7:33)! Steven said that God told Moses that he would send him back to Egypt: "This is the same Moses that they [the Israelites] had rejected," although God himself had sent him to be their ruler and deliverer (Acts 7:35). Moses led them out of Egypt and *performed wonders and signs in Egypt, at the Red Sea, and for forty years in the wilderness* (Acts 7:36).

As Stephen continues his irritating description of their ancestors as foreigners, how they rejected, abused, and disobeyed Moses and the law like an unruly mob, he assailed their nonsensical view of a "holy land and temple"—his irony did not escape his listeners; they were furious. After quoting the prophets who said God rejected them (Israel) and sent them into exile (Acts 7:42–43), Stephen zeroes in on their corrupt view of the "temple" and "the presence of God." He reminded them that the "*tabernacle of the covenant law* was with their ancestors in the wilderness" (a tent), as *God directed Moses to construct, according to the pattern that God gave them—it was the will of God* (Acts 7:44). In the tabernacle, the presence of God moved with the people of God. Furthermore, it was the whim of David to build a temple to provide "a dwelling place for the God of Israel."[38] After Solomon built it, he said, "However, the Most High does not dwell in houses [the temple] made by human hands." Then, quoting the prophet Isaiah, Stephen ceases subtlety altogether and directly confronts the Sanhedrin and their gaslighted view of a corrupt Judaism, accusing them of rejecting Jesus the suffering Messiah-redeemer and his good news of the spiritual kingdom of God that revealed the *Holy Spirit dwelling in Christians.*

> You stiff-necked people! Your hearts and ears are still uncircumcised. You are just like your ancestors: *You always resist the Holy Spirit!* Was there ever a prophet your ancestors did not persecute? They even killed those who predicted the coming of the Righteous One. And now you have betrayed and murdered

---

37. Gen 49:29–30; Acts 7:14–15.

38. 1 Kgs 8:12–61.

him—you who have received the law that was given through angels but have not obeyed it.[39]

Anger built up in the members of the Sanhedrin as Stephen dismantled their history and revealed their rebellion against God, Moses, the law, and their supposed holy places; it finally exploded and they murdered him.

Hellenist Stephen was a man ahead of his times in understanding the gospel's international heavenly kingdom and international mission of the church. *Fifteen years would pass before the Jewish apostles would understand Jesus' gospel and mission like Stephen.* In a sense, the charges against Stephen were true, but they were reported by false witnesses to make them sound "anti-Israel"; he was merely declaring the reality of Jesus' international good news of the kingdom of God. He was saying that Moses the lawgiver and the nation of Israel were no longer the main focus of God's salvation. Now, *Jesus the Messiah* and his church were the focus; Jesus fulfilled the law and established an international kingdom of God where the people of God were from every tribe and nation.[40] The temple was no longer the "Holy Place"; now the inner lives of Christians were the residence of God's Holy Spirit. The earthly city of Jerusalem and the land were now mere symbols for the "heavenly Jerusalem and heavenly kingdom."[41] Jesus, Paul, and Peter proclaimed the same message as Stephen did—and they all were killed for it.

The major issue in the predominantly Jewish early church was maintaining Christian identity against the efforts of the Judaizing gaslighters to insert torah-life alongside the gospel. The Circumcision party in the church imposed and perpetuated Jewish identity that compromised the gospel. The apostle Paul, the *chief anti-gaslighter of the New Testament*, addressed this in his letter to Galatian Christians:

> I am astonished that you are so quickly deserting the one who called you to live in the grace of Christ and are turning to a different gospel—which is really no gospel at all. Evidently some people are throwing you into confusion and are trying to pervert the gospel of Christ. You foolish Galatians! Who has bewitched you? Before your very eyes *Jesus Christ was clearly portrayed as crucified*. Did you *receive the Spirit* by the works of the law or by *believing* what you heard? Are you so foolish? After beginning

39. Acts 7:51–53, emphasis mine.

40. Gal 6:15–16; Acts 2:1–11; Matt 28:1–20.

41. Heb 11:10, 13–16, 35; 12:22; Gal 4:24–26. The hopes and veneration for an earthly Jerusalem are typical of the first-century corrupt stream of Judaism, just as Christian Zionism is today.

by means of the Spirit, are you now trying to finish by means of the flesh?[42]

Contrary to evangelical tradition, the emphasis of the New Testament is on continuing to believe, not belief at the crisis point of conversion, as important as that evangelical tradition is. Unfortunately, it has caused some evangelicals to think that continuing to believe, having a vital relationship in following Jesus, is optional. The example of the Galatian church above is but one example among many in the New Testament concerning this truth. John, the author of the Fourth Gospel, in an anti-gaslighting treatise clearly stated his purpose for writing his Gospel: "Jesus performed many other signs in the presence of his disciples which are not recorded in this book. *But these are written that you may continue to believe that Jesus is the Messiah, the Son of God, and that by believing you may have life in his name.*"[43] The gaslighted message of a corrupt Judaism challenging the gospel in the early church was such a major problem that John dedicated his entire Gospel to it. The topic of continuing to believe is a theme that *dominates the entire New Testament.*[44]

WHY ARE CHRISTIANS SO MEAN TODAY?

The above examples of biblical gaslighting show which side of the Judaism-gospel conflict in the New Testament evangelicals should be on—a *Jesus-centered faith* in which all of salvation history points to Jesus the Messiah-redeemer and his gospel of the spiritual kingdom of God for everyone. As the first few paragraphs of this chapter suggests, gaslighting in the history of the evangelical movement has resulted in many evangelicals taking the opposite side of the above New Testament examples—an "Israel-focus." In the quote from Galatians above, the apostle Paul says an Israel-centered faith is not "good news."

In an article entitled, "Why Are Christians So Mean?" evangelical pastor Keith Mannes points to an unusual Israel-influence among evangelicals today. He illustrates it by noting a Christian in his neighborhood who was flying a flag showing Rambo's body with Trump's head superimposed

42. Gal 1:6–7, 3:1–3; emphasis mine.

43. John 20:30–31, my emphasis. This alternate reading is from the New International Version notes, indicating the present continuous tense of the Greek language; the best New Testament manuscripts have "continue believing."

44. A full account of the conflict between "gaslighted corrupt Judaism" and "Jesus' gospel of the kingdom of God" is the subject of my book *American Evangelical-Pentecostal Elephant.*

holding a rocket launcher. Mannes asks, "How did the Rambo-Trump flag-flyer, and the church with him, get so mean?" He notes Christians readily imagine themselves as Israelites and Old Testament heroes rather than Christians of the New Testament that *reflect the spirit of Jesus*. Pastor Mannes says by some "weird circuitry with the slip of a few words, images and brain synapses," Christians imagine themselves fervently as ancient Israelites. He says, "These people would vote for Samson for president." Imagining themselves as ancient Israelites is "how evangelicals get to the place where a devout, church-going, Bible-reading, prayer-offering, Jesus-talking man imagines the work of God is best done with Rambo-Trump as president." Pastor Mannes states, "We desperately need to *rewire the motherboard with Jesus*" (my emphasis).[45] It appears that the vengeance and warfare of the Old Testament burns in the hearts of many evangelicals, not the love of Jesus. "Rewiring the motherboard with Jesus" means to return to what the apostles of the New Testament say is the model for Christians—regaining a Jesus-focus. The apostles say (1) "Examine yourselves to see whether you are in the faith; test yourselves. Do you not realize that Christ Jesus is in you—unless, of course, you fail the test?" (2 Cor 13:5). (2) "Whoever claims to live in him must live as Jesus did" (1 John 2:6). (3) "Therefore, holy brothers and sisters, who share in the heavenly calling, fix your thoughts on Jesus (Heb 3:1). (4) "Let us run with perseverance the race marked out for us, fixing our eyes on Jesus, the pioneer and perfecter of faith" (Heb 12:2).

I state a theological reason here for Pastor Mannes's practical observations of why evangelicals have this unusual Israel-connection. As mentioned at the beginning of this chapter, throughout their history evangelicals have been gaslighted with an Old-Testament-oriented, Israel-centered theology that dominates evangelical thinking today. For the past 170 years, evangelicals have embraced a popular, influential Israel-centered Dispensational theology. It was introduced to America by an English ex-clergyman, John Darby, in the early 1830s. The theology promoted an *Israel-centered tradition very similar to the Israel-centered tradition of first-century Judaism and Judaizers in the church.* Evangelicals continued to embrace the Israel-centered theology as an ad hoc theology, *until it evolved to the point where it dominated evangelical thinking.* The similarities between the first-century's gaslighting a corrupt Israel-tradition with today's popular ad hoc evangelical theology are surprising and unavoidable.

---

45. Mannes, "Why Are Christians So Mean?"

An Israel-Centered Evangelical Theology

Darby's system of theology was novel in the history of the Christian faith; it challenged centuries of Reformation theology and the central beliefs of the church in history.[46] It was not received in America by theologians and theological analysis but by a second tier of evangelical pastors, Bible teachers, and revivalists because of its emphasis on Israel in the end times.[47] The evangelical movement was intensely interested in the modern State of Israel at that time; events taking place in modern Israel were thought to be the fulfillment of biblical prophecy. The Israel-focused system of theology morphed into Christian Zionism in the 1960s. Dispensational theology and a radical Christian Zionism were *Israel-centered, not Christ-centered;* nevertheless, for almost two centuries evangelicals have been subtly gaslighted with the theology primarily because of its eschatology. A Christ-centered theology focuses on a crucified Messiah-Savior and a heavenly kingdom's power; the apostle Paul stated that Christ's cross was "God's power and wisdom."[48] However, an Israel-centered theology focuses on a messiah-king and an earthly Jewish eschatological kingdom. It does not hold *the crucifixion, resurrection of Jesus Christ, and his sending the gift of the Holy Spirit as the mid-point of salvation history, the decisive point of all of God's efforts to provide salvation* with the "already" present, powerful kingdom of God. Therefore, it empties the cross of Christ of its power[49] and confuses the "not yet" kingdom of God with Israel, rather than the revelation of Jesus Christ at his second coming. To expect no harmful results from such a long-standing serious theological error influencing the minds of evangelicals is only wishful thinking.

The surprising similarities of Dispensational theology in the nineteenth century and Christian Zionism in the twentieth century with the first-century corrupt stream of Judaism that plagued Jesus, his disciples, and the early Jewish church *cannot be ignored.*[50] Theological analysis shows that the similarities are not a coincidence; all three theologies maintain:

1. An *Israel-centered theology*

---

46. Pomerville, *New Testament Case*, 10–32.

47. Pomerville, *New Testament Case*, 17–18.

48. 1 Cor 1:17.

49. 1 Cor 1:17.

50. A full account of the theological analysis of Dispensational theology and Christian Zionism vis-à-vis Reformation theology and the New Testament is in my book *New Testament Case against Christian Zionism: A Christian View of the Israeli-Palestinian Conflict.*

2. That Jesus' present spiritual kingdom is viewed as *secondary* to hopes of a restored earthly Jewish kingdom

3. A promotion of Jewish particularism—*separation* of Israel and the church—giving primacy to Jewish ancestry, the temple, its sacrificial system, and "the land" (Palestine)

4. An Israel-identity and Israel-focused gospel that *stifles* the church's mission and its reception in the gentile world

5. A *separate* track of salvation for Israel and the church

6. A belief that Christ *plus* torah-obedience was/is a superior salvation

7. The continued *separation* of Jew and gentile in theological thought, even after Jesus broke down the wall of hatred between Jew and gentile through *his suffering and death on the cross*

8. Belief that Jewish ancestry constitutes the people of God today (even the *unrepentant* modern State of Israel)

9. Belief that God was/is restoring a Jewish earthly kingdom in Palestine

The similarities are not coincidental. They mean that evangelicals tolerate the same Israel-centered theology, the same theological error that was a major problem for the early church—and they continue to do so today. Compromise of *the central role of Jesus Christ as the suffering Messiah-Savior*[51] compromises evangelical spirituality as well as the gospel message.

Dispensational theology has been a popular, long-standing evangelical self-contradiction in the minds of evangelicals that subtly robs Jesus Christ and his cross of their central role in salvation history as well as the Pentecostal and charismatic Christian's belief in the renewal of the Pentecostal experience of the Spirit today. Both are set aside because of the imposition of an extrabiblical system of Israel-focused dispensations on Scripture. If the gaslighting of a corrupt Israel tradition in the early church was a major problem and perverted the gospel, why would evangelicals think *the same influence in their history and same error would not impact them today*? Focus on this historic Israel-centered theology has seriously impacted the personal relationship of some evangelicals with Jesus Christ, affecting their capacity for truth, causing incredible gullibility, and leading them to spiritual decline. A crucified Christ is the unexchangeable center of the Christian faith, but this Israel-centered theology maintains the nation of Israel is central. There is no excuse for gentile Christians today, following the corrupt Israel

---

51. 1 Cor 1:17–18; Rom 1: 16–17; in effect, these verses recognize the importance of a suffering Messiah-Savior and identify Christ crucified as the power and wisdom of the Christian faith—*its theological center.*

tradition found in an Israel-centered Dispensational theology and Christian Zionism. It is a cultural blind spot among evangelicals that affects their view and interpretation of the whole New Testament.

At the peak of Christian Zionism's influence in the 1960s, the Jews for Jesus movement emerged in America.[52] The movement of Jewish Christians resisted the idea of a "Christian" Zionism. If anyone should have responded to a Christian Zionism, it should have been *Jewish Christians*! However, the movement's focus was in the opposite direction; they used Jewish culture *to introduce Jews to Jesus*. They emphasized that Jesus was the Savior-Messiah and the fulfillment of the law of Moses, Jewish culture, and Jewish hope. Jesus was kosher! The movement was extremely successful with their Jesus-focus. They were not deceived by pseudo-"Christian" Zionism precisely *because they were "Christian Jews."* They did not look to evangelical history for their theological guidance (Dispensational theology), but to *the history of the early Jewish church in the New Testament* (biblical theology)! They immediately recognized the gaslighting of a corrupt Judaism in the narrative of the Acts of the Apostles, *contradicting Jesus' gospel of the spiritual kingdom of God—a suffering, crucified Messiah-Savior who gives the gift of the Holy Spirit.* They readily recognized the Judaism-gospel conflict narrative in the New Testament and all its cultural implications, *because they were Jews!* As Christian Jews, they saw the danger of an extreme Israel-focus. Their cultural familiarity with the books of Moses, the prophets, and Israel's sacrificial system assisted them in recognizing Jesus the suffering Savior-Messiah. They also recognized the necessity of the gift of the indwelling Holy Spirit for continuing spiritual life. Due to the extraordinary manifestations of the Spirit in the charismatic movement in all Christian churches in the 1960s, many of the "Jews for Jesus" were charismatic Christians. It was a natural response for Jewish Christians who were familiar with the ancient faith of Israel, knowing the promises of salvation in the prophets involved the promised Holy Spirit; reading the Acts of the Apostles confirmed it. As Jewish Christians, they saw the significance of Stephen's ironic defense in the Acts and could understand the effect of six hundred years of gaslighting on the first-century generation of Jews. *Because they were Jews*, they could understand and empathize with the slow realization of Jewish Christians in accepting Christian identity apart from torah-life and fighting other Jews who claimed to be Christians but were influenced by a corrupt Judaism.

The biblical gaslighting examples presented in this chapter are relevant today. They suggest that many evangelicals have been gaslighted, not just by Donald Trump but by evangelical history and its Israel-centered

---

52. Pomerville, *New Testament Case*, 145–50.

Dispensational theology. Many have engaged in a self-deception, allowing a personal erosion of the truth of the gospel to take place until their capacity for truth has been compromised, leading them to follow a sociopath that cares nothing for American or biblical values and faith. *Evangelicals must ask themselves if a historic "Israel extremism" has become a shroud on the centrality of Jesus Christ and his cross and has resulted in an erosion of their evangelical faith and spirituality.* Has the long history of evangelicals holding to Dispensational theology that deprived Jesus and his cross of their central role *now deprived them of his central role in their hearts?* It is the view of both psychology and Christian theology that America was significantly impacted by the gaslighting of Donald Trump; some evangelicals did not see him coming and were susceptible, due to their loss of Jesus-focus.[53] Evangelical involvement in the deception and seduction of the Republican party unleashed a powerful partisan cultural dynamic and depraved president that caused many to accept Trump's anti-American, antidemocratic reality, compromising their evangelical faith in the process. Many failed to apply the truth of the gospel revealed in Jesus' teachings to their politics and assessment of Donald Trump, not taking the apostle Paul's warning and encouragement to heart: "Be on your guard; stand firm in the faith; be courageous; be strong. Do everything in love."[54] *Evangelicals should have seen him coming.* What psychologists have argued is true: The self-deception of narcissistic evangelicals (a biblical oxymoron) has taken place, because they liked what they heard Trump say. Many made their choice and gave their political allegiance to an immoral, lawless, psychopathic liar, a deranged sociopath; this only strengthens the argument that their narcissism led to self-deception and the disablement of their capacity for truth.

The prophet Isaiah observed Israel in their self-deception saying, "Give us no more visions of what is right! Tell us pleasant things, prophesy illusions."[55] The psalmist warned, "How long will you love delusions and seek lies?"[56] The apostle Paul speaks of those who "refused to love the truth," so God sent them "a powerful delusion that they would believe a lie."[57] There is a reason why Fox News has the highest ratings of editorial news outlets— it responds to the appetites of narcissistic Americans, telling them what they

---

53. A similar loss of Jesus-focus was found among Jewish Christians in Rome; see Heb 2:9; 3:1; 4:14; 7:22; 10:10, 19–22; 12:2, and 13:15.

54. 1 Cor 16:13.

55. Isa 30:10.

56. Ps 4:2b; variant translation in NIV.

57. 2 Thess 2:10–16.

want to hear.[58] Fox News is the center for knowingly propagating Trump's lies, misinformation, disinformation, and conspiracy theories for ratings.[59] A narcissistic society is comfortable with Trump's Big Lie and his antidemocratic reality. In its high ratings, Fox News represents what a sick narcissistic society wants to hear; 61 percent of white evangelicals watch the Trump propaganda center;[60] it is like a magnet, drawing narcissistic Americans and evangelicals who hear exactly what they want to hear. Fox News supports Trump's gaslighting, repeating his bold, audacious, over-the-top absurdist reality, and the lies entertain Americans.[61] In the Roman Coliseum, where ferocious animals tore apart human beings, it also was a popular forum in Roman society, Christians were not in the stands; they were *in the arena*. The downside for many evangelicals today is that Fox News has contributed toward their suspending Christian belief and the guidance of the Scriptures in their political lives, replacing indispensable biblical standards with the pathological absurd reality of a sociopath.

The next chapter reveals the time when evangelicals and all Americans should have seen Donald Trump coming; it shows the way a sociopath tyrant president reacted to the onset of a highly contagious, deadly coronavirus. *He gaslighted Americans!* In the early months of the spread of the virus, Trump said that it was harmless and began a gaslighting campaign, saying there was nothing to worry about. He intentionally contradicted public health experts and delayed a professional emergency response by politicizing the virus and sabotaging efforts to interdict it, to protect his "re-election image" while the virus ravaged America and quickly turned into a pandemic that resulted in the unnecessary deaths of hundreds of thousands of Americans.

58. Froomkin, "Fox News Isn't News."

59. Leonnig and Rucker, *I Alone Can Fix It*, 203–4; Bump, "Unique Role of Fox News"; Lahut, "We Watched Tucker Carlson's"; Rossi, "2 Longtime Fox News Contributors"; Taylor, "Bret Baier and Chris Wallace Complained"; Skolnik, "'Throw a Fake'"; Collier, "Gene Therapy: Fox Is Getting"; Baragona, "Kevin McCarthy Promises"; Stelter, "Fox Stays Silent"; Whitney, "Commentary: Private Texts Confirm"; Howe, "'Journalistic Scandal'"; Durkee, "Here Are the Most Explosive Comments."

60. Burge, "Faith in Numbers."

61. Rom 1:32; 1 Cor 13:6.

PART III

Fascism American Style

Chapter 8

A Fascist Tyrant's Reaction to a Deadly Pandemic—Gaslighting Americans

"Alex, testing is killing me; it's going to lose me the election. If you test, the number of COVID-19 infections increase!"

SOCIOPATH DONALD TRUMP[1]

"I will sound the alarm in any case of disorder or emergency."

US ARMED FORCES GENERAL ORDERS, NUMBER THREE

THE COVID-19 PANDEMIC DESCENDED upon America in the last year of Donald Trump's presidency. The malignant narcissistic sociopath had been gaslighting America from a position of presidential power for three years and it resulted in a chaotic, toxic White House.[2] His response to the deadly virus? He gaslighted Americans! He was not alone in his gaslighting at the arrival of the COVID-19 virus; other malignant narcissists had attached themselves to Donald Trump along with most Republican congressional sycophants that were wholly focused on maintaining their jobs and staying connected with presidential power.[3] Then, of course, there was Trump's dangerous fanatical base of "true believers" that he wielded like a weapon, intimidating whoever did not do what he wanted. All in this "toxic triangle of Trumpism" joined together in proclaiming Trump's twisted, absurdist

1. Leonnig and Rucker, *I Alone Can Fix It*, 85.
2. Leonnig and Rucker, *I Alone Can Fix It*, 1, 7, 33.
3. DeVega, "Trump and His Regime."

reality to a narcissistic society. *There could not have been a worse time for a pandemic to hit America.*

Michelle Obama accurately summed up Donald Trump's presidency when she said: "Being president doesn't change who you are, it reveals who you are."[4] The pressures of the COVID-19 pandemic on Trump revealed who he was repeatedly: a gaslighting, malignant narcissistic sociopath focused solely on his reelection, even when a deadly virus was claiming the lives of hundreds of thousands of Americans. His response was to tell more lies. Sociopath Trump was devoid of empathy during this carnage, continuing to lie and deceive Americans about the COVID-19 virus. Christians should have noticed.[5] The one personality trait that defines Donald Trump *is deception.* It was the main strategy of his presidency. As "Deceiver in Chief" and saboteur of democracy, his purpose was to gaslight Americans about the volatility of the coronavirus that happened on his watch; he had to maintain an image of electability for a second term.[6] However, the pandemic crisis revealed the evil pathological personality behind the sociopath's gaslighting; he just did not care about the carnage. This is the fourth chapter emphasizing Donald Trump's extraordinary method of deception—gaslighting. This repetition is intentional. Gaslighting is used by fascists, abusers, and cult leaders to steal others' reality. Fascists use mass violence to stay in power. Fascist Trump was no different—he employed gaslighting during a deadly pandemic that resulted in massive loss of life; *it was fascism "American style."*

The sociopath tyrant was obsessed with only one thing in his last catastrophic year as president: *winning the upcoming presidential election in November of 2020.*[7] Unfortunately, the COVID-19 virus descended on America in the beginning of that year. The election was not just a "distraction" for Trump, it was a single overwhelming obsession dominating his thinking. All issues, including a deadly pandemic, passed through that election filter. The desperate fascist tyrant would do anything to win the election and remain in power; he would not let the COVID-19 crisis interfere with his goal. Trump knew that the virus claiming American lives during his presidency would make him look bad, weak, and not like the strongman dictator he aspired to be. After contracting the virus, when he was barely able to breath and stand on his own, he acted out his White House balcony Il Duce posturing scene for his base, ripping off his mask so that they would see him as the strongman. His denial that the virus was deadly, his urgent

4. Paz, "Full Transcript of Michelle Obama's."

5. Heb 10:16; John 14:16.

6. ABC Staff, "2020 Election COVID Effort."

7. Leonnig and Rucker, *I Alone Can Fix It*, 33.

and dangerous rush for a vaccine before the election, and his advocacy of bizarre "cures" for the virus showed that he was not concerned with saving American lives—it was the reckless rush of a sociopath to preserve an electable image at any cost. Therefore, with the 2020 election dominating his and his toxic White House's attention, *he and his narcissistic sycophants conspired to politicize the deadly virus and gaslight the American people about it.* Trump not only lied about the coronavirus, saying it was harmless and would just go away, he intentionally implemented his five-step gaslighting strategy, streaming lies and deception with the goal of *changing the reality of the deadly virus in the eyes of Americans, challenging public health measures, and declaring war on science itself.*

AN APT ANALOGY: FAILING TO REACT TO IMMINENT DANGER

The surprise attack at Pearl Harbor was an unforgettable disaster in the history of the United States. It is an apt analogy illustrating the tragedy of Donald Trump's failure to react appropriately to the imminent danger of the COVID-19 virus. The Pearl Harbor attack involved warnings that were not heeded and a neglect that was not characteristic of a professional US military defending an American navy base in the middle of the Pacific Ocean. There also had been warnings of war with Japan at the highest level of the military that were not expeditiously communicated to the Pearl Harbor Navy Base as well as high-level faulty intelligence decisions. In addition to these high-level failures of government, there were actual alert warnings to the military that went unheeded on Oahu and off shore on December 7, *one hour before the arrival of Japanese planes.* The warnings were neglected; they did not reflect a US military response with a professional edge. Had there been such a professional response, it would have significantly changed the story of the Pearl Harbor attack and history itself. A failed professional response to imminent danger also characterized Trump and his administration's response to the COVID-19 pandemic, bringing a disastrous loss of American lives.

At 1300 EST mainland time (0632 PST) Hawaii time, one hour before the bombing, the leadership of the US Army in Washington, DC, was convinced that the Japanese Empire would attack Pearl Harbor. However, due to a jumble of errors, navy radio communications was not used; rather, the warning was sent *via telegram that arrived six days after the attack*! Disregarding warnings and an uncharacteristic lack of a professional edge to an impending disaster led to my linking the Pearl Harbor attack, that destroyed

America's Pacific Fleet with a loss of two thousand, four hundred lives, to the COVID-19 pandemic.

Early warnings concerning the dangers of the virus should have put America on a war footing to deal with a pandemic, but Trump intentionally ignored the warnings. Trump's reaction to the COVID-19 virus was far from being proportionate with the danger it posed for Americans; his bumbling response demonstrated an even greater jumble of errors, cavalier attitudes, and lack of professionalism than the Pearl Harbor attack. In fact, Donald Trump's reaction to the pandemic included intentional, counterproductive, and negative actions that made it a much greater disaster than Pearl Harbor. President Franklin Roosevelt called the Japanese surprise attack at Pearl Harbor "December 7, 1941—a date which will live in infamy." Donald Trump's failure to respond to the COVID-19 virus with a professional edge will live in infamy, because more people died in the pandemic than in *all the military casualties of World War II*. A sociopath president focused on himself and winning the next election instead of the dangers the virus held for Americans.[8]

Of course, the Pearl Harbor attack took place during peacetime on an early Sunday morning at a naval base in the middle of the Pacific Ocean where a sense of readiness, a professional edge, usually prevailed in the US Armed Forces; it is part of their core values as an institution sworn to protect the nation, and those values permeate the Armed Forces at every level. There are written orders requiring a professional edge even at the low level of military sentry duty. There are "eleven general orders" that sentries commit to memory to fulfill their duty even in peacetime: to always be alert, reporting danger, safeguarding lives and property, and giving alarm. There were two US Navy-related incidents that should have spread the alarm and alerted the Pearl Harbor base. A minesweeper, the USS Condor, spotted a mini Japanese submarine at the entrance of the harbor at 0342 hours; they alerted the destroyer USS Ward, which resulted in the Ward sinking *another* Japanese mini submarine outside the harbor at 0637 hours. In addition, the US Army security force on the island of Oahu had the responsibility for defending the naval base but did not demonstrate a professional edge in responding to a radar warning *one hour prior to the attack*. In November of 1941, there were navy maneuvers off Oahu in which a simulated air attack on the base was enacted, and the radar system was used and worked perfectly.[9] Although radar was a new technology and was not supposed to

8. Wikipedia, "United States Military Casualties"; a year after Trump's presidency, the casualties from COVID-19 approached *one million* Americans dead.

9. Wikipedia, "Radar Warning of Pearl Harbor."

be in operation on that fateful Sunday morning; at 0702 hours a new radar operator was learning to use the scope and saw a "large haze" on the scope, indicating a large number of aircraft[10] approaching Pearl Harbor from the north. This warning was confirmed by an operator more senior, and he reported it to the Aircraft Warning Information Center, to a new second lieutenant who had no experience with radar. He told the radar operator that he would check it out. He called back, telling the operator not to worry about it, because there was a "flight of B-17s" (bombers) that was coming from the mainland. So, the radar operators shut down the radar station and went to breakfast. The incidents and warnings were sufficient to put the base on alert prior to the impending "surprise attack," but they did not produce the alarm they should have; a lack of professional edge caused by a lackadaisical mindset snuffed out the urgency of the warnings. The bombs started falling at 0748 hours.[11]

Several what-ifs need to be added to the Pearl Harbor disaster to show how much worse Donald Trump's unprofessional, deceptive reaction was to the COVID-19 pandemic. Of course, those failing to respond with a professional edge in the Pearl Harbor attack were neglectful, not responding as they should have, but *none of their actions or inaction was intentional in the face of a known danger*. What if there had been military personnel that knowingly gave false information about the attack, intentionally preventing an alarm? What if there had been saboteurs that destroyed key defense capabilities such as the Aircraft Warning Information Center, the radar stations, and base communications prior to the attack? What if there had been personnel that conspired to facilitate and abet the attack by communicating "targeting information" for the enemy planes? What if there had been those who spread propaganda, false information, to give a sense of safety when they knew there was danger and a deadly attack was imminent? What if there had been subversive elements that wanted to see the American government fall, not concerned with American casualties, and conspired with others for personal gain and power? All of these what-ifs appear absurd and unthinkable, especially considering intentional seditious and traitorous acts in the context of the Pearl Harbor surprise attack, *but all the what-if acts describe exactly how sociopath Donald Trump and his White House responded to the arrival of the deadly COVID-19 virus and the pandemic that followed.* They intentionally gaslighted Americans about the virus and pandemic, making it decidedly worse, until hospital beds across the country were full and staff

10. Later in the day, calculations determined the "large haze" represented approximately 180 aircraft.

11. Wikipedia, "Radar Warning of Pearl Harbor."

were unable to manage the dead bodies of those who died from the virus. What kind of person would deliberately lie and deceive, engaging in such treacherous acts in the face of imminent danger? Only an enemy, the kind of man that would incite a violent insurrection on the Capitol of the United States to overthrow a democratic election to remain in power—narcissistic sociopath fascist Donald J. Trump.

DONALD TRUMP GASLIGHTING DURING A PANDEMIC?

President Donald Trump's manic reaction to the deadly COVID-19 pandemic should have revealed to everyone that he was unlike any other president. He responded to the deadly virus without empathy and with the unthinkable response of gaslighting and deceiving Americans so he could be reelected. His pathological behavior, ignorance, and lies about the COVID-19 virus were not done in a corner, but in the naked light of day for all to see daily on television—while the death toll was mounting. The excuse for his dereliction in the face of the pandemic offered by some—"He's just an odd guy, not a politician type"—does not cut it. His gaslighting failed to get him the election image he wanted; the impact of the pandemic on America was too great, and he lost the election. A year after leaving office, with nearly one million dead from the COVID-19 virus in America, Trump shifted his gaslighting from the virus to a continuous stream of lies that he did not lose the election; yet Americans still followed him, not missing a beat, continuing to believe whatever he claimed.

As though the delusional stolen election claim was normal, Trump was discussed in a gaslighted media, in a sycophant Republican Congress, and in the public forum as though he were just like any other ex-president, with no mention of his delusional, delayed, and demented response to the pandemic. Was it because his gaslighting about the pandemic was so successful, or was it mindless "politically correct" restraint that caused almost everyone to avoid mentioning an ex-president's mismanagement of the pandemic and the numerous examples of his pathological personality disorders in doing so? Donald Trump was, and still is, a malignant narcissistic sociopath, but no one mentions it or acts like it. Society ignores his continuous alternate reality about having won the election, "normalizing" him when there is nothing normal about Donald Trump or his disastrous presidency. Small demonstrations of sanity, like kicking him off social media sites because of a delusional Big Lie, a variety of state and federal investigations into his crimes, and a damning investigation into his incitement of an insurrection at the Capitol, revealed that Trump's blanket of delusion did not affect everyone. However, the Trump normalizing phenomenon is widespread in narcissistic America, indicating that his gaslighting *has penetrated deeper into the American psyche than anyone thought possible.*

Gaslighting: Changing Pandemic Reality

The intentional implementation of a strategy to deceive Americans about the reality of a deadly virus is evidence of the mental derangement and diabolical nature of Donald Trump. It is the same gaslighting strategy that he used in his presidential election campaign and repeatedly in his presidency. *Gaslighting is the signature of a narcissistic sociopath fascist tyrant.* Trump's five-step strategy became prominent again in his last year in office when the COVID-19 virus appeared, during the pandemic, and even after he lost the 2020 election. The gaslighting steps were step one: stake a claim; step two: advance and deny; step three: create suspense; step four: discredit opponents; step five: win. A difference in implementing the strategy in his last year was that Trump's pathological personality disorders became worse under the pressure of a silent, rapidly spreading COVID-19 virus; his lies could not keep up with the spread of the virus and its impact on society. However, the emergence of an unknown deadly virus fit the circumstances for launching step one: stake a claim—that the virus was harmless. No one knew anything about it; the virus was new and unknown to the scientific community, invisible and airborne; therefore, Trump could make the bold and bizarre claim that it was harmless—this was what people wanted to hear. They might think, Maybe it's true. In the beginning Trump pressed the narrative that the virus was like the flu and not dangerous. After three years of autocratic fascist rule, firing those who opposed him, creating an atmosphere of fear, and with a grandiose view of himself, Trump took full charge of managing the virus—despite his ignorance. It was clearly the domain and responsibility of virologists, scientists, and public health experts to manage a response to the deadly virus. Nevertheless, Trump and the White House took control of the COVID-19 virus, giving his political aides authority over the medical and public health experts so they could control the narrative of the coronavirus and freely politicize it. In Trump's devious mind, having control of the virus narrative meant that he could move on to step two: advance and deny, vacillating on virus issues like testing, the necessity for public vaccination, safe vaccine production, and public health measures that were necessary (masks, social distancing, washing hands); this allowed for the ping-pong back and forth of advance and deny. At the same time, he advanced ridiculous bogus cures and did not wear a mask himself, causing confusion among Americans, delaying the crucial initial response to the spreading virus.

Public confusion over advance and deny efforts and a mounting death toll led to step three: create suspense, when there was such a need for solid health information on an unknown virus; instead, *Trump put a continuous question mark on the virus.* The pathological narcissist imposed himself on the scientific discussions of doctors, virologists, and public health experts, sharing his ignorance and contradicting the experts. He presided over press conferences monitoring experts reporting on the virus, and his staff closely monitored the Centers for Disease Control and Prevention's (CDC) announcements by the virologist experts, contradicting them publicly.[12] Trump's absurd resistance to the doctors and experts—due to his narcissistic, grandiose view of himself—accelerated when the scientific experts insisted on following "time-consuming" scientific procedures and protocols for safe vaccine production *that did not fit Trump's election timetable.* Malignant narcissist Trump's battle with science continued throughout the year, even after he and his family became infected.

Necessary vaccine development delays were the occasion for Trump to completely sideline the experts, bringing him to step four: discredit opponents—discrediting not just the doctors, virologists, and public health officials but the few "adults" in the room from his staff who tried to keep him from making disastrous decisions in interdicting the virus. Of course, his pathological, grandiose arrogance made it easy for him to confront experts publicly, boldly, and with a straight face as he discredited them. This made it difficult for the virologists and experts to go against the president. Trump discrediting them opened a can of worms for conspiracy theorists and sycophants to get his attention, claiming "special knowledge" without having appropriate scientific credentials (*other* malignant narcissists) to jump in adding to the confusion. To succeed, they only had to be the last person to speak to him. The clueless president leaned on his go-to media source, Fox News hosts, who were also pushing conspiracy theories about the virus. With the variety and cascade of misinformation from so many sources, people did not know what to believe. From the beginning of the COVID-19 virus, Fox News switched from an opinion media organization to supporting and promoting conspiracy theories.[13] An ignorant narcissistic president politicizing the COVID-19 crisis not only prevented the scientific community from dealing with the virus on a war-footing, but all

12. Leonnig and Rucker, *I Alone Can Fix It,* 5.

13. Hayes, "Levitz: 'Fox News Is Literally Killing"; Acosta, "'This Is Not Going to End Well"; Melber, "Fox News Lies Debunked."

of the above politicizing actions *unnecessarily delayed scientific progress for months in getting fundamental COVID-19 safety prevention issues in place to interdict the virus.*[14] Trump and his chaotic White House's mismanagement of the new COVID-19 virus then faced a *pandemic, and it was too late to prevent a rapidly multiplying American death toll.*

The last step, step five: win—declaring victory whatever the outcome—of course did not mean that Trump won over the COVID-19 virus; instead, the virus entered the rapidly spreading pandemic stage. Trump's arrogance and grandiose self-assertion drove him to take charge, making control of the virus impossible; his delays, misinformation, and ignorance in defying the virus experts and sidelining them, politicizing vaccine production to co-incide with his election plans, added up to outright sabotage[15] that resulted in an increased virus death toll.[16] Since the beginning of the COVID-19 virus (December 2019), 876,636 American lives have been lost, with millions more having been infected, and COVID-19 variants were multiplying in the American population. In this dark period, Donald Trump *claimed victory* for the quick production of a vaccine—a final absurdity and display of no empathy to cap a sociopath president's bumbling delusional reaction to the COVID-19 virus and pandemic.

A CHAOTIC CHRONOLOGY: POLITICIZING THE PANDEMIC

I do not attempt a complete chronology of the COVID-19 pandemic; rather I single out dates and incidents that show Trump's politicizing the virus, mismanaging it, and sabotaging it. In his personality disordered pathological arrogance, Trump took a "public health issue" from doctors of virology and public health experts and politicized it, slowing the nation's management of a deadly pandemic; his pathological arrogance resulted in the unnecessary carnage of American lives. The first part of the chronology covers steps one to three of Trump's five-step gaslighting strategy that took place during the crucial early months of detecting the virus when there was a chance of containing it. Step three: create suspense starts early on and continues through 2020 to the end of Donald Trump's presidency. The full-blown politicization of the virus by the White House begins with step four: discredit opponents,

---

14. Weixel and Choi, "Health Care—Trump Staffers Interfered."

15. Saletan, "Evidence of Trump's Pandemic Sabotage."

16. Fung, "Birx Estimates Trump Administration;" Luscombe, "NIH Director Francis Collins."

as Trump and his toxic administration sideline the medical experts and virologists and the White House takes over the virus narrative.

December 31, 2019

A curious email arrived in the boxes of ranking officials of the CDC in Atlanta; it was from an outpost in Beijing warning of an "unexplained pneumonia" reported in the port city of Wuhan on the Yangtze River. The scientists at the outpost reported they were trying to learn more. Dr. Robert Redfield, director of the CDC, a virologist and infectious disease physician for decades, was concerned and ordered a "sit-rep" be written, and the next day Redfield briefed a senior staffer at the National Security Council. On January 3, Redfield called his counterpart in China's CDC, Dr. George Fu Gao, questioning him about the Wuhan incident, but Gao was evasive in his answers, saying the pneumonia originated in a marketplace in Wuhan where exotic animals were sold. Redfield said the usually gregarious Gao sounded like a "prisoner talking in some sort of code because someone was listening."[17] Redfield phoned Gao again and told him that he should look for cases beyond the radius of the marketplace; when he did, Gao found hundreds of cases with no link to the market. Finally, Gao broke down on the phone and told Redfield, "We may be too late" (to stop the spread). On January 6, Redfield sent a formal request to China's Department of Health asking about the virus; he received no reply. Later, Redfield found out that a week before his January 3 call to Gao, the Chinese Department of Health had significant anecdotal evidence of human-to-human transmission.[18]

Over several days, Redfield called Dr. Gao, asking specific questions about his cases, and discussed the information with Dr. Fauci; they concluded the information Gao gave them meant that the virus was a natural jump from an infected animal to human, then moving from infected human to human. This question of origins of the virus was Dr. Anthony Fauci's and Dr. Francis Collins's of the National Institutes of Health (NIH) belief from the beginning; they still held it two years later. Fox News's Bret Baier gave a review of the history of the origins of COVID-19, cherry picking an obscure memorandum giving the view of a scientist that believed the virus was created in the Wuhan laboratory. In Fox tradition, Baier continued to promote misinformation about the virus as well as conspiracy theories two years later. In January of 2022, Dr. Collins repeated his anti-lab view on origins of the COVID-19 virus, saying he did not think it was possible to

17. Leonnig and Rucker, *I Alone Can Fix It*, 12–13.
18. Leonnig and Rucker, *I Alone Can Fix It*, 14–16.

create the virus from scratch in a lab.[19] The lab theory of COVID-19 origins was not played down as Fox News insinuated, but it was not Drs. Fauci and Collins's view of origins. It was racist Trump's view. In the same month, Dr. Fauci said that "evidence leans very, very strongly towards COVID-19 being a natural occurrence," like SARS and MERS turned out to be, and that "real card-carrying molecular virologists" feel the same.[20]

Early January 2020

US intelligence agencies had been giving warnings about a novel coronavirus and its contagious spread in the president's daily oral brief at the White House, *but Trump ignored them.* In addition, he rarely read his written briefings. He later claimed that the coronavirus did not rise to his attention in those early days.[21] On January 10, Matthew Pottinger, the White House deputy security advisor, had been monitoring Redfield's reports; he had previously lived through the SARS (severe acute respiratory syndrome) coronavirus outbreak in 2002, covering it from China as a foreign correspondent for the *Wall Street Journal.* He knew the Communist government would try to conceal key information. He told Anthony Ruggiero to have daily National Security Council (NSC) meetings to provide information on the virus, starting January 14, 2020. On January 10, a Shanghai public health clinical center, that cooperated with Wuhan hospitals, published the "genome sequence of the virus," using samples from Wuhan patients; they uploaded it on a publicly available website to share information with medical investigators seeking information about the virus. The Chinese government had told laboratories not to publish any information. When Dr. Anthony Fauci received the news of the genome sequencing of the virus, he called the Virus Research Center and told them to use the Chinese genome sequencing information to begin developing a vaccine.[22] Dr. Fauci and Dr. Francis Collins discussed the lab origins theory and consulted with other experts on the evolution of the virus—both accidently and intentionally—and they ruled it out; *their opinion was that the virus was from nature and its spread was human-to-human.*[23]

19. Leonnig and Rucker, *I Alone Can Fix It,* 13; Korab, "Dr. Fauci Opens Up"; Baier, "New International Documents."

20. Mediaite Staff, "Dr. Fauci Tells Fox News."

21. Leonnig and Rucker, *I Alone Can Fix It,* 19.

22. Leonnig and Rucker, *I Alone Can Fix It,* 20.

23. Leonnig and Rucker, *I Alone Can Fix It,* 20.

January 13, 2020

Fauci and Redfield noted that the COVID-19 virus had spread from Wuhan to Thailand. The first US patient with COVID-19 entered America: A sixty-year-old woman returning from Wuhan who had been taking care of her sick father arrived at Chicago's O'Hare Airport; days later she fell ill with the virus and infected her husband.[24] On January 14, the Chinese health minister announced that the COVID-19 virus was on the way to becoming a pandemic. Mid-January the COVID-19 virus was silently pouring into the US. It was too late to stop the contagion; the cases were spreading asymptomatically.[25]

January 18, 2020

Alex Azar, secretary for health and human services, told Mick Mulvaney, Trump's acting chief of staff, that the COVID-19 virus was a global threat and that he was worried that Trump was not briefed on it. Mulvaney said nothing about notifying the president; subsequently, Mulvaney had the role of a "saboteur" in suppressing a timely professional response to the virus. Azar called the president and warned him, saying, "It's really a big deal." All Trump could do was obsess and rant about Azar's prior warnings about vaping; Azar could not get him off the topic. Trump asked no questions about COVID-19, was peeved, and told Azar he had to go to a ball at Mar-a-Lago; the president hung up the phone.[26] On January 21, the second person known to have the virus, a thirty-five-year-old businessman, entered the United States via Seattle-Tacoma Airport in Washington State after a business trip to the area just outside Wuhan. When reporters asked Trump about the new COVID-19 virus at Davos, Switzerland, during the World Economic Forum, he responded, "Everything's under control."[27] Public health officials could not believe what he said; they were getting information daily about its danger and rapid spread. At the same time, Dr. Francis Collins, director of the NIH, was in Davos for meetings with other leading global infectious disease experts about the coronavirus, persuading them

---

24. Leonnig and Rucker, *I Alone Can Fix It*, 21.

25. Leonnig and Rucker, *I Alone Can Fix It*, 21, 27, 37; "asymptomatically" means people without symptoms spread the virus.

26. Leonnig and Rucker, *I Alone Can Fix It*, 29.

27. Leonnig and Rucker, *I Alone Can Fix It*, 30.

to declare "an international public health emergency," *but the urgency was undercut by what his boss said.*[28]

January 28, 2020

In early January, *Trump knew from his advisors, the CIA, and Matthew Pottinger that COVID-19 was worse than SARS in 2003 and more like the Spanish flu epidemic of 1918 that killed fifty million people.*[29] China admitted on January 28 that they had six thousand cases of COVID-19 and 132 deaths; US officials suspected that the numbers were much higher. Fauci, Collins, and Pottinger were convinced there should be a travel ban on those coming to the United States from Wuhan; they felt the virus was galloping past them and China was holding back information on it. They also agreed to endorse the State Department's plan to fly four more evacuation flights for Americans to leave Wuhan and surrounding areas; the plan included US diplomats and permanent residents, along with protocol to keep them from spreading the virus when they returned. When they presented this to plan to Trump, he asked how many people would be involved, and when they told him hundreds, perhaps a couple thousand, Trump blew up; he did not want to risk "his numbers" (of COVID-19 cases) going up. Trump did not want sick Americans landing on US soil, even if they were working for the State Department, or else the government would have to report a rise in infections and that would make the public—the voters—nervous. The president was always thinking about the political ramifications for himself, even during a national crisis. He was talking about Americans who had gone to China to serve the US government, but he spoke as if they had irresponsibly or illegally crossed into a foreign country! The sociopath president had to be persuaded to allow those serving in government service back into their home country with arguments like: "It would be like leaving a man on the field of battle, and reminding him of his America First mantra (as if their lives mattered to the sociopath), and that refusal would make him look bad."[30] Trump also suggested that Americans who traveled overseas and caught COVID-19 should be sent to *Guantanamo* rather than returning to the United States![31] On the same day, the World Health Organization (WHO) finally declared the coronavirus a global health emergency. At a

28. Leonnig and Rucker, *I Alone Can Fix It*, 31.

29. Leonnig and Rucker, *I Alone Can Fix It*, 32–37.

30. Leonnig and Rucker, *I Alone Can Fix It*, 41–43.

31. Reid, "Authors of New Book Allege."

rally in Warren, Michigan, *Trump lied to a roaring rally crowd, saying that they had nothing to worry about with the COVID-19 virus.*[32]

February 29, 2020

While the rest of the world was calling the COVID-19 virus a pandemic, two crucial months into the COVID-19 crisis, Alex Azar told Vice President Mike Pence (in charge of the Coronavirus Task Force) that the task force needed to start using the word "pandemic" because that was what it was. *Trump refused; he was worried about the markets and reelection.* Nancy Messonnier of the clinical decision support (CDS) gave an accurate warning on television about how a pandemic would impact everyday life in America. The Dow Jones dropped 879 points. Trump was angry with Messonnier, saying, "She's scaring people, this is killing me."[33] For the crucial first two months of the US knowing about the deadly coronavirus, the country was not on a war footing in facing it, but political forces resisted calling the deadly contagious virus for what it was—a pandemic. *This is the reason why the United States, one of the foremost scientifically oriented nations in the world, has the highest death rate of any nation on the globe* (876, 291 COVID-19 deaths),[34] and the runner-up is Brazil, led by a dictator (623,636 COVID-19 deaths); fourth place is Putin's Russia (320,178 COVID-19 deaths).[35]

March 2, 2020

On her first day on the job as White House Coronavirus Response Coordinator, Dr. Deborah Birx was interviewed on MSNBC and stated the deadly coronavirus in the US "now has reached outbreak proportions, and likely pandemic proportions." The interview was followed by an interview with Dr. Anthony Fauci, who said not only was it a pandemic in the US, but "there were multiple sustained transmissions of a highly infectious agent in multiple regions of the globe"—it was a *global pandemic.*[36] Mike Pence was Birx and Fauci's boss and his top aides, Marc Short and Katie Miller, were tasked with silencing alarmism to keep Fauci and other professional health experts from scaring the public. Short and Miller tightly controlled which

32. Leonnig and Rucker, *I Alone Can Fix It*, 44.
33. Leonnig and Rucker, *I Alone Can Fix It*, 61–65.
34. The date of this writing is February 2, 2022.
35. Murphy and Wu, "Map: Track Coronavirus Deaths."
36. Leonnig and Rucker, *I Alone Can Fix It*, 68.

task-force members could speak to the media; Miller was a narcissistic fanatic in protecting Trump and sidelining experts of the COVID-19 virus, but she was not the only one.[37] The White House politicians handling the virus response focused on Trump's reelection, not the virus's deadly impact on Americans. When the subject of a timeline for the development of a vaccine emerged in a discussion with pharmaceutical executives, Trump asked, "So you're talking over the next few months, you think you can have a vaccine?" Dr. Fauci interjected, telling him that he would have a vaccine in a few months, but "like I've been telling you, Mr. President," it would be "a year to a year and a half" until the vaccine could be injected safely into someone's arm. It was clear that Trump did not understand how vaccines were developed, tested, approved, and then injected; he was also clueless about the time involved. He shrugged off the information, saying, "*I like the sounds of a couple of months better.*"[38]

The End of March 2020

Three months into the COVID-19 crisis in America, Fauci and others said that the virus was airborne, spreading even asymptomatically, and requested that mask use should be announced! When the virus dominated the news cycles, *"take-charge Trump" started attending the Coronavirus Task Force Meetings not wearing a mask, making trivial and ignorant observations.* Trump was against the public health measure of testing that would determine the seriousness of the COVID virus and provide tracking information. He told Alex Azar, "Testing is killing me; it's going to lose me the election." If you test, the number of COVID-19 infections increase![39] Trump said, "CDC should never have done this" (testing). In seven weeks the US tested only eleven thousand Americans, while South Korea tested twenty thousand a day.[40] Trump complained about Federal Drug Administration guidance, saying, "The scientists wanted him to fail,"[41] as though testing was all about Trump and not science and the safety of Americans. It is important to note that in Trump's sabotaging the implementation of measures that would slow the spread of the virus, he was assisted by other malignant narcissists on his

---

37. Leonnig and Rucker, *I Alone Can Fix It*, 71.

38. Leonnig and Rucker, *I Alone Can Fix It*, 69–70.

39. Leonnig and Rucker, *I Alone Can Fix It*, 201.

40. Leonnig and Rucker, *I Alone Can Fix It*, 83–86.

41. Leonnig and Rucker, *I Alone Can Fix It*, 284.

staff: Peter Navarro, Mick Mulvaney, Mark Meadows, Scott Atlas, and Katie Miller, to mention a few obvious cases.[42]

This second part of the COVID-19 chronology covers steps four to five of Trump's gaslighting plan. Trump and the White House politicians overruling the virologists and public experts amounted to sabotaging interdiction of the virus at crucial points and the political resistance turning into an "anti-science movement," both in the White House and in the public arena. Important issues arose such as a travel ban from Europe and cruise ship operations. *The virologists* said that cruise ship operations should be shut down, because they were "floating COVID cities," but *the politicians* made the decision to continue because they said shutting operations down would ruin the economy. Trump's reason for allowing them to continue was clear—his reelection.[43] *Mounting deaths due to the virus did not stop the politicians' resistance to the virologists and public health experts' advice, because that was not their priority—preserving Donald Trump's electable image was.* Mike Pence, the head of the task force, refused Redfield's suggestion that a sail ban remain on cruise ships until February 2021. Redfield was going to resign over the issue; however, he came up with a conditional sail order that would allow cruise ships to begin a return to sailing in phases, with a drastically limited number of passengers and with firm social distancing, testing, and quarantine rules.[44] Redfield won on this occasion, but cruise ships as super-spreaders of the virus continued into the second year of the coronavirus, even after the COVID-19 vaccine was available.[45]

April 2020

COVID-19 deaths reached thirty thousand. Finding a pre-election scapegoat was important, so sociopath Trump employed his favorite tactic of "projection" to divert attention from his failure to protect the American people to someone else; he chose the *WHO and China*. Being a pathological liar also helped this gaslighting effort. Trump's scapegoat hunt, and subsequent focus on them, released tons of misinformation, disinformation, and conspiracy theories that in 2023 are still in the public mind. The China scapegoat—Trump's focus on calling COVID-19 "the Asian-virus/

42. Leonnig and Rucker, *I Alone Can Fix It*, 71, 77–79, 99, 110, 129, 218–19, 228, 229–30, 275.

43. Leonnig and Rucker, *I Alone Can Fix It*, 77–81.

44. Leonnig and Rucker, *I Alone Can Fix It*, 285–87.

45. McCormick, "'Not the Cruise I Signed Up For.'"

China-virus"—turned into a deadly racist reaction from Trump's "crazy-base," as they are assaulting and killing Asian-Americans.[46]

May 20, 2020

The United Kingdom developed the first COVID-19 vaccination with As-traZeneca at Oxford University. Trump's response to the worldwide break-through was that it was a terrible development: A British company was first with a vaccine! He told Azar, "No press; I'm going to get killed" (at the election). Hicks, Kushner, and Scavino said it was great news and asked the sociopath why he yelled at Azar for reporting it.[47] On May 28, coronavi-rus deaths in the US reached one hundred thousand. Just a few days prior, Trump had said, "Within a couple of days it's going to be down to zero"; the next day he said, "It's going disappear one day—it's like a miracle—it will disappear."[48] Five months into the coronavirus crisis, Trump made these statements! He also said that it would never reach one hundred thousand deaths. Michael Gerson, George Bush's speechwriter, said in an interview with the *Washington Post*'s Ashley Parker, "There's maybe a fundamental problem here in the ability [of Trump] to feel and express empathy, and that's a serious problem in the aftermath of loss of life and a kind of crisis that involves the loss of American lives."[49] Gerson's comment appears to be the understatement of the year, a tendency of politicians to understate er-rors when referencing a US president.

In their book *I Alone Can Fix It*, Leonnig and Rucker do not use the term "sociopath," but opt for using the term "transactional" for Trump's lack of feelings behind his decisions and behavior. However, it can be mislead-ing, implying that he may be just a cagey businessman, "crazy like a fox." A brief review of typical characteristics of Trump's personality disorders clearly show his uncanny fit as a sociopath; he (1) is incapable of under-standing and responding in an empathic way to how others feel; (2) has not developed respect for the thinking of others, relationships, or efforts, not valuing the accomplishments of others; (3) has no appreciation for orga-nizations, government structures, conventional practices, and laws; (4) has a monomania of sorts, a me-orientation; (5) and has a limited capacity to distinguish the real from the wished for or imagined, and because of this

46. Leng, "Violence against Asian Americans"; Ruiz et al., "One-Third of Asian Americans"; Avlon, "Why Anti-Asian American Violence."

47. Leonnig and Rucker, *I Alone Can Fix It*, 143–44.

48 Leonnig and Rucker, *I Alone Can Fix It*, 152.

49. Leonnig and Rucker, *I Alone Can Fix It*, 151.

demonstrates a ready willingness to distort the truth. *These all point to a "crazy like crazy" sociopath.*[50]

July 11, 2020

Donald Trump and his White House aides started a campaign to discredit and sideline Dr. Anthony Fauci, the nation's leading infectious disease expert and most trusted spokesman for the federal government's pandemic response.[51] The next day, Dan Scavino, White House communications director—like another infamous minister of communication in Germany—posted a cartoon on Facebook mocking Fauci: It was of "Dr. Faucet," with a Pinocchio-like nose, saying, "Indefinite lockdown, schools stay closed this Fall . . . Shut-up and obey."[52] Typical Joseph Goebbels Nazi-style propaganda went unnoticed in the Trump White House. The discrediting of the experts by fascist Trump and his White House was the beginning of the anti-vax/anti-science movement in the US that continues to plague America two years later. A few days later, one of the White House's other unqualified malignant narcissists, Peter Navarro—an economist—attacked Fauci, saying, "You've got blood on your hands." He published an op-ed in *USA Today* headlined "Anthony Fauci Has Been Wrong about Everything I Have Interacted with Him On."[53] Leonnig and Rucker said, "The Fauci-bashing underscored Trump's hostility toward medical expertise and produced a chilling effect among government scientists and public health professionals. Most importantly, it hampered the nation's efforts to combat the virus at the very moment it was spreading wildly across the Sun Belt."[54]

Early September 2020

Trump and his aides pulled the plug on regular virus briefings, blocked many media appearances for Fauci and other health experts, and carried on normal campaigning and governing. Trump all but abdicated responsibility for ending the pandemic.[55] Leonnig and Rucker state:

50. Covitz, "Health, Risk, and the Duty," §3744–56; Wehner, "Trump Is Obsessed."
51. Leonnig and Rucker, *I Alone Can Fix It*, 217.
52. Leonnig and Rucker, *I Alone Can Fix It*, 217.
53. Leonnig and Rucker, *I Alone Can Fix It*, 217. 18.
54. Leonnig and Rucker, *I Alone Can Fix It*, 217. 18.
55. Leonnig and Rucker, *I Alone Can Fix It*, 257.

Starting in June, as Redfield conferred with congressional ap-
propriators about growing the Center for Disease Control [*sic*]
(CDC) budget with supplemental funds, Meadows proactively
stepped into the budget discussions to say the White House objected. Redfield learned from a legislative aide that at Meadows's
direction the White House's legislative affairs staff dive-bombed
a negotiated increase for the CDC's budget. Meadows just took
the money out, the aide told Redfield.[56]

When requests for funding the distribution of the vaccine and other virus-
mitigating equipment went unheeded from the beginning of the onset of
the coronavirus, Meadows was the "chief saboteur" of funding for CDC,
especially when it came to the last mile effort that provided for infrastructure to distribute the vaccines when they would be available to the states.
The plans for this last mile effort were made early in January 2021, but there
was no money for distribution mechanisms for the states. On September
16, Redfield met with senators, asking for six billion dollars for the last mile
effort, but when Senator Murray asked about the state of the CDC budget, Redfield revealed that the Trump administration had transferred three
hundred million dollars from the CDC to the Department of Health and
Human Services's public affairs office. Almost all that money was slated to
be used for a public relations campaign to defeat despair and inspire hope
ahead of the elections.[57]

Redfield informed the senators "about gaps in the country's public
health system to handle this [distribution of vaccines] wartime endeavor"[58]
of the last mile. "By September, Redfield could no longer be silent. He took
a public stand. First, he had a series of private calls with Blunt and Murray
to tell them time was running out and the whole country was in trouble if
the CDC didn't snag emergency funds in the billions of dollars."[59] Concerning when the vaccine would be available for distribution, Trump lied, stating, "100 million doses would be distributed at the end of 2020"—around
election time. Redfield contradicted him, stating the one hundred million
doses would be distributed mid-2021. Noting the discrepancy, reporters
mentioned this to Trump; he said that Redfield, who had been planning
the last mile for months, might not have had all the facts. Trump's efforts
to overrule, contradict, and discredit the public health experts was again
assisted by Mark Meadows, as he told hosts of *Fox & Friends* that "he didn't

56. Leonnig and Rucker, *I Alone Can Fix It*, 271–74.
57. Leonnig and Rucker, *I Alone Can Fix It*, 271–74.
58. Leonnig and Rucker, *I Alone Can Fix It*, 272.
59. Leonnig and Rucker, *I Alone Can Fix It*, 273.

know where Redfield [the CDC director] got his timetable, but it was not based on those who were closest to the process."[60]

October 1, 2020

Trump and his complicit White House's efforts to have the vaccine before the election was impossible. He contracted the virus before the election, ten months into the coronavirus crisis and pandemic. Contracting the virus himself did not stop his anti-virus antics, misinformation, and childlike macho demonstrations. Hope Hicks contracted the virus around noon-time, but Trump and Meadows wanted the news hidden from the public because Trump planned to take a New Jersey trip to raise five million dollars for his reelection. His traveling violated the White House protocol that anyone in close contact with a virus-infected person confirmed positive would be isolated for forty-eight hours. Trump went on the trip anyway, and the meeting was in indoors with donors. Then he continued to New York where he proclaimed, "I just want to say that the end of the pandemic is in sight." Eight hours later, Trump revealed via Twitter that he and Melania had COVID-19.[61] On the morning of October 2, Trump was in bad shape; both Dr. Sean P. Conley, Trump's physician, and Redfield knew that Trump could quickly deteriorate and die. Trump was advanced in age, was overweight, had high blood pressure, and had hardening of the arteries in his heart. He was immediately given supplemental oxygen because his SpO2 readings were low, and aggressive treatment had to be implemented: "experimental yet promising treatments, including a single eight-gram dose of Regeneron's cocktail of two monoclonal antibodies which was in experimental stage were given to him. In the evening he was given Gilead Sciences's Remdesivir and the next day dexamethasone, a steroid for serious cases."[62] *It appears Trump received world-class triage that saved his life.* He resisted being hospitalized, because it would make him look weak. At 6:00 p.m., Trump was hospitalized; he was flown via helicopter to Walter Reed Medical Center to occupy the presidential suite. Dr. Conley could only report information that Trump authorized about his condition, therefore he lied about Trump's condition throughout his stay at Walter Reed, giving a rosy picture of his physical condition.

60. Leonnig and Rucker, *I Alone Can Fix It*, 275.

61. Leonnig and Rucker, *I Alone Can Fix It*, 297–99.

62. Leonnig and Rucker, *I Alone Can Fix It*, 301–2.

October 4, 2020

Trump became bored quickly at Walter Reed and, against Dr. Conley and Redfield's advice, he decided to take a "joy ride" around the area of the hospital in the presidential limousine, putting Secret Service agents in danger of contracting COVID-19. It was Mark Meadows's job to stop such a foolhardy stunt, but he and Scavino planned it with Trump at lunch. Like other macho fascist leaders, Trump wanted to show strength and virility. Dr. James Phillips, chief of disaster medicine at George Washington University, was consulting at Walter Reed and tweeted: "Every single person . . . in the vehicle during that completely unnecessary presidential drive-by just now must be quarantined for fourteen days. They might get sick. They may die. For political theater. Commanded by Trump to put their lives at risk for theater. This is insanity."[63] Two months later, he was removed from Walter Reed's consulting list. Trump wanted to leave the hospital after three nights. However, Dr. Redfield said it would be "foolhardy."[64] On October 5, at 6:30 p.m., Trump left Walter Reed Hospital; the fascist sociopath president's message to America about COVID-19 was "don't be afraid of COVID, don't let it dominate your life." *He said this after receiving world-class medical treatment that saved his life that no American would ever be able to have.*[65]

Upon arrival at the White House, Trump set up a "made-for-television" appearance from the White House balcony, a replica balcony scene that many older Americans remembered seeing numerous times of Il Duce, Benito Mussolini. With a defiant removal of his mask and the same signature arrogance of Il Duce's lifted chin, Trump saluted and gave a thumbs up; he had the imitation down pat, but he could not hide that he looked sick, was gasping for breath, and was barely able to stand. Trump enacted his parody of Il Duce while his White House was ravaged by a virus outbreak that many officials traced to the Barrett nomination event in the Rose Garden. The list of Trump aides and associates who tested positive around this time totaled more than thirty and included Bill Stepien; Kayleigh McEnany; Kellyanne Conway; Stephen Miller; Nick Luna, the president's bodyguard and director of Oval Office operations, Republican National Committee Chairperson Ronna McDaniel; Chris Christie; and Senators Ron Johnson, Mike Lee, and Thom Tillis.[66] After the way that Donald Trump and his White House gaslighted the American people about the coronavirus, it appears that in

---

63. Leonnig and Rucker, *I Alone Can Fix It*, 307–8.
64. Leonnig and Rucker, *I Alone Can Fix It*, 306.
65. Leonnig and Rucker, *I Alone Can Fix It*, 309.
66. Leonnig and Rucker, *I Alone Can Fix It*, 310–11.

a disproportionate, small way poetic justice visited the gaslighters. Trump returned to the campaign trail, but on November 3, 2020, Joe Biden won the presidential election with 306 electoral votes and 81,268,924 popular votes, and Donald Trump lost with 232 electoral votes and 74,216,154 popular votes.[67] He was not the only loser: eight hundred thousand Americans lost their lives due to Trump's neglect of the virus and Trump's reelection focus.

After Donald Trump's COVID-19 virus campaign of gaslighting, many Americans would no longer be convinced the virus was deadly, and the importance of vaccinations in the American public health tradition would no longer exist, nor would Americans trust the institution of science that formerly contributed to America's greatness. If the gaslighting of Donald Trump with the COVID-19 pandemic did not convince America that he was a malignant narcissistic sociopath, his immediate post-election deranged actions and rhetoric should have. Trump's gaslighting did not stop with the changed reality of the COVID-19 virus pandemic. His narcissistic, grandiose view of himself drove him on to more focused attempts to regain power. He would continue the attempt to change the reality of "democratic elections" in America, changing the reality of democracy itself, along with changing the reality of truth itself, by denying that he lost the 2020 presidential election. A denial of reality in such monumental terms is usually associated with mentally deranged, grandiose personalities. This was fascism American style; *the fascist did not commit outright physical mass executions; rather mass deaths came by way of stealth, neglect, and deception.*

TRUMP'S UNTHINKABLE PANDEMIC REACTION

Previously, I considered the Pearl Harbor disaster an apt analogy for Trump's disastrous, failed reaction to the pandemic. However, none of the military's actions or inaction at Pearl Harbor was intentional. I asked a series of what if questions in using the Pearl Harbor disaster incident to illustrate how bad Trump's failed response was to the imminent danger of the pandemic. The questions hypothesized, What if it was not just neglect and a lack of professionalism at Pearl Harbor, but the military intentionally committing seditious and traitorous acts at a time of imminent danger? It was a bizarre, absurd, and unthinkable hypothesis. But the analogy revealed something about Donald Trump—he did intentionally downplay the imminent danger, he did gaslight about the virus's volatility and threat, and he did prevent a timely professional response, sacrificing eight hundred thousand American lives to the pandemic. What about that unthinkable response? Were

67. Federal Election Commission, *Official 2020 Presidential General Election*, 1–2, 8.

Trump's pathological personality disorders merely a human disfunction in the psychological sense, or does this scientific discipline again fall short in describing an even more dangerous disfunction of humanity—*a spiritually corrupt human nature with an evil, supernatural edge*? The widespread penetration and success of Trump's gaslighting and incredible grip he still has on Americans raises the question of whether a supernatural dimension of evil was involved in a man dominated by it.

When Captain Gilbert, the psychologist at the Nuremberg war crime trials, heard the Nazi defendants' blasé explanations for the atrocities they committed in the holocaust, he concluded that "evil" was the absence of empathy. There is no doubt that Gilbert knew the defendants were sociopaths, but in using the term "evil" he provided a possible conceptual bridge from a psychological diagnosis to a biblical theology diagnosis. I discussed that Gilbert's insight revealed that extreme self-centeredness (no empathy) also represents theology's view that a corruption of human nature has potential for such atrocities when considering the influence of supernatural evil. No empathy is the polar opposite of "loving others as yourself." The words "love your neighbor as yourself" in James's epistle are in the context of the subject of "true religion" (Jas 1:26–27; 2:8–10) where it is described as "looking after orphans and widows" and deeds toward others, an others-orientation as opposed to a self-orientation. *Donald Trump was the epitome of the absence of empathy as the American death toll increased to the hundreds of thousands, and his focus was on getting reelected.* Considering that Trump's gaslighting was motivated by supernatural evil does provide answers for (1) his bizarre, non-empathetic reaction to a deadly pandemic and its human carnage, (2) his continuing to gaslight the nation in such dire circumstances, and (3) his being driven solely by selfish political purposes—to win an election. Captain Gilbert saying "evil is the absence of empathy" is his profession's equivalent of Jeremiah's prophetic statement about corrupt human nature's being open to demonic influence: "The heart is deceitful above all things and beyond cure. Who can understand it? I the Lord search the heart and examine the mind."[68] James also states in his epistle, "Each person is tempted when they are dragged away by their own evil desire and enticed. Then, after desire has conceived, it gives birth to sin; and sin, when it is full-grown gives birth to death."[69] There is a progression indicated in the corruption of human nature.

Christian theology reaches beyond what psychology describes as basic flaws in humanity its pathological personality disorders, which they even refer to as "evil." The biblical story of corrupt human nature delves into

68. Jer 17:9–10.
69. Jas 1:14–15.

the origins of supernatural evil, where the power of sin incites a rebellious response to any attempt to curtail self and its desires.[70] Political science's "toxic triangle," in which a malignant narcissistic tyrant connects with a narcissistic society in a narcissistic collusion in gaslighting, corresponds to Christian theology's understanding of a self-centered, rebellious tyrant at an advanced stage of corrupt human nature connecting with a self-centered society in which human nature is also compromised. Theology considers it a collusion with supernatural evil. It is the dog-whistle phenomenon, one corrupt human communicating subtly to another corrupt human being's lower angels, using the language of grievance and rebellion. In other words, *millions of vulnerable Americans did see him coming and, liking what they saw and heard, they chose to follow him*; the two were bound together by a rebellious human nature and its self-centered desires.

Donald Trump's gaslighting tapped into the negative feelings, grievances, and resentments that a narcissistic society felt about life in America; he tapped into corrupt human nature "deceitful above all things" and incurable. His gaslighting resulted in the release of the worst side of sinful human nature in many Americans, as they showed intolerance, racism, incivility, rebellion, and an inexplicable rage toward others in society. These self-centered behaviors coincide with a corrupt human nature,[71] the Bible referring to them as "acts of the flesh" or acts of the corrupt "old self." The apostle Paul says they are obvious: "sexual immorality, impurity, debauchery; idolatry [extreme self-focus that rules out God] witchcraft, hatred, discord, jealousy, fits of rage, selfish ambition, dissensions, factions [partisanship] and envy, drunkenness, orgies, and the like."[72] Therefore, the Christian view holds that in malignant narcissist Trump's gaslighting of society, his corrupt human nature was at work in a progressive development of evil.[73] In previous chapters on the gaslighting phenomenon, I illustrated how the daily news media reported the effect of Trump's gaslighting on American behavior. Those incidents did not support just a theory about America, they supported *the reality of a progressive evil in human nature at work in Americans that was incited by Trump's gaslighting.*

In the pandemic, Trump's corrupt human nature set in motion a dynamic process of evil: (1) By a self-serving, gaslighting deception about the volatility of the coronavirus, (2) scientific truth about the virus perished and confusion reigned, (3) resulting in the unnecessary deaths of hundreds

70. Rom 6:15—7:25; Gal 5:1–26.
71. Col 3:5–8.
72. Gal 5:19–21.
73. Rom 6:13—7:23.

of thousands of Americans. The idea of a progressive development of evil pervades the biblical story of salvation: (1) The progressive development of evil principle emerges in the Bible when extreme self-centeredness is left unchecked in an individual or society; (2) truth is then compromised and perishes under the onslaught of deception, and the result is (3) the destruction of spiritual life—even physical life. The prophet Jeremiah spoke of this progression of evil at the point of Israel's going into captivity and exile. He said Israel had been following the "stubborn inclinations of their evil hearts," having an extreme self-centeredness (cultural and national) that led them into idolatry (literally, worship of self rather than God)—they were "stiff-necked" and were more evil than their ancestors. Israel did not listen to God as he spoke through the prophets until "truth perished, vanishing from their lips" and then they began to engage in extremely destructive behavior to human life, and "burn their sons and daughters in the fire."[74] Contemporary violence toward children is also characteristic of American violence, excessive violence of parents toward their children and mass shootings targeting children in primary schools. All three elements of the progressive development of evil are at work in American society. Trump's gaslighting and the perilous state of American society is a contemporary example of the progressive development of evil principle.

A narrative in John's Gospel provides a biblical example of gaslighting that plumbs the depths of its evil nature; it illustrates the progressive development of evil.[75] His Gospel focuses uniquely on the Christian necessity of always making a right response to the truth—"believing."[76] John records Jesus' confrontation with (1) the hardened, self-centered *gaslighters* of first-century, Pharisees, (2) who are known by their *rejection of the truth* that Jesus was the heavenly Messiah from God; and (3) all the other Gospels say the confrontation of the Pharisees with Jesus was motivated by envy and they were looking for ways *to murder him*. Jesus said they were "doing the works of their father" Satan.[77] He attributed their motivation to supernatural evil, pointing out Satan's rejection of truth, "not holding the truth for there is no truth in him." Jesus spoke of Satan foremost as a *liar*: "When he lies, he speaks his native language, for he is a liar and the father of lies,"[78] but Jesus noted that beyond being the ultimate *deceiver of humankind*, Satan

74. Jer. 7:24, 28, 31.

75. John 8:13–59; 2 Thess 2:10–12.

76. John 1:1–17; 3:21; 4:24; 6:32–40; 7:37–39; 8:12; 9:5; 10:27; 12:35–36; 14:6, 15–16; 15:9; 16:13; 17:17; 18:37; 20:31.

77. John 8:37–41.

78. John 8:44.

was also the ultimate *destroyer of humanity,* "a murderer from the beginning." Cain's inspiration to kill Abel was the inspiration of Satan in salvation history; Satan is in an epic struggle with God to corrupt and *destroy God's redemptive purpose and his creation* (especially humans).[79] Jesus told his disciples to "beware of the leaven of the Pharisees" because they had been overcome by Satan and were his gaslighters; their hearts were hardened by rejecting the truth, they had no capacity for truth, and they became Satan's conduit for the progressive development of supernatural evil in the attempt to destroy God's redemptive purpose in Jesus Christ.

Therefore, in the view of biblical theology, it is reasonable to assume that there was and is a supernatural dimension of evil influencing Donald Trump's gaslighting—it explains his phenomenal hold on Americans. Trump reveals an extremely self-centered, corrupt human nature without a capacity for truth, someone open to the influence of supernatural evil. This belief in a supernatural evil does not rule out psychology's diagnosis and description of Trump displaying all the pathological attributes of a malignant narcissistic personality disorder; rather, it provides a viewpoint that probes deeper and qualifies the personality disorders *as having a supernatural, evil edge.* Donald Trump was and is a source of danger because of his narcissistic traits, but he is also open to the inspiration and manipulation of supernatural evil, making him especially dangerous. This man was (1) a self-centered sociopath with an evil-influenced mindset that had responsibility for facing America's deadly COVID-19 pandemic; (2) the mouthpiece of deception and misinformation in the pandemic—an instrument of evil—deceiving and giving misinformation about a deadly virus through his gaslighting, and (3) responsible for the unnecessary deaths of millions of Americans. Trump's anti-coronavirus gaslighting replaced the historic American reality of common sense, public health values, and a concern for others. His demented and deadly reality resulted in millions resisting vaccination and public health measures and rejecting the findings of science. Having no capacity for truth, no conscience, and no empathy or concern for the welfare of others, Donald Trump had a singular focus—*himself and maintaining ultimate political power by winning the next election.*

In a final fascist desperation move, Trump's self-imposed grandiosity manifested itself in planning and inciting a violent insurrection at the Capitol, a last-ditch chance to overthrow the certification of the election results and remain in power, but it failed. After mishandling the pandemic and losing the election in 2020, the fascist tyrant continued gaslighting but switched targets to steal American reality of free, democratic elections. His

79. Rom 8:18–39.

goal was to make sure elections and democratic rule would no longer be trusted in Republican circles and by millions of Americans. Trump's false claim that he won the election became his MAGA mantra—a "stolen election"; he believed that if you say something long enough to a gaslighted, gullible people, they will believe it. His pathological personality disorders have worsened since his election loss, and his fanatical base and the Republican party have also become a more violent, dangerous cult following.

Today, America is not the country it was before Donald Trump came to presidential power. With his diabolical gaslighting, he has transformed scores of millions of Americans, turning them into his own immoral and rebellious image, damaging American democratic reality for decades to come. Donald Trump's four years of gaslighting in the Oval Office have destroyed the capacity of truth for millions by casting doubt on whether truth was even important anymore. After Trump's lies are debunked, they are raised again and again; they still dominate media outlets, and truth is elusive; conspiracy theories are rampant and are even espoused by Republican members of Congress. In two impeachments, the Republican party helped Trump to remain untouchable for crimes in office. With his inherited fortune, he was able to weaponize lawsuits in abusing courts of law, evading justice, and escaping accountability. Who would have thought that a president of the United States would be allowed to engage in a crime wave inflicting such damage to American democracy and its people? Trump's one-man crime wave in the White House and his continuing unaccountability promotes a continuation of his deception and lawlessness in America—the subject of the next chapter.

Chapter 9

Crime Wave in the White House— But an Unaccountable President?

Get Out of Jail Free: This card may be kept until needed or sold.
MONOPOLY CARD

They make many promises, take false oaths and make agreements; therefore, lawsuits spring up like poisonous weeds in a plowed field.
But you have neglected the more important matters of the law— justice, mercy, and faithfulness.
THE PROPHET HOSEA[1] AND JESUS OF NAZARETH[2]

The Strongman's rogue nature also draws people to him. He proclaims law-and-order, yet enables lawlessness. This paradox becomes official policy as government evolves into a criminal enterprise, Hitler's Germany being one example and Putin's Russia another.
RUTH BEN-GHIAT IN STRONGMEN[3]

1. Hos 10:4.
2. Matt 23:23–24.
3. Ben-Ghiat, *Strongmen*, 251.

THE DANGER OF NORMALIZING DONALD TRUMP

Who would even imagine that American democracy would reach the point where the government became a criminal enterprise, the White House a crime scene, and the American president responsible for a crime wave against democracy *who then escapes American justice*? Yet that is precisely what Americans experienced in Donald Trump's presidency, and when he left office *nothing changed for him*. Instead of facing federal law enforcement officers with arrest warrants at Mar-a-Lago for federal crimes he committed in attempting to turn democracy into a fascist state, the public criminal is unaccountable and a free citizen. He does not face society's widespread condemnation for gross lawlessness; American society acts as though it did not even happen! The media speaks of the ex-president like he is just another president, asking him for his opinion on current events, comparing him with other presidents, and delusional American donors continue to give him money when he is caught committing crimes![4] What is the reason for this extraordinarily gullible American behavior condoning lawlessness? Prior to Donald Trump's presidency, Americans held that no one was above the law. Now, the crimes of the former leader of the nation are ignored. Why isn't he indicted for any of his crimes?

After four years of Donald Trump's fascist criminal assault on democratic rule and institutions, we should not be surprised that there are problems with reestablishing the administration of American justice—there is something fundamentally broken about it. During Trump's presidency, he flaunted the rule of law repeatedly, subjecting it to every possible manipulation, corrupting the Department of Justice until it became a "get out of jail free" card for him and a weapon to use against his enemies. Four years of his gaslighting, lies, deception, and propaganda have left American society numb to injustice—*and no one seems to care*. Unaccountability for his crimes *has a narcotic effect on an increasingly toxic and narcissistic society*. Justice officials bear the responsibility to counter the effect a lawless Trump-era has had on American society. Are they up to it? They must show a renewed vision for the rule of law and justice that recognizes and responds effectively to the malignant normality of Trump's criminal subculture. American justice must revive the tradition of equal enforcement of the law for all citizens and the prosecution of criminals whoever they are, and wherever facts of a criminal investigation lead. It is time for American justice to make a comeback. Society is on a lawless precipice and needs a clear demonstration of the rule of law in the case of Donald Trump to deter crime.

4. Relman, "Trump Solicits Cash."

From the beginning of Donald Trump's entry into American politics
and throughout his presidency, he was engaged full time in committing
crimes to dismantle democracy. In the position of ultimate power, he was a
saboteur of America's democratic republic as he engaged in "a constitutional
crime spree"[5] in the attempt to bring America to her knees. His fascist-
related crime wave focused on key democratic institutions upon which he
relentlessly declared war, discrediting elections and bringing the rule of law
into disrepute—even corrupting the Department of Justice itself. Trump
burrowed deep in corrupting the fabric of American democracy, not just by
signing an excessive number of presidential Special Orders to reverse Barak
Obama's Democratic policies, but committing offenses against presidential
traditions—laws with no teeth—designed for honorable ethical presidents,
and then moving on to committing *a variety of serious federal crimes*. In
his revered position of public trust, he showed complete disdain for any
rule, law, or regulation that limited what *he wanted to do*; the malignant
narcissistic sociopath rejected any power or authority but his own. His
pathological personality disorders left him with no conscience, no moral
standard, and no concern for social norms. The result was complete lawless
behavior, without hesitancy or remorse, until his criminality found its way
into every nook and cranny of American democracy—*corrupting everything
in his path*. At the end of his term of office, he proceeded beyond the pale
by planning and boldly inciting an insurrection at the US Capitol to stay in
power, just like any other fascist leader.

According to the American Constitution, such abuse of the office of the
president should never have happened. An open door to massive criminal
action was provided Trump by Attorney General William Barr and White
House lawyers, who told him that he had "absolute immunity" no matter
what he did. It was a ridiculous legal notion, an affront to the Constitution,
which holds that no one is above the law. Any legal notion of presidential
immunity from prosecution was intended to protect *ordinary, law-abiding
presidents* from lawsuits that would impede *the ordinary conduct of the presidential office*. Nevertheless, Trump's corrupt associates cited presidential
immunity repeatedly *for federal crimes the president committed in office!* AG
Barr applied the so-called presidential immunity doctrine of the DOJ's OLC
"to not prosecute a sitting president" to serial criminal Donald Trump.[6] The
irony was that this immunity doctrine was merely an outdated and poorly

5. Swalwell, *Endgame*, 251.

6. Reviewing chapter 4, "Plucking the Bald Eagle," may be helpful here, for the discussion of "absolute presidential immunity" and the Mueller investigation and report.

reasoned internal policy directive that did not even have "the force of law."[7] The policy was not a law embodied in the Constitution or a legal statute; it was only an internal personnel policy of the DOJ.[8] The personnel policy was treated as constitutional law by AG Barr and President Trump's lawyers who told Trump that he was immune from prosecution, leaving the *sociopath president free to do whatever he wanted*. It is no wonder that he created such chaos and his corruption penetrated so deeply in American democracy. It was like handing a child a loaded and cocked pistol with the safety off and telling him to go out and "play cops and robbers" with his friends.

The legal issue of presidential immunity for a rogue president like Donald Trump had not yet been adjudicated in the courts; there was *no case law focused on a rogue president like Trump*. The policy was applied to him only because his White House lawyers said that it should be; then, AG Barr and Trump's lawyers added the idea of *absolute* immunity to the policy! According to Trump's lawyers, even if the president were to shoot someone on Fifth Avenue in New York City, he would be unaccountable under American law![9] At the time of Trump's chaotic lawless presidency, this ridiculous claim of absolute immunity was not challenged by anyone. Making a bad situation worse, the American public did not know absolute presidential immunity was unconstitutional. Trump's unaccountability for criminal actions and his constant public gaslighting about being a victim, "the only president who was treated so unfairly," he claimed, confirmed his innocence in the eyes of an uninformed public at the peak of his deceptive gaslighting in office.

The Constitution holds an ex-president responsible for crimes committed while in office; when he leaves, his status as an ordinary citizen resumes. Crime-committing presidents are supposed to be accountable. However, Donald Trump *still walks free after he left office, unaccountable for his crimes*, smiling and thumbing his nose at American justice. After his crime wave in office, nothing changed for him. Two years later, he continues to abuse and manipulate the justice system and courts by a wave of lawsuits that allow him to escape accountability, still claiming presidential immunity. He continues to propagate the malignant normality of a stolen election in his hate rallies, with crowds of Americans cheering him on as he repeats the Big Lie. Trump pardoned his aides and associates convicted of felonies before he left office, so *they too are at liberty in society*, joining him in spreading his antidemocratic values, stirring hatred, and inciting

7. Wehle, "Law and the OLC's Article II."
8. Wehle, "Law and the OLC's Article II."
9. Pierson, "Trump Could Shoot Someone."

violence.[10] The news media responds to the phony "Make America Great Again" propaganda by *normalizing him*, continuing to interview the ex-president—whom they know to be a pathological liar—asking him for his opinion on foreign affairs,[11] justice issues (!), and a variety of other political issues. They know reporting about him has entertainment value. In sync with Trump's delusional claims of a stolen election is the appearance that he is still legally president[12] and a viable candidate for the 2024 presidential elections—provided he does not launch another coup to regain power in the interim. A delusional fantasy continues in American society because he is unaccountable. Trump's effective gaslighting of Americans for four years still holds society captive. Proof of the effectiveness of his gaslighting is society normalizing him; he is not normal and never has been. *Trump's criminal unaccountability leaves society without a deterrence to crime, and social morality continues to deteriorate.*

Psychoanalyst Mary Trump, who perhaps knows Donald better than anyone, says that the danger and heart of the legal unaccountability issue is normalizing Donald Trump; it promotes the message that no one can stop him.[13] If normalizing Trump continues, his gaslighting spell continues and he appears a victim like any other honorable ex-president, wrongly persecuted, instead of a man who was responsible for a fascist crime wave against American democracy in the attempt to bring it down. If given the opportunity, he will do it again and probably succeed. *Donald Trump will be stopped only by holding him accountable for his crimes in an American court of law*; if not, his indelible, falsely innocent impression in gaslighted America remains—an unjustly persecuted president who was not guilty of anything. After the first impeachment, Trump called the Russian investigation a hoax.[14] Always escaping justice, he remains a viable candidate for president in 2024 and free for another attempt to overthrow democracy. Donald Trump's crimes cry out for American justice.

10. DeVega, "Trump's Latest Hate Rally."

11. Palmer, "Donald Trump Condemns NATO."

12. Papenfuss, "Trump Still Acting Like Imperious President."

13. Wallace, "Mary Trump."

14 Bump, "Trump Presented His Russia Hoax Theory"; Schiff, *Midnight in Washington*, 150.

THE DAMAGING PARADOX OF TRUMP'S UNACCOUNTABILITY

Today, a historic test of the rule of law has arrived in "the American experiment." A critical time in the nation's history has arrived for a test of the legal axiom "No one is above the law." It is test of democracy itself. The unaccountability of former president Donald Trump for his crime wave in office and attempt to overthrow a democratic election strikes at the heart of democracy. Elections and the rule of law are what fascist dictators aim to destroy; without them, you do not have democracy. The popular affirmations that (1) American democracy stands on the rule of law, (2) no one is above the law, and (3) "crime doesn't pay" are the antithesis of an unaccountable president of the United States that has engaged in a crime wave. Trump mocks the American system of justice with his unaccountability. His lawlessness and unaccountability have left Americans with *a delusional sense of justice.* In the article "Trump's Greatest Triumph Is Convincing America that Crime Pays," Jonathan Chait speaks of the power of Trump's example of lawlessness on American society, as he reminisces about the pre-Trump era. Chait says, "I happen to believe that when you help yourself to money that you aren't legally entitled to, that is called *stealing.* People who routinely engage in stealing are called *crooks.*"[15] The clarity of the pre-Trump era of crime is refreshing, but it has slipped away in the wake of Trump's crime wave and unaccountability. It shows him to be above the law and, without question, *Trump's criminal unaccountability is a powerful example that readily transfers to the American public.* Trump repeatedly playing the "get out of jail free" card has seriously diminished the notion of crime and consequences in American society, making justice fuzzy in the minds of Americans, even to the point where his unaccountability is perceived as permission to commit crime and engage in violence just like he does, with people expecting the same unaccountability.

Contrary to normalizing that overlooks Trump's crimes and attempts to erase them is the existence of an overwhelming amount of evidence of his crimes in the public domain: (1) two congressional impeachments that essentially were indictments for crimes; (2) a two-year-long special counsel investigation by Robert Mueller indicting many of Trump's associates for federal crimes, with ten counts of obstruction of justice against Trump himself; and (3) numerous civil and criminal, state and federal ongoing investigations. Therefore, a reasonable question is, What keeps the knowledge of Trump's crimes from sinking into public consciousness? Why does the

---

15. Chait, "Trump's Greatest Triumph."

public continue to normalize him? The public sees no indictments of Donald Trump, no trials, and no incarceration. The lingering paradox of Trump's wave of fascist crimes yet unaccountability makes the American justice system and democracy look weak and his fascist/authoritarian system look invincible. *How the justice system functions today vis-à-vis Donald Trump is important for society's return to belief in the American justice system, as well as for healing a society racked with violence and lawlessness.* Trump's unaccountability for any of his crimes, the drumbeat of his gaslighting about democracy's weaknesses and rigged elections, his untouchable legal status, and the fact that he faces no indictments, no prosecutions, is a powerful social influence. It all leaves the dangerous impression that he is innocent. An obvious question arises: Where is American justice in all of this?

In an interview with Michael Kruse of *Politico*, Ruth Ben-Ghiat explains how nothing changes for Trump's followers either; the Big Lie that Trump won the election helps his gaslighted followers from having to face a lost election; he remains their hero, their winner, invincible Trump, while at the same time *wronged* Trump, *victim* Trump.[16] As a president in exile—in his twisted mind—Trump continues conducting social and political events at Mar-a-Lago, the new White House. His influence continues; he is also highlighted as preferred speaker and hero at Republican events like the Conservative Political Action Conference (CPAC) and with the powerful gun lobby of the NRA, as he continues proclaiming the delusional Big Lie with a violent rhetoric that they all love to hear—let's also give them guns! Trump stokes violence in society and creates the notion of a coming civil war. It appears his delusional, violent alternate reality is unstoppable. A disgraced cult-like Republican party is in lock-step with fascist Trump along with scores of millions of Americans under the spell of his gaslighting.

Ben-Ghiat, an expert on fascist leaders, explains how autocratic personality cults like Trump's are deflated: "Ballot victories alone don't stop autocrats, but *the law can*; it takes *prosecution and convictions* to deflate their personality cults . . . that's what it takes."[17] Accountability for Trump's crimes in an American court of law, the institution of justice that he tried so hard to destroy, is the beginning point of dispelling his gaslighting spell. A demonstration of the rule of law and accountability can put a stop to Trump's lawlessness and, in turn, society's delusion of lawlessness and injustice. The latter delusion is by far the more difficult to reverse and will take more time than indicting and prosecuting Donald Trump for his crimes. The hope for a return from Trump's damage to democracy rests with the proper function

16. Kruse, "One Way History Shows."

17. Kruse, "One Way History Shows," emphasis mine.

of America's judicial system and reestablishing the rule of law. *The country must be reminded what the rule of law was like before Donald Trump became president.*

If a war would have followed Trump's presidential gaslighting of America, as it did with Nazi propaganda in German society in 1939, perhaps Americans would have recognized the seriousness of Trump's fascist crimes and the damage done to democracy. In America, however, there was no public awareness that democracy narrowly escaped destruction with Trump's fascist crime wave and failed fascist coup. In Germany, the people experienced the *consequences of propaganda in a war*—a long, horrific, painful destruction of their country with great loss of life, along with the socioeconomic results of conducting and losing a war. In addition, after Germany's trauma of war, the Nuremberg war crimes trials took place, which publicly revealed the atrocities of fascist Naziism and an anti-Semitic Holocaust involving the execution of six million Jews. The German people saw the evils of fascism and its perpetrators on display in a court of international law, and from that firm ground of legal reality, *the country was able to recover from the deceitful spell of Nazi propaganda.*

In stark contrast, in the aftermath of fascist Trump's gaslighting America and his failed coup on January 6, 2021, there was no war, no justice meted out in a court of law, and no revealing Trump's guilt and the evils of his fascist reign; he did not meet his end with an ignominious suicide in a Berlin bunker like Adolf Hitler. Instead, two years later sociopath Donald Trump walks about freely in American society as a folk hero—protected by the very democratic laws he formerly discredited and shielded by the democracy that he attempted to destroy. He has impunity and is supported by the white supremacists and a far-right-influenced Republican party; he continues his gaslighting of America, with his racist anti-American rhetoric of a stolen election and his efforts to suppress the vote. *Trump's fascist crime wave is publicly unanswered and unrecognized by American justice.* Therefore, the spell of his gaslighting and lies remains intact. Millions of Americans view the violent Capitol insurrection he incited as just "normal political discourse"! He continues his manipulative delay tactics with the court system, having his lawyers file multiple baseless lawsuits and legal motions, and he does not appear in a court of law under oath to answer for his crimes. In June of 2022, this is happening *in America*, the bastion of freedom and democracy where formerly the iron-clad rule of law was renowned, and no one was above the law. Now, there is the example of unaccountable Donald Trump above the law, trashing America's democracy, its legal heritage, and rule of law.

If democracy is to survive in America, the legal paradox of Trump's crime wave and unaccountability must end. However, it is abundantly clear that closure of the fascist era of Donald Trump's gaslighting deception will not occur *until he is indicted for his crimes, tried, and convicted in an American court of law.* Donald Trump will be revealed as a power-hungry fascist that enriched himself with the American presidency, committing multiple anti-American felonies in the effort to dismantle American democracy.[18] A trial and conviction will break the spell of Trump's gaslighting for millions of Americans, just as the post-war Nuremberg war crimes trials did with Nazi propaganda in Germany. No such trial will take place in America, until justice officials stand up with a sense of courage, fearlessness, and patriotic duty, calling out Trump for his crimes and contempt for American justice and indict him. There should be a public outcry demanding his accountability. Or, is American justice broken without remedy? Common responses like "an American president has never been charged before" or "the indictment of an ex-president will divide the country"[19] are pathetic. They fail to comprehend the gravity of not indicting Trump and its effect on the rule of law and American society. The core issue is that America has never seen a notorious sociopath serial criminal attacking democracy at every turn, committing crime after crime in the office of the American presidency. Shocked and overwhelmed by his criminal blitzkrieg, justice officials appear to be caught flat footed. In military terms, a blitzkrieg is not stopped without resolute courage, and it calls for sacrificial confrontation.

A WEAK AMERICAN JUSTICE RESPONSE TO TRUMP'S CRIME WAVE

In an article entitled "Donald Trump's Longtime Legal Strategy May Be Catching Up with Him," Chris Cillizza reports that in the past three decades Trump has been involved in 4,095 lawsuits where he was either suing someone or being sued.[20] A minimum of thirty of the lawsuits took place while he was president. Clearly, the large number of lawsuits are evidence of his chief legal strategy: sue, sue, sue and delay, delay, and delay![21] Barbara Res, former executive vice president of the Trump Organization for decades, says about Trump, "He sues, that's his M.O. He sues."[22] He has perfected the weap-

18. Salant, "You're Still Paying."
19. Samuels, "Pence Says DOJ Charges."
20. Cillizza, "Donald Trump's Longtime Legal Strategy."
21. Cillizza, "Donald Trump's Longtime Legal Strategy."
22. Kruse, "Trumpology: Can Trump Still Sue?"

onization of lawsuits to harass, deflect, retaliate, delay prosecution, and to punish his opponents (including those who sue him), protecting his brand, his money, his image, and himself.[23] He just "sues his way out of trouble." Trump himself is not that affected by the lawsuits—his golf outings probably consumed more of his time—due to his team of lawyers handling them; he spent almost a year on golf courses.[24] Not without reason, it has been noted that as president he did not spend much time governing.

Trump frequently sues or threatens to sue government officials and prosecutors that investigate him and attempt to prosecute him. *Salon's* Heather Digby Parton said about Trump's lawsuits, "His corruption is so blatant that he floods the zone with so much bizarre and unconventional behavior for a public figure that it becomes difficult to discern the difference between what is criminal and what is unethical and what is merely performance." Parton says that Trump's threats to prosecutors are more powerful and persuasive "after his long-road of manipulating the justice system and escaping—it spooks the legal system—making the threats both political and actual for prosecutors and government officials due to his fanatical base actually going after people." She says about Trump's threats, "It is not his dog whistle, it is a bullhorn."[25] Trump does not care about conventional practices, any law, or what happens to the people he sues—he is a sociopath. When he sues or is sued, his sociopathic personality disorders take over and he has no shame; he only experiences personally satisfying grandiose and sadistic entertainment in the game. In addition, prosecutors are overwhelmed by a flood of counter-lawsuits and legal motions, and Trump enjoys winning over his opponents and the justice system. For Trump the malignant narcissist, lawsuits are weaponized for the purpose of getting his own way in controversies that he continuously creates or uses to get out of a crime. When his criminal blitzkrieg is confronted, he throws a legal tantrum and yells at his lawyers, "Sue, sue, sue!" Representative Eric Swalwell says that in his weaponization of lawsuits, "Trump is like a legal terrorist."[26] Prosecutors are like railroad switchman standing on the tracks of a rapidly approaching freight train; they needn't panic, but merely pull the switch to a spur where the train's journey must end.

The reality is that after President Trump's example in corrupting justice, his overwhelming lawlessness, and manipulation of the legal process,

23. Cillizza, "Donald Trump's Longtime Legal Strategy."

24. Burke, "Donald Trump Spent Almost a Year"; Kasprak, "Has Trump Spent '278.5 Years'?"

25. Parton, "Can Anyone Stop Trump?"

26. Swalwell, *Endgame*, 308.

it often leads prosecutors and justice officials to think about the political ramifications of a criminal indictment, instead of fulfilling their public duty to remove a criminal from society that is a public threat. When the crimes involve powerful public figures, not indicting degrades the democratic principle of liberty and justice for all and sends a message to the American public that encourages criminal activity. Chicago in the 1930s was a time of widespread political corruption and violence, but a federal prohibition agent, Eliot Ness, and his colleagues were called the "Untouchables," due to their legendary, fearless, and incorruptible pursuit of mob boss Al Capone. After the St. Valentine's Day Massacre, when seven members of Bugs Moran's North Side Gang were lined up against a wall and machine gunned, Capone became the FBI's public enemy number one for ordering the massacre. Even though Ness knew Capone was a dangerous gangster and public menace, he was single-minded and fearless in his efforts to indict Capone for his crimes and flaunting the law. Ness finally settled on charging the murderous mob boss with *twenty-two counts of tax evasion, removing him from society for eleven years.* Capone's sentence ended while he was incarcerated on Alcatraz Island, but when released he was immediately sent to a hospital for treatment of syphilitic paresis from which he sustained brain damage. Capone ended his days with the mentality of a twelve-year-old in his mansion on Palm Island, Florida.[27] Ness is both a model and reminder for justice officials today to pursue justice with Donald Trump.

Against all efforts to normalize Donald Trump and his presidency is the inordinate and unprecedented number of felony cases filed against Trump in criminal courts and serious civil cases (often financial-related crimes) that are evidence of his crime wave in office. Justice officials and Congress have compiled a mountain of evidence against him. However, in the outstanding thirty cases filed against Trump dating back to 2015, *not one of them has come to trial.*[28] Rarely does Trump even appear for a pre-trial deposition under oath to answer for his crimes. For a layperson unfamiliar with the intricate procedures of charging and court scheduling, there appears to be something wrong with the time element in the cases. The legal equation of thirty unresolved cases against Trump in seven years without one going to trial is puzzling. The delays in the justice system are excessive, even when considering the COVID-19 pandemic that slowed progress in the courts. Precisely why is it that Trump escaped accountability for his crimes for so long? In chapter 4, I suggested that Trump may

27. History.com Editors, "Al Capone Goes to Prison."

28. Everson, "Tracking Trump"; no case has yet come to trial at the date of this writing in May 2022.

have found the Achilles heel of the American justice system. The example of Donald Trump's thirty ongoing lawsuits with no indictments or trials, no courageous confrontation of his criminal blitzkrieg, is strong evidence that this legal maxim is no longer true.

The current thirty investigations of Donald Trump break down into twelve congressional, ten federal, and eight state and local cases,[29] yet those lawsuits only represent the tip of the iceberg of his crimes. The same is true about the number of crimes and offenses Trump committed in office. He may never be held accountable for all the offenses committed in office, such as (1) receiving illegal donations; (2) illegal fundraising;[30] (3) unlawful communications with foreign governments and refusing to hand over records to Congress; (4) failing to respond to lawful subpoenas; (5) witness tampering in impeachment hearings; (6) illegally suppressing bank documents, failing to turn over personal financial documents to Congress in investigation of alleged money laundering; (7) failing to hand over personal and business tax returns to Congress, (8) granting top secret clearances to relatives when they have been officially denied (numerous offenses of nepotism in office); (9) misuse of campaign funds; (10) misuse of charitable assets; (11) mishandling of classified documents and other breaches of White House security;[31] (12) multiple counts of obstruction of justice; (13) IRS audits of his enemies[32] and countless side-hustles and financial grifts. These are only some his other crimes and offenses, and they do not include Trump's ethical violations of standing traditional rules for a United States president,[33] which lawless sociopath Trump continuously ignored. The allegation that Trump was responsible for a crime wave in office is not hyperbole.[34] *It is an accurate description of his lightning-like multiple criminal strikes in the storm of his presidency.*

What is unprecedented is Trump's avoidance of indictment. His main legal strategy has always been weaponizing lawsuits—flooding the courts with time-consuming legal motions and appeals to avoid criminal indictment—most of them made in bad faith and without legal merit. Yet for

29. Buchanan, "Tracking 30 Investigations."

30. Hall and Levinthal, "Federal Officials Donald Trump."

31. Dorman, "Donald Trump Used"; Borger, "Trump's Unorthodox Phone Habits"; Litman, "Another Case Where Trump Flagrant Misconduct"; Leary, "National Archives Retrieves 15 Boxes"; Graham, "Incredible Vanishing Trump Presidency."

32. Figliuzzi, "'Random' IRS Audit"; Paris and Katz, "Comey and McCabe Audits"; Melber, "After Trump Demands Comey Punishment."

33. Shafer, "Opinion: How Trump Flushed"; D'Antonio, "Opinion: How We Can Repair."

34. Swalwell, *Endgame*, 251, 269, 271.

the most part, judges have responded to Trump's legal foolishness and bad faith stalling with forbearance and tolerance. For the average person, this is especially confusing; they do not understand this forbearance of judges, observing the principle of law that blindfolded Lady Justice illustrates—*treating all without bias and fairness*, even a serial offender like Donald Trump with a history of bold contempt for the law. For laymen, it just appears that Lady Justice is blind; common sense dictates justice should *focus* on him. As judges respond in this manner repeatedly, it sets the scene for long-drawn-out litigations that inevitably allow him to escape justice. The legal system appears unable to prevent Trump's strategy of weaponizing lawsuits; it allows him to delay justice and sue his way out of trouble, proving the maxim "justice delayed is justice denied."

The problem with getting justice may be not as simple as a layperson may think. As judges confront the lawlessness of sociopath Trump, they have a certain disadvantage. They must follow the letter and spirit of the law while Trump, a manipulating serial criminal, does not. Police officers understand this disadvantage because they face it every day—following the rule of law when lawbreakers do not. They are governed by some of the same legal principles as those in higher levels of the justice system, but in a certain sense they are at an even greater disadvantage. First, they are not lawyers. Second, every legal decision or action they make in an arrest or during a criminal investigation must conform to the rule of law, but sometimes their decisions or actions may result in life or death and call for instantaneous action that afterward attorneys meticulously examine for weeks or longer in court. Every police officer is familiar with this disadvantage. However, both judges and police officers know that Lady Justice holds a double-edged sword in her left hand. Both must approach their duty without bias and fairness, but they are not defenseless in enforcement of the law. Both have the solemn authority and weight of the law behind them; those who commit crimes and show contempt for the law face consequences—fines, physical arrest, and incarceration. When contempt for the law emerges at any level, officials have discretion; there are legal remedies and consequences that necessarily should follow—swiftly. The law does have teeth. Consequences for lawbreaking provide an important deterrent effect in law enforcement at all levels of the justice system.[35] But this appears to be the failure of the justice system at the highest levels—inaction—it does not use its discretion to swiftly apply the law, legal remedies bringing consequences and respect for the rule of law. Often, they are swayed by political reaction. Intuitively, at

---

35. The Christian viewpoint is described by the apostle Paul in Rom 13:1–7, especially 13:4, "for rulers do not bear the sword for no reason." Law-abiding citizens do not have to worry about the sword, but lawbreakers do.

a lower level, police officers know that if such inaction is frequent on their beat, it becomes physically dangerous, human nature being what it is. They are like railroad switchmen, freezing at the approaching freight train.

The deterrent effect and swift legal consequences is the point in this discussion about Trump's abuse of the law and an appropriate response from the criminal justice system; it is not only important for the integrity of the criminal justice system, but it has a practical effect for deterrence and crime prevention, even the wellness of society itself. Trump's historic successes in boldly and contemptuously weaponizing lawsuits in abuse of the legal system must be met by courageous justice officials stepping up and becoming "prosecutorial thorns" in Trump's side *just by doing their jobs.* Men and women of conviction and personal dedication are needed who follow the truth and the rule of law, "standing out," considering that justice is worth risking a negative mark on their careers and indicting Donald Trump for his crimes. The courage and risk I speak of should not be considered extraordinary for prosecutors and law enforcement officials; even officials at a lower level of the profession—police officers—demonstrate courage by doing their jobs every day, putting not only their personal reputations at risk but also *their physical lives.* Unfortunately, Trump has brought the specter of violence to prosecutors and judges personally; they know the danger they face in investigating, indicting, and prosecuting him. He only needs to play the victim publicly and his dangerous MAGA base will retaliate for him. When justice officials do not swiftly implement legal remedies at their disposal for offenders with careers in manipulating justice, putting them at a disadvantage, serial criminals like Trump learn from this, continue to escape justice, and are emboldened to escalate criminal activity. Prosecutorial inaction, failure to indict with sufficient evidence, is even more egregious; it is a failure of duty to enforce the law with dire consequences.

In today's legal environment, both prosecutors and district attorneys are aware of the historic abuses that Trump has perpetrated in the law community; they know Trump's claims about being an unjustly persecuted president and an innocent victim of partisan politics are manipulation. Prosecutors know that the volume of Trump's crimes, unaccountability, and contempt for the law even surpass that of mob bosses; one remedy they have for this is called racketeering influenced and corruption organizations (RICO) investigations. They also know that Trump continues to manipulate the justice system to avoid indictment and to avoid being put under oath, because as a compulsive liar he would not be unable to stand up to the questioning of an able prosecutor under the rigors of legal procedures that are designed to get to the truth in a trial. Prosecutors and judges are fully aware of the crucial need to indict Donald Trump, *but he remains unindicted.*

Through media reporting, Trump's multiple crimes in a four-year term of office and evidence that he has enriched himself by the presidency have also become public knowledge;[36] this has put public pressure on the justice system to make an effective response to his contempt for the law and hold him accountable.

In the post-Donald Trump presidency, a problem associated with his crime wave and criminal unaccountability is his continuing with a life-long strategy of bold and aggressive weaponizing lawsuits. Trump's shock and awe legal blitzkrieg, a sort of "so-much-crime-you-can-hardly-keep up," along with multiple frivolous legal motions—all of it emanating from just *one person* is novel. It is not novel for crime bosses—but it is for an ex-president of the United States! A multiplicity of crimes and lawsuits flow from Trump's pathological grandiosity; for him everything must be big, the greatest con, the most audacious theft, the perfect phone call; everything is done "bigly," as Trump would say. The unending lawsuits filed and court motions on his behalf are often without merit and frivolous, bringing the reprimand of judges,[37] especially when the serial criminal claims the ridiculous issues of presidential privilege, absolute immunity, or a stolen election. In one such case, where a "Trumper" colluded with the ex-president in election fraud in Georgia, the judge responded to a baseless motion, "Hell no" and laughed the case out of court.[38]

The volume of Trump's crimes and lawsuits have made him the embodiment of a malignant normality in the American justice system. For a justice system and courts that are accustomed to dealing with one crime at a time and then meticulously grinding out justice according to the rule of law, Trump's strategy of weaponizing lawsuits—fighting cases with multiple frivolous motions and counter lawsuits—spooks prosecutors and the justice system. In the first impeachment of Donald Trump, prosecutor Adam Schiff suggested that the framers of the Constitution may have anticipated a rogue president—they were not naïve about human nature—quoting the words of Alexander Hamilton from 1792:

> When a man unprincipled in private life, desperate in his fortune, bold in his temper, possessed of considerable talents, having the advantage of military habits, despotic in his ordinary demeanor, known to have scoffed in private at the principles of

36. Date, "Last Call at Trump's Monument."

37. Stempel, "Judge's Order Releasing Trump's Tax Returns"; Dwyer, "Supreme Court Rejects Trump's Claim"; Melber, "Trump Loses His Bid"; Larson, "Sidney Powell, Lin Wood."

38. Shuham, "Georgia Judge Laughs."

liberty, when such a man is seen to mount the hobby horse of popularity, to join in the cry of danger to liberty, to take every opportunity of embarrassing the general government and bringing it under suspicion, to flatter and fall in with all the nonsense of the zealots of the day, it may justly be suspected that his object is to throw things into confusion that he may ride the storm and direct the whirlwind.[39]

After quoting Hamilton, Schiff states, "I would say that the founders could have little imagined that a single President might have done all of these things except that the evidence has sadly proved this is exactly what this President has done [first Trump impeachment]."[40] We also could add, nor would the framers have imagined that after a president "rode the storm and directed the whirlwind," committing numerous felonies, that he would be *unaccountable under American law*! Schiff's reference to Trump's criminal activity only pertained to his crimes committed up to the first impeachment in 2019, because he had yet to experienced his inciting an insurrection on the Capitol of the United States to overthrow the results of a democratic election!

HOPE FOR A RETURN TO AMERICAN JUSTICE

From a lay perspective of the criminal justice system, the wave of lawlessness of Donald Trump demands that justice officials stand up, do their sworn duty, and confront him by applying the law, indicting and prosecuting the former president. They are the last resort for restoring justice in America. The legal baggage left by Trump, his continuing abusive legal tactics and contempt for the law, demands a courageous and robust response of the American justice system. With his corruption of the DOJ, Attorney General William Barr left a legal mess in his wake. It seems unfair for so much to land on AG Garland's plate with so many political ramifications. However, the way to remedy political damage done by the former attorney general is to function as the nation's chief prosecutor, confronting him with the rule of law, indicting and prosecuting Donald Trump. Garland must not delay in indicting Trump for any political reasons; he is not primarily a politician or judge; he is America's chief prosecutor. The following criminal and civil cases cited below only represent a few of the many cases against Donald Trump. They may lead AG Garland to a RICO investigation and prosecution

39. Swalwell, *Endgame*, 269.
40. Swalwell, *Endgame*, 269.

for the federal crimes;[41] it is only one of many prosecutorial strategies that he may employ for Trump's inciting an insurrection.

The Hindrance of Delayed Prosecutions

Trump's unaccountability for multiple crimes and history of weaponizing lawsuits should not cause prosecutors to avoid indicting him. Rather, his abuse of the justice system should lead them to seek and adopt procedural legal strategies swiftly, using their discretion in drawing justice's double-edged sword and applying legal remedies to negate Trump's delay tactics to expedite his indictment and prosecution. While the success of a prosecution in Trump's cases will have significant impact on society (both good and bad), years of delay and failure to indict him have had devastating consequences for society. There are prominent examples that show Trump's high-profile status and weaponizing lawsuits seemed to have intimidated prosecutors in delaying prosecution or declining to indict even when sufficient evidence was available. Legal analysts suggest a reason for reluctance to indict is the effect that the loss of a high-profile case would have on a prosecutor's career. I cite two high profile cases where there has been inordinate delay when apparent sufficient evidence to convict was present: (1) the Fulton County Georgia DA Fani Willis's criminal case against Trump for election interference crimes, dating back to late 2020, and (2) the Manhattan District Attorney Alvin Bragg's criminal case against Donald Trump for tax evasion, dating back to August 23, 2018.

In an article, "Opinion: How Real Is the Chance of Criminally Prosecuting Donald Trump," legal analyst Elie Honig of CNN states that prosecutor Fani Willis waited one and a half years to convene a special grand jury,[42] while the evidence against Trump was supported by phone recordings and other important evidence that is public knowledge. Prosecutor Willis has examined fifty witnesses, but reluctant key witnesses refused to voluntarily appear. According to Georgia law, she must convene a regular grand jury that has subpoena power. Whenever the "special grand jury" finishes, it cannot vote to indict but can only issue a report recommending its findings. Then, if prosecutor Willis chooses to indict, she would have to convene a regular grand jury. Whenever Trump's time-consuming appeals are exhausted, the district attorney's office will try the case in court, to get a "beyond a reasonable doubt" verdict. Of course, all the legal actions above

---

41. An exception to trying multiple crimes of a criminal conspiracy is a RICO investigation and trial.

42. Honig, "Opinion: How Real Is the Chance."

will be subjected to Trump's "fun and games," with empty appeals, legal motions, and counter lawsuits prolonging the whole process. If Trump is found guilty, he will certainly appeal the court's finding and sentence, consuming many months. Honig states, "Prosecutor Willis has thus far moved at an inexplicably slow pace."[43]

To the eyes of a layman, Willis does not appear to be swiftly seeking an indictment and adopting procedural strategies that would avoid or negate Trump's historic delay tactics. There may be an unusually complex legal system in Georgia; however, Willis does not appear to be concerned with timeliness in pursuing the indictment of Donald Trump. Using the previously discussed law enforcement officers doing their jobs, risking reputation and life daily and swiftly applying the law, prosecutor Willis appears to be spending too much time in the police station preparing to "hit the street." What message will an inordinate delay have on the American public? What mischief will Trump work given the delay?

Manhattan DA Alvin Bragg had a case with a good chance of indicting Trump criminally for complex tax-related crimes, but he has become notorious for not indicting Trump. Former DA Cyrus Vance had pursued the tax case for three years, hiring highly qualified lawyers Mark F. Pomeranz and Carey R. Dunne, with specialized experience in prosecuting complex financial cases. Vance and his experts all believed there was sufficient evidence to indict Trump on numerous felony violations of New York penal law. Less than two months after, new DA Alvin Bragg replaced Vance, and Pomeranz and Dunne abruptly resigned. MSNBC legal analyst Ari Melber stated that simultaneous resignations of attorneys is a "message"; the new DA, Bragg, disagreed with the two highly qualified attorneys about indicting Donald Trump.[44] The Manhattan prosecutor's office refused to release the two attorneys' resignation letters, but reporters stated they contained information about a stalled investigation.[45] Bragg stated that the investigation is ongoing, but legal analysts say it is stalled.[46] In a *Washington Post* article, "Opinion: If Prosecutors Are Finished Investigating Trump, They Should Say So," Norman Eisen says Bragg has a duty to the public to explain why he is not prosecuting the high-profile Trump case. He has not responded. Attorneys for Donald Trump and Allen Weisselberg, the Trump organization financial officer, filed a motion to dismiss the case in February 2022. The appearance

43. Honig, "Opinion: How Real Is the Chance."

44. Jones, "Irritated Ari Melber Declares"; Gottlieb and Lefcourt, "D. A. Bragg, Explain Why."

45. Pagliery, "Top Trump Prosecutors." As of June 11, 2022, Bragg had not responded.

46. Gottlieb and Lefcourt, "D. A. Bragg, Explain Why."

of the Manhattan Trump prosecution is that after Bragg took over as a newly appointed DA, he did not want the loss of a high-profile case on his career.[47] On August 18, 2022, Bragg finally negotiated an "unexpectedly favorable" plea bargain with Weisselberg: If he pled guilty, he would only serve five months in Rikers Island New York jail (as opposed to fifteen years in prison for fifteen felony counts) and pay two million dollars in back taxes—without implicating Donald Trump.[48] Bragg has delayed justice and failed to indict Trump with tax crimes for which Trump was clearly personally responsible.[49] Again, the legal maxim "Justice delayed is justice denied" comes to mind. Seven years later, Bragg appears to be starting over by investigating other Trump crimes—like the hush money Trump paid to prostitute Stormy Daniels. Bragg took the old no-risk case in which Trump was an unnamed co-conspirator and in which Michael Cohen, Trump's lawyer, had already been convicted and sent to prison. As prosecutions go, Bragg's new case represents low hanging fruit.[50]

The New York Attorney General Letitia James's civil investigation of Trump illustrates his contempt for the law and the American justice system, but it also illustrates an attorney general that has used her discretion and applied procedural strategies to defeat Trump's delay tactics. Trump's finances are crucial in exposing his massive civil criminality, but he has always been aggressive in hiding them from public and legal scrutiny. In the post-Trump presidency period, there has been more legal activity in attempting to expose his finances. AG James's investigation started August 24, 2020. Subpoenas for documents were first served September 30, 2021.[51] James has probed Trump's personal finances, those of the Trump organization, and his properties, but has been waiting ten months for documents from Trump. On December 21, 2021, Trump sued AG Letitia James to halt her investigation and have her removed, a legal retaliation that was a cheap publicity stunt.[52] Racist Trump attacked James, who is African American, both personally and professionally, using bold, shameless projection, saying that *she* is a racist and *her* racism has motivated *her* legal actions against *him*. AG James responded in a professional manner with courage and legal

47. "Bragg's Bad Choice," editorial.

48. Badash, "Former Trump CFO Nearing"; Helmore, "Trump's 'Eyes and Ears'"; Cohen and Freifeld, "Trump Organization Defense Rests Case."

49. Pierides, "Trump Org. Exec Just Dropped."

50. Rashbaum et al., "Manhattan Prosecutors Again Consider"; Scannell, "First on CNN: Trump Org. Controller."

51. Italiano, "New York AG Blasts."

52. Balk, "Donald Trump Sues NY Attorney General"; Bromwich et al., "Judge Holds Trump in Contempt."

expertise, imposing legal sanctions to stop his stalling the investigation. Trump has filed more than twelve affidavits attempting to stop James's ten-thousand-dollar-a-day fine imposed in a contempt finding against him for withholding documents. Judge Arthur Engoron[53] first set March 3, 2022, for Trump to turn over documents or be fined; then he extended it to March 31 and, when Trump was dismissive, saying "I don't have any documents," the fine ran from April 25 to May 6 until it reached 110,000 dollars—Trump had to pay the fine. But he did not comply with the judge's third party search order, mandating a non-Trump company search for the documents and electronic devices and other types of evidence that would be followed up with a report. By May 20, the ten-thousand-dollar-a-day fine had resumed retroactive to May 7 (amounting to 130,000 dollars) and civil enforcement was to follow the failure to obey Judge Engoron's order to produce documents.[54] As of May 29, 2022, there had been no news of a report being received by AG James. It is helpful to note that this probe of Trump's finances began almost seventeen months ago, and Judge Engoron's order for Trump to produce documentation went on for eleven weeks.

On August 10, 2022, Donald Trump sat for a deposition before AG James and attorneys from her office; he invoked the Fifth Amendment of the Constitution four hundred and forty times in four hours, refusing to testify based on self-incrimination. Sociopath Trump used his usual strategy of projection as an excuse for "taking the Fifth," and he said, "The current administration and many prosecutors in this country have lost all moral and ethical bounds of decency"[55]—a perfect description of Donald Trump's character! In a civil case, invoking "the Fifth" may be taken as a *confession*; the recording of pleas of "the Fifth" may be played in open court for the jurors to hear in a civil trial, and the judge instructs the jurors that they may draw an adverse inference.[56] A civil trial requires only a preponderance of evidence to convict.

If Trump is convicted, the ruling would hit him where it hurts—his money and business in New York. Not only would there be hundreds of millions of dollars in fines to pay, but a New York law AG James has used will result in the dissolution of Trump's business! On September 21, 2022, James filed a lawsuit (indictment in a civil case) against Trump and his children,

53. Rashbaum et al., "Manhattan Prosecutors Again Consider"; Breuninger, "Trump Asks Judge."

54. Kates, "Judge Lifts $10,000-a-Day Contempt Ruling"; Mangan, "Judge Says Trump Contempt Ruling"; in April of 2023, Ivanka Trump still withholds documents.

55. Sheth and Italiano, "Trump Invoked His Fifth Amendment Right."

56. Severi, "Trump Repeated 'Witch Hunt' Answer"; Breuninger, "Trump Took Fifth Amendment."

alleging two hundred instances of fraud and a baseline of 250 million dollars in illegal profits had to be paid (actual fines would be 750 million dollars to one billion dollars) and a five-year ban on the family from buying real estate or receiving commercial real estate loans from any New York bank. AG James's filing is an essential death sentence on the Trump organization if they are found guilty in trial; Trump claiming "the Fifth" four hundred and forty times amounts to nails in his coffin.[57] A guilty as charged trial would act as a decisive revelation for releasing Trump's gaslighting grip on the American public. Trial is set for 2023.

Hindering a Return to Justice: John Durham's Red Herring Investigation

The Special Counsel Robert Mueller investigation into Russian interference in the 2016 presidential election reveals Trump's evasive legal tactics; it appears to have been left behind in Trump's criminal history. The abuse of the Mueller investigation by Trump is a legal commentary of his corrupt presidency and criminal acts. Trump abused his power of office in politicizing the DOJ, appointing a political sycophant, William Barr, as attorney general, who then corrupted the justice system in multiple ways. One of the ways Trump deflected public attention from Mueller's investigation and crimes of obstruction of justice was instructing Barr to appoint Special Counsel John Durham to "investigate the FBI investigators" in Mueller's probe of Russian interference in the 2020 elections. Durham's investigation was an extension of the corrupt DOJ under Barr; three years later, Durham's investigation was still ongoing in May of 2022.[58] Trump intended that Durham's investigation provide a counter-story, a distraction to the truth that in his Russia investigation Mueller uncovered crimes of Trump and his associates in their contacts with Russian FSB agents.

Robert Mueller's two-year investigation, assisted by seventeen lawyers and a great number of FBI agents, indicted thirty-five people and three Russian companies for over one hundred crimes during the peak of corruption in Trump's presidency. However, Mueller's investigation was quickly neutralized by corrupt AG Barr;[59] Trump used Barr and the DOJ to protect himself and assail his enemies. The threat of Mueller's investigation to Trump was that it not only showed his election campaign's massive contact with

57. Khullar, "'Art of the Steal.'"

58. On May 18, 2022, the first trial of the Durham investigation, Michael Sussmann, had been in session two days.

59. Schiff, *Midnight in Washington*, 431–32.

Russians, but it also *documented evidence of Trump's ten felony counts of criminal obstruction of justice.* Therefore, Barr quashed Mueller's report, protecting Trump from prosecution, but equally important for Trump was that it suppressed all the Russia contact information that contradicted Trump's stream of lies about "no contact with Russia." Although Trump's other associates were indicted, tried, and convicted, Donald Trump was not. Mueller did not indict him, because he was legally bound by the DOJ's Office of Legal Counsel policy memo "that a sitting president cannot be indicted." The memo was a phony "get out of jail free" card, and Trump still is unaccountable for committing obstruction of justice; Mueller compiled sufficient evidence to indict him.[60] Barr lied about his reason for not charging Donald Trump.[61]

The Mueller investigation may be the case with the longest delay yet, due to Trump's evasive delay tactics, but Mueller's charges are not dead and just a matter of judicial history; Trump may still be indicted. The statute of limitations for a federal crime is five years, and the last date of Trump's criminal conduct in Mueller's investigation was January 18, 2019. AG Garland could file an indictment any time before January 18, 2024. If Trump claimed any presidential immunity now, his claim would be rejected by the courts, as they have already ruled against the issue. Trump's repeat offender status is documented—ten counts of obstruction of justice in the Mueller investigation as well as investigations of the same nature in his two presidential impeachments—which in effect were "congressional indictments." This is not to mention the special congressional investigation record of Trump's inciting an insurrection at the Capitol and his stealing classified documents, violations of the Espionage Act.

The Mueller special counsel investigation is a stark contrast to the ongoing Special Counsel John Durham's investigation *that was initiated under corrupt AG William Barr and ordered by Donald Trump in the middle of the first impeachment hearings.*[62] It was a desperate political ploy of the sociopath president to discredit the Russia investigation, divert attention from it, and fix the public's attention on Hillary Clinton's email controversy. It was a pure psychological projection to deflect attention from the Russian investigation and his ties to Russia. As an investigation of the investigators, *it amounted to looking for a crime among FBI investigators,* hoping to find members in the top echelons of the FBI and CIA or US officials that

60. Boggioni, "Former US Attorney Spills the Beans."

61. Kurtz, "Bill Barr Was Just as Bad."

62. Schiff, *Midnight in Washington*, 431–32; Polantz, "Federal Judge Blasts"; Kahardori, "Beware Bill Barr"; Dress, "Former Manhattan Prosecutor Alleges."

committed crimes. Durham found no such high officials. However, this did not matter, because the success of Trump's psychological projection with the investigation did not depend on finding any guilty top officials, only the perception that they existed. The perception buttressed Trump's gaslighting about the Mueller Russia investigation being a hoax. Adam Schiff refers to the president's use of psychological projection when he said, "Trump was aggressively trying to flip the script [in the Russia investigation]; *he* wasn't colluding with Russia *Hillary* was; *he* hadn't done anything wrong *the FBI* had; the Justice Department shouldn't be investigating *him* they should be investigating *the FBI.*"[63] Today, the projection sounds childish, but at the time it won the day. After Trump fired FBI Director James Comey, he had the DOJ fire FBI Director Andrew McCabe and fast-track the firing so that he would lose part of his pension.[64] Such audacious, bold actions against opponents had never come out of the Oval Office before, and it tended to make them believable. Who would have suspected that it was a "tantrum," a childish response from the Toddler in Chief: "*I'm* not a crook; *you're* a crook!" But it worked; a gaslighted, gullible American public forgot about all of Trump's Machiavellian plots, scheming, and yelling at Hillary, "Lock *her* up."

Three years later, John Durham and his attorneys were still employing the same projection ploy in the Michael Sussmann trial, saying the defendant lawyer Sussmann was part of a conspiracy—an "October Surprise"[65] against Trump in 2016—trying to establish that Hillary Clinton triggered the Russia probe! The historic truth now known is that the whole Durham investigation *was and still is* an effort to deflect from Trump's complicity with Russia and focus guilt on Hillary.[66] Durham's inquiry is a complete embarrassment. Trump was not held accountable at the time, and today Durham's phony investigation is trying to re-litigate the Russia probe, changing the historical narrative and rehashing Trump's lies about having no Russia contacts in a renewed attempt to discredit Mueller's investigation. Durham should not be allowed to continue his nonsensical, shameless investigation of the investigators. The Durham investigation's original purpose was purely political; today, it is Trump propaganda rooted in the corrupt DOJ under Bill Barr and sociopath Trump's manipulation of the DOJ to protect himself.

63. Schiff, *Midnight in Washington*, 150, emphasis mine.

64. Schiff, *Midnight in Washington*, 150; McCabe won back his full pension in a wrongful termination lawsuit.

65. Legare, "Prosecutors Allege Michael Sussmann Planned."

66. Bump, "Again: There's No Evidence"; Connor, "Federal Judge Stomps"; Bump, "Trump Presented His Russia Hoax."

After three years of investigation, on the eve of the statute of limitations expiring, *Durham filed a last-minute indictment of Michael Sussmann for allegedly lying to the FBI.* To file the indictment, of a former federal prosecutor in a myopic, weak case, Durham resorted to a technical application of the law, alleging Sussmann hid who he was representing when he spoke to the FBI—that was his alleged lie! Sussmann was a whistleblower on Trump. This long-running Durham failure left one FBI lawyer that pled guilty to "changing an email" when he took a shortcut in filing a Foreign Intelligence Surveillance Act application for a wiretap. The case was charged by two of Durham's associates (Durham personally did not convict anyone in the three-year-long investigation). Another attempt at indictment was Igor Dancenko, a paid confidential informant of the FBI. Durham charged him with lying to the FBI, but he was acquitted in a trial on October 18, 2022. All Durham's efforts hardly amounted to finding top officials of the FBI, CIA, and US government complicit in committing crimes! When the results of his miserable failure are compared with Mueller's investigation and indictment of thirty-five people and three Russian companies for over one hundred crimes, Durham's poisoned purpose is exposed; *it was nothing more than a three-year-long fruitless political charade, launched by a corrupt DOJ to distract from Trump's crimes.* On other occasions in court, judges noted Durham's duplicity and ruled against him for extending the scope of his charges in court, attempting to rehash the Russia investigation as a "conspiracy" when Sussmann was not charged with one.[67] Overall, legal analysts conclude John Durham's investigation did not pass "the smell test."[68] Sussmann was found not guilty in Durham's first special counsel trial on May 30, 2022.[69] Philip Bump of *The Washington Post* said, "John Durham Dumps a Small Bucket of Water on the Forest Fire He Sparked"[70]; he describes the investigation aptly. Durham's limitless investigative nitpicking should have been stopped, as it projects the poisonous, deceptive Trump era and a corrupt DOJ into present efforts to indict Trump by using a false, gaslighted history. Four years after Durham's 6.5 million dollar investigation, it was discovered that he and AG Barr, "the worst AG in fifty years,"[71] had con-

67. Sheth and Barber, "Federal Judge Called Out"; Dunleavy, "Judge Restricts Durham Evidence."

68. Jansen, "John Durham Continues Investigating"; Goldsmith and Sobel, "Durham Investigation."

69. Legare, "Attorney with Ties to 2016 Clinton Campaign."

70. Dilanian and Winter, "Special Counsel Named by Trump"; Cillizza, "Is This All John Durham Has?"; Gerstein, "Durham Prosecution Rests"; Bump, "John Durham Dumps a Small Bucket."

71. Kurtz, "Worst Attorney General."

spired together in hiding information showing Trump's financial crimes while they were in Italy looking for evidence to charge the investigators in the Russia investigation. The Italians had no evidence to share on Russia, but gave them tips on Trump's financial crimes, which they did not pursue. Durham's top investigator, Nora A. Dannehy, and two other prosecutors resigned during the investigation, due to Durham's unethical practices and spreading disinformation.[72]

In large part, hope for a return to American justice by a criminal indictment of Donald Trump rests with Attorney General Merrick Garland. Lawrence Tribe, professor emeritus of constitutional law at Harvard University, said, "If Garland doesn't prosecute Trump, the rule of law is out the window."[73] Professor Tribe's comment on the January 6 investigation warns of all that is riding in holding Trump accountable for his fascist crimes. An indictment, trial, and guilty verdict *for any one of Trump's crimes would begin to break the spell of Trump's gaslighting of America.* American democracy narrowly escaped an end in Trump's attempted coup, but *democratic society did not escape.* It did not get relief from his insidious gaslighting and criminal unaccountability; his violent anti-American influence remains embedded in the minds of Americans with disastrous effects.[74] The transfer of Trump's sick, narcissistic reality to Americans by his gaslighting has resulted in a toxic, narcissistic society splitting at the seams. Unprecedented violence, mass shootings, and fits of rage are common as the ethical and moral restraints of society continue to crumble under Trump's influence. American democratic society cannot wait forever for justice in the case of Donald Trump.[75] Breaking the spell of Trump's gaslighting deception requires an infusion of legally verifiable truth about his crimes and testimony given under oath—*trials in the American justice system are the place where this happens.*

In the meantime, a reprieve for Americans is the special congressional panel's investigation of the insurrection. Televised live hearings provided testimony of what happened on that fateful day from Republican witnesses under oath—Trump's White House staff, his lawyers, and those administrative aides present with Trump on and before the January 6 insurrection. While the hearings are not the same as a trial that leads to a conviction,

72. Savage et al., "How Barr's Quest"; Wu, "Why Merrick Garland Should Fire"; Parton, "Durham Investigation Goes Bust"; Griffing, "Bombshell Report Reveals Durham Probe"; Badash, "Top Legal Experts."

73. DeVega, "Lawrence Tribe: If Garland Doesn't Prosecute."

74. Landen, "Family of Elderly Man Beaten"; Haddon, "Starbucks Shuts Sites."

75. Stone, "Is Trump in His Sights?"; Blitzer, "Law Professor Who Taught Merrick Garland."

congressional fact-finding has brought an avalanche of facts about the January 6 insurrection to the attention of the American public *and* to the Department of Justice to assist in their investigation. The public knows there is more than sufficient evidence to indict Donald Trump for numerous federal crimes. The fact-finding of the congressional hearings is crucial for breaking the spell of Trump's deceptive gaslighting, because tens of millions of Americans not only did not see him coming, but they did not see him going either. They still believe Trump's gaslighting about a stolen election and attempt to justify the January 6 insurrection.

American justice is turning the corner in exposing Donald Trump's crimes but must find its way through the deceptive fog that Trump's gaslighting inflicted on the minds of Americans. The issue is not just Trump's web of lies about his inciting a violent insurrection. The fascist president's machinations and crimes during four years that led up to that event are also involved—*the insurrection is not an isolated event.* The truth is that we are not commenting about a man that "is presumed innocent until proven guilty." Donald Trump's track record of criminal investigations in this chapter shows that he is a lawless, hard-core career criminal, motivated by pathological personality disorders and corrupt morals; he is schooled in avoiding legal culpability and has no intention of stopping or reforming; he has been "lawyered-up" for decades in his crime wave; he knows his Miranda rights. The DOJ has already convicted lower-level participants for their role in the insurrection. The congressional hearings are only a stopgap measure for society's relief from the lawless example of Donald Trump; the only real remedy to restore justice is an indictment, trial, and conviction of Trump for his anti-American crimes committed while president. *The country needs this to escape his deceptive spell, bring healing to society, and return to American justice.*

Chapter 10

The Inevitable Downfall
of a Fascist Tyrant

A *"Tyrant" is a dictator gone bad.*

ELIZABETH MIKA, PSYCHOANALYST[1]

Truth has stumbled in the streets, honesty cannot enter.
Truth is nowhere to be found.

THE PROPHET ISAIAH[2]

WHEN BARACK OBAMA PRESIDED over the presidential portrait unveiling of George and Laura Bush in 2012 and when Joe Biden hosted Barack and Michelle Obama for their portrait unveiling in 2022, former president Obama likened the portraits of former presidents lining the walls to a relay race. After a president takes the baton from the former president, he does the best he can to make American democracy live up to its ideals and then hands off the baton to the next president to continue the race. Obama said in this way every president realizes his work is incomplete and will be finished by other presidents; then, shifting to another metaphor, he said that every president that occupies the White House recognizes they "are renters and will leave when the lease runs out." In her remarks, former first lady Michelle Obama added, "Once our time is up, we move on." *Donald Trump, the forty-fifth president, interrupted the relay race, a runner that refused to hand off the*

1. Mika, "Who Goes Trump?," §5196, §5191.
2. Isa 59:14b–15.

haton and ran in the opposite direction; he treated the White House like he owned it. Obama's metaphor described out-going *democratic* presidents; Donald Trump portrayed an out-going *fascist tyrant.*

AMERICANS SEDUCED BY A FASCIST TYRANT

On November 3, 2020, Donald Trump lost the presidential election to Joe Biden. Biden won by receiving 306 electoral college votes, and in the popular vote he received 81,268,924 votes. Donald Trump lost the election, receiving only 232 electoral votes and receiving 74,216,154 popular votes. This presidential election marked an unprecedented, bizarre place in American election history, because the incumbent president, Donald Trump, lost reelection but *refused to leave office and transfer power to the lawfully elected winner.* When the ex-president finally physically moved out of the White House, the Republican party still considered him the rightful, lawful president! Why? Because the fascist sociopath continued to act like he was still president, and he told them the election was "stolen from him"! What will history say about such gullible people? Most Americans rejected the demented fascist tyrant's Big Lie. Still, in addition to the Republican party there were tens of millions of "Americans" who believed him. It is a memorable, historic moment when truth is so scarce in the streets of America that millions accept the un-American reality that losing a presidential election does not mean the president leaves office! Americans have been overcome by the signature characteristic of a fascist tyrant—they lie profusely. It is not just that sociopath Trump is a compulsive liar but what he did to dismantle American democracy that is so memorable. History will not judge Donald Trump's presidency as a legitimate example of "the American experiment."

Other nations are familiar with banana republics and have experienced fascist coups and fascist tyrants using nefarious means to get into office, lying to their people, and then doing everything in their power to stay there. However, when Donald Trump campaigned for president in 2016, enlisting Russian help to win the election, for the first time the United States of America experienced the frightening un-democratic reality of a sick fascist tyrant. Many Americans and a major political party were just waiting for someone like Trump to come along. The new president immediately weaponized the internet, gaslighting Americans, replacing their American reality with his own pathological fascist reality. He covered up his demented character and tyrannical fascist ways with lies. Americans didn't see him *coming* and, long after he was voted out of office, they didn't see him *going* either.

Trump turned lies into an art form with his gaslighting. The social reality in America today is that Americans still believe the election was stolen from Donald Trump—two years after Joe Biden took office! Yale professor Timothy Snyder explains it: "Post-truth is pre-fascism."[3] A pall of falsehood darkened America and "truth stumbled in the streets." Trump destroyed America's capacity for truth by his gaslighting, until it was "nowhere to be found." America is now a lie-based society where shiny objects—conspiracy theories—dominate the political radar of Americans. When malignant narcissistic fascist Trump left the White House, a substantial part of a sick narcissistic society thought he was still the legitimate president. In other words, the tyrant left behind a society still under the spell of four years of his gaslighting; he had successfully transferred his sick, pathological, un-American reality to Americans. Two years after his election loss, millions of Americans do not accept his election loss, do not know he is a mentally deranged sociopath, and do not realize he dismantled democracy![4] They were seduced by a "dictator gone bad."

The Republican party knew he was an autocrat consumed with destroying American democracy, and they were still complicit in his campaign against democratic elections, against the right to vote, even to the point of supporting a violent coup on the Capitol to stay in power. Today, Republicans remain clueless—or want to appear so—that this is how fascist tyrants remain in power. The wake-up call of a violent insurrection at the US Capitol did not dissuade them. Trump's cult following includes almost the entire Republican party.[5] His presidency was one grandiose deceptive projection—*he* did not steal the election from Hillary Clinton in 2016 with Russia's help; *Joe Biden* stole the election from him in 2020![6] Republicans were sucked in by Trump's gaslighting great deception. Lies not only roam the streets of America and truth is nowhere to be found, or at least very hard to come by, but Trump's fascist Big Lie about a stolen election easily permeates the Republican party and democratic elections and stalks the halls of Congress. The explanation for all this is that *Trump's deceptive gaslighting is an ugly fact of sick American society today.*

3. Snyder, *On Tyranny*, 71; DeVega, "Dr. Lance Dodes."

4. DeVega, "Trump Dances for the NRA;" Bump, "Riot Is Not the Point."

5. Teh, "Anti-Trump Conservative Group"; Wagner, "'Republicans Have Become a Cult"; Gettys, "GOP 'Tripled Down' on Trump's 'Toxicity.'"

6. Davis and Sheth, "Trump Files Grievance-Filled Lawsuit."

A Culture of Lies and Gullible Anti-Americans

How "Americans" could tolerate such bold, nonsensical, continuous lies and antidemocratic behavior from Donald Trump for almost six years is testament to the effectiveness of his gaslighting society with an anti-American Big Lie.[7] The big liar's gaslighting about a stolen election captivated the collective psyche of millions, and he transferred his sick, pathological, anti-American reality to Americans. Tom Nichols of the *Atlantic* explains how Trump did it:

> Donald Trump is central to this fraying of public sanity, because he has done one thing for such people that no one else could do: He has made their lives interesting. He has made them feel important. He has taken their itching frustrations about the unfairness of life and created a morality play around them, and cast himself as the central character. Trump, to his supporters, is the avenging angel who is going to lay waste to the "elites," the smarty-pantses and do-gooders, the godless and the smug, the satisfied and the comfortable.[8]

Nichols's description, eighteen months after Trump left the White House, indicates the damage the tyrant inflicted on society was lasting; it did not disappear when he left office. He describes the psychological captivity of society and toxic lies that brought lawlessness and long-term damage of "pro-Trumpers" who accepted his demented reality: "Now, they are saying they believe that Trump broke the law—but that they don't care." Wait a minute! They don't care he broke the law, a fundamental American value that formerly both Republicans and Democrats held? Nichols says, "They see Trump and his crusade—their crusade against evil, the drama that gives their lives meaning—as more important than the law."[9] Was not that sociopath Trump's view of the rule of law—a fascist tyrant's goal? Chapter 5, "'Gaslighting'—Stealing America's Reality," and chapter 6, "Gaslighting Disables Your Capacity for Truth," gave the psychological theory for what Nichols reports. The gaslighting theme presented throughout this book has shown that a significant portion of American society crumbled under the influence of Trump's fascist lies and that he destroyed their capacity for truth. I speak specifically here about American society's loss of respect for the rule of law—*something to which every fascist tyrant aspires*—but truth itself also suffers terribly under tyrants.

7. The time of writing this chapter is August 2022.
8. Nichols, "New Era of Political Violence."
9. Nichols, New Era of Political Violence."

In gaslighted, gullible American society today, there is not only widespread acceptance of lies but also a boldness to lie anywhere and any time without fear of consequences:[10] in personal relationships, social media, cable news networks, the US Congress, and even in a court of law. It reveals a loss of personal honor in truth telling and a degrading of humanity. The toxic strain of lying was demonstrated in the civil defamation trial of Alex Jones in August of 2022. Caught in lies under oath in a court of law, Jones was repeatedly admonished by Judge Maya Guerra Gamble to respond truthfully: "It seems absurd to instruct you again that you must tell the truth while you testify," she said, "yet here I am."[11] After being caught in an obvious lie that contradicted email evidence held in the opposing counsel's hand, Jones was asked if he knew the meaning of perjury. Jones was unmoved. In the civilized atmosphere of a court of law with rules concerning witnesses responding truthfully, Alex Jones appeared extremely out of place. His responses were like those of an uncontrollable primitive human being, instinctively animal-like, completely unconcerned with truth. He was gaslighted and delusional, showing human nature operating at its lowest level with no concern or capacity for truth.

Jones is representative of a sick society shot through with lies. He epitomized America's conspiracy-oriented culture, making money by telling lies in the most despicable, dishonorable way. In the Sandy Hook mass shooting of forty school children, he continuously lied about the shooting, saying it was a hoax! Jones appeared subhuman, having gone beyond the pale of humanity. The punitive financial judgment against him in the civil trial was not sufficient to cover the tragic loss of children's lives and the immense suffering of their parents; Jones was ordered to pay forty-five million dollars for his lies. It was just the start of his financial doom; other parents and another trial awaited him, where he finally received a one-billion-dollar judgment.[12] His judgments will reverberate in America's conspiracy culture of lies, signaling a warning to conspiracy theorists and news channels like Fox News that parrot lies.[13]

A Sick, Fascist Tyrant's Big Lie

On a much larger scale of political damage, the former Conspirator in Chief captivated tens of millions of Americans and an entire political party with

10. Supica, "'They Weren't Mad at All.'"
11. Queen, "7 Key Moments."
12. Culhane, "Real Reason Alex Jones."
13. Rubin, "Dominion Files $1.6 Billion Lawsuit."

the Big Lie of a stolen election.[14] As the 2020 election results were coming into the White House, fascist Trump heard the announcement that red Arizona had turned blue and he said, "They're stealing this from us."[15] Trump's tortured mind created the idea of a stolen election that would become his mantra and rallying cry during his last two months in office. With the bad news coming in on key electoral states, he saw his self-concocted, grandiose, alternate reality bubble was bursting and he was not going to get his way. Trump knew that he was losing but did not want to accept the election loss; his personality disorders led him not to accept it.[16] Proof of this assertion is that at a Texas rally—after his failed coup attempt—Trump freely admitted that it was his intention to overturn the 2020 election![17] With his compulsive, unscripted macho chatter he was, and is, his own worst enemy. Eventually, he will talk himself into jail and discover that his presidential "get out of jail free" card was a delusion.[18]

Trump listened to election results come in, surrounded by Republican sycophants who feared his wrath and tried to avoid him; they knew the Toddler in Chief was going to throw a tantrum. Of course, there were other malignant narcissists in the room with Trump, like inebriated, compulsive liar Rudy Giuliani[19] who told him exactly what he wanted to hear: "Just say we won!"[20] *Just lie!* Giuliani had no moral compass and no capacity for truth; others in the room were shocked at his audacity. Did he not even have a shred of honor? Giuliani's response that night was just like Trump's response; after the election, he pled with the Department of Justice, "*Just say* the election was corrupt and leave the rest to me and the Republican party." The sociopath who had no concept of honor was saying, "*Just tell the Big Lie.*" It was a tacit admission that he knew he lost the election fair and square but wanted to have the DOJ's endorsement of the Big Lie. When Trump called Georgia's election official Brad Raffensperger and said, "*Just find me 11,780 votes*," it revealed the same sick mindset and criminal intent—*just lie.* Trump found that his sick reality had not corrupted every Republican when he tried to corrupt Raffensperger, asking him to find nonexisting Trump votes, and he refused to lie for Trump. However, Giuliani and other Trump crazies would

14. Parsley, "Donald Trump Demands"; Elrod, "Forever Coup."

15. Leonnig and Rucker, *I Alone Can Fix It*, 345.

16. Wehner, "Trump Is Obsessed."

17. Wallace, "Trump Confesses to the Whole Plot"; Blake, "Trump Makes the Coup Deniers."

18. See the stolen classified documents case at the end of this chapter.

19. Blasi, "Rudy Giuliani Says Being Slapped."

20. Leonnig and Rucker, *I Alone Can Fix It*, 340.

assist him in unravelling a criminal conspiracy to defraud America with the Big Lie, joining the fascist's purpose of nullifying a democratic election.

From the beginning, Donald Trump's primary intention was to remain in power beyond the limits of his term—no matter what. His whole time in office was consumed with boldly attacking and discrediting the key democratic institution of free and fair elections just like any other fascist tyrant; he did not see how this anti-American path might ultimately backfire. For malignant narcissist sociopath Trump, the election loss only meant that by his boundless arrogance, bluster, and grandiose view of himself, he would ultimately get his way. He would double down, dig in his heels, and *just say the election was stolen from him, gaslighting his way back into the Oval Office.* Supreme confidence is a trait of Trump's malignant narcissism. By means of the Big Lie, he would (1) resist the presidential transition of power; (2) continue his gaslighting about a stolen election; and (3) continue to abuse the courts with claims of election fraud, even knowing full well that he could not win the cases without evidence.[21] Seasoned in the manipulation of the courts, Trump used and abused them as a propaganda tool for a pseudo-legal basis for his actions in gaslighting gullible Americans on a stolen election. Mark Aronchick, a Pennsylvania attorney, accused Giuliani of a similar strategy, saying that his court presentations of a stolen election were "like he was living in some fantasy world, making wild allegations that were disgraceful in an American courtroom and worst of all revealing his ignorance of the law."[22] Giuliani did not care if he lied in court or lost. Trump did not care about the law either; both knew the whole point of the frivolous lawsuits was appearance, not reality.

Donald Trump considered the loss of the election a mere public-relations-marketing problem, even though he was surrounded by lawyers telling him that changing the results of the election was illegal; they could not change his mind. He didn't listen to anyone. The grandiose, narcissist ex-president routinely rejected any constraint on what he wanted. The theological view of Trump's motivation—his corrupt human nature—is that he only listens to the whispering of his corrupt self, with the supernatural prompting of unlimited evil that is fundamentally destructive.[23] The psychological view focuses on Trump's fundamental human weakness, sociopathic malignant narcissism; it is why he rejects advice and is also the source of his pathological lying. Supremely confident in his lies, he would just launch his deceptive

21. Leonnig and Rucker, *I Alone Can Fix It*, 390.

22. Leonnig and Rucker, *I Alone Can Fix It*, 389.

23. See chapter 8 on Trump's response to the pandemic, the section entitled "Trump's Unthinkable Pandemic Reaction."

five-step gaslighting strategy and lie to regain power. He would mobilize his base and the cult-like Republican party along with other gullible followers by a flood of lies about the election being stolen from him. Why not? Lying always worked for him; however, he did not have the slightest inkling that his personality disorders could lead to his fall from power. Like any other fascist tyrant, he thought he was above the law and invincible; there was no limit to what he would say or do to stay in power. It was not that he did not know he lost the election—he would let people think that was true, as an ace in the hole court defense for his crimes should he be held accountable later. He did not know his pathologies were no defense. Criminals do not go free just because they are in self-denial. Dr. Lance Dodes states that "sociopath Trump knows what he is doing, but this is not the same as his having personal insights into his own behavior. He does not know he is a sociopath; he is just out of touch with reality about his view of himself as a god-like figure with his grandiose statements; he has not lost touch with the reality of his actions—he knows what he is doing."[24] Unfortunately, the same is true of the sick, narcissistic society that he gaslighted.

AN ANTI-AMERICAN POLITICAL PARTY

A curious political equation developed with Republicans regarding the Big Lie: More than eighty judges of both political parties concluded Trump had no leg to stand on about a rigged stolen election, but polls showed two-thirds of Republican voters believed the election was illegitimate![25] The real question is, How much anti-American talk and activity will Americans tolerate? Unfortunately, currently they have an immense capacity. Under the gaslighting influence of Donald Trump, Republicans proudly wear the MAGA baseball hat, believing they are "Making America Great Again" when Trump is making them *anti-American*. Republican voters are captivated by Trump's fascist lies. Congressional Republicans used the anti-American Big Lie as a platform for election primaries—and won. Impeachment prosecutor Adam Schiff stated that Donald Trump had completely remade the GOP in his own flawed image and that it had no political platform; Republicans just did what Trump said, no longer believing in conservative American values.[26] This is another way of saying that Trump thoroughly gaslighted them with his stolen election lies; his anti-American reality is now their

24. DeVega, "Dr. Lance Dodes."

25. Leonnig and Rucker, *I Alone Can Fix It*, 436; Papenfuss, "Trump Demands to Be Declared"; Greenberg, "Most Republicans Still Falsely Believe."

26. O'Donnell, "Rep. Schiff: Trump Completely Remade."

reality. A sick, fascist, anti-American tyrant subtly attacked and destroyed a core measure of what it is to be "American" in the Republican party.

Trump told Republicans not to vote in the 2022 and 2024 elections, saying the most important thing for them to focus on was not voting! Trump's grandiosity was showing; he told Republicans that if the matter of stealing the election from him was not settled, they should not vote in future elections![27] A malignant narcissistic fascist tyrant revealed his priority; it was not democracy's demise that concerned him, but himself and his power. There were various reactions to his bizarre statement on the cable news networks. One stated it was a threat aimed at the GOP to get with him totally on the election fraud issue or his crazy MAGA supporters wouldn't vote in the elections.[28] Another view was that Trump made it plain that democratic elections were so hopeless that measures outside the authority of the Constitution and law—anti-American measures—were the only resort.[29] The *Daily Beast* reported that Trump was against the efficacy of the vote, stating that he doesn't care about elections and not voting was a stunt to demean elections.[30] One media source cited a detailed history of scores of anti-election voter suppression efforts that Trump and Republicans committed during his presidency, and his statement now was to confuse voters and bring discredit on the upcoming elections.[31] One take on the "don't vote" statement was that it was aimed at minority communities during a pandemic; Trump's election strategy was to "pollute the water, sow doubt, sow confusion, depress voters from having any confidence"[32]—it's enough for them (struggling minorities) to just survive, let alone have a hard time voting. A Republican fascist tyrant was attacking the democratic institution of elections and an anti-American party followed him in lock-step.

The Republican party became more fascist-like under the Big Lie, as they resorted to fascist thug politics; they were complicit in Trump's threats to unleash his crazy base. Episodes where his base did commit violence gave credence to Trump's threats, especially his bold incitement of an insurrection of the Capitol; the violence made the public and politicians afraid. Judges were threatened and intimidated by Trump's base as well as candidates for Republican office, attempting to bring them in line with Trump's will. He was purging the Republican party of those who opposed him or had voted

27. Everson, "Trump Urges Republicans to Sit Out."

28. Earle, "Trump Threatens MAGA Backers."

29. Kilgore, "Trump Says Republicans Must Solve."

30. Lewis, "Trump Tells GOP."

31. Lim et al., "Trump and the Republicans."

32. Lithwick, "Why Donald Trump's Attacks."

to impeach him.[33] The Republicans engaged in shock politics with political election ads that had violent messaging; candidates were shown with pistols and rifles firing at supposed democratic targets. One ad had Marjorie Taylor Greene shooting a high caliber rifle with a scope at an automobile with "socialism" written on the side, blowing it up. *CNN's* Jim Acosta said, "If they [Republicans] really want to shock us, they should tell the truth about the 2020 election!"[34] The shock ads were like throwing gasoline on the fire in a society that was already ablaze and violence prone. Prior to the midterm elections, Republican activist Charlie Kirk at a Tea Party event was asked, "How many elections are they gonna steal before we kill these people?"[35] Surprisingly, no one connected the dots; threats and violence were how fascists think and work. A "dictator gone bad" and his mob were preparing for future election violence leading up to the 2022 and 2024 elections; their gaining a slim Republican majority in the House in the 2022 midterm elections guaranteed revenge politics in Congress as well as a surge of racist violence in American society.

Given the Republican party's focus on restricting the vote, transferring power to fake local state electors to decertify their state's voter ballots, and following Trump's stolen election lie, it appears that *the Republican party has given up on voting in elections as a means for gaining power.*[36] It is giving up on democracy in exchange for fascism. Trump's pathological certainty in the success of his gaslighting scheme created an alternate reality in people's minds that penetrated the Republican party and transformed it into a cult.[37] It is a personality cult of fascist tyrant Donald Trump, a party gaslighted thoroughly on his lie that democratic elections are dishonest, rigged, and not to be trusted.[38] They have earned the title "the anti-American party." Trump is not alone in his fascist anti-American value campaign; there are many other narcissists in the Republican party,[39] some at the malignant stage that readily joined him in a fascist criminal conspiracy for an authoritarian government—even launching an insurrection to get one. Two hundred and

33. Cohen and Lybrand, "'We're Getting All Kinds of Threats'"; Foran and Rogers, "Anthony Gonzalez Is Retiring."

34. Acosta, "Acosta: If Republicans Really Want."

35. Idliby, "Charlie Kirk Gets Asked."

36. Christopher, "Trump Effect."

37. Wagner, "Republicans Have Become a Cult."

38. Marcotte, "Republicans Pick Putin over Democracy"; DeVega, "Don't Be Fooled"; House and Litran, "GOP Vows Revenge for Trump Probes."

39. Berstein, "Accused of Leading Pre-Riot Tour"; Leonnig and Rucker, *I Alone Can Fix It*, 447–52.

three Republican House members voted "no" on a coup prevention bill.[40] Another election coup on or before the 2024 presidential elections would be in keeping with all the preparations that sick, fascist tyrant Donald Trump and his Republican party have made. The MAGA crazies in the party pledge violence toward the FBI,[41] the agency that would battle a future surge of white supremacy and violence, putting them squarely in the fascist camp. Americans need to remember how important the FBI was in the 1960s civil rights movement.

The Rise of the Crazies

Nobel prize-winning Paul Krugman, of the *New York Times*, summed up the state of the Republican party by describing its MAGA cultists as "crazies and cowards." He said that they are probably the minority of GOP politicians, but says "for every Lauren Boebert or Marjorie Taylor Greene there are most likely several Kevin McCarthys, careerists, *apparatchiks*,"[42] a different kind of fanatic, fascist-like as their only concern is to remain in power. Some other GOP members that could be added to the careerist list are Matt Gaetz, Ted Cruz, Mark Meadows, Ron Johnson, Rick Scott, Josh Hawley, and Lindsey Graham. Krugman's mention of cowards describes most of the Republicans in Congress that are merely cogs in the political party machine with unswerving loyalty to Trump.[43] For a variety of reasons and in various degrees of commitment, these Republicans remained loyal to and followed Trump beyond the end of his presidency. "Crazies" are those gaslighted Americans who believe the election was stolen and would do anything Trump asks to keep him in power, even something illegal, like planning and implementing the overthrow of a democratic election. Trump's cult-following of enablers, both crazies and *apparatchiks*, set the scene for what happened in the last two months of his presidency when he became truly desperate to stay in power.

On December 18, 2020, several crazies were gathered with President Trump in a notable, unauthorized midnight meeting illegally convened; they were let into the Oval Office by Peter Navarro's aide.[44] Michael Flynn, Sidney Powell, Emily Newman, and chief executive officer of Overstock.com, Patrick Byrne, were gathered around the Resolute desk; they suggested that

40. Wilkins, "'Siding with Insurrectionists.'"
41. Gettys, "Republicans Plan to Make."
42. Krugman, "Opinion: Crazies, Cowards."
43. Tapper, "Longtime GOP Official."
44. Melber, "Trump Coup Exposed."

Trump declare martial law and proposed crazy conspiracy theories. Only one of the four crazies had security clearance to be there; two of them, Flynn and Byrne, had compromising relationships with the Russians—Byrne had dated lawyer Natalia Veselnitskaya, a Russian agent.[45] One of Trump's lawyers, Eric Herschmann, saw the parties walking in the hallway and followed them into the Oval Office; sitting at the rear of the room, Herschmann challenged the crazies' conspiracy theories that had already been debunked in federal courts across the nation. He phoned lawyer Cipollone and he came running. When he entered the room, he saw people he did not know. He asked Byrne who he was, warning the president that their theories had no legal basis. The meeting quickly turned chaotic, with yelling and cursing that created an impasse between Trump's crazies and the adults in the room. Flynn was yelling at Herschmann, saying the lawyers were not loyal enough and calling them quitters. Herschmann told Flynn to stop yelling at him and challenged him to a physical fight; Flynn then turned on Cipollone, who just shook his head. The lawyers won the night.[46] The question is, How much craziness will Americans tolerate?

A Crazy Plot to Overthrow Election Results

Trump hoped that his violent public rhetoric would create enough civil unrest that he could invoke the Insurrection Act and use the military. He knew that he had to get the governmental agencies with the guns, the FBI, the CIA, and the military, under his control.[47] Crazies like pardoned Michael Flynn were calling for martial law and were ready to invoke the Insurrection Act,[48] but those calls were effectively stopped by a true patriot, General Mark Milley, chairman of the joint chiefs of staff. Milley recognized that the US government was experiencing its "Reichstag moment" just prior to a full-blown coup; fascist Trump was creating circumstances in which he could step in and declare martial law and use the military.[49] When Trump failed at declaring martial law, he committed to a "crazy false elector's plot" to control the count of electoral college votes on January 6, supported by a violent insurrection of his followers at the Capitol. The crazy notion of the false elector's strategy was proposed by lawyer John Eastman.[50] True

45. O'Donnell, "Strzok: 'Triple Russian Threat.'"
46. Leonnig and Rucker, *I Alone Can Fix It*, 425–27.
47. Leonnig and Rucker, *I Alone Can Fix It*, 385, 414–15, 437.
48. Leonnig and Rucker, *I Alone Can Fix It*, 424.
49. Leonnig and Rucker, *I Alone Can Fix It*, 437.
50. KCAL News Staff, "Former Chapman Law School Dean."

to his fascist mindset, tyrant Trump opted for Eastman's plan that would neutralize the people's vote, controlling the outcome of individual state elections with local governments setting up illegal electors supported by Republican members of Congress. Professor Timothy Snyder, historian and expert on authoritarian governments, said the Russians have a phrase, "administrative resource," which refers to the people running an election having the power to determine the outcome![51] It was a fascist strategy for fake electors to thwart "the will of the people," neutralizing their votes. Fiona Hill, Trump's former national security advisor and expert on Russia, warned that Donald Trump was following his role model Vladimir Putin—the one who stays in power permanently by manipulating people and elections.[52]

Eastman's bogus alternate electors theory held that Vice President Mike Pence had unilateral authority to send the votes back to the states where false electors would determine the state vote outcome. Just days before the insurrection (January 2–8), Rudy Giuliani, Steve Bannon, and John Eastman had set up "war rooms" in the Willard Hotel in Washington, DC, to work through the clock searching for ideas on how to implement the plan. On January 2 alone, three hundred state legislators were contacted on conference calls (involving Trump, Giuliani, and Eastman), telling them there was evidence of election fraud and asking them to decertify the election results in their states.[53] The alternate elector plan was illegal, unfounded, junk law; yet on January 4, Eastman and Giuliani presented it to Trump as gospel.[54] Ironically, it was fascist Trump's desperate bid to steal the election from Joe Biden. Prior to the insurrection, Pence called former vice president Dan Quayle for advice. Quayle told Pence to have nothing to do with such a scheme.[55] Pence was the key to the plan; Trump pressured him to invalidate the counting of the votes when Congress was in session on January 6. On insurrection day, assisted by the Proud Boys and Oath Keepers, Trump incited his crazed base to "fight like hell," and the armed crowd stormed the US Capitol to stop the certification of Joe Biden's win. Hours after the violence of the insurrection subsided, members returned to congressional chambers along with Vice President Pence, and he performed his duty certifying the electoral college vote of Joe Biden's win of the 2020

51. Melber, "It Can Happen Here."

52. Lemon, "Trump Wanted to 'Stay in Power.'"

53. Martinez, "Trump's 'War Room.'"

54. Alemany et al., "Ahead of Jan. 6, Willard Hotel"; Leonnig and Rucker, *I Alone Can Fix It*, 447.

55. Alemany et al., "Ahead of Jan. 6, Willard Hotel"; Leonnig and Rucker, *I Alone Can Fix It*, 447.

national election. The false electors plan failed to bring about the results that Trump and the Republicans expected, *but the plan was not shelved.*

The failed violent insurrection of January 6, 2021, did not mean that Donald Trump and the Republican party were finished with Eastman's strategy. Eighteen months later, the ex-president and his party were still pushing the idea of political power shifting to state legislators by targeting Republican secretaries of state and governors, Big Lie candidates in the upcoming November 2022 midterm elections, Republicans that would have a central role in determining state election results.[56] Professor of law and constitution at Yale University Akhil Reed Amar said the Republican party was not finished with Eastman's strategy, but that it might be the means for dealing a final, fatal blow to democracy in the 2024 presidential election.[57] The false elector scheme became a powerful movement with momentum in the Republican party, especially in key electoral states, because they saw such fascist strategies as the only road to regain power. The anti-American shift of power away from voters and voting in the false elector's scheme was supplemented by a fascist focus on instigating violence against the FBI, the DOJ, and federal judges.[58] The hope was that combining false electors with increasing social violence would ensure that the DOJ would not risk an indictment of Donald Trump for inciting the January 6 insurrection. However, the question was not just how much violence the public would tolerate, but how much anti-American violence and crimes Americans would tolerate before they turned on Donald Trump.

CRIMES AMERICANS WILL NOT TOLERATE

I take up the story of Trump's surge of crimes in the last two months of his presidency. His anti-American crimes were a bridge too far, crimes that Americans would not tolerate. He projected this overreaching battle by saying he would never leave the White House because he won the election![59] Ironically, I am not describing an American president leaving office but a sick fascist tyrant refusing to leave. In his last two months, the Toddler in Chief threw a tantrum that created an incredible amount of chaos and harm to American democracy with lightening occurrences of fascist-like crimes:

56. Todd, "Full Schiff: Worst Case Scenario."

57. Velshi, "Debunking 'Democracy Vs. Republic.'"

58. Figliuzzi, "Body Count Grows"; Murphy, "How Dangerous Is Today's Republican Party?"; Bobic, "House GOP Candidate Carl Paladino."

59. Kwong, "Terrifying New Details."

(1) refusing to authorize the presidential transition of power;[60] (2) planning an insurrection; (3) coercing Department of Justice and state election officials to declare election fraud;[61] (4) launching a string of baseless election fraud cases in federal courts;[62] (5) conducting "stop the steal" rallies that fomented public unrest and violence; (6) firing administration officials that would not go along with his anti-American actions; (7) issuing a wave of pardons to convicted felons of his administration;[63] (8) *destroying and removing secret government documents;*[64] and (9) *inciting a violent insurrection on the US Capitol that resulted in loss of life and injuries to one hundred and forty Capitol police*—the occasion for Trump's second impeachment. Item number eight appears to be an insignificant crime, but in fact it vies with item number nine for bringing about the inevitable downfall of Donald Trump. In the end, they would both prove to be crimes Americans would not tolerate.

I do not give the details here of what is already public knowledge about the January 6 insurrection. At the time of this writing,[65] a more detailed picture of what happened is still unfolding. The picture available is this:

- First, Americans saw the insurrection on television: Trump inciting the insurrection with his speech from the Ellipse, his crazy followers attacking the Capitol police and breaking into the congressional chambers to stop certification of Joe Biden's win.

- Second, from June 9 to July 21 2022, eight congressional hearings were televised for the American public that showed a bipartisan congressional panel interviewing key Republican witnesses, giving testimony in a professionally produced video that showed Donald Trump inciting the insurrection with armed violent insurrectionists assaulting police at the Capitol building.[66] Witness testimony had Trump watching the violence of the insurrection on television for 187 minutes, refusing pleas to stop it.[67] The congressional panel's hearings are not finished and are to resume in October 2022.

60. Leonnig and Rucker, *I Alone Can Fix It*, 398.

61. Balz, "What Is Defensible?"

62. Davis and Sheth, "Trump Files Grievance-Filled Lawsuit."

63. Leonnig and Rucker, *I Alone Can Fix It*, 383, 429.

64. Alemany et al., "Boxes of Trump White House Records."

65. August 2022.

66. Feuer and Schmidt, "Jan 6 Panel"; Wikipedia, "Public Hearings of the United States House."

67. Herb, "What We Knot about Trump's Inaction."

- Third, in the Department of Justice's ongoing January 6 investigation, 928 people have been arrested and charged, and 417 have entered guilty pleas.[68] Full details of January 6 will be revealed when the DOJ indicts Donald Trump and associates for their role in the insurrection; their testimony will be under oath backed by the full weight of the law, according to its rules and procedures for getting the truth.[69]

Crimes That Exposed a Thief and Traitor

After Trump left the White House, an unexpected turn of events occurred in August 2022 that brought the momentum of the Republican Trump reelection with false electors and path to the 2024 presidential elections for Trump to an abrupt halt. Suddenly, the probability that Trump would be indicted became a near certainty and public attention swiftly shifted 180 degrees to the truth that Donald Trump had been a thief and traitor from the beginning. Despite his four-year-long pathological machinations to cover up his identity and crimes, he is who he is—a thief and a con man. It was inevitable that his pathologies would expose and destroy him in the high-profile role of the presidency that was open to intense public scrutiny. His pathologies gave him a false sense of entitlement that led him to misuse and abuse the presidential office; inevitably, his pathologically grandiose view of himself backfired and did him in. The natural instincts of a thief led him to commit the unthinkable crime of stealing the nation's secrets.

On August 8, 2022, the FBI served a search warrant on Trump's residence at Mar-a-Lago, and missing classified and Defense documents were found. This treasonous crime in addition to his incitement of an insurrection pointed to the unavoidable truth that fascist tyrant Donald Trump was a traitor. Any personal credibility that rational people may have had evaporated along with any notion that he was fit for a future presidential run. *He committed crimes that Americans would not tolerate.* The events following the search warrant were seismic on American public opinion. The view of an ex-president trying to cope with leaving office shifted to Trump the thief and traitor who was stealing America blind and betraying the country. The investigation of the stolen secret documents unveiled the depth of Trump's massive betrayal of America, a betrayal starting in his election campaign with Russian help and continuing throughout his presidency as he assailed

68. Mascaro et al., "Jan 6 Panel Probes"; Hall et al., "At Least 1,003 People Have Been Charged."

69. Blitzer, "Law Professor Who Taught Merrick Garland"; Press, "Bill Press: January 6 Hearing."

democracy. The bookends of his presidency, two impeachments involving election crimes, indicated that he was always a traitor to democracy. Signs that Republican momentum had stalled with the search warrant revelation were that (1) the red wave for the upcoming primaries came crashing down; (2) Trump was no longer on the ballot for 2024; (3) Trump's phony defense and reelection funds started drying up; (4) approval ratings of Joe Biden increased; (5) Fox News suddenly was no longer a pro-Trump network; (6) the phony John Durham investigation began winding down;[70] and (7) Trump's multiple legal battles surged forward. If just a search warrant at Mar-a-Lago jarred loose Trump's gaslighting façade so that a small beam of light broke through the darkness revealing his true character, what could public reaction be when he is indicted for insurrection and crimes under the Espionage Act? The whole façade of his lies and gaslighting deception will come crashing down under the illuminating truth that *Donald Trump is not only a thief and a con man but a traitor.*

The service of the search warrant at Trump's Mar-a-Lago residence was a natural legal step to recover evidence in an FBI criminal investigation that had been ongoing for eighteen months—the theft of classified documents from the White House. Agents found a trove of classified, top secret and Department of Defense documents in an unsecured place adjacent to where the ex-president entertained foreign visitors![71] The warrant was issued by Federal Judge Bruce Reinhart of Florida and approved by US Attorney General Merrick Garland. Nevertheless, the search caused a bogus uproar in the Republican party and with Trump's crazy base. There was no reason for it. Not only was serving a warrant routine law enforcement activity in a criminal investigation, but the government's national archives had been trying to get Trump to hand over classified documents over a year![72] Despite the routine legal warrant service, immediately threats of violence were made against the FBI, issuing Judge Reinhart, the Department of Justice, the attorney general, and the national archives. The search warrant incident exposed Donald Trump for what he was—a thief and fascist traitor—but it also exposed an anti-American Republican party that unleashed disproportionate fascist-like violence against America's democratic government.[73]

70. Reed, "Durham Probe into Trump-Russia Investigation"; Griffing, "Bombshell Report Reveals Durham Probe."

71. Crane and Chamberlain, "FBI Seized 11 Sets"; Visser, "Trump Had 300 Classified Documents."

72. Brigham, "Yikes: Experts Stunned"; Haberman and Schmidt, "How Trump Deflected Demands."

73. Papenfuss, "National Archives Now Targeted"; Goldman, "Hard Right Stokes Outrage."

Typically, Trump appealed to victim status, engaging in his usual irresponsible audacious rhetoric and a flood of lies.[74] The revengeful violence Trump stoked was focused squarely on law enforcement and the Department of Justice. The sociopath fascist tyrant even publicly named the FBI agents in the search, exposing their identity, targeting them for violent reprisal just for doing their jobs. Subsequently, an FBI office in Cincinnati was attacked by a man clothed in body armor carrying an AR-15 assault rifle; a car chase ensued and the man was killed in a shoot-out with the FBI. Another FBI office in Chicago recorded a violent incident.[75] The fascist incitement of violence targeting government was the same kind that Trump incited at the insurrection on January 6. The fascist violence was condoned and defended by Republicans. Senator Lindsey Graham gave his support with a fascist-like warning on national television: "If Trump is prosecuted for theft of the documents, 'riots would fill the streets.'"[76] *Fascists incite violence against government authority and rage against the rule of law.* Was this an omen of a fascist anti-American Republican future? Far from viewing the incident as an anti-American intolerable crime, congressional Republicans saw the insignificant documents charge as a mere "storage issue," but it may have invoked the fearful memory of crime boss Al Capone's insignificant income tax charge that brought his downfall. They may have seen the search warrant as handwriting on the wall for the party and Trump; a road map writ large for the downfall of the con man and quintessential thief caught red-handed with national defense and top-secret documents, revealing America's deepest held secrets.[77] Why would Trump retain the documents except for their political and monetary worth—leverage to make a deal?[78] Is this a bald statement of opinion and conjecture? Or, is it consistent with everything this book has chronicled about Donald Trump so far?

74. Boggioni, "Trump Demands FBI Return."

75. Dreisbach, "Attempted Attack on an FBI Office."

76. Vlamis and Teh, "Sen. Lindsey Graham Said"; Nichols, "New Era of Political Violence"; Melber, "GOP Goes from Condemning Looting."

77. Boggioni, "Trump Facing a 'Substantial Criminal Case'"; Crane and Chamberlain, "FBI Seized 11 Sets."

78. Haberman and Schmidt, "How Trump Deflected Demands"; Graham, "Art of the Self-Deal"; Cattley, "Donald Trump's Business Partner"; Korecki, "Johnson's Campaign Is Paying."

Recalibrating Thinking about Donald Trump's Guilt

Before reviewing roller-coaster information and often frenzied piecemeal reporting of "breaking news" about the Mar-a-Lago search warrant, we need to recalibrate our thinking about Donald Trump's guilt. Throughout the book, I have documented a malignant narcissist sociopath serial-criminal, transferring his sick reality to the public in multiple legal cases where Trump was *always* presumed to be innocent. Too often the devious sociopath, schooled in avoiding detection for his crimes and manipulating the legal system, drove media reporting with his worn-out strategy of victimization, absurd lies, projection, weaponizing the courts with phony delay motions, and his lawyers' bizarre claims creating the impression that he is innocent. Trump is a deceiver adept at swaying the court of public opinion with his branding/marketing experience. He always claims victim status and asserts the protections of the law like an innocent citizen—the same law that he ignores and abuses everyday—*when the truth is that he is a career criminal that continually abuses the law and the legal system, escaping accountability.*[79]

Sometimes, the news media mimics a court of law, reporting all the protections and rights of a person under investigation—as though preserving Trump's legal rights was ever the issue. He does not need someone to read Miranda rights to him. He knows he has "the right to remain silent" and "the right to an attorney." He has rejected the right to be silent—to his lawyer's chagrin—and no one has been able to stop him from making foolish legal gaffs and manic tirades that often amount to confessions. In his unfathomable arrogance, he repeatedly spews out foolish defenses and diversions that are consistent with a hard-core criminal. He has abused the right to an attorney like no other, making "lawyering-up" an art form. He has been successful in repeatedly suckering the public and the media into a roller-coaster ride with his deceptive gaslighting and deflections of guilt, resulting in confusion. With American justice failing to indict him, Trump has had all the time he wants to perfect avoiding justice; the wisdom of Solomon proclaims, "When the sentence for a crime is not quickly carried out, people's hearts are filled with schemes to do wrong" (Eccl 8:11). I will avoid Trump's obvious delay tactics and not grapple with every bold psychological projection, bizarre excuse, and rabbit hole he and his lawyers offer for his unlawful possession of stolen classified documents.

We need not allow a career criminal and sociopath to dictate our narrative, chasing Trump's pathological responses, lies, distractions, and

---

79. Johnson, "Mystal: What Does Trump Have to Do?"

manipulation of the media that treats each of his new crimes as though he is "presumed innocent until proven guilty." I do not presume Donald Trump's innocence. This book is not a court of law, nor is the media's "breaking news." We are not in court presenting evidence under the obligation to exclude any notion of prejudice. Therefore, I will not avoid applying what we already know of Trump and his possession of stolen classified documents and will not avoid mentioning the obvious guilt of a career criminal, pretending that he is innocent of crimes for which he has escaped accountability. His guilt has not only been substantiated by the legal community reporting on multiple criminal investigations and by a congressional select committee's investigation of the January 6 insurrection, *but frequently Trump confirms his guilt by his own mouth.* Being a sociopath both helps and hurts him. Further, he has appealed to the Fifth Amendment against self-incrimination over four hundred times in a major civil case where, according to civil law, claiming the Fifth Amendment can be taken as a tacit admission of guilt. Therefore, I choose to rely on what we already know about Donald Trump— what we have seen with our own eyes and what we have chronicled about him—information from professional psychologists, historians, politicians, and legal experts in the media during the years of his presidency.

With the two crimes that Americans won't tolerate, in the first crime, congressional hearings have presented ample evidence to show Trump guilty of inciting an insurrection along with other federal crimes, and hundreds of participants in the insurrection he incited have been found guilty in a court of law. In the second crime, the theft and retention of classified documents his guilt is obvious. He knowingly and willfully committed crimes against the Espionage Act and obstructed justice; it has been confirmed by the legal community's experts, the intelligence community, and law school professors. Up to this point, his delay tactics have worked, but they have finally reached an intolerable level for Americans. In both anti-American crimes, Donald Trump should be indicted without unnecessary delay in the first half of 2023. In the book's closing chapter, to ignore and exclude Trump's criminal history and guilt previously chronicled in its pages would not only be ironic and silly, but would betray the book's purpose in showing he is a career criminal and how he dismantled American democracy.

Prior to the actual trial of Donald Trump, therefore, I choose to depend on what we have already chronicled about Donald Trump's criminal behavior and continue to rely on expert legal analysts in the media, intelligence experts, respected prosecutors, and professors of law to boil down legal arguments in the complex documents case. They are necessary sources when there is so much misleading legal flak in media reports surrounding the explosive case—mainly due to its unprecedented nature and Trump sowing lies and confusion about his obvious guilt and the media rushing to give undeveloped breaking news. Our attention will not be diverted from what we already know about Donald Trump; he is (1) a deceptive gaslighter of American society; (2) a pathological liar and con man who distorts, deflects, and deceives; 3) a lawless, successful abuser and manipulator of courts and the justice system; 4) a racist; 5) a sadistic sociopath that threatens, incites, and *enjoys* violence and its effects; and 6) a fascist anti-American tyrant who committed multiple felonies in dismantling American democracy. There is sufficient evidence to indict Donald Trump for the unthinkable crimes of planning and inciting an insurrection, as well as betraying the nation's national security by stealing, retaining and converting classified government documents—a commission of espionage. At this point in the book, it would also be silly to avoid an elephant in the room.

THE OPEN BOOK OF A SOCIOPATH TYRANT'S CRIMES

In an *MSNBC* interview, Nicolle Wallace asked Mary Trump, based on her personal and professional knowledge of him, why Donald took the classified documents and kept them at Mar-a-Lago. His psychoanalyst niece replied with a coy smile, "Of course he did!"[80] She implied, "Why would anyone think anything else!" She warned of the dangers of his pathological personality disorders worsening and his not stopping his criminal activity. Mary Trump also said, "We need to recalibrate our thinking about the danger of the man; everything that he did before, there is worse to come." This ominous statement comes from Mary Trump's professional viewpoint of her uncle the sociopath; she even fears the end of "the American experiment."[81] The damage Trump has inflicted on democracy's institutions is incalculable and will take generations to repair. Of course, Fox News erroneously blames Joe Biden for it all, the one they call "sleepy Joe," as if he could inflict such massive destruction in two years! However, in one presidential four-year term and afterwards, a sociopath dictator gone bad could and did. Trump corrupted everything he touched. Mary Trump's explanation of Donald's pathological personality disorders in chapter 1 made him, his behavior, and his presidency virtually an open book. The extent of damage that sociopath Trump did to America by stealing and keeping the classified documents is undetermined, but there are reports of deep damage occurring to the country's intelligence efforts—agents in the field, national security, and the trust of America's allies.

80. Wallace, "Trump's Niece on Why He Kept Documents."
81. Wallace, "Trump's Niece on Why He Kept Documents."

A Realistic View of the Classified Documents Case

While the Department of Justice will finally decide the issue of Trump's guilt with the classified documents,[82] intelligence and legal experts agree that mere possession of Department of Defense documents (NDI)[83] is prima facie evidence of a crime under the Espionage Act. Such a crime depends on the factors of knowledge, intent, and willfulness. The Espionage Act does not use the term "classified," but rather criminalizes the *willful, unlawful retention of information relating to national defense.*[84] This is not just a thief possessing stolen property. With NDI, the incriminating issue is not their markings but their content.[85] It is a crime to have NDI documents outside a secure government facility and to willfully retain possession of them. Ex-president Trump not only stole and retained them but played a shell game with them and fought to retain possession of them by extorting the National Archives and Records Administration (NARA) for years, demanding the exchange of documents he wanted for those he possessed![86] In 2018, with the Hillary Clinton email scandal in mind, Trump signed into law a bill that made it a felony to remove or retain classified documents.[87] Trump knew and willfully retained the documents, trying to strike a deal with them; this is clear evidence of intent in the federal crime of espionage. Also, Trump's complicit and duplicitous team of lawyers and aides transmitted the classified documents to a third party, putting classified information on a thumb-drive and uploading it on a computer.[88] All of these actions illustrate Trump's pathological grandiosity in committing crimes—so much you can't keep up—even with the crime of espionage. Documents marked "classified" that FBI agents recovered *were* classified, property of the US government. Without question, Trump knowingly, intentionally, and willfully retained them and refused to give them back; he even confessed to trying to strike a deal with NARA for them! Declassification of the documents is a red

82. Wallace, "Andrew Weissmann Predicts."

83. "NDI" are National Defense Information documents under the Director of National Intelligence.

84. Rohrlich and Sollenberger, "Unsealed Affidavit"; Boggioni, "Specific Espionage Act Provision;" Mordowanec, "What Is NDI?"

85. Mordowanec, "What Is NDI?"

86. Watson "National Archives Head Defends."

87. Arkin, "Exclusive: Informer Told FBI"; Haberman, "Trump Was Warned Late Last Year."

88. Reimann, "Trump Lawyers Turned over More"; Willmer and Tillman, "Trump Lawyers in Mar-a-Lago Search"; Collins et al., "Trump Team Turns over Additional."

herring, a Trump diversion; they are not and could not be ex-president Trump's property.

All of Trump's claims to own the documents are false, diversionary noise, and proof of (1) his gross ignorance of the presidency; (2) his pathological personality disorders; and (3) Trump and his attorneys' guilt, having obstructed giving the documents to NARA and the Department of Justice for several years. Specifically, their actions mean they are guilty of felony obstruction of justice. Trump *knew* it was a crime to have them and he was given warnings that he should not have them. In finally serving a search warrant, the FBI sought stolen materials that a judge deemed was evidence of a crime, and FBI agents found numerous boxes containing over one hundred stolen NDI and other classified documents in Trump's home. *His possession of the documents at Mar-a-Lago, conspiracy to retain possession of them, and their sheer numbers indicate Trump's commission of federal crimes.*

Basic legal facts regarding the documents case are in the following timeline from Eugene Kiely's article on FactCheck.org. It is a compilation of facts derived from legal documents: DOJ filings, motions, affidavits, NARA records, quotes from Judge Cannon's order, Trump's lawyer's motions, and the Eleventh Circuit Court orders.

January 18, 2021

With two days left in his presidency, Donald Trump moved boxes of documents from the White House to Mar-a-Lago.

February 18, 2022

After a year of continuous but unheeded requests from NARA for missing classified documents, they finally received fifteen boxes from Mar-a-Lago (MAL) containing highly classified documents mingled with other records, and some had been torn up.[89] NARA contacted the DOJ because among the materials in the boxes were over one hundred documents with classification markings, comprising more than seven hundred pages, and some had the highest levels of classification, including special access program (SAP) materials. After Trump possessed the documents for a year, his lawyer Evan Corcoran, delayed requests from NARA and the DOJ wanting to review the documents in their investigation of Trump. Corcoran responded with specious counterclaims (Trump declassified them, has executive privilege over

---

89. Kiely, "Timeline of FBI Investigation."

them, Trump said he owned them, etc.) and delayed inspection of them (April 29, May 1, and May 24 in 2022). Regarding Trump's counter claims of executive privilege, acting archivist of NARA Debra Steidel Wall denied the claim, saying, "The 'protective' claim of privilege" was not even close to being valid. The Trump team's compliance with a grand jury subpoena to hand over other remaining classified documents was incomplete and evasive. Corcoran finally said DOJ officials could meet him at MAL on June 3, 2022, to receive more classified materials.[90]

June 3, 2022

Jay Bratt, chief counterintelligence and export control secretary in the DOJ's National Security division, and three FBI agents visited MAL to receive all classified documents. An unnamed Trump attorney presented them with a single Redweld envelope containing documents the attorney believed were classified. Later, in a secure place, the FBI found the contents of the envelope were "38 unique documents bearing classified markings: 5 marked CONFIDENTIAL, 16 marked SECRET, 17 marked TOP SECRET."[91] The FBI agents toured the storeroom at MAL, which contained fifty to fifty-five boxes of documents, but "critically, the former President's counsel explicitly prohibited government personnel from opening or looking inside any of the boxes that remained in the storage room, giving them no opportunity to confirm that no documents with classification markings remained."[92] Also, Trump's counsel claimed all records from the White House were in one location—the storage room—and there were no other records in private office space or other locations on the premises. The president's custodian of records gave the FBI a signed certification letter attesting a diligent search was made for all documents in response to the grand jury subpoena and no copies, written notations, or reproductions of any kind were retained from any document.[93] It is also critical to note that despite the assurances Trump attorneys gave, this did not preclude that the classified documents were concealed or removed before the arrival of the federal officials.

90. Kiely, "Timeline of FBI Investigation."
91. Kiely, "Timeline of FBI Investigation."
92. Kiely, "Timeline of FBI Investigation."
93. Kiely, "Timeline of FBI Investigation."

August 8, 2022

An FBI search warrant was served at MAL. Agents found items named in the warrant for crimes of which Judge Reinhart said there was probable cause: "willful retention of national defense information" (18 U.S.C. § 793), "concealment or removal of government records" (18 U.S.C. § 2071), and "obstruction of a federal investigation" (18 U.S.C. § 1519).[94] The facts listed in the timeline are derived from various legal documents, so the precise connections and details of the story the documents tell must be filled in by the DOJ investigation. However, some implications of obstruction and lying by the Trump team stand out. When comparing the assertions attorneys gave at MAL on June 3 with facts revealed by the DOJ search warrant on August 8, (1) the search warrant resulted in the recovery of over three hundred classified documents, more than was presented in the single envelope (thirty-eight documents);[95] *therefore, they did not surrender all documents*; and (2) the FBI located documents in Trump's office; therefore either the attorneys lied on June 3 or the classified documents were concealed or moved before the search warrant on August 8.[96] Lies about no documents remaining and concealing/moving them are both federal crimes; Trump and his attorneys will be held accountable for this subterfuge.[97]

September 2, 2022

A more detailed list of the classified documents was released by the DOJ. The list included forty-eight empty folders marked as having once containing "classified" material, including forty-three of the folders from Trump's office. The search also turned up forty-two empty folders marked as "Return to Staff Secretary/Military Aide" (NDI documents), including twenty-eight in Trump's office.[98] No one possesses Defense documents in their private residence. A fundamental question that the DOJ, the Special Master, and the Eleventh Circuit Appeals Court have asked is, Why did Donald Trump have the classified documents in his possession? He has never given a rational

94. Kiely, "Timeline of FBI Investigation"; Schonfeld and Beitsch, "DOJ: Classified Documents."

95. Visser, "Trump Had 300 Classified Documents."

96. Herb et al., "Justice Department Says Classified Documents"; Arkin, "Exclusive: Informer Told FBI."

97. Griffing, "Trump 'Played Role' in Lawyer Falsely Telling"; Reiser, "Joyce Vance: Trump Testing Out"; Gerstein and Cheney, "Trump Team Likely Sought to Conceal."

98. Kiely, "Timeline of FBI Investigation."

answer to this question—as to what his interest is in them. The sheer volume of classified documents begs the question—over three hundred documents.[99] The DOJ investigation will reveal the precise answer to why Trump had the documents. However, the empty folders and the following October 7 incident provide a provisional answer—*espionage.*

October 7, 2022

Jay Bratt, chief counterintelligence of the DOJ, told Trump lawyers they were seeking more classified documents removed from the White House,[100] and FBI agents were questioning people about whether classified documents were at Trump Tower and his New Jersey club; such questions are usually asked when agents are building probable cause for a search warrant.[101] Previous chapters indicate everything malignant narcissist Donald Trump has done has been to increase his personal power[102] and add to his personal wealth in launching numerous financial grifts.[103] The political and monetary value of the documents suggests what Trump might do with them. The above timeline evidence indicates that team Trump not only retained the classified and defense documents but they were concealed and moved in and out of MAL.[104] What we already know about Donald Trump is that he a thief and betrayer of American democracy. It all could indicate violations of the Espionage Act. However, the DOJ trial will give a definitive answer as to what happened to the NDI and other classified documents.

September 5, 2022

The complication of the document case reached a critical point when Judge Aileen Cannon, a Trump appointee, caused a typical Trump delay with an utterly lawless ruling in appointing a Special Master to review the documents seized in the FBI search warrant.[105] She blatantly gave Trump

99. Maddox, "*NYT*: Trump Had 300+ Documents."

100. Mangan, "DOJ Suspects Trump Still Has."

101. Suebsaeng and Rawnsley, "Justice Department Asking If Trump Stashed."

102. Bernstein, "For Donald Trump, Information."

103. Dawsey and Arnsdorf, "Trump Rakes in Millions"; Leonard, "Trump Says Mar-a-Lago Documents Coverage."

104. Reilly et al., "DOJ Says Trump Likely 'Concealed.'"

105. Korecki et al., "Judge Grants Trump's Special Master Request."

special treatment with a bizarre ruling untethered to law.[106] Judge Cannon
proved to be a "loose cannon," giving Trump special treatment because he
was an ex-president rather than a ruling that considered everyone equal
under the law. An unprecedented move was discovered regarding the instal-
lation of Cannon in the case. Trump's lawyer went "judge shopping" and
filed in person for a judge outside of the MAL and search warrant issuing
area, a district forty-four miles away, without mentioning that there was
other litigation connected with the filing.[107] Subsequently, Cannon's ruling
was condemned by the Eleventh Circuit District Appellate Court, because
it not only gave Trump special treatment but stalled the investigation and
imperiled national security. After a rebuke from the Circuit Court and the
nation's law community, Judge Cannon was unfazed and continued to give
Donald's case special treatment by an appeal to Supreme Court Justice Clar-
ence Thomas to delay even further. Professor of law Lawrence Tribe said
that the Eleventh Circuit Court basically ruled "she had no business being
there"; that is, making rulings in the documents case, let alone involving the
Supreme Court. Cannon's involvement ended with her ruling repudiated
and her removal from the case.[108]

How the Trump Story Ends

The intervention of corrupt judge Aileen Cannon in the high-profile documents case made it seem that Donald Trump would not be held accountable
for anything he did. A news article addressed the point, "What Does He
Have to Do to Go to Jail?"[109] He appeared unstoppable; however, Ruth Ben-
Ghiat said, "The law can."[110] All of Trump's efforts to corrupt democratic
institutions in the last two months of his presidency were about trying to
corrupt and co-opt the FBI and the armed forces (those with the guns), but
he failed because two American patriots opposed him—FBI Director James
Comey and General Mark A. Milley. The proof of fascist Trump and an
anti-American Republican party's current intentions to destroy the FBI is

106. Weissmann, "Ruling Untethered to the Law"; Melber, "DOJ Hits Back"; Pagliery, "Court Screwup Reveals"; O'Donnell, "Lawrence: DOJ Tells Trump-Picked
Judge"; Brigham, "Experts Slam Judge Cannon's"; Palmer, "Aileen Cannon Decision to
Give Trump."
107. Derysh, "'I Find It Bizarre'"; Pagliery, "Trump Went Judge Shopping."
108. Legare and Quinn, "Appeals Court Agrees to Speed Up."
109. Johnson, "Mystal: What Does Trump Have to Do?"
110. Kruse, "Trumpology: Can Trump Still Sue?"

their ongoing campaign of violence directed at the FBI.[111] However, General Mark Milley is still in his position, and both institutions are in place to deal with the troubles coming from white supremacists. Notably, AG Merrick Garland has declared unequivocally that Donald Trump will be prosecuted for his involvement in the January 6 insurrection along with his other crime that Americans will not tolerate—espionage. Two years after being on the case, however, it is not a question of if but when Garland will indict Trump. Another indication of his end is that New York AG Leticia James has already sued (indicted) Trump in a civil case that will come to trial in 2023; a conviction of his financial crimes in that case will ruin the Trump organization. Legal accountability for Donald Trump appears to be on the horizon.

Returning to Nicolle Wallace's interview with Mary Trump, Wallace noted the long pattern of Donald's influence over Republicans and she asked Mary "how he was able to co-opt the whole Republican party." Mary did not say he gaslighted them. As a psychoanalyst, she reached deeper, explaining that Donald's sociopath father never corrected him for any of his deviant behavior as a child, instead praised him for it, resulting in Donald mirroring his father's sociopath reality. She pointed to Donald's pathological personality disorders. She said Donald had never been held accountable for anything in his entire life. Her concurrence with the psychological view expressed throughout this book, that Donald's pathologies are fundamentally important for understanding him and his ability to influence others (his gaslighting), is not a coincidence. Mary's explanation of Donald's pathological personality disorders in chapters 1 and 2 made his criminal career as president an open book. They were the key to understanding him and his presidency. At the end of the interview, Wallace asked how she saw the Trump story ending. Mary chuckled at the difficulty of Nicolle's question, but did not hesitate, "*Donald must be indicted, tried, and adequately punished swiftly!*"[112] Mary's answer to this question is also in concurrence with this book. Indeed, what will break his gaslighting spell over both the Republican party and a narcissistic society is when for the first time he will be held accountable for his crimes, marking a significant deterrent to crime in American society and the return to American justice. Imprisonment would be a serious narcissist wound for sociopath Trump, severely restricting him from having his way, but it is not a cure for his pathologies nor does it negate any possibility of his continuing influence in some measure even from prison.

111. Gettys, "Republicans Plan to Make."
112. Wallace, "Trump's Niece on Why He Kept Documents."

AG Merrick Garland's appointment of a special counsel to pursue the indictment of Trump for crimes that America will not tolerate is a crucial step toward his end. The Select House Committee investigation has submitted its January 6 insurrection report to the DOJ. However, the new House Republican leader, Kevin McCarthy, has already announced and shown the party's revengeful intentions to attack the Department of Justice and AG Garland's investigation of Trump, to create chaos in Congress.[113] AG Garland countered Republican intentions by safeguarding the investigation and pursuit of indicting Trump by appointing Special Counsel Jack Smith. The same line-prosecutors working on Trump's indictment will continue; they only have been given a new boss. Jack Smith is uniquely qualified. He was a war crimes prosecutor in The Hague and convicted over one hundred persons in the Kosovo war crimes trials, including prosecuting former presidents as well as the mafia when he worked in the DOJ's ethical standards division. The Special Counsel rules are clear: Jack Smith is "not subject to day-by-day supervision by any official" and has autonomy in supervising the investigation of Trump. AG Garland still has the final say, but if there is any disagreement between Smith and Garland it becomes public and Garland is required to report it to Congress.[114] In spite of an anti-American Republican party's view to cause chaos in Congress, the investigation and indictment of Donald Trump will not be interfered with even by the election of a new president and appointment of a new attorney general in 2024. However, a delay of a year to the already two-year investigation of the January 6 insurrection makes no sense, as there is sufficient evidence to indict him now. Credibility will return to the DOJ when Merrick Garland, as the nation's chief prosecutor, *indicts Donald Trump for crimes that America will not tolerate.* His act will secure America's democracy, restore public confidence in the rule of law, and break the spell of Trump's gaslighting in America. It all depends on what the nation's chief prosecutor will tolerate.

113. Beitsch, "McCarthy's Planned Expulsion."
114. Melber, "MSNBC's Melber: Garland Can't 'Punt' Decision."

Conclusion

*I expect there will be more such grief in our days as human depravity
continues to irk the Omnipotent.*

MERCY DUKE, PENOBSCOT BAY, MAINE (CIRCA 1766)[1]

You should not be surprised at my saying, "You must be born again."

JESUS OF NAZARETH[2]

IN HER BOOK *BARKSKINS*, Annie Proulx's historical novel about early America, her character Mercy Duke was concerned about the influence of human
depravity and made a prediction at the dawning of American democracy.
Both Mercy and the framers of the American Constitution were realistic
about the obvious danger of human depravity. At the time, the gospel of Jesus Christ was taking hold in the country, bringing an unusual awareness of
fallen human depravity. Christian historians and theologians call the times
the period of the Great Awakenings or the "evangelical revivals." Christian
scholars identify three or sometimes four periods of the revivals when
the power of the gospel transforming corrupt human nature was called "a
born-again experience." Mercy Duke's concern about human depravity took
place in the period leading up to the second evangelical revival; the revivals
played an important role in shaping American culture and the American
Constitution.[3]

At the close of the fourth evangelical revival (1960 to 1980), I was preparing a doctoral dissertation from which the definition of "evangelical" was
taken and used in the introduction to this book. The descriptions denoting

1. Proulx, *Barkskins*, 215.
2. John 3:7.
3. Lepore, *These Truths*, 43–45, 49–54, 59, 67–68, 72–75, 86, 92, 106, 135; Meacham,
American Gospel, 3–12, 67–76, 146–78.

evangelical centered on personal salvation through faith in Jesus and his gospel. Jesus' victory overcoming fallen human depravity became a reality for his followers as they were empowered by God's gift of the indwelling Holy Spirit. Therefore, the book's title, *Why Didn't Evangelicals "See Him Coming"?*, is paradoxical. How could evangelical Christians experiencing the reality of God's salvation, schooled in biblical morality, and living in a free democracy not recognize an immoral anti-American president—how could they not "see him coming"? Not recognizing the danger of Donald Trump when he displayed all the earmarks of human depravity, being deceived by him, and then committing allegiance to him gives a clue to the paradox. It is a *stark contradiction of what evangelicals believed it was to follow Jesus as Lord.* It indicated a spiritual compromise had taken place, forgetting what Jesus said about spiritual conversion overcoming corrupt human nature and the importance of continuing in faith. It indicated a lapse in believing that impaired their spiritual discernment.

Nearly two-and-a-half centuries after, Mercy Duke's statement still holds true for Donald Trump. He illustrates how human depravity can still deceive Christians and other Americans, destroy American democracy, and divert Christians from following Jesus as Lord. Biblical theology presented the case for Trump as a slave to human depravity, a prisoner of a corrupt human nature that is open to the power of sin, motivated and controlled by supernatural evil.[4] The Trump story is a study in corrupt human nature and evil flowing through him, corrupting others on a national scale. Without an appropriate continuing response of faith to the omnipotent God's salvation, Mercy Duke's prediction holds true, corrupt human nature continues, remaining the same, and people are vulnerable to evil and its influence— Christians included when they stop "believing," stop following the Lord of life. Throughout this book, biblical theology suggested the intervention of supernatural evil in describing the depth of Trump's deception and dismantling of American Democracy. Psychology, law, and political science played an important role in this portrait of evil but did not penetrate deep enough into the question of Donald Trump's corruption, people's reaction to him, and the devastating results. Biblical theology plumbs the depths of questions about corrupt human nature regarding Trump's gaslighting, society's vulnerability to it, and the deadly results. The paradox is that evangelical Christians had already personally resolved the matter of a corrupt human nature through their faith in Jesus and his gospel, yet some listened to Trump's dog whistle, hearing a bullhorn and responding to him; they were overcome by his gaslighting and not able to access the power of the gospel.

4. 2 Pet 2:2, 10, 12–14, 18–21.

Their faith response to Jesus and the power of his gospel was interrupted and compromised. The theological question is not if this interruption could occur, but why it occurred, because *continuing faith in Jesus matters.*

It is a mistake to think Donald Trump is a genius at deception—that he is "crazy like a fox"—in his ability to deceive. This is contrary to what people who know him and work with him say. A multitude of illustrations from his presidency indicate the toddler in chief demonstrating his stupidity and lack of understanding about almost everything. Psychology presented a strong case, showing his arrested cognitive development and inability to devise and launch a complex plan of deception. As helpful as the secular solutions of the psychology, law, and political science are for understanding and healing society after Trump, they are complex, tenuous, and do not probe deep enough, as Holocaust psychologist Captain Gilbert discovered at the Nuremberg trials. Furthermore, law has never been the solution for corrupt humanity, as the law of Moses demonstrated; instead, it brought "awareness" of what sin was, "inciting" the desires of the flesh from a corrupt human nature, bringing spiritual death when it was intended to lead Israel to embrace Jesus the Messiah as a solution for a righteous life. A corrupt human nature made the law function that way.[5] Faith in Jesus and his salvation is the only solution to the powerful corruption of human nature. Human knowledge and understanding does not penetrate the supernatural dimension where the problem of human depravity resides—sin against a Holy God.[6] Nevertheless, followers of Jesus should lead the way in secular society as engaged citizens, even though the ultimate solution to corrupt humanity is spiritual and beyond the reach of human efforts; they should participate with other Americans, giving a clear witness to Jesus' gospel in confronting white supremacy and racism.[7] Jesus himself is the best example of this "redemptive engagement" in society, as the New Testament shows; Christians should follow him.

After mental health professionals stood up to Trump, declaring him a danger to society as a sociopath and malignant narcissist, their profession and the terms they use to describe him are now beginning to get the attention of Americans. There is a reason why the term "gaslighting" was Merriam-Webster's word of the year in 2022. Americans accessed the word online every single day of the year, and its impact on the English language rose quickly in the last four years,[8] due to the gaslighting of pathological

5. Rom 3:19–20; 7:9–11; Gal 3:19–22.

6. 1 Cor 1:17–30; 2:10–16.

7. Rom 13:1–10; Titus 3:1–8; 1 Pet 2:11–17; Heb 13:15–16, 18.

8. Italie, "'Gaslighting' Is Merriam-Webster's Word."

liar Donald Trump and his impact on American society. The sociopath ex-president has no empathy, no oath, no creed, or ideology—his only allegiance is to himself. Therefore, it should be no surprise that his pathological personality disorders inevitably led him to be exposed as a traitor and a thief. A pathological entitlement and grandiose view of "self" led him to abuse the presidency by amassing personal wealth and destroying any power other than his own; all these actions were indicated clearly in the definition of "sociopath." Trump did what sociopaths do. A simple equation explains the tragedy of his presidency. A sociopath gained ultimate power in the American presidency plus the fact that he was given total immunity and not held accountable for crimes plus the fact that his abuse of office and ineptitude for the task meant he followed his malignant narcissistic impulses in deceiving Americans equals a corrupt and chaotic presidency that nearly destroyed democracy.

Donald Trump does not seek help for his pathologies, and they only become worse as they continue to serve his voracious, corrupt human nature. What does he do after leaving office? Not having learned a thing, the dangerous sociopath declares that he is running for president again, ignoring criminal indictments closing in on him and spurred on by his Teflon, grandiose self-image, he doubles down on gaslighting that still holds America in its spell, ignoring his party's pleas not to run and giving himself a second chance to destroy American democracy. Yale historian Timothy Snyder said, "Many reasonable people make a mistake of assuming that rulers who came to power through institutions cannot change or destroy those very institutions—even when that is exactly what they have announced that they will do."[9] Donald Trump became president in a democratic election, even though he declared his fascist intentions to destroy democratic institutions. Throughout his presidency he continued to announce those intentions in word and deed, but he did it without causing undue alarm or political consequences! He declared he was going to Make America Great Again, and with that lie he was able to cover up his fascist intentions to destroy democracy with *gaslighting*, plucking it one feather at a time.

A fundamental trait of Donald Trump's pathology-ridden character is that he is a deceiver. His deceptive speech has the quality of enigma and riddle. As enigma, his words have hidden meaning under obscure or ambiguous allusions, so that we can only guess at their significance. At times, his speech has a riddle quality, involving contradictory statements with a hidden meaning to be guessed at.[10] Both of these dictionary definitions describe

9. Snyder, *On Tyranny*, 24.

10. "Enigma" and "riddle," in Jewell, 261, 720.

the pattern of Trump's devious speech throughout his life. Psychoanalysts call such speech "gaslighting"; all the deception in his language immediately translates when people's fears, grievances, and corrupt human nature provide a connection with the gaslighting malignant narcissist and he steals their truth and their reality. His gaslighting is like a dog whistle; the deceptive speech carries a subliminal message understood by vulnerable people who choose to believe his lie, *because it is what they want to hear*; falsehood is "in the eye of the beholder." The key to Professor Snyder's paradoxical statement about the mistake of reasonable people seeing someone elected in a democratic election while declaring he would destroy it is they suspend reason and like hearing the candidate's lies. He put his finger on how Trump could campaign for the American presidency saying he wanted to Make America Great Again while at the same time declaring his intentions to destroy democracy. Trump's pathological personality disorders enabled him to gaslight America and attack democratic institutions, even doubling down by boldly eulogizing and consorting with fascists and dictators. Two years after leaving office, he was doing the same thing, boldly announcing that the United States Constitution should be terminated and he should be restored as president![11] Along with many others, *CNN*'s legal analyst Elie Honig said such a statement was "wrong, crazy, and dangerous," adding that would leave us without democracy.[12] Most Republicans were silent after hearing Trump's treasonous declaration, but some gaslighted Republicans agreed with the statement and defended it!

In the early days of deciding the title for the book, *Why Didn't Evangelicals "See Him Coming"? Donald J. Trump's Deception and Dismantling of American Democracy*, I was aware that evangelicals and other Americans did not see him coming because of the powerful gaslighting deception he launched in the internet age and that, from the beginning of his political life, his purpose was to dismantle democracy. However, it was not until Donald Trump left the White House that the incredible depth of his deception and how meticulously he dismantled democracy became clear as well as how close he came to destroying it. Two years after Trump left office, reports in the media continue to reveal the depth of his duplicity and crimes, and I expect this revelation will continue for many years to come. His Big Lie that the election was stolen was successfully transferred to tens of millions of Americans, even becoming the platform for Republicans running for Congress in the midterm elections—and they won control of the House of Representatives! Today, politicians from both parties, journalists, constitutional

11. Reed, "Trump Doubles down on Calls"; Feinberg, "Trump Falsely Claims."
12. Reed, "'Wrong, Crazy, Dangerous.'"

scholars, and experts in the legal community say that democracy is on the brink and that we are seeing the end of "the American experiment." The spell of Trump's gaslighting still has a grip on Americans; the presence of an anti-American Republican party in Congress is the proof.

President Biden was criticized for his preelection speech before the 2022 midterm elections because he warned Americans that they could lose democracy. His message was not preelection scare tactics and hyperbole but an accurate assessment of American democracy in its "dismantled state." However, a silent majority of democracy-loving Americans heard the speech, and their votes stopped a predicted red wave. It was not his speech alone that stopped the wave, but it became a catalyst for *a silent majority of Americans that realized an anti-American minority was running roughshod over them*; the tail was wagging the dog. The moment arrived when the accumulation of anti-American rhetoric, Trump's election denials, anti-voting rights, the attack on objective truth and core American values—especially the blatant revival of white supremacist racism, both in society and in Congress—political violence aimed at the Department of Justice and the FBI, and an anti-American president inciting an insurrection and involving himself in espionage *all merged in the minds of Americans, and it was just too much*! The pathological audacity and hypocrisy of anti-American Trump droning on about a stolen election, wearing the symbol of his biggest lie, a MAGA hat, registered with the electorate, and a silent majority of Americans voted their conscience. Democracy-loving Americans found their tolerance level for just how much anti-American rhetoric and actions they would take and expressed their indignation in the vote.

With increasing awareness of the loss of democracy, the silent majority's indignant action in the midterm elections may turn into a red, white, and blue wave of Americans that are determined to defend democracy against the assault of white supremacy and racism on every front. The blatant Republican threats of a civil war against democracy in Congress, repeated by Donald Trump and his violent anti-American base, must be taken seriously. In times of profound uncertainty and collective feelings of anxiety about America's ability to meet these anti-American challenges, Americans must resolve to fight and win this ideological war. The ideological bombs of white supremacists aimed at American institutions by Oath Keepers and members of Congress should be considered as real as the bombs that fell on Pearl Harbor that awakened "the sleeping American giant" eighty-one years ago today. The clear provocations of white supremacists in word and violent deed call for preparedness and will to undertake the ideological war until they are defeated. Individual Christians and the church have a critical role in this ideological war against white supremacy, not least because it falsely claims allegiance to Christianity.

As helpful as the secular disciplines are for understanding the era of sociopath Donald Trump, they do not give a complete answer to the fundamental question of the book: Why didn't *evangelicals* see him coming? The historic definitions of evangelical in the introduction all reach for what is true and authentic about the Christian faith, ultimately pointing to the gospel of Jesus Christ in the first century, to find what was true and authentic in the life and teachings of Jesus of Nazareth, in the lives of his apostles, and in those who believed. When speaking of himself as the "good shepherd" (John 10:1–30), Jesus addressed our question about how evangelicals didn't see Donald Trump coming. He said, "My sheep *listen to my voice*; I know them, and they *follow me*" (v. 27, emphasis mine) and "they will never follow a stranger but will run from him because they do not recognize his voice" (v. 5). Christians listening to his voice and following him can distinguish between the voice of the good shepherd and the "thief and robber who comes only to steal and kill and destroy" (v. 10a). Jesus said, "No one can snatch them away from the Father's hand" (vv. 28b–29). Therefore, if Christians listened to the voice of Donald Trump, *they chose to follow him and listen to his voice*. Not recognizing he was a morally and spiritually bankrupt human being showed they were not even trying to distinguish good from evil or *could not do so*. Those who have been enlightened by salvation and "have tasted the heavenly gift sharing the Holy Spirit" that are unable to tell the vast difference between a depraved human being and biblical righteousness have suffered spiritual impairment and have drifted away from following Jesus as Lord and the authentic gospel of salvation they once believed, turning to follow another and a "different gospel which is really no gospel at all."[13] A major contributing influence that has weakened many evangelicals in their Jesus-focus as the Lord of life and center of New Testament Christianity is the 170-year relationship with a Dispensational theology in its history that emphasizes an extreme Israel-focus and a Pollyanna view of the early church in the New Testament. It has left many with a corrupt "Rambo" view of the Christian faith in an Old Testament context, where the suffering servant of the Lord and a suffering church have slipped away, along with their Jesus-centered faith, replaced with visions of a "Christian nation" instead of Jesus' spiritual "heavenly kingdom" of power.

The Bible is a mine of clear information for distinguishing between good and evil. It frequently describes the surrender of self to corrupt human nature, like Donald Trump's example, "boasting about evil all day long,

13. Heb 5:11—6:1; Gal 1:6–7; 3:1–6.

loving evil rather than good, falsehood rather than speaking the truth, and loving every harmful word."[14] Its description of the response of divine love in Christians, the "others-focus" of redeemed human nature, is also clear:

> Love must be sincere. Hate what is evil; cling to what is good. Be devoted to one another in love. Honor one another above yourselves. Never be lacking in zeal, but keep your spiritual fervor, serving the Lord. Be joyful in hope, patient in affliction, faithful in prayer. Share with the Lord's people who are in need. Practice hospitality. Bless those who persecute you; bless and do not curse. Rejoice with those who rejoice; mourn with those who mourn. Live in harmony with one another. Do not be proud, but be willing to associate with people of low position. Do not be conceited . . . Do not be overcome with evil, but overcome evil with good.[15]

Evangelicals and other Christians knew the difference between Donald Trump and the Christian faith; it was obvious—he stuck out like a sore thumb. Yet many, whether intentionally or unintentionally, were blind to the difference. Committing the grievous spiritual choice of turning away from Jesus as Lord, setting aside the grace of God in disobedience to his word, they unlocked the potential influence of corrupt human nature that brings devastating spiritual consequences.[16] As they experienced the dark abyss of Donald Trump, for some the abyss gazed back and they were vulnerable and influenced by him to the extent that their faith-contact with Jesus was broken.[17] Committing allegiance to Donald Trump, which he constantly demanded, someone so obviously contrary to personal faith in Jesus and the righteousness that comes from believing in him, inevitably leads to disavowing the word and Spirit of Christ, marking the reassertion of the "old self" and returning to the desires of the flesh that bring serious consequences for spiritual life.[18]

The simple message that Jesus and his disciples proclaimed was "repent and believe."[19] In the dark times of the first century, reception of the simple gospel message was followed by demonstrations of the power of heaven transforming sinful human nature, healing the sick, raising the

---

14. Ps 52:1–4; 2 Pet 2:1–22; Lev 19.

15. Rom 12:9–16.

16. 1 John 1:5–7; 2:4–6; Matt 12:29–45.

17. 1 John 5:21.

18. John 12:35b–36; Gal 5:16–21.

19. Mark 1:14–15.

dead, and overcoming the forces of darkness.[20] In the darkest moments of Donald Trump's influence today, believing the gospel message brings the same demonstration of the power of heaven. The inner transformation of flawed human nature from an omnipotent God is so powerful that Jesus spoke of it as "being born again" and the result was receiving a new human nature.[21] The unfailing factor of this inner transformation is that it includes *the gift of Jesus' powerful indwelling Spirit in the heart of whoever believes.*[22] Continuing faith in Jesus, eyes fixed on the pioneer and perfecter of faith, is critical;[23] he or she that believes faces life in this world with a renewed self and power to control their body of flesh in overcoming its desires and for loving others. The only failure with this great salvation is on the human side; an interruption of believing is the human choice that breaks *a faith-connection with Jesus the Lord of life.*

Christians in any period of salvation history that have turned away from Jesus only need to call upon God as they did in the beginning of their profession of faith, repent, and return to him. The simplicity of this message provides a glimpse into God's amazing grace and the unfailing love that Jesus exemplifies. The prophet Hosea spoke about God's promise of unfailing love, even to the people of God who rejected him repeatedly in their wilderness wanderings: "I led them with cords of human kindness, with ties of love. To them I was like one who lifts a little child to the cheek, and I bent down to feed them."[24] The apostle Paul referred to the wilderness wanderings of Israel also, applying that image as a warning to all generations of Christians; he instructed that what happened to Israel in their wilderness wanderings were examples of those who had experienced God's grace but set their hearts on evil things, focusing on themselves and the desires of the flesh, grumbling, and testing Christ; yet Paul emphasizes the faithfulness of God in dealing graciously with those who strayed.[25] The truth of the gospel has been inserted throughout this book as a redemptive thread, a message of hope as I reviewed the repeated examples of Trump's corrupt human nature. It brings the only release from the influence of corrupt human nature, bringing refreshing insight and perspective for assessing Trump and his evil influence on America. The prophet Hosea's promise of unfailing love and grace is a reminder for those who have been damaged by their wandering

20. John 1:1–5; 9–13; 11:43–44.
21. John 1:13; 3:3–8.
22. Rom 8:5–11; John 20:23.
23. Heb 12:2.
24. Hos 11:4.
25. 1 Cor 10:1–13.

from Christ and their gaze into Trump's dark abyss. Solomon captures the
sobering ethical lesson for those who have strayed onto the wrong path:

> Do not set foot on the path of the wicked
> or walk in the way of evildoers.
> Avoid it, do not travel on it;
> turn from it and go on your way.
>
> For they cannot rest until they do evil;
> They are robbed of sleep till
> they make someone stumble.
> They eat the bread of wickedness
> and drink the wine of violence.
>
> The path of the righteous is
> like the morning sun,
> shining ever brighter till
> the full light of day.
> But the way of the wicked is
> like deep darkness,
> *they do not know*
> *what makes them*
> *stumble.*[26]

26. Prov 4:14–19, emphasis mine.

Bibliography

Acosta, James. "Acosta: If Americans Really Want to Shock Us, Then Do This." YouTube video. CNN, Oct 23, 2021. https://www.youtube.com/watch?v=Ut3mEq-bfmU .

———. "Acosta to Trump: Take Your Fake White House Seal and Play President Somewhere Else." CNN, Jul 10, 2021. https://www.edition.cnn.com/videos/politics/2021/07/10/trump-pretender-in-chief-acosta-hold-on-nr-sot-vpx.cnn.

———. "'This Is Not Going to End Well': Former Fox News Anchor Reacts to Recent Rhetoric." CNN, Jan 28, 2022. https://www.cnn.com/videos/media/2022/01/28/gretchen-carlson-fox-rhetoric-russia-ukraine-sot-dip-vpx.cnn.

Albert, Victoria. "Comey: 'Trump Eats Your Soul in Small Bites.'" *Daily Beast*, May 1, 2019. https://www.thedailybeast.com/comey-trump-eats-your-soul-in-small-bites.

Albright, Madeleine. *Fascism: A Warning*. New York: HarperCollins, 2018.

Alemany, Jacqueline, et al. "Ahead of Jan. 6, Willard Hotel in Downtown D.C. Was a Trump Team 'Command Center' for Effort to Deny Biden the Presidency." *Washington Post*, Oct 23, 2021. https://www.washingtonpost.com/investigations/willard-trump-eastman-giuliani-bannon/2021/10/23/c45bd2d4-3281-11ec-9241-aad8e48f01ff_story.html.

———. "Boxes of Trump White House Records Found at Mar-a-Lago Resort." *Washington Post*, Jan 9, 2022. https://www.washingtonpost.com/politics/2022/02/07/boxes-trump-white-house-records-found-mar-a-lago-resort/.

Alexander, Dan, and Richard Behar. "The Truth behind Trump Tower Moscow: How Trump Risked Everything for a (Relatively) Tiny Deal." *Forbes*, May 23, 2019. https://www.forbes.com/sites/danalexander/2019/05/23/the-truth-behind-trump-moscow-how-the-president-risked-everything-for-a-relatively-tiny-deal/?sh=109e7005bc32.

Applebaum, Anne. *Twilight of Democracy: The Seductive Lure of Authoritarianism*. New York: Doubleday, 2020.

Arkin, William M. "Exclusive: An Informer Told FBI What Documents Trump Was Hiding, and Where." *Newsweek*, Aug 10, 2022. https://www.newsweek.com/exclusive-informer-told-fbi-what-docs-trump-was-hiding-where-1732283.

Associated Press. "George Clooney Says He Won't Run for Office, Calls Trump a 'Knucklehead.'" *Hollywood Reporter*, Oct 10, 2021. https://www.hollywoodreporter.com/news/politics-news/george-clooney-donald-trump-knucklehead-1235029412/.

Avlon, John. "Why Anti-Asian American Violence Is Rising—Along with White Supremacist Propaganda." *CNN Opinion*, Mar 17, 2021. https://www.cnn.com/2021/03/17/opinions/asian-hate-crimes-us-avlon/index.html.

Badash, David. "Former Trump CFO Nearing 'Unexpectedly Favorable' Plea Deal with Manhattan DA." *New Civil Rights Movement*, Aug 15, 2022. https://www.thenewcivilrightsmovement.com/2022/08/former-trump-cfo-nearing-unexpectedly-favorable-plea-deal-with-manhattan-da-nyt/.

———. "Top Legal Experts Call for Ethics Probe into Bill Barr's Handpicked Special Counsel John Durham." *AlterNet*, Oct 19, 2022. https://www.alternet.org/2022/10/actual-witch-hunt-john-durham.

Baier, Bret. "New Internal Documents Reveal COVID Origins Downplayed." Fox News, Jan 25, 2022. https://www.foxnews.com/video/6293658048001.

Balk, Tim. "Donald Trump Sues NY Attorney General Letitia James in Bid to Halt Probe of His Business." *New York Daily News*, Dec 20, 2021. https://www.nydailynews.com/news/politics/us-elections-government/ny-trump-sues-letitia-james-ag-20211220-qq2g7aawrvczlh2dbrb5u7fszu-story.html.

Balz, Dan. "What Is Defensible in the Case against Trump?" *Washington Post*, Jun 25, 2022. https://www.washingtonpost.com/politics/2022/06/25/trump-jan6-hearings-sundaytake/.

Baragona, Justin. "Kevin McCarthy Promises to 'Pass on All of Hannity's Messages' to McConnell." *Daily Beast*, Oct 28, 2021. https://www.thedailybeast.com/kevin-mccarthy-promises-to-pass-on-all-of-sean-hannitys-messages-to-mitch-mcconnell.

Beals, Monique. "Poll: 50 Percent of Republicans Don't Believe Their Vote Will Be Counted Accurately." *The Hill*, Nov 2, 2021. https://thehill.com/homenews/campaign/579527-poll.

Beitsch, Rebecca. "Democrats Say GOP Lawmakers Implicated in Jan 6 Should Be Expelled." *The Hill*, Oct 25, 2021. https://thehill.com/policy/national-security/578377-democrats-say-gop-lawmakers-implicated-in-jan-6-should-be-expelled/.

———. "McCarthy's Planned Expulsion of Intel Democrats Prompts Howls." *Yahoo! News*, Nov 22, 2022. https://news.yahoo.com/mccarthy-planned-expulsions-intel-democrats-010854634.html?fr=sycsrp_catchall.

Ben-Ghiat, Ruth. *Strongmen: Mussolini to the Present*. New York: Norton, 2020.

Benen, Steve. "The Investigation into the Russia Investigation Isn't Going Well." Maddow Blog, MSNBC, Oct 1, 2021. https://www.msnbc.com/rachel-maddow-show/maddowblog/investigation-russia-investigation-isn-t-going-well-n1280593.

———. "Court Suspends Giuliani's Law License over Bogus Fraud Claims." Maddow Blog, MSNBC, Jun 25, 2021. https://www.msnbc.com/rachel-maddow-show/maddowblog/court-suspends-giuliani-s-law-license-over-bogus-fraud-claims-n1272298.

Bernstein, Andrea. "For Donald Trump, Information Has Always Been about Power." *ProPublica*, Sep 14, 2022. https://www.propublica.org/article/why-trump-hoarded-documents-information.

———. "Accused of Leading Pre-Riot Tour, GOP Reps Story Evolves (Again)." Maddow Blog, MSNBC, May 24, 2022. https://www.msnbc.com/rachel-maddow-show/maddowblog/accused-leading-pre-riot-tour-gop-reps-story-evolves-rcna30357.

Bidar, Musadiq. "Obama Blames Social Media for 'Turbocharging Some of Humanity's Worst Impulses.'" CBS News, Apr 21, 2022. https://www.cbsnews.com/news/obama-disinformation-speech-social-media/.

Blake, Aaron. "Trump Makes the Coup Deniers Look Silly Again." *Washington Post*, Jan 1, 2022. https://www.washingtonpost.com/politics/2022/01/31/trump-makes-coup-deniers-look-silly-again/.

Blasi, Weston. "Rudy Giuliani Says Being Slapped on the Back by a ShopRite Employee Felt 'As If a Boulder Hit Me.'" *MarketWatch*, Jul 1, 2022. https://www.msn.com/en-us/news/politics/rudy-giuliani-being-slapped-by-shoprite-employee-felt-as-if-a-boulder-hit-me/ar-AAYVpOH.

Blitzer, Wolf. "Law Professor Who Taught Merrick Garland Predicts He Will Indict Trump." CNN, Jul 2, 2022. https://www.cnn.com/videos/politics/2022/07/02/merrick-garland-trump-possible-indictment-ac360-vpx.cnn.

Bobic, Igor. "House GOP Candidate Carl Paladino Said Merrick Garland 'Probably Should Be Executed.'" *HuffPost*, Aug 18, 2022. https://www.huffpost.com/entry/carl-paladino-merrick-garland-executed_n_62fe499ae4b063894830e640.

Boggioni, Tom. "Former US Attorney Spills the Beans on 'Thuggish' Bill Barr's Interference in SDNY Cases." *Raw Story*, Sep 9, 2022. https://www.rawstory.com/bill-barr-donald-trump-2658171533.

———. "A Specific Espionage Act Provision Could Seal Trump's Fate: Former NSA Counsel." *Raw Story*, Aug 27, 2022. https://www.rawstory.com/donald-trump-espionage.

———. "Trump Demands FBI Return Seized Documents back 'to the Location from Which They Were Taken.'" *Raw Story*, Aug 14, 2022. https://www.rawstory.com/donald-trump-mar-a-lago-2657861053.

———. "Trump Facing a 'Substantial Criminal Case' after 'Theft' of NSA Documents: Legal Analyst." *Raw Story*, Aug 29, 2022. https://www.alternet.org/2022/08/trump-documents-2657902193.

Borger, Gloria. "Trump's Unorthodox Phone Habits Complicate January 6 Investigation." CNN, Feb 13, 2022. https://www.cnn.com/2022/02/13/politics/trump-telephone-records-capitol-riot-investigation/index.html.

"Bragg's Bad Choice: A Prosecutor Shares New Light on Manhattan D.A.'s Trump Decision." Editorial. *New York Daily News*, Jul 31, 2022. https://www.nydailynews.com/opinion/ny-edit-bragg-trump-20220731-ehi3oykm5nhlxd55q6v36m5mau-story.html.

Breuninger, Kevin. "Trump Asks Judge Not to Hold Him in Contempt, Says He Complied with Subpoena for NY Attorney General." CNBC, Apr 20, 2022. https://www.cnbc.com/2022/04/20/trump-asks-judge-to-reject-ny-ag-letitia-james-contempt-request.html.

———. "Trump Took Fifth Amendment More Than 440 Times in Refusing to Answer New York Attorney General's Questions." CNBC, Aug 10, 2022. https://www.cnbc.com/2022/08/10/trump-says-he-refused-to-answer-ny-attorney-generals-questions-in-probe-of-his-business.html?utm_content=Main&utm_medium=Social&utm_source=Twitter#Echobox=1660182397.

Brigham, Bob. "Experts Slam Judge Cannon's Latest Pro-Trump Rulings: 'Hilarious, Corrupt, Shameless, and Obvious.'" *Raw Story*, Sep 29, 2022. https://www.rawstory.com/aileen-cannon-scandal.

———. "'Yikes': Experts Stunned after Trump's Late-Night Release of NARA Document." *Raw Story*, Aug 23, 2022. https://www.rawstory.com/trump-nara.

Bright, John. *The Kingdom of God: The Biblical Concept and Its Meaning for the Church*. New York: Abingdon, 1953.

Bromwich, Jonah, et al. "Judge Holds Trump in Contempt over Documents in New York A.G's Inquiry." *New York Times*, Apr 25, 2022. https://www.nytimes.com/2022/04/25/nyregion/trump-investigation-letitia-james-contempt.html.

Bruce, F. F. *The Gospel of John*. Grand Rapids: Eerdmans, 1983.

Buchanan, Larry. "Tracking 30 Investigations Related to Trump." *New York Times*, May 13, 2019. https://www.nytimes.com/interactive/2019/05/13/us/politics/trump-investigations.html?mtrref=www.google.com&gwh=5364461B9C9AA0B781233 2F91ECoF615&gwt=pay&assetType=PAYWALL.

Bump, Philip. "Again: There's No Evidence Hillary Triggered the Russia Probe." *Washington Post*, May 23, 2022. https://www.washingtonpost.com/politics/2022/05/23/again-theres-no-evidence-hillary-clinton-triggered-russia-probe/.

———. "John Durham Dumps a Small Bucket of Water on the Forest Fire He Sparked." *Washington Post*, Feb 18, 2022. https://www.washingtonpost.com/politics/2022/02/18/john-durham-dumps-small-bucket-water-forest-fire-he-sparked/.

———. "The Riot Is Not the Point." *Washington Post*, Jun 9, 2022. https://www.washingtonpost.com/politics/2022/06/09/riot-is-not-point.

———. "Trump Presented His Russia Hoax Theory to a Court. It Went Poorly." *Washington Post*, Sep 9, 2022. https://www.washingtonpost.com/politics/2022/09/09/trump-2016-russia-clinton/.

———. "The Unique Role of Fox News in the Misinformation Universe." *Washington Post*, Nov 9, 2021. https://www.washingtonpost.com/politics/2021/11/08/unique-role-fox-news-misinformation-universe/.

Burge, Ryan. "Faith in Numbers: Fox News Is Must-Watch for White Evangelicals, a Turnoff for Atheists . . . and Hindus, Muslims Really Like CNN." *The Conversation*, May 24, 2021. https://theconversation.com/faith-in-numbers-fox-news-is-must-watch-for-white-evangelicals-a-turnoff-for-atheists-and-hindus-muslims-really-like-cnn-161067.

Burke, Lauren Victoria. "Donald Trump Spent Almost a Year Playing Golf during Presidency." *Milwaukee Courier*, Jan 9, 2021. https://milwaukeecourieronline.com/index.php/2021/01/09/donald-trump-spent-almost-a-year-playing-golf-during-presidency/.

Carey, Matthew. "'Trump Is No Hitler, but . . .': 'The Meaning of Hitler' Directors on Parallels between the Führer and 45." *Deadline*, Aug 14, 2021. https://deadline.com/2021/08/the-meaning-of-hitler.

Carpenter, Amanda. *Gaslighting America: Why We Love It When Trump Lies to Us*. New York: HarperCollins, 2018.

Cattley, Alice. "Donald Trump's Business Partner Fires Billion-Dollar Bombshell." *Lovemoney*, Oct 18, 2022. https://www.msn.com/en-us/news/politics/donald-trumps-business-partner-fires-billion-dollar-bombshell/ss-AA133vXl?ocid=U305DHP#image=4.

Chait, Jonathan. "Trump's Greatest Triumph Is Convincing America That Crime Pays." *Intelligencer, New York Magazine*, Mar 24, 2022. https://nymag.com/intelligencer/article/trumps-greatest-triumph-is-convincing-america-crime-pays.html.

Choi, Joseph. "One-Third of GOP Candidates Have Embraced Trump Election Claims: Report." *The Hill*, Jul 6, 2021. https://thehill.com/homenews/campaign/561664-one-third-of-gop-candidates-have-embraced-trump-election-claims-report/.

Christopher, Tommy. "Trump Effect: Whopping 60 Percent of Republicans Think 2020 Election Should Be Overturned." *Mediaite*, Oct 27, 2021. https://www.mediaite.

com/news/trump-effect-whopping-60-percent-of-republicans-think-2020 election-should-be-overturned/.

———. "Watch: Mary Trump Goes Off on Media for Normalizing Trump, Says Dems Should Call for Him to Be Prosecuted." *Mediaite*, Aug 28, 2021. https://www. mediaite.com/news/watch-mary-trump-goes-off-on-media-for-normalizing-trump-says-dems-should-call-for-him-to-be-prosecuted/.

Cillizza, Chris. "Donald Trump's Longtime Legal Strategy May Be Catching Up with Him." CNN, Apr 25, 2022. https://www.cnn.com/2022/04/25/politics/trump-legal-strategy-history.

———. "Is This All John Durham Has?" CNN, Sep 17, 2021. https://www.cnn. com/2021/09/17/politics/john-durham-probe/index.html.

———. "Kayleigh McEnany Is Gaslighting America." CNN, Aug 25, 2021. https://www. cnn.com/2021/08/25/politics/kayleigh-mcenany-crises-trump-biden/index.html.

———. "Yet More Evidence Donald Trump Is Running a Shadow Presidency." CNN, Sep 9, 2021. https://www.cnn.com/2021/09/09/politics/donald-trump-13-military-members-killed-afghanistan/index.html.

CNN Staff. "Read: Justice Department's Response to Trump's Supreme Court Appeal." CNN, Oct 11, 2022. https://www.cnn.com/202210/11/politics/justice-department-responds-to-tump-appeals-supreme-court-mar-a-lago/index.html.

Cohen, Luc, and Karen Freifeld. "Trump Organization Defense Rests Case in Criminal Tax Fraud Trial." Reuters, Nov 29, 2022. https://www.reuters.com/legal/trump-organization-defense-rests-case-criminal-tax-fraud-trial-2022-11-28/.

Cohen, Marshall, and Holmes Lybrand. "'We're Getting All Kinds of Threats.' Judge Says Defiant US Capitol Rioters Are Fueling Anger from Disgruntled Trump Supporters." CNN, Oct 22, 2021. https://www.cnn.com/2021/10/22/politics/judge-capitol-riot-threats/index.html.

Cohen, Michael. *Disloyal: A Memoir; The True Story of the Former Personal Attorney to President of the United States.* New York: Skyhorse, 2020.

Cole, Brendan. "Donald Trump Sent Record 12,200 Tweets in 2020, Ends Year with Stock Market Boast." *Newsweek*, Jan 1, 2021. https://www.newsweek. com/donald-trump-record-12200-tweets-2020-stock-market-boast-1558415 #:~:text=Unconventional-,Donald%20Trump%20Sent%20Record%2012%2C 200%20Tweets%20in%202020,Year%20With%20Stock%20Market%20Boast &text=President%20Donald%20Trump%20ended%20his,of%207%2C700%20 set%20in%202019.

Collier, Gene. "Gene Therapy: Fox News Is Getting People Killed, but You Knew That." *Pittsburg Post-Gazette*, Sep 8, 2021. https://www.post-gazette.com/opinion/gene-collier-columns/2021/09/08/Fox-News-is-getting-people-killed-but-you-knew-that/stories/202109080029.

Collins, Kaitlan, et al. "Trump Team Turns over Additional Classified Records and Laptop to Federal Prosecutors." *CNN Politics*, Feb 10, 2023. https://www.cnn. com/2023/02/10/politics/trump-classified-records-laptop.

Collinson, Stephen. "The GOP's Devotion to Trump Threatens to Destroy American Democracy." CNN, May 4, 2021. https://www.cnn.com/2021/05/04/politics/donald-trump-gop-democracy/index.html.

Comey, James. *A Higher Loyalty: Truth, Lies, and Leadership.* New York: MacMillian, 2018.

Concepcion, Summer. "Report: Presidential Diarist Says Trump 'Iced Out' WH Record-Keepers Days before Insurrection." *Talking Points Memo*, Apr 3, 2022. https://talkingpointsmemo.com/news/trump-white-house-record-keepers-presidential-diarist-january-6.

Connor, Tracy. "Federal Judge Stomps All over Trump's Russiagate Lawsuit against Hillary." *Daily Beast*, Sep 9, 2022. https://www.thedailybeast.com/federal-judge-david-middlebrooks-disembowels-donald-trump-russiagate-lawsuit-against-hillary.

Cooper, Anderson. "'There Has Been a Coup': Bernstein Reacts to New Evidence on Trump's Role in Riot." CNN, Oct 8, 2021. https://www.cnn.com/videos/politics/2021/10/08/bernstein-trump-executive-privilege-january-6-ac360-vpx.cnn.

Coppins, McKay. "The Man Who Broke Politics." *Atlantic*, Oct 15, 2018. https://www.theatlantic.com/magazine/archive/2018/11/newt-gingrich-says-youre-welcome/570832/.

LoveProperty Staff. "The Shocking Secrets of Trump Tower." *LoveProperty*, Jul 21, 2021. https://www.loveproperty.com/gallerylist/112888/the-shocking-secrets-of-trump-tower.

Covitz, Howard. "Health, Risk, and the Duty to Protect the Community." In *The Dangerous Case of Donald Trump: 27 Psychiatrists and Mental Health Experts Assess a President*, edited by Bandy X. Lee, §3685–838. New York: St. Martin's, 2017. Kindle ed.

Crane, Emily, and Samuel Chamberlain. "FBI Seized 11 Sets of Classified Documents in Trump Mar-a-Lago Raid." *New York Post*, Aug 12, 2022. https://nypost.com/2022/08/12/fbi-seized-11-sets-of-classified-documents-in-trump-mar-a-lago-raid/.

Crane-Newman, Molly, and Chris Sommerfeldt. "Trump Organization, Allen Weisselberg Charged with 'Sweeping' Tax Fraud Crimes in NYC." *New York Daily News*, Jul 1, 2021. https://www.nydailynews.com/news/politics/new-york-elections-government/ny-manhattan-da-trump-org-allen-weisselberg-2021 0701-j6xbedefyvadzjplg4nhjrw7ne-story.html.

Culhane, John. "The Real Reason Alex Jones Was Hit with a Nearly $1 Billion Sandy Hook Judgment." *Slate*, Oct 14, 2022. https://slate.com/news-and-politics/2022/10/alex-jones-billion-dollar-sandy-hook-judgment-justified.html.

Cummings, William, et al. "Mueller's Investigation Is Done. Here Are the 34 People He Indicted along the Way." *USA Today*, Mar 25, 2019. https://www.usatoday.com/story/news/politics/2019/03/25/muellers-russia-report-special-counsel-indictments-charges/3266050002/.

Daily Beast Staff. "Ivanka Just Might Flip on Her Dad, Mary Trump Says." *Daily Beast*, Jul 6, 2021. https://www.thedailybeast.com/ivanka-trump-just-might-flip-on-her-dad-mary-trump-says.

D'Antonio, Michael. "Opinion: How We Can Repair the Damage of the Trump Presidency." CNN, Sep 21, 2021. https://www.cnn.com/2021/09/21/opinions/after-trump-presidency-qa-dantonio/index.html.

Date, S. V. "Last Call at Trump's Monument to Corruption." *HuffPost*, May 3, 2022. https://www.huffpost.com/entry/donald-trump-hotel-corruption_n_62707be5e4 b04a9ff89ef131.

Davis, Anthony. "Interview of Dr. Bandy X. Lee." YouTube video. *Meidas Touch, the Weekend Show*, Aug 7, 2002. https://www.youtube.com/watch?v=DREKGn4nPhQ.

Davis, Charles R., and Sonam Sheth. "Trump Files Grievance-Filled Lawsuit Accusing Hillary Clinton and Democrats of Carrying out an 'Unthinkable Plot' to Tie His Campaign to Russia." *Business Insider*, Mar 25, 2022. https://www.businessinsider.com/trump-lawsuit-alleges-unthinkable-plot-to-tie-him-to-russia-2022-3.

Dawsey, Josh, and Isaac Arnsdorf. "Trump Rakes in Millions off FBI Search at Mar-a-Lago." *Washington Post*, May 7, 2022. https://www.washingtonpost.com/politics/2022/08/17/trump-fundraising-fbi-raid.

Delkic, Melina. "How Times Journalists Uncovered the Original Source of the President's Wealth." *New York Times*, Oct 18, 2018. https://www.nytimes.com/2018/10/02/insider/donald trump-fred-tax-schemes-wealth-html.

Derysh, Igor. "'I Find It Bizarre': Experts Think It's Fishy How Trump Judge Aileen Cannon Landed the Mar-a-Lago Case." *Salon*, Oct 18, 2022. https://www.salon.com/2022/10/18/i-find-it-bizarre-experts-think-its-fishy-how-aileen-cannon-landed-mar-a-lago-case/.

DeVega, Chauncy. "Don't Be Fooled: The GOP Love Affair with Putin Is Worse Than It Looks." *Salon*, Mar 3, 2022. https://www.salon.com/2022/03/18/dont-be-fooled-the-love-affair-with-putin-is-worse-than-it-looks/.

———. "Dr. Lance Dodes: Trump Is a Dangerous Sociopath—But He's Sane Enough to Stand Trial." *Salon*, Jun 27, 2022. https://www.salon.com/2022/06/27/dr-lance-dodes-is-a-sociopath--but-hes-sane-enough-to-stand-trial/.

———. "Lawrence Tribe: If Garland Doesn't Prosecute Trump, the Rule of Law Is 'Out the Window.'" *Salon*, Aug 30, 2021. https://www.salon.com/2021/08/30/laurence-tribe-if-garland-doesnt-prosecute-trump-the-rule-of-law-is-out-the-window.

———. "Philosopher Jason Stanley: Fascism's Definitely Not Beaten—But There's Reason for Hope." *Salon*, Mar 29, 2021. https://www.salon.com/2021/03/29/philosopher-jason-stanley-fascisms-definitely-not-beaten--but-theres-reason-for-hope/.

———. "Trump Dances for the NRA: America's Emotional Health Is Critical and Getting Worse." *Salon*, Jun 9, 2022. https://www.salon.com/2022/06/09/dances-for-the-nra-americas-emotional-health-is-critical-and-getting-worse/.

———. "Trump and His Regime Committed—or at Least Condoned—Mass Murder. America Just Doesn't Care." *Salon*, Nov 12, 2021. hhttps://www.salon.com/2021/11/18/and-his-regime-committed--or-at-least-condoned--mass-murder-america-just-doesnt-care/.

———. "Trump's Latest Hate Rally: A Master Class in Cult Mind Control." *Salon*, Apr 28, 2022. https://www.salon.com/2022/04/08/latest-hate-rally.

Dhaliwal, Shivdeep. "Barack Obama Says People 'Dying,' Democracy 'Under Threat' Due to Disinformation on Social Media." *Benzinga*, Apr 22, 2022. https://www.benzinga.com/news/22/04/26755123/people-dying-democracy-under-threat-dye-to-misinformation-on-social-media-says-obama.

Diaz, Jaclyn. "2 Years Later, Former White House Counsel Don McGahn Agrees to Testify." *NPR*, May 13, 2021. https://www.npr.org/2021/05/13/996419615/years-later-former-white-house-counsel-mcgahn-agrees-to-testify.

Dilanian, Ken, and Tom Winter. "Special Counsel Named by Trump DOJ Charges Democrat Lawyer Sussmann with False Statement to the FBI." *NBC News*, Sep 16, 2021. https://www.nbcnews.com/politics/justice-department/special-counsel-appointed-trump-doj-may-indict-democratic-lawyer-sussmann-n1279353.

Dodes, Lance. "Sociopathy." In *The Dangerous Case of Donald Trump: 27 Psychiatrists and Mental Health Experts Assess a President*, edited by Bandy X. Lee, §1931–2068. New York: St. Martin's, 2017.

Doliner, Anabelle. "Father Allegedly Shoots Son Because He Wouldn't Stop Playing Guitar." *Newsweek*, Oct 7, 2021. https://www.newsweek.com/father-allegedly-shoots-son-because-he-wouldnt-stop-playing-guitar-1642416.

"Donald Trump and the Self-Made Sham." Editorial. *New York Times*, Oct 2, 2018. https://www.nytimes.com/2018/10/02/opinion/donald-trump-tax-fraud-fred.html.

Dorman, John L. "Donald Trump Used a Secret Service Agent's Phone to Call Melania Trump after Stormy Daniels Allegations Broke: Report." *Business Insider*, Feb 13, 2022. https://africa.businessinsider.com/politics/donald-trump-used-a-secret-service-agents-phone-to-call-melania-trump-after-the/nfrj9gz.

Dreisbach, Tom. "An Attempted Attack on an FBI Office Raises Concerns about Violent Far-Right Rhetoric." NPR, Aug 12, 2022. https://www.npr.org/2022/08/l2/1117275044/an-attempted-attack-on-an-fbi-office-raises-concerns-about-violent-far-right-rhe.

Dress, Brad. "Former Manhattan Prosecutor Alleges Trump Tried to Undermine Integrity of Office." *The Hill*, Apr 28, 2022. https://thehill.com/policy/healthcare/politics-elections/3469954-former-manhattan-prosecutor-alleges-trump-tried-to-undermine-integrity-of-office/.

Drezner, Daniel W. *The Toddler in Chief: What Donald Trump Teaches Us about the Modern Presidency.* Chicago: University of Chicago Press, 2020.

Dunleavy, Jerry. "Judge Restricts Durham Evidence on Clinton Campaign 'Joint Venture' in Sussmann Trial." *Washington Examiner*, May 8, 2022. https://www.washingtonexaminer.com/news/justice/judge-restricts-durham-evidence-on-clinton-campaign-joint-venture-in-sussmann-trial/.

Durkee, Alison. "Here Are the Most Explosive Comments Fox News Stars—Carlson, Ingraham, Hannity—and Murdoch Made Off-Camera about Trump and the 2020 Election." *Forbes*, Mar 10, 2023. https://www.forbes.com/sites/alisondurkee/2023/03/10/dominion-v-fox-news-here-are-the-most-explosive-comments-anchors-and-rupert-murdoch-made-about-the-2020-election-behind-the-scenes/?sh=5eae24c1aaeb.

———. "Ethics Complaint against Rudy Giuliani Seeks to Disbar Him in New York." *Forbes*, Jan 21, 2021. https://www.forbes.com/sites/alisondurkee/2021/01/21/ethics-complaint-against-rudy-giuliani-seeks-to-disbar-him-in-new-york/.

Dutton, Jack. "Donald Trump Jr. Selling Shirts That Say 'Guns Don't Kill People, Alec Baldwin Kills People.'" *Newsweek*, Oct 25, 2021. https://www.newsweek.com/donald-trump-jr-selling-alec-baldwin-shirts-after-rust-shooting-1642229.

Dwyer, Devin. "Supreme Court Rejects Trump Claim of 'Absolute Immunity' from Grand Jury Subpoena for Tax Returns." ABC News, Jul 9, 2020. https://abcnews.go.com/Politics/scotus-rules-trump-financial-records-subpoenas/story?id=71382157.

Earle, Geoff. "Trump Threatens MAGA Backers Won't Vote If GOP Won't Take on 'Fraud.'" *Daily Mail*, Oct 13, 2021. https://www.dailymail.co.uk/news/article-10089759/Trump-warns-Republicans-supporters-wont-vote-party-doesnt-make-voter-fraud-priority.html.

Eisen, Norman, et al. "Opinion: If Prosecutors Are Finished Investigating Trump, They Should Say So." Washington Post, Mar 26, 2022. https://www.washingtonpost. com/outlook/2022/03/26/trump-alvin-bragg-manhattan/.

Elrod, Alan. "The Forever Coup: Trump's Big Lie Is the Coin of the GOP Realm in Arizona." AZ Mirror, Aug 6, 2022. https://www.azmirror.com/2022/08/05/the-forever.

Epps, Garrett. "No, You Can't Carry a Gun on the Floor of the House." Washington Monthly, Jan 22, 2021. https://washingtonmonthly.com/2021/01/22/no-you-cant-carry-a-gun-on-the-floor-of-the-house/.

Everson, Zach. "Tracking Trump: A Rundown of All the Lawsuits and Investigations Involving the Former President." YouTube video. Forbes, May 30, 2023. https:// www.youtube.com/watch?v=DjhkQ7RQv_A.

———. "Trump Urges Republicans to Sit Out Coming Elections." National Review, Oct 13, 2021. https://www.nationalreview.com/news/trump-urges-republicans-to-sit-out-coming-elections/.

Fahrenthold, David A., et al. "Ballrooms, Candles and Luxury Cottages: During Trump's Term, Millions of Government and GOP Dollars Have Flowed into His Properties." Washington Post, Dec 28, 2020. https://www.washingtonpost.com/ politics/ballrooms.

Federal Election Commission. Official 2020 Presidential General Election Results. 2021. https://www.fec.gov/resources/cms-content/documents/2020presgeresults.pdf.

Feinberg, Andrew. "Trump Falsely Claims He Never Called to 'Terminate' US Constitution Despite Having Said Exactly That." Independent, Dec 6, 2022. https:// www.independent.co.uk/news/world/americas/us-politics/trump-constitution-terminate-denies-b2239336.html.

Feuer, Alan, and Michael S. Schmidt. "The Jan 6 Panel after 8 Hearings: Where Will the Evidence Lead?" New York Times, Jul 22, 2022. https://www.nytimes. com/2022/07/22/us/politics/jan-6-committee.html.

Figliuzzi, Frank. "The Body Count Grows as Trump Followers Put Their Lives on the Line for Him." Yahoo! News, Aug 14, 2022. https://news.yahoo.com/body-count-grows-trump-followers-165911016.html.

———. "The 'Random' IRS Audit of Trump's Enemies Leaves Me Deeply Suspicious." MSNBC, Jul 9, 2022. https://www.msnbc.com/opinion/msnbc-opinion/irs-audit ing-james-comey-andrew-mccabe-concerning-n1296936.

Firozi, Paulina. "Eric Trump in 2014: 'We Have All the Funding We Need out of Russia.'" The Hill, May 7, 2017. https://thehill.com/homenews/news/332270-eric.

Foran, Clare, and Alex Rogers. "Anthony Gonzalez Is Retiring. Here's What Has Happened to the House Republicans Who Voted to Impeach Trump." CNN, Sep 17, 2021. https://www.cnn.com/2021/09/17/politics/house-republicans-impeach ment-trump-anthony-gonzalez-retirement/index.html.

Free Dictionary. "Case Law." Accessed 2016. https://legal-dictionary.thefreedictionary. com/Case+Law.

———. "Psychopathy." Accessed 2021. https://www.thefreedictionary.com/psychopathy.

Froomkin, Dan. "Fox News Isn't News." NBC News, Apr 10, 2022. https://www. nbcnews.com/think/opinion/fox-news-study-comparing-fox-cnn-highlights-cable-tvs-harm-rcna23620.

Frum, David. "Revenge of the Donald." Atlantic, Oct 28, 2021. https://www.theatlantic. com/ideas/archive/2021/10/trump-running-president-2024-election/620502/.

Fung, Katherine. "Birx Estimates Trump Administration Could Have Prevented 30 to 40 Percent of Covid Deaths." *Newsweek*, Oct 26, 2021. https://www.newsweek. com/birx-estimates-trump-admin-could-have-prevented-30-40-percent- covid-deaths-1642753#:~:text=Birx%20Estimates%20Trump%20Admin%20 Could,40%20Percent%20of%20COVID%20Deaths.

Gartner, John D. "Donald Trump Is: A) Bad, B) Mad, C) All of the Above." In *The Dangerous Case of Donald Trump: 27 Psychiatrists and Mental Health Experts Assess a President*, edited by Bandy X. Lee, §2079–292. New York: St. Martin's, 2017.

Gazis, Olivia. "Senate Intelligence Committee Releases Final Report on 2016 Russian Interference." CBS News, Aug 18, 2020. https://www.cbsnews.com/news/senate- report-russian-interference-2016-us-election/.

Gerstein, Josh. "Durham Prosecution Rests on Shaky Legal Ground." *Politico*, Sep 17, 2021. https://www.politico.com/news/2021/09/17/durham-prosecution-legal-512 525.

Gerstein, Josh, and Kyle Cheney. "Trump Team Likely Sought to Conceal Classified Docs at Mar-a-Lago, DOJ Tells Judge." *Politico*, Aug 30, 2022. https://www.politico. com/news/2022/08/30/trump-justice-department-filing-warrant-00054319.

Gettys, Travis. "GOP 'Tripled Down' on Trump's 'Toxicity'—And 'It's Making Them All Seem Like Lunatics.'" *Raw Story*, Aug 17, 2022. https://www.rawstory.com/ donald-trump-toxic.

———. "Republicans Plan to Make 'Life as Difficult as Possible' for FBI When They Are Back in Control: Report." *Raw Story*, Sep 26, 2022. https://www.rawstory.com/fbi- republicans/.

Gilligan, James. "The Issue Is Dangerousness Not Mental Illness." In *The Dangerous Case of Donald Trump: 27 Psychiatrists and Mental Health Experts Assess a President*, edited by Bandy X. Lee, §3185–335. New York: St. Martin's, 2017.

Glass, Leonard L. "Should Psychiatrists Refrain from Commenting on Trump's Psychology." In *The Dangerous Case of Donald Trump: 27 Psychiatrists and Mental Health Experts Assess a President*, edited by Bandy X. Lee, §2921–3038. New York: St. Martin's, 2017.

Goldman, Adam. "Hard Right Stokes Outrage after Search of Mar-a-Lago." *New York Times*, Aug 30, 2022. https://www.nytimes.com/2022/08/30/us/politics/trump- search-violence.html.

Goldsmith, Jack, and Nathaniel Sobel. "The Durham Investigation: What We Know and What It Means." *Lawfare*, Jul 9, 2020. https://www.lawfareblog.com/durham- investigation-what-we-know-and-what-it-means.

Gottlieb, Robert C., and Gerald B. Lefcourt. "D. A. Bragg, Explain Why You Dropped the Case against Trump." *New York Daily News*, Mar 29, 2022. https:// www.nydailynews.com/opinion/ny-oped-bragg-trump-explain-20220329- 6fa77vsvhfbytikdbpjwt2fi7e-story.html.

Gourguechon, Prudence. "Is the Commander in Chief Fit to Serve? A Nonpartisan Test That Marries U.S. Army Leadership Standards with Psychoanalytic Theory." In *The Dangerous Case of Donald Trump: 27 Psychiatrists and Mental Health Experts Assess a President*, edited by Bandy X. Lee, §7558–684. New York: St. Martin's, 2017.

Graham, David A. "The Art of the Self-Deal." *Atlantic*, Oct 17, 2022. https://www. theatlantic.com/ideas/archive/2022/10/trumps-secret-service-grift/671767/.

———. "The Incredible Vanishing Trump Presidency," *Atlantic*, Feb 9, 2022. https://www.theatlantic.com/ideas/archive/2022/02/the-incredible-vanishing-trump-presidency/621633/.

English Grammar Lessons. "The Best Laid Plans of Mice and Men." Accessed 2022. https://english-grammar-lessons.com/the-best-laid-plans-of-mice-and-men-mea.

Greenberg, Jon. "Most Republicans Still Falsely Believe Trump's Stolen Election Claims." *Poynter*, Jun 16, 2022. https://www.poynter.org/fact-checking/2022/70.

Griffing, Alex. "Bombshell Report Reveals Durham Probe Included Criminal Investigation of Trump Financial Deals after 2019 Tip from Italian Officials." *Mediaite*, Jan 26, 2023. https://www.mediaite.com/news/bombshell-report-reveals-durham-probe-included-criminal-investigation-of-trump-financial-deals-after-2019-tip-from-italian-officials/.

———. "Trump 'Played Role' in Lawyer Falsely Telling DOJ He Had No More Documents, Legal Analyst Says Unsealed Affidavit Indicates." *Mediaite*, Sep 13, 2022. https://www.mediaite.com/tv/trump-played-a-role-in-lawyer-falsely-telling-doj-he-had-no-more-docs-legal-analyst-says-unsealed-affidavit-indicates/.

Haberman, Maggie. "Trump Was Warned Late Last Year of Potential Legal Peril over Documents." *New York Times*, Sep 19, 2022. https://www.nytimes.com/2022/09/19/us/politics/trump-herschmann-documents.html#:~:text=Trump%20warned%20him%20late%20last,sought%20to%20impress%20upon%20Mr.

Haberman, Maggie, and Michael S. Schmidt. "How Trump Deflected Demands for Documents, Enmeshing Aides." *New York Times*, Oct 8, 2022. https://www.nytimes.com/2022/10/08/us/politics/trump-documents-lawyers.html.

Haddon, Heather. "Starbucks Shuts Sites over Safety Concerns." *Wall Street Journal*, Jul 12, 2022. https://www.wsj.com/articles/starbucks-closing-some-stores-citing-safety-concerns-in-certain-cafes-11657588871.

Haidt, Jonathan. "Why the Past 10 Years of American Life Have Been Uniquely Stupid." *Atlantic*, Apr 11, 2022. https://www.theatlantic.com/magazine/archive/2022/05/social-media-democracy-trust-babel/629369/.

Hall, Madison, et al. "At Least 1,003 People Have Been Charged in the Capitol Insurrection So Far." *Insider*, Feb 16, 2023. https://news.yahoo.com/least-948-people-charged-capitol-192631254.html.

Hall, Madison, and Dave Levinthal. "Federal Officials to Donald Trump: Your Political Money Numbers Don't Make Sense." *Business Insider*, Jul 17, 2022. https://www.businessinsider.com/donald-trump-money-political-committee-fec-federal-election-commission-2022-7.

Haslett, Cheyenne, and Anne Flaherty. "Trump's Focus on 2020 Election Got in the Way of COVID Response during Deadly Winter, Birx Says." ABC News, Jun 24, 2022. https://abcnews.go.com/Politics/trumps-focus-2020-election-covid-response-deadly-winter/story?id=85594085.

Hayes, Chris. "Levitz: 'Fox News Is Literally Killing Its Viewers' with Covid Lies." MSNBC, Jan 27, 2022. https://www.msnbc.com/all-in/watch/levitz-fox-news-is-literally-killing-its-viewers-with-covid-lies-131787333992.

Helmore, Edward. "Trump's 'Eyes and Ears' Walks Fine Line as Trial Lays Bare Business Practices." *Guardian*, Nov 20, 2022. https://www.theguardian.com/us-news/2022/nov/20/trump-organization-tax-fraud-trial-allen-weisselberg.

Herb, Jeremy, and Marshall Cohen. "What We Know about Trump's Inaction during the 187 Minutes of January 6." CNN, Jul 20, 2022. https://www.cnn.com/2022/07/20/politics/what-we-learned-trump-187-minutes/index.html.

Herb, Jeremy, et al. "Justice Department Says Classified Documents at Mar-a-Lago Were Likely 'Concealed and Removed' to Block Investigation." *CNN Politics*, Aug 30, 2022. https://www.cnn.com/2022/08/30/politics/mar-a-lago-justice-department-response/index.html.

"Hillary Clinton Email Investigation." Ballotpedia, Oct 8, 2015. https://ballotpedia.org/Hillary_Clinton_email_investigation.

History.com Editors. "Al Capone Goes to Prison." *History.com*, Oct 17, 2021. https://www.history.com/this-day-in-history/capone-goes-to-prison.

Holmes, Jack. "They Were Going to Bulldoze the American Republic for This Guy." *Esquire*, Sep 21, 2021. https://www.esquire.com/news-politics/a37676088/.

Honig, Elie. "Opinion: How Real Is the Chance of Criminally Prosecuting Donald Trump?" CNN, May 2, 2022. https://edition.cnn.com/2022/05/02/opinions/georgia-grand-jury-trump-legal-challenges-honig/index.html.

House, Billy, and Laura Litran. "GOP Vows Revenge for Trump Probes as Pillar of Congress Takes Over." *Bloomberg*, Aug 11, 2022. https://www.bloomberg.com/news/articles/2022-08-10/gop-vows-revenge-for-trump-probes-as-pillar-of-congress-takeover#xj4y7vzkg.

House Intelligence Committee. *The Impeachment Report: The House Intelligence Committee's Report on Its Investigation into Donald Trump and Ukraine.* New York: Broadway, 2019.

Howe, Caleb. "'Crime of the Century!' Trump Goes Ballistic over Election Again, Bashes Fox News, Newsmax, and Mike Pence as Cowards." *Mediaite*, May 15, 2021. https://www.mediaite.com/politics/crime-of-the-century-trump-goes-ballistic-over-election-again-bashes-fox-news-newsmax-and-mike-pence-as-cowards/.

———. "'Journalistic Scandal of Magnitude Not Seen in Very Long Time': Aidan McLaughlin Tells Ari Melber Fox Debacle Isn't Mere Media Bias." *Mediaite*, Apr 28, 2023. https://www.mediaite.com/tv/journalistic-scandal-of-magnitude-not-seen-in-very-long-time-aidan-mclaughlin-tells-ari-melber-fox-debacle-isnt-mere-media-bias/.

Idliby, Leia. "Charlie Kirk Gets Asked at TPUSA Event: 'How Many Elections Are They Gonna Steal before We Kill These People?'" *Mediaite*, Oct 26, 2021. https://www.mediaite.com/news/charlie-kirk-gets-asked-at-tpusa-event-how-many-elections-are-they-gonna-steal-before-we-kill-these-people/.

Italiano, Laura. "New York AG Blasts Cushman & Wakefield for Blowing Trump-Probe Subpoena Deadline; Asks Judge to 'Enforce' Compliance." *Business Insider*, Jul 5, 2022. https://www.businessinsider.com/ny-ag-blasts-trump-appraisers-cushman-wakefield-blowing-subpoena-deadline-2022-7.

Italie, Leanne. "'Gaslighting' Is Merriam-Webster's Word of the Year for 2022." Associated Press, Nov 28, 2022. https://apnews.com/article/word-of-the-year-2022-80d02a3e0a347e54246657 1ca9cdb2ef.

Jackson, Hollie. "Ex-Trump Organization CFO Allen Weisselberg Pleads Guilty to Tax Fraud." NBC News, Aug 18, 2022. https://www.nbcnews.com/politics/donald-trump/ex-trump-org-cfo-weisselberg-expected-plead-guilty-cooperate-company-t-rcna43679.

Jankowicz, Mia. "Marjorie Taylor Greene Chased AOC down a Corridor in Congress, Yelling at Her about Terrorists and Radical Socialists." *Business Insider,* May 13, 2021. https://www.businessinsider.in/politics/world/news/marjorie-taylor-greene-chased-aoc-down-a-corridor-in-congress-yelling-at-her-about-terrorists-and-radical-socialists/articleshow/82606518.cms.

Jansen, Bart. "John Durham Continues Investigating 2016 Campaign and Trump, Russia Accusations. What Has He Found?" *USA Today,* May 17, 2022. https://www.usatoday.com/story/news/politics/2022/03/17/john-durham-special-counsel-donald-trump-russia/6938335001/?gnt-cfr=1.

Jewell, Elizabeth J., ed. *The Pocket Oxford Dictionary and Thesaurus, Second American Edition.* New York: Oxford University Press, 2002.

Johnson, Jason. "Mystal: What Does Trump Have to Do to Go to Jail?" MSNBC, Aug 27, 2022. https://www.msnbc.com/cross-connection/watch/mystal-what-does-trump-have-to-do-to-go-to-jail-147140677848.

Jones, Kipp. "Irritated Ari Melber Declares, 'This Case Is Stalling Out' after Trump Investigators Abruptly Resign." *Mediate,* Feb 23, 2022. https://www.mediaite.com/tv/irritated-ari-melber-declares-this-case-is-stalling-out-after-trump-prosecutors-abruptly-resign/.

Kahardori, Ankush. "Beware Bill Barr." Intelligencer, *New York Magazine,* May 18, 2022. https://nymag.com/intelligencer/2022/03/beware-bill-barr.html.

Kanefield, Teri. "New Evidence of Trump Election Illegality Also Has a Silver Lining." NBC News, Aug 3, 2021. https://www.nbcnews.com/think/opinion/new-evidence-trump-election-illegality-also-has-silver-lining-ncna1275755.

Kaplan, Rebecca. "Nancy Pelosi: 'The Enemy Is Within' the House of Representatives." CBS News, Jan 29, 2021. https://www.cbsnews.com/news/nancy-pelosi-enemy-within-house-of-representatives/.

Karem, Brian. "Why Won't Donald Trump Go Away? Because Americans Can't Tell Appearance from Reality." *Salon,* Sep 9, 2021. https://www.salon.com/2021/09/09/why-wont-donald-trump-go-away-because-americans-cant-tell-appearance-from-reality/.

Kasprak, Alex. "Has Trump Spent '278.5 Years' of Salary on Taxpayer-Funded Golf Outings?" *Snopes,* Sep 21, 2020. https://www.snopes.com/fact-check/278-years-golf.

Kates, Graham. "Judge Lifts $10,000-a-Day Contempt Ruling against Trump, with Conditions." CBS News, May 12, 2022. https://www.cbsnews.com/news/trump-contempt-judge-lifts-conditions.

Kaufmann, Yehezkiel. *The Religion of Israel.* New York: Schocken, 1972.

KCAL News Staff. "Former Chapman Law School Dean Faces Disbarment." CBS News, Jan 26, 2023. https://www.cbsnews.com/losangeles/news/former-chapman-law-school-dean-faces-disbarment/.

Kelly, Caroline. "Liz Cheney Says Some GOP Members Voted against Impeachment out of Fear for Their Lives." CNN, May 14, 2021. https://www.cnn.com/2021/05/14/politics/liz-cheney-republican-party-cnntv.

Kessler, Glenn. "Trump's False or Misleading Claims Total 30,573 over 4 Years." *Washington Post,* Jan 24, 2021. https://www.washingtonpost.com/politics/2021/01/24/trumps-false-or-misleading-claims-total-30573-over-four-years/.

Khullar, Samaa. "'Art of the Steal': Experts Say Trump Pleading the 5th in NY AG Probe Backfired—Now He's 'Screwed.'" *Salon* Sep 21, 2022. https://www.salon.

com/2022/09/21/art-of-the-steal-experts-say-pleading-the-5th-in-ny-ag-probe-backfired--now-hes-screwed/.

Kiely, Eugene. "Timeline of FBI Investigation of Trump's Handling of Highly Classified Documents." *FactCheck.org,* Aug 30, 2022. https://www.factcheck.org/2022/08/timeline-of-fbi.

Kilgore, Ed. "Trump's Long Campaign to Steal the Presidency: A Timeline." Intelligencer, *New York Magazine,* Jul 14, 2022. https://nymag.com/intelligencer/article/trump-campaign-steal-presidency-timeline.html.

———. "Trump Says Republicans Must Solve the Big Lie or Their Voters Will Not Vote." Intelligencer, *New York Magazine,* Oct 13, 2021. https://nymag.com/intelligencer/2021/10/trump-demands-republicans-solve-the-big-lie.html.

Korab, Alek. "Dr. Fauci Opens Up about Origins of Covid-19 Virus." *Eat This, Not That!* Jan 26, 2022. https://www.yahoo.com/video/dr-fauci-opens-origins-covid-170120558.html.

Korecki, Natasha. "Johnson's Campaign Is Paying the Law Firm of a Trump Attorney Allegedly Connected to Jan. 6 Fake Elector Plot." NBC News, Oct 17, 2022. https://www.nbcnews.com/politics/2022-election/johnsons-campaign-paying-law-firm-trump-attorney-allegedly-connected-j-rcna52517.

Korecki, Natasha, et al. "Judge Grants Trump's Special Master Request, Delays Parts of Criminal Probe." NBC News, Sep 5, 2022. https://www.nbcnews.com/politics/judge-grants-trumps-request-special-master-rcna46321.

Krugman, Paul. "Opinion: Crazies, Cowards and the Trump Coup." *New York Times,* Jan 30, 2022. https://www.nytimes.com/2022/06/30/opinion/republicans-trump-coup.html.

Kruse, Michael. "The One Way History Shows Trump's Personality Cult Will End." *Politico,* Apr 16, 2022. https://www.politico.com/news/magazine/2022/04/16/history-shows-trump-personality-cult-end-00024941.

———. "Trumpology: Can Trump Still Sue His Way out of Trouble?" *Politico,* Jun 3, 2019. https://www.politico.com/magazine/story/2019/06/03/donald-trump-lawsuits-white-house-227036/.

Kurtz, David. "Bill Barr Was Just as Bad as We Thought and Maybe Worse." *Talking Points Memo,* Aug 25, 2022. https://talkingpointsmemo.com/morning-memo/bill-barr-olc-memo-mueller-report.

———. "The Worst Attorney General in 50 Years Was Even More Corrupt Than We Thought." *Talking Points Memo,* Jan 27, 2023. https://talkingpointsmemo.com/morning-memo/bill-barr-john-durham-special-counsel-investigation.

Kwong, Jessica. "Terrifying New Details of Donald Trump's Final Hours in the White House Revealed." *Metro,* Sep 13, 2022. https://www.msn.com/en-us/news/politics/terrifying-new-details-of-donald-trumps-final-hours-in-the-white-house-revealed/ar-AA11KLIc?ocid=UP97DHP&li=BBnb7Kz.

Lahut, Jake. "We Watched Tucker Carlson's Jan. 6 Documentary So You Don't Have To. Here's Why Its Whitewash of the Capitol Insurrection Makes No Sense." *Business Insider,* Nov 23, 2021. https://www.businessinsider.com/tucker-carlsons-jan-6-documentary-so-you-dont-have-to-2021-11.

Lambe, Jerry. "Steve Bannon Suggests Merrick Garland, FBI Involved in 'Coup' Plot to Oust Trump." *Patabook News,* Oct 26, 2021. https://patabook.com/news/2021/10/26/steve-bannon.

———. "Texas Man Sentenced to Life in Prison for Beating Toddler to Death after She Put Her Shoes on Wrong Feet, Days before Her Birthday." *News Break*, Oct 25, 2021. https://lawandcrime.com/crime/texas-man-sentenced-to-life-in-prison-for-beating-toddler-to-death-after-she-put-her-shoes-on-wrong-feet-days-before-her-birthday/amp/.

Larson, Eric. "Sidney Powell, Lin Wood Ordered to Pay $175,250 for 'Frivolous' Michigan Election Lawsuits." *Bloomberg*, Dec 2, 2021. https://www.bnnbloomberg.ca/sidney-powell-lin-wood-ordered-to-pay-175-250-for-frivolous-michigan-election-lawsuits-1.1690469.

Landen, Xander. "Family of Elderly Man Beaten to Death by Teens Speaks Out: 'Who Does This?'" *Newsweek*, Jul 9, 2022. https://www.newsweek.com/family-man-beaten-traffic conc-speaks-out-whats-happened-us-1723184.

Leary, Alex. "National Archives Retrieves 15 Boxes of Documents from Trump Residence." *Wall Street Journal*, Feb 7, 2022. https://www.wsj.com/articles/national-archives-retrieves-15-boxes-of-documents-from-trump-11644267295.

Lee, Bandy X., ed. *The Dangerous Case of Donald Trump: 27 Psychiatrists and Mental Health Experts Assess a President*. New York: St. Martin's, 2017.

———. "Dr. Bandy X. Lee in Conversation with Dr. Mary L. Trump." YouTube video. Sep 5, 2018. https://www.youtube.com/watch?v=M9__k6ivm7E.

———. "Our Duty to Warn and to Protect." In *The Dangerous Case of Donald Trump: 27 Psychiatrists and Mental Health Experts Assess a President*, edited by Bandy X. Lee, §719–980. New York: St. Martin's, 2017.

Lee, Ella. "Humanity's Worst Impulses: Obama Says Online Disinformation Puts Democracy at Risk." *USA Today*, Apr 22, 2022. https://www.usatoday.com/story/news/politics/2022/04/22/obama-online-disinformation-democracy-at-risk/7408070001/#:~:text=%27Humanity%27s%20worst%20impulses%27%3A%20Obama%20says%20online%20disinformation%20puts%20democracy%20at%20risk&text=Former%20President%20Barack%20Obama%20warned,fueled%20by%20unchecked%20technology%20companies.

Legare, Robert. "Attorney with Ties to 2016 Clinton Campaign Acquitted in First Durham Special Counsel Trial." CBS News, May 31, 2022. https://www.cbsnews.com/news/michael-sussmann-trial-durham-verdict.

———. "Prosecutors Allege Michael Sussmann Planned 'October Surprise' against Trump in September 2016 FBI Meeting, as Trial Gets Underway." CBS News, May 17, 2022. https://www.cbsnews.com/news/john-durham-michael-sussman-trial-donald-trump/.

Legare, Robert, and Melissa Quinn. "Appeals Court Agrees to Speed up Justice Department's Appeal of Order Appointing Outside Arbiter in Trump Documents Case." CBS News, Oct 5, 2022. https://www.cbsnews.com/news/trump-mar-a-lago-documents-case-special-master-appeals-court-agrees-to-speed-up-justice-department-appeal/.

Leiter, Brian. "Nietzsche's Moral and Political Philosophy." In *Stanford Encyclopedia of Philosophy*, edited by Edward N. Zaita. Summer 2021 ed. https://plato.stanford.edu/archives/sum2021/entries/nietzsche-moral-political/.

Lemon, Jason. "Christian Pastor Claims Biden Surrounded by 'Demonic Hedge of Protection.'" *Newsweek*, Apr 1, 2021. https://www.newsweek.com/christian-pastor-claims-biden-surrounded-demonic-hedge-protection-1580476.

———. "Christian 'Prophet' Johnny Enlow Claims Trump 'Anointed' by God to Take down Billionaires Who 'Really Control' World." *Newsweek*, Apr 22, 2021. https://www.newsweek.com/christian-prophet-johnny-enlow-claims-trump-anointed-god-take-down-billionaires-who-really-1585825.

———. "Evangelical 'Prophet' Claims 'Power Came to Earth' on Ides of March to Remove Biden." *Newsweek*, Mar 24, 2021. https://www.newsweek.com/evangelical-prophet-claims-power-came-earth-ides-march-remove-biden-1578536.

———. "Pastor Johnny Enlow Says People Will Understand Donald Trump's Bravery When They Get to Heaven." *Newsweek*, Apr 14, 2021. https://www.newsweek.com/pastor-johnny-enlow-says-people-will-understand-donald-trumps-bravery-when-they-get-heaven-1583612.

———. "Trump Wanted to 'Stay in Power Forever' Like Putin, Says His Ex-National Security Advisor." *Newsweek*, Oct 10, 2021. https://www.newsweek.com/trump-wanted-stay-power-forever-like-putin-says-his-ex-national-security-adviser-1637376.

Leng, Jada. "Violence against Asian Americans." PBS, Dec 7, 2022. https://www.pbs.org/articles/violence-against-asian-americans.

Leonard, Kimberly. "Trump Says Mar-a-Lago Documents Coverage Has Given the Palm Beach Club '$5 Billion-Worth of Free Publicity.'" *Business Insider*, Oct 6, 2022. https://www.businessinsider.nl/trump-says-mar-a-lago-documents-coverage-has-given-the-palm-beach-club-5-billion-worth-of-free-publicity/.

Leonnig, Carol, and Philip Rucker. *I Alone Can Fix It: Donald J. Trump's Final Year*. New York: Penguin, 2021.

Lepore, Jill. *These Truths: History of the United States*. New York: Norton, 2018.

Lewis, Matt. "Trump Tells GOP: Back My Big Lie or I'll Burn the Party Down." *Daily Beast*, Oct 15, 2021. https://www.thedailybeast.com/trump-tells-gop-back-my-big-lie-or-ill-burn-the-party-down.

Levitsky, Steven, and Daniel Ziblatt. *How Democracies Die*. New York: Broadway, 2018.

Lifton, Robert Jay. "Our Witness to Malignant Normality." In *The Dangerous Case of Donald Trump: 27 Psychiatrists and Mental Health Experts Assess a President*, edited by Bandy X. Lee, §487–554. New York: St. Martin's, 2017.

Lim, Clarissa-Jan, and Ryan Brooks. "Trump and the Republicans Are Doing Everything They Can to Confuse Voters before the Election." *Buzzfeed News*, Sep 24, 2021. https://www.buzzfeednews.com/article/clarissajanlim/trump-republicans-confuse-voters.

Lithwick, Dahlia. "Why Donald Trump's Attacks on Voting Have Ramped Up." *Slate*, Oct 6, 2020. https://slate.com/news-and-politics/2020/10/election-meltdown-voter-suppression-depression-donald-trump-power.html.

Litman, Harry. "Another Case Where Trump's Flagrant Misconduct Won't End in Charges." *Los Angeles Times*, Feb 16, 2022. https://www.latimes.com/opinion/story/2022-02-16/donald-trump-presidential-records-act-national-archives.

Lowell, Hugo. "'Just Say the Election Was Corrupt,' Trump Urged DOJ after Loss to Biden." *Guardian*, Jul 30, 2021. https://www.theguardian.com/us-news/2021/jul/30/donald-trump-doj-officials-2020-election-memos-house-oversight.

———. "Trump Plans to Sue to Keep White House Records on Capitol Attack Secret." *Guardian*, Sep 29, 2021. https://www.theguardian.com/us-news/2021/sep/29/donald-trump-6-january-records-sue#:~:text=Donald%20Trump%20is%20preparing%20to,extended%20legal%20battle%20over%20disclosure.

Lozda, Carlos. *What Were We Thinking: A Brief Intellectual History of the Trump Era.* New York: Simon & Schuster, 2020.

Luscombe, Belinda. "NIH Director Francis Collins Is Leaving with a Warning for Some Politicians." *Time*, Feb 4, 2022. https://time.com/6141545/nih-director-francis-collins-exit-interview/.

———. "Why Everyone Is So Rude Right Now." *Time*, Dec 15, 2021. https://time.com/6099906/rude-customers-pandemic.

Maddow, Rachael. "Federal Judge Calls out Barr for Lying, Orders Previously Withheld Documents Released." MSNBC, May 5, 2021. https://www.msnbc.com/rachel-maddow/watch/federal-judge-calls-out-barr-for-lying-orders-previously-withheld-documents-released-111358533515.

Malkin, Craig. "Pathological Narcissism and Politics." In *The Dangerous Case of Donald Trump: 27 Psychiatrists and Mental Health Experts Assess a President*, edited by Bandy X. Lee, §1442–673. New York: St. Martin's, 2017.

Manderson, Nathaniel. "So Who Are 'Evangelicals'? And How Did They Become Such Massive Hypocrites?" *Salon*, Jun 4, 2022. https://www.salon.com/2022/06/04/so-are-evangelicals-and-how-did-they-become-such-massive-hypocrites/.

Mangan, Dan. "DOJ Suspects Trump Still Has Classified Documents He Removed from White House, Even after the FBI Mar-a-Lago Raid." CNBC, Oct 7, 2022. https://www.cnbc.com/2022/10/07/doj-suspects-trump-has-classified-documents-he-took-from-white-house.html.

———. "Judge Says Trump Contempt Ruling Lifted If He Pays $110K Fine, Provides Other Information." CNBC, May 12, 2022. https://www.cnbc.com/2022/05/11/judge-says-trump-contempt-ruling-can-be-lifted-if-he-pays-110k-fine-provides-other-info.html.

———. "Tax Firm Mazars Fires Trump Organization as Client, Says Former President's Financial Statements Are Unreliable." CNBC, Feb 14, 2022. https://www.msn.com/en-us/news/politics/tax-firm.

Mannes, Keith. "Why Are Christians So Mean?" *Reformed Journal*, Oct 23, 2020. https://blog.reformedjournal.com/2020/10/23/why-are-christians-so-mean.

Marcotte, Amanda. "Republicans Pick Putin over Democracy—Rick Scott's Creepy Blueprint for America Shows Why." *Salon*, Feb 4, 2022. https://www.salon.com/2022/02/24/pick-putin-over-democracy--and-rick-scotts-creepy-blueprint-for-america-shows-why/.

Martinez, Gina. "Trump's 'War Room' to Overturn the Election." *Daily Mail*, Oct 23, 2021. https://www.dailymail.co.uk/news/article-10123821/New-details-emerge-war-room-meetings-DCs-Willard-hotel-ahead-Jan-6.html.

Mascaro, Lisa, et al. "Jan 6 Panel Probes Trump's 187 Minutes as Capitol Attacked." Associated Press, Jul 21,2021. https://www.kcra.com/article/jan-6-panel-trumps-187-minutes-as-capitol-attacked/40680202.

Mazzetti, Mark. "G.O.P.-Led Senate Panel Details Ties between 2016 Trump Campaign and Russia." *New York Times*, Aug 18, 2020. https://www.nytimes.com/2020/08/18/us/politics/.

McAuliff, Michael, and Leonard Greene. "'I Am Someone's Daughter, Too': AOC Trashes Apology from Congressman Who Called Her a 'F---ing B--ch.'" *New York Daily News*, Jul 23, 2020. https://www.iolaregister.com/author/michael.

McCormick, Erin. "'Not the Cruise I Signed up For': 30-Fold Increase in Covid Cases Upends Industry." *Guardian*, Jan 13, 2022. https://www.theguardian.com/world/2022/jan/12/cruise-covid-cases-ship-industry.

Meacham, Jon. *American Gospel: God, the Founding Fathers, and the Making of a Nation*. New York: Random House, 2006.

Mediaite Staff. "Dr. Fauci Tells Fox News Doctor Evidence Leans 'Very, Very Strongly' towards Covid Being a 'Natural Occurrence.'" *Mediaite*, Jan 27, 2022. https://www.mediaite.com/radio/dr-fauci-tells-fox-news-evidence-leans-very-very-strongly-towards-covid-being-a-natural-occurrence/.

Melber, Ari. "After Trump Demands Comey Punishment, Trump-Run IRS Busted for Suspicious Comey Audit." MSNBC, Jul 8, 2022. https://www.msnbc.com/the-beat-with-ari/watch/-after-trump-demands-comey-punishment-trump-run-irs-busted-for-suspicious-comey-audit-143621701598.

———. "DOJ Hits Back in Trump Criminal Probe, Appealing Review for Secrets Trump Stole." MSNBC, Sep 9, 2022. https://www.msnbc.com/the-beat-with-ari/watch/doj-hits-back-in-trump-criminal-probe-appealing-review-for-secrets-trump-stole-148037701937.

———. "Fox News Lies Debunked: Viewers Know Less Than If They Watched No News at All." MSNBC, Jan 28, 2022. https://www.msnbc.com/the-beat-with-ari/watch/fox-news-lies-debunked-viewers-know-less-than-if-they-watched-no-news-at-all-131875397839.

———. "GOP Goes from Condemning Looting to Warning of 'Riots' for Trump." MSNBC, Aug 30, 2022. https://youtu.be/qk8lwfaFBYM.

———. "It Can Happen Here: Expert on Tyranny Warns of GOP Extremism." MSNBC, Oct 23, 2021. https://www.msnbc.com/the-beat-with-ari/watch/it-can-happen-here-expert-on-tyranny-warns-of-gop-extremism-124405829813.

———. "MSNBC's Melber: Garland Can't 'Punt' Decision on Indicting Trump." MSNBC, Nov 18, 2022. https://www.msnbc.com/the-beat-with-ari/watch/msnbc-s-melber-garland-can-t-punt-decision-on-indicting-trump-154254405742.

———. "'Trolls' and 'Liars': The Definitive Debunking of Trump AG Bill Barr." MSNBC, Jan 26, 2023. https://www.msnbc.com/the-beat-with-ari/watch/-trolls-and-liars-the-definitive-debunking-of-trump-ag-bill-barr-161814085810.

———. "Trump's Business Was Just Labeled a 'Criminal Organization.'" MSNBC, Jul 2, 2021. https://www.msnbc.com/11th-hour/watch/trump-s-business-was-just-labeled-a-criminal-organization-115877957944.

———. "Trump Collusion Exposed in 2021: Aide Caught Red-Handed in Russia Back Channel." MSNBC, Aug 16, 2021. https://www.msnbc.com/the-beat-with-ari/watch/trump-collusion-exposed-in-2021-aide-caught-red-handed-in-russia-back-channel-110281797702.

———. "Trump Coup Exposed: Midnight Military Meeting Led to Jan 6 Rally, Navarro Plot." MSNBC, Jul 15, 2022. https://www.msnbc.com/the-beat-with-ari/watch/trump-coup-exposed-midnight-military-meeting-led-trump-to-jan-6-rally-navarro-plot-144069189815.

———. "Trump Loses His Bid to Chuck Testifying as Judge Dismisses His 'Orwell-Humpty Dumpty' Defense." YouTube video. MSNBC, Mar 16, 2022. https://www.youtube.com/watch?v=lrAvOl3snsc.

Mika, Elizabeth. "Who Goes Trump? Tyranny as a Triumph of Narcissism." In *The Dangerous Case of Donald Trump: 27 Psychiatrists and Mental Health Experts*

Assess a President, edited by Bandy X. Lee, §5175–453 New York: St. Martin's, 2017.

Mordowanec, Nick. "What Is NDI? Affidavit Reveals Trump Had Defense Documents." *Newsweek*, Aug 26, 2022. https://www.newsweek.com/what-ndi-affidavit-reveals-trump-had-defense-documents-1737496.

Mueller, Robert S. *The Mueller Report: The Final Report of the Special Counsel into Donald Trump, Russia, and Collusion.* Vols. 1 and 2. New York: Skyhorse, 2019.

"Mueller Report: US Congress Given Key Findings from Attorney General Barr." BBC News, Mar 24, 2029. https://www.bbc.com/news/world-us-canada-47683309.

Murphy, Joe, and Jiachuan Wu. "Map: Track Coronavirus Deaths around the World." NBC News, Jan 21, 2022. https://www.nbcnews.com/news/world/world-map-coronavirus-deaths-country-covid-19n1170211.

Murphy, Mike. "How Dangerous Is Today's Republican Party? Very, Former CIA Director Michael Hayden Believes." *MarketWatch*, Aug 19, 2022. https://www.marketwatch.com/story/how-dangerous-is-todays-republican-party-very-ex-cia-director-michael-hayden-believes-11660785930.

Neuharth, Dan. "What Exactly Is 'Malignant Narcissism'?" *Psychology Today*, May 25, 2019. https://www.psychologytoday.com/us/blog/narcissism-demystified/2019 05/what-exactly-is-malignant-narcissism.

Ngan, Mandel. "North Korea Slams Feeble Biden." *Agence France Presse*, Apr 9, 2022. https://www.barrons.com/news/north-korea-slams-feeble-biden-01649552708.

Nichols, Tom. "The New Era of Political Violence Is Here." *Atlantic*, Aug 15, 2022. https://www.theatlantic.com/newsletters/archive/2022/08/the-new-era-of-political-violence-is-here/671146/.

Niedzwiadek, Nick. "McCarthy after Ousting Cheney: 'I Don't Think Anybody Is Questioning the Legitimacy of the Presidential Election.'" *Politico*, May 12, 2021. https://www.politico.com/news/2021/05/12/mccarthy-2020-election-legitimacy-487612.

Obeidallah, Dean. "Why the Explosion in Unruly Air Passengers?" CNN, Jun 14, 2021. https://www.cnn.com/2021/06/13/opinions/unruly-air-passengers-masks-trump-obeidallah/index.html.

O'Donnell, Lawrence. "Goldman on Trump Keeping and Destroying White House Documents: What's He Hiding?" MSNBC, Feb 8, 2022. https://www.msnbc.com/the-last-word/watch/goldman-on-trump-keeping-and-destroying-wh-docs-what-s-he-hiding-132658757590.

———. "Lawrence: DOJ Tells Trump-Picked Judge She's Risking National Security. MSNBC, Sep 9, 2022. https://news.yahoo.com/lawrence-doj-tells-trump-picked -031938028.html.

———. "Rep. Schiff: Trump Completely Remade GOP in His Own Flawed Image." MSNBC, Oct 9, 2021. https://www.msnbc.com/the-last-word/watch/rep-schiff-trump-completely-remade-gop-in-his-own-flawed-image-123403845518.

———. "Strzok: 'Triple Russian Threat' at 'Unhinged' Trump WH Meeting." MSNBC, Jul 26, 2022. https://www.msnbc.com/the-last-word/watch/strzok-triple-russian-threat-at-unhinged-trump-wh-meeting-144781381504.

O'Neill, Brian. "Evil, I Think, Is the Absence of Empathy." *Slugger O' Toole*, Jun 19, 2018. https://sluggerotoole.com/2018/06/19/evil-i-think.

Pagliery, Jose. "Court Screwup Reveals Mar-a-Lago Judge's Latest Legal Absurdity in Trump Case." *Daily Beast*, Oct 6, 2022. https://www.thedailybeast.com/court-screwup-reveals-judge-aileen-cannons-latest-legal-absurdity-in-trump-case.

———. "Top Trump Prosecutors Cited Stalled Investigation in Resignation Letters." *Daily Beast*, Feb 28, 2022. https://www.thedailybeast.com/top-donald-trump-prosecutors-carey-dunne-mark-pomerantz-cited-stalled-investigation-in-resig nation-letters.

———. "Trump Went Judge Shopping and It Paid off in Mar-a-Lago Case." *Daily Beast*, Sep 6, 2022. https://www.thedailybeast.com/donald-trump-went-judge-shopping-and-it-paid-off-in-mar-a-lago-case.

Palmer, Ewan. "Aileen Cannon Decision to Give Trump Special Master 'Utterly Lawless'—Tribe." *Newsweek*, Sep 6, 2022. https://www.newsweek.com/judge-aileen-cannon-trump-special-master-fbi-1740063.

———. "Donald Trump Condemns NATO When Asked about Russia's 'Evil' Actions." *Newsweek*, Apr 14, 2022. https://www.newsweek.com/trump-putin-nato-russia-sean-hannity-ukraine-1697852.

Papenfuss, Mary. "National Archives Now Targeted by Threats after Trump Attacks: Report." *HuffPost*, Aug 30, 2022. https://www.huffpost.com/entry/national-archive-threats-trump-lies_n_630bf31de4b088f74235504f.

———. "Trump Demands to Be Declared President Nearly 2 Years after Election." *HuffPost*, Aug 29, 2022. https://news.yahoo.com/trump-demands-declared-presi dent-nearly-005409924.html#:~:text=Trump%20Demands%20To%20Be%20 Declared%20President%20Nearly%202%20Years%20After%20Election,-Mary%20 Papenfuss&text=If%20anyone%20needed%20more%20evidence,also%20open%20 to%20another%20option.

———. "Trump Still Acting Like Imperious President in Mar-a-Lago 'Barbie Dream House': Report." *HuffPost*, Dec 19, 2022. https://news.yahoo.com/trump-still-acting-imperious-president-035428452.html.

Paris, Francesca, and Josh Katz. "Comey and McCabe Audits: How Likely That They Were Coincidental?" *New York Times*, Jul 7, 2022. https://www.nytimes. com/2022/07/07/upshot/comey-mccabe-tax-audits.html.

Parsley, Aaron. "Donald Trump Demands to Be Declared 'Rightful Winner' of 2020 Election Nearly 2 Years after Losing." *People*, Aug 30, 2022. https://people.com/ politics/donald-trump-demands-declared-rightful-winner-2020-election-2-years-after-losing/.

Parton, Heather Digby. "Can Anyone Stop Trump? The Most Promising Case against Him Fizzles Out." *Salon*, Mar 25, 2022. https://www.salon.com/2022/03/25/can-anyone-stop-trump-the-most-promising-criminal-case-against-him-fizzles-out/.

———. "Durham Investigation Goes Bust: Bill Barr Blew up Mission to Expose the Deep State—To Save Trump." *Salon*, Feb 1, 2023. https://www.salon.com/2023/02/01/ durham-investigation-goes-bust-bill-barr-blew-up-mission-to-expose-the-deep-state--to-save/.

———. "The Trump Administration Drained the Swamp—Into the White House." *Salon*, Jun 24, 2019. https://truthout.org/articles/the-trump-administration-drained-the-swamp-into-the-white-house/.

Paz, Isabella Grullon. "Full Transcript of Michelle Obama's D.N.C. Speech." *New York Times*, Aug 19, 2020. https://www.nytimes.com/2020/08/17/politics/Michelle-Obama-speech-transcript-video.html.

Peck, Adam, and Danielle McLean. "Mueller Report Rules Were Written to Give Congress Access, Say Experts." *Think Progress*, Apr 5, 2019. https://archive.thinkprogress.org/mueller-report-rules-were-written-to-give-congress-access-say-experts-8f9619d3a430/.

Pierides, Maria. "Trump Org. Exec Just Dropped a Major Bombshell about Donald Trump in Court: He 'Authorized' Rent in Tax Fraud Scheme." * SheFinds*, Nov 20, 2022. https://www.shefinds.com/collections/donald-trump-former-cfo-testifies-tax-fraud/.

Pierson, Brenden. "Trump Could Shoot Someone and Escape Prosecution, His Lawyer Argues." Reuters, Oct 23, 2019. https://www.reuters.com/article/us-usa-trump-vance-idUSKBN1X218U.

Polantz, Katelyn. "Ex WH Counsel McGahn to Testify behind Closed Doors about Trump efforts to Obstruct Russia Investigation." CNN, May 13, 2021. https://www.cnn.com/2021/05/12/politics/don-mcgahn-house-testimony/index.html.

———. "Federal Judge Blasts William Barr for Mueller Rollout, Asks If It Was Meant to Help Trump." CNN, May 5, 2020. https://edition.cnn.com/2020/03/05/politics/judge-mueller-report-barr/index.html.

Pomerville, Paul A. *An American Evangelical-Pentecostal Elephant in the Room: The Neglect of a New Testament Narrative*. Seattle: Amazon Kindle Direct, 2020.

———. *The Cross-Cultural American: Ending America's Obsession with Race*. Charleston: CreateSpace, 2009.

———. *The New Testament Case against Christian Zionism: A Christian View of the Israeli-Palestinian Conflict*. Seattle: Amazon Kindle Direct, 2014.

———. *The Third Force in Missions: A Pentecostal Contribution to Contemporary Mission Theology*. Peabody, MA: Hendrickson, 2016.

Pramuk, Jacob. "Trump Committed 'Outright Fraud' on 'Dubious Tax Schemes,' According to a Big, New Investigation from the *New York Times*." CNBC, Oct 2, 2018. https://www.cnbc.com/2018/10/02/trump-committed-fraud-in-tax-schemes-new-york-times-says.html.

Press, Bill. "Bill Press: January 6 Hearings: Only One Possible Take-Away." *Tribune Content Agency*, Jul 14, 2022. https://tribunecontentagency.com/article/bill-press-january-6-hearings-only-one-possible-take-away/.

———. "Press: Breaking News: Media's Frame Is Helping Trump." *The Hill*, Dec 14, 2021. https://thehill.com/opinion/campaign/585656-press.

Proulx, Annie. *Barkskins*. New York: Scribner, 2016.

Queen, Jack. "7 Key Moments from Alex Jones Sandy Hook Defamation Trial." Reuters, Aug 4, 2022. https://www.reuters.com/business/media-telecom/7-key-moments-alex-jones-sandy-hook-defamation-trial-2022-08-04/.

Rashbaum, William K., et al. "Manhattan Prosecutors Again Consider a Path toward Charging Trump." *Seattle Times*, Nov 21, 2022. https://www.seattletimes.com/nation-world/manhattan-prosecutors-again-consider-a-path-toward-charging-Trump/.

Reed, Brad. "Durham Probe into Trump-Russia Investigation to Wind Down with No Further Charges: New York Times." *Raw Story*, Sep 14, 2022. https://www.rawstory.com/john-durham-2658209848.

———. "Trump Doubles down on Calls to 'Terminate' Constitution in Furious All-Caps Truth Social Post." *Raw Story*, Dec 3, 2022. https://www.rawstory.com/trump-coup-2658827194.

———. "'Wrong, Crazy, Dangerous': CNN Legal Analyst Aghast by Trump Call to 'Terminate' Constitution." *Raw Story*, Dec 3, 2022. https://www.rawstory.com/trump-coup-2658827241.

Reid, Joy. "Authors of New Book Allege Trump Recommended Sending Covid-Infected Americans Returning from Overseas to Guantanamo." MSNBC, Jun 22, 2021. https://www.msnbc.com/the-reidout/watch/trump-allegedly-recommended-sending-infected-americans-returning-from-overseas-during-covid-surge-to-guantanamo-115226181905.

———. "Political Analyst Tells Joy Reid: Forget Trumpism, It's Neo-Fascism." MSNBC, Jul 5, 2021. https://www.msnbc.com/the-reidout/watch/democrats-optimism-for-bipartisanship-clashes-with-increasingly-outlandish-gop-116100165523.

Reilly, Ryan, et al. "DOJ Says Trump Likely 'Concealed and Removed' Classified Docs at Mar-a-Lago." NBC News, Aug 30, 2022. https://www.nbcnews.com/politics/justice-department/doj-says-special-master-trump-case-harm-national-security-interests-rcna45515.

Reimann, Nicholas. "Trump Lawyers Turned over More Classified Materials and a Laptop to DOJ, Report Says." *Forbes*, Feb 10, 2023. https://www.forbes.com/sites/nicholasreimann/2023/02/10/trump-lawyers-turned-over-more-classified-materials-and-a-laptop-to-doj-report-says/?sh=73a3c60b3107.

Reiser, Lindsey. "Joyce Vance: Trump Testing out a 'Shifting Array of Potential Defenses' Following FBI Investigation." MSNBC, Aug 14, 2022. https://www.youtube.com/watch?v=TFHrln2u36U.

Relman, Eliza. "Trump Solicits Cash Right after the January 6 Committee Votes to Subpoena Him and Tells Supporters He's Fighting for Their 'Heritage.'" *Business Insider*, Oct 13, 2022. https://www.businessinsider.nl/trump-solicits-cash.

Rohrlich, Justin, and Roger Sollenberger. "Unsealed Affidavit: Agents Thought They'd Find 'Evidence of Obstruction' at Mar-a-Lago." *Daily Beast*, Aug 26, 2022. https://www.yahoo.com/entertainment/feds-release-search-warrant-affidavit-162938775.html.

Rosenberg, Eli, et al. "A Record Number of Workers Are Quitting Their Jobs, Empowered by New Leverage." *Washington Post*, Oct 12, 2021. https://www.washingtonpost.com/business/2021/10/12/jolts-workers-quitting-august-pandemic/.

Rossi, Rosemary. "2 Longtime Fox News Contributors Resign over Tucker Carlson's Capitol Riot Special." *The Wrap*, Nov 21, 2021. https://www.thewrap.com/fox-news-contributors.

Rubin, Olivia. "Dominion Files $1.6 Billion Lawsuit against Fox News over False Fraud Claims." ABC News, Mar 26, 2022. https://abcnews.go.com/US/dominion-files-16-billion-lawsuit-fox-news-false/story?id=76699634.

Ruiz, Neil, et al. "One-Third of Asian Americans Fear Threats, Physical Attacks and Most Say Violence against Them Is Rising." *Pew Research Center*, Apr 21, 2021. https://www.pewresearch.org/short-reads/2021/04/21/.

Salant, Jonathan D. "You're Still Paying for Trump's Visits to His N.J. Golf Club. Here's the Cost to Taxpayers." *NJ.com*, May 7, 2022. https://www.nj.com/politics/2022/05/youre-still-paying-for-trumps-visits-to-his-nj-golf-club-heres-the-cost-to-taxpayers.html.

Saletan, William. "The Evidence of Trump's Pandemic Sabotage Keeps Piling Up." *Slate*, Jun 22, 2021. https://slate.com/news-and-politics/2021/06/trump-covid-pandemic-sabotage-evidence.html.

Samuels, Brett. "Pence Says DOJ Charges against Trump for Jan. 6 Would Be
    Terribly Divisive." *The Hill*, Dec 19, 2022. https://thehill.com/homenews/
    administration/3780783-pence-says-doj-charges-against-trump-for-jan-6-
    would-be-terribly-divisive/.
Sarkis, Stephanie A. "11 Red Flags of Gaslighting in a Relationship." *Psychology
    Today*, Jan 22, 2017. https://www.psychologytoday.com/us/blog/here-there-and-
    everywhere/201701/11-red-flags-of-gaslighting-in-a-relationship.
Savage, Charlie, et al. "How Barr's Quest to Find Flaws in the Russia Inquiry Unraveled."
    New York Times Daily, Jan 23, 2023. https://thenewyorktimedaily.com/how-barrs-
    quest-to.
Savage, Charlie, and Mark Joseph Stern. "Judge Calls Barr's Handling of Mueller Report
    'Distorted' and Misleading." *New York Times*, Mar 5, 2020. https://www.nytimes.
    com/2020/03/05/us/politics/mueller-report-barr-judge-walton.html.
Scannell, Kara. "First on CNN: Trump Org. Controller to Testify to Manhattan Grand
    Jury Investigating Hush Money Payments." CNN, Feb 1, 2023. https://www.cnn.
    com/2023/02/01/politics/trump-organization-controller-grand-jury/index.html.
Schiff, Adam. *Midnight in Washington: How We Almost Lost Our Democracy and Still
    Could*. New York: Random House, 2022.
Schonfeld, Zach, and Rebecca Beitsch. "DOJ: Classified Documents at Mar-a-Lago
    'Likely Concealed and Removed.'" *The Hill*, Aug 31, 2023. https://thehill.com/
    policy/national-security/3622203-doj-classified-documents-at-mar-a-lago-
    likely-concealed-and-removed/.
Senate Intelligence Committee. *Final Report on 2016 Russian Interference*. Washington,
    DC, 2020.
Severi, Misty. "Trump Repeated 'Witch Hunt' Answer All throughout NY AG Deposition,
    Attorney Says." *Millennial Press*, Aug 10, 2022. https://themillennialpress.
    com/2022/08/10/trump-repeated-witch-hunt-answer-all-throughout-ny-ag-
    deposition-attorney-says/.
Shafer, Jack. "Opinion: How Trump Flushed the Presidential Honor System
    down the Toilet." *Politico*, Feb 11, 2022. https://www.politico.com/news/
    magazine/2022/02/10/trump-flushed-record-system-disregard-history-00008055.
Shammas, Brittany. "A Man Reported Killing a Man in His Driveway, Authorities Say.
    He Was Arrested 11 Days Later." *Washington Post*, Oct 25, 2021. https://www.
    washingtonpost.com/nation/2021/10/25/texas-driveway-killing/.
Shamsian, Jacob. "Trump's Apparent Confirmation of His Company's Tax Schemes
    Could Burn Him in Court." *Business Insider*, Jul 7, 2021. https://www.
    businessinsider.in/international/news/trumps-apparent-confirmation-of-his-
    companys-tax-schemes-could-haunt-him-in-court/articleshow/84212869.cms.
Sheth, Sonam. "The U.S. Officially Designates Paul Manafort's Associate Konstantin
    Kilimnik as a 'Known Russian Agent.'" *Business Insider*, Apr 15, 2021. https://www.
    businessinsider.com/us-sanctions-manafort-associate-russian-agent-konstantin-
    kilimnik-2021-4.
Sheth, Sonam, and C. Ryan Barber. "A Federal Judge Called out John Durham's
    Prosecutors for Creating a 'Sideshow' with a Court Filing That Sent Trump World
    into a Frenzy." *Business Insider*, Mar 10, 2022. https://www.businessinsider.com/
    federal-judge-durham-prosecutors-created-sideshow-sussmann-filing-2022-3.
Sheth, Sonam, and Laura Italiano. "Trump Invoked His Fifth Amendment Rights in
    His Long-Awaited Deposition with the NY Attorney General's Office." *Business

Insider, Aug 10, 2022. https://www.businessinsider.com/trump-invoked-fifth-5th-amendment-rights-during-ny-ag-deposition-2022-8.

Shuham, Matthew. "Georgia Judge Laughs David Perdue's 2020 Election Lawsuit out of Court." *Talking Points Memo*, May 13, 2022. https://talkingpointsmemo.com/news/georgia-judge-dismisses-david-perdue-2020-election-lawsuit.

———. "Intelligence Committee's 1,000 Page Russia Report Ends with Dueling GOP and Dem Appendices." *Talking Points Memo*, Aug 18, 2020. https://talkingpointsmemo.com/news/intel-committees-1000-page-russia-report-ends-with-dueling-gop-and-dem-appendices.

Singer, Thomas. "Trump and the American Collective Psyche." In *The Dangerous Case of Donald Trump: 27 Psychiatrists and Mental Health Experts Assess a President*, edited by Bandy X. Lee, §4921–5140. New York: St. Martin's, 2017.

Sizer, Stephen. *Christian Zionism: Road-Map to Armageddon?* Eugene, OR: Wipf & Stock, 2021.

Skolnik, Jon. "'Throw a Fake': Rudy Giuliani Reveals to the FBI How He Used Fox News to Push Lies about Hillary Clinton." *Salon*, Aug 13, 2021. https://www.salon.com/2021/08/13/throw-a-fake-rudy-giuliani-reveals-to-fbi-how-he-used-fox-news-to-push-lies-about-hillary-clinton/.

Slisco, Aila. "'Guilty as Sin': Jamie Raskin Promises Trump Will Answer for 'Crime Wave.'" *Newsweek*, Feb 14, 2022. https://www.newsweek.com/guilty-sin-jamie-raskin-promises-trump-will-answer-crime-wave-1679131.

Smith, Allan, et al. "Trump Begs Georgia Secretary of State to Overturn Election Results in Remarkable Hourlong Phone Call." NBC News, Jan 4, 2021. https://www.nbcnews.com/politics/donald-trump/trump-begs-georgia-secretary-state-overturn-election-results-remarkable-hourlong-n1252692.

Sneed, Tierney, and Josh Kovensky. "Unsealed Manafort Docs Shed New Light on Sharing of 2016 Data with Alleged GRU Officer." *Talking Points Memo*, May 24, 2021. https://talkingpointsmemo.com/news/manafort-kilimnik-2016-campaign-trump-data-mueller.

Snyder, Timothy. *On Tyranny: Twenty Lessons from the Twentieth Century*. New York: Tim Duggan, 2017.

Stelter, Brian. "Fox Stays Silent about New Texts That Expose Hannity and Ingraham's Jan. 6 Hypocrisy." *CNN Business*, Dec 14, 2021. https://www.cnn.com/2021/12/14/media/january-6-fox-news-reliable-sources.

Stempel, Jonathan. "Judge's Order Releasing Trump's Tax Returns and Blasting 'Repugnant' Immunity Claim Put on Hold." Reuters, Oct 7, 2019. https://www.reuters.com/article/us-usa-trump-vance-idUSKBN1WM1DK.

Stephanopoulos, George. "Trump Decimated the Intelligence Community: DHS Whistleblower." ABC News, Sep 26, 2021. https://w.w.w.youtube.com/watch?v=YmUBGjCokqs.

Stern, Mark Joseph. "Federal Judge Says He Needs to Review Every Mueller Report Redaction Because Barr Can't Be Trusted." *Slate*, Mar 3, 2020. https://slate.com/news-and-politics/2020/03/barr-mueller-report-redactions-foia.html.

Stone, Peter. "Is Trump in His Sights? Garland under Pressure to Charge Ex-President." *Guardian*, Apr 10, 2022. https://www.theguardian.com/us-news/2022/apr/10/merrick-garland-charge-donald-trump-january-6.

Strzok, Peter. *Compromised: Counterintelligence and the Threat of Donald J. Trump*. New York: Houghton Mifflin Harcourt, 2020. Kindle ed.

Suebsaeng, Asawin, and Adam Rawnsley. "Justice Department Asking If Trump Stashed Documents in Trump Tower." *Rolling Stone*, Oct 7, 2022. https://www.rollingstone.com/politics/politics-news/trump-maralago-raid-fbi-tower-bedminster-1234607008/.

Supica, Vladmir. "'They Weren't Mad at All, and They Tipped $60. Lie to Your Tables': Restaurant Server Encourages." *Daily Dot*, Aug 24, 2022. https://www.dailydot.com/irl/restaurant-server-lies-to-customers.

Suskind, Amy. *The List: A Week-by-Week Reckoning of Trump's First Year.* London: Bloomsburg, 2018.

Swalwell, Eric. *Endgame: Inside the Impeachments of Donald J. Trump.* New York: Abrams, 2021.

Tansey, Michael J. "Why Crazy Like a Fox Versus Crazy Like a Crazy Really Matters: Delusional Disorder, Admiration of Brutal Dictators, the Nuclear Codes, and Trump." In *The Dangerous Case of Donald Trump: 27 Psychiatrists and Mental Health Experts Assess a President*, edited by Bandy X. Lee, §2341–570. New York: St. Martin's, 2017.

Tapper, Jake. "Longtime GOP Official: Republican Leaders Are Cowards." CNN, Sep 6, 2022. https://www.cnn.com/videos/politics/2022/09/06/peter-wehner-trump-gop-mccarthy-biden-sot-lead-sot-vpx.cnn.

Taylor, Drew. "Bret Baier and Chris Wallace Complained to Fox News Heads about Tucker Carlson Capitol Riot Special (Report)." *The Wrap*, Nov 22, 2021. https://www.thewrap.com/bret-baier-chris-wallace-fox-news-complained.

Teh, Cheryl. "Anti-Trump Conservative Group Says the GOP Has Become an 'Authoritarian Nationalist Cult That Worships Donald Trump." *Business Insider*, Aug 18, 2022. https://sports.yahoo.com/anti-trump-conservative-group-says-08 2213214.html.

Teng, Betty P. "Trauma, Time, Truth, and Trump." In *The Dangerous Case of Donald Trump: 27 Psychiatrists and Mental Health Experts Assess a President*, edited by Bandy X. Lee, §3969–4181. New York: St. Martin's, 2017.

Tillman, Zoe. "Mueller Memo Advising Barr on Trump Findings Is Ordered Released." *Bloomberg*, Aug 19, 2022. https://www.bloomberg.com/news/articles/2022-08-19/mueller-memo-from-justice-department-to-barr-is-ordered-released.

Timm, Jane C. "Trump Vs. the Truth: The Most Outrageous Falsehoods of His Presidency." NBC News, Dec 31, 2020. https://www.yahoo.com/now/trump-vs-truth-most-outrageous-093019719.html.

Todd, Chuck. "Full Schiff: Worst Case Scenario Would Be Trump 'Runs and Loses and Then Overturns the Election' in 2024." NBC News, Jun 26, 2022. https://www.nbc.com/meet-the-press/video/full-schiff-worst-case-scenario-would-be-trump-runs-and-loses-and-then-overturns-the-election-in/NBCN859845886.

Trump, Mary L. *Too Much and Never Enough: How My Family Created the World's Most Dangerous Man.* New York: Simon & Schuster, 2020.

Vaillancourt, William. "Homeland Security Secretary Altered Report on Russian Election Interference to Help Trump, Watchdog Says." *Rolling Stone*, May 3, 2022. https://www.rollingstone.com/politics/politics-news/chad-wolf-homeland-security-russian-interference-report-1347046/.

Velshi, Ali. "Comity in Congress after 1/6 Impeded by Republican Boosters of Trump's Big Lie." YouTube video. MSNBC, Apr 16, 2021. https://www.youtube.com/watch?v=qri73NASbLI.

———."Debunking 'Democracy Vs. Republic': The Legal Theory Firing Up GOP State Legislators." MSNBC, Aug 20, 2022. https://www.msnbc.com/ali-velshi/watch/debunking-democracy-vs-republic-the-legal-theory-firing-up-gop-state-legislators-146629701813.

———. "*NYT*: Trump Had 300+ Classified Documents at Mar-a-Lago." MSNBC, Feb 10, 2022. https://www.msnbc.com/rachel-maddow-show/maddowblog/trump-took-materials-mishandle-classified-info-rcna15689.

Visser, Nick. "Trump Had 300 Classified Documents at Mar-a-Lago, Called Boxes 'Mine': Report." *HuffPost*, Aug 23, 2022. https://www.huffpost.com/entry/trump-300-classified-documents-mar-a-lago_n_630420fde4bof72c09d9f987.

Vlamis, Kelsey, and Cheryl Teh. "Sen. Lindsey Graham Said If Trump Is Prosecuted for Mishandling Classified Information, 'There Will Be Riots in the Streets.'" *Business Insider*, Aug 29, 2022. https://www.businessinsider.com/lindsey-graham-trump-prosecution-for-classified-info-will-cause-riots-2022-8.

Von Rennenkampff, Marik. "Republicans Incriminate Trump, Decimate His 'Russia Hoax' Narrative." *The Hill*, Aug 25, 2020. https://thehill.com/opinion/white-house/513499-republicans-incriminate-trump-decimate-his-russia-hoax-narrative/.

Vuleta, Branka. "35 Encouraging Stats on the Divorce Rate in America 2021." *Legaljob*, Mar 30, 2021. https://legaljobs.io/blog/divorce-rate-in-america.

Wagner, Alex. "'The Republicans Have Become a Cult': Rep. Kinzinger on Escaping and Saving the GOP." MSNBC, Aug 17, 2022. https://www.msnbc.com/alex-wagner-tonight/watch/-the-republicans-have-become-a-cult-rep-kinzinger-on-escaping-and-saving-the-gop-146345029761.

Wallace, Nicolle. "Andrew Weissmann Predicts 'the Former President Will Be Prosecuted.'" MSNBC, Aug 26, 2022. https://www.msn.com/en-us/news/politics/andrew.

———. "Judge Details What Daniel Goldman Calls 'Unfathomable Conduct' from Former AG Barr." MSNBC, May 6, 2021. https://www.msnbc.com/deadline-white-house/watch/judge-details-what-daniel-goldman-calls-unfathomable-conduct-from-former-ag-barr-111406149857.

———. "Mary Trump: 'Democracy Is on a Knife's Edge.'" MSNBC, Apr 7, 2022. https://www.msnbc.com/deadline-white-house/watch/mary-trump-democracy-is-on-a-knife-s-edge-137257541663.

———. "Trump Confesses to the Whole Plot to Overturn the 2020 Election." MSNBC, Jan 31, 2022. https://www.msnbc.com/deadline-white-house/watch/trump-confesses-to-the-whole-plot-to-overturn-the-2020-election-132110917917

———. "Trump's Niece on Why He Kept Documents at Mar-a-Lago." MSNBC, Oct 4, 2022. https://www.youtube.com/watch?v=34yooTiazFc.

Wang, Amy B., and David A. Fahrenthold. "Trump-Appointed Ambassador Directed Government Business to His Hotel, Emails Show." *Washington Post*, Sep 2, 2021. https://www.washingtonpost.com/politics/2021/09/02/trump-appointed-ambassador-directed-government-business-his-hotel-emails-show/.

Watson, Kathryn. "National Archives Head Defends Agency's 'Non-Political' Work." CBS, Aug 30, 2022. https://sports.yahoo.com/national-archives-head-defends-agencys-002207590.html.

Wehle, Kimberly. "Law and the OLC's Article II Immunity Memos." *Stanford Law & Policy Review* 32.1 (2020). https://law.stanford.edu/publications/law-and-the-olcs-article-ii-immunity-memos.

Wehner, Peter. "Trump Is Obsessed with Being a Loser." *Atlantic*, Feb 27, 2022. https://www.theatlantic.com/ideas/archive/2022/02/trump-obsessed-being-loser-2020-election/621505/.

Weissmann, Andrew. "A Ruling Untethered to the Law." *Atlantic*, Sep 6, 2022. https://www.theatlantic.com/ideas/archive/2022/09/judge-cannon-trump-mar-a-lago-special-master/671349/.

Weixel, Nathaniel, and Joseph Choi. "Health Care—Trump Staffers Interfered in CDC Guidance, Report Finds." *The Hill*, Oct 17, 2022. https://thehill.com/newsletters/health-care/3693335-health-care-trump-staffers.

Whitney, Jake. "Commentary: Private Texts Confirm: Fox Isn't a News Network." *Tribune News Service*, Mar 10, 2023. https://thebrunswicknews.com/news/business/commentary-private-texts-confirm-fox-isn-t-a-news-network/article_29083cd3-8d56-51dd-9162-f1361e46fa8a.html.

Widmer, Ted. "Draining the Swamp." *New Yorker*, Jan 19, 2017. https://www.newyorker.com/news/news-desk/draining-the-swamp.

Wikipedia. "Al Capone." Accessed Apr 19, 2022. https://en.wikipedia.org/wiki/Al_Capone.

———. "Talk:Sociopath." Accessed 2021. https://en.wikipedia.org/wiki/talk:sociopath.

———. "Gaslight (1944 Film)." Accessed 2021. https://en.wikipedia.org/wiki/Gaslight_(1944_film).

———. "Lady Justice." Accessed 2021. https://en.wikipedia.org/wiki/Lady_Justice.

———. "Malignant Narcissism." Accessed 2021. https://en.wikipedia.org/wiki/Malignant_narcissism.

———. "Precedent." Accessed 2012. https://en.wikipedia.org/wiki/Precedent.

———. "Public Hearings of the United States House Select Committee on January 6 Attack." https://cn.wikipedia.org/wiki/Public_hearings_of_the_United_States_House_Select_Committee_on_the_January_6_Attack.

———. "Radar Warning of Pearl Harbor Attack." Accessed 2021. https://en.wikipedia.org/wiki/Radar_warning_of_Pearl_Harbor_attack.

———. "United States Military Casualties of War." Accessed Dec 20, 2021. https://en.wikipedia.org/wiki/United_States_military_casualties_of_war.

Wilkins, Brett. "'Siding with Insurrectionists,' 203 House Republicans Vote No on Coup Prevention Bill." *Salon*, Sep 22, 2022. https://www.salon.com/2022/09/22/siding-with-insurrectionists-203-vote-no-on-coup-prevention-bill_partner/.

Williams, Juan. "Juan Williams: Trump Is Killing American Democracy." *The Hill*, Oct 25, 2021. https://thehill.com/opinion/campaign/578235-juan.

Willingham, AJ. "The Truth behind the 'He Gets Us' Ads for Jesus Airing during the Super Bowl." CNN, Feb 11, 2023. https://www.cnn.com/2023/02/11/us/he-gets-us-super-bowl-commercials-cec/index.html.

Willmer, Sabrina, and Zoe Tillman. "Trump Lawyer in Mar-a-Lago Search Appeared before Grand Jury." *Bloomberg*, Feb 11, 2023. https://news.bloomberglaw.com/white-collar-and-criminal-law/trump-lawyer-in-mar-a-lago-search-appeared-before-grand-jury-1.

Wire, Sarah D. "Threats against Members of Congress Are Skyrocketing. It's Changing the Job." *Los Angeles Times*, Sep 20, 2021. https://www.latimes.com/politics/story/2021-09-20/threats-members-of-congress.

Wu, Shan. "Why Merrick Garland Should Fire Special Counsel Durham Now." *Daily Beast*, Jan 27, 2023. https://www.thedailybeast.com/shan-wu-on-why-merrick-garland-should-fire-special-counsel-durham-now.